Facilities Management Handbook

Frank Booty
(General Editor)

LexisNexis™ UK

Members of the LexisNexis Group worldwide

United Kingdom	LexisNexis UK, a Division of Reed Elsevier (UK) Ltd, Halsbury House, 35 Chancery Lane, LONDON, WC2A 1EL, and 4 Hill Street, EDINBURGH EH2 3JZ
Argentina	LexisNexis Argentina, BUENOS AIRES
Australia	LexisNexis Butterworths, CHATSWOOD, New South Wales
Austria	LexisNexis Verlag ARD Orac GmbH & Co KG, VIENNA
Canada	LexisNexis Butterworths, MARKHAM, Ontario
Chile	LexisNexis Chile Ltda, SANTIAGO DE CHILE
Czech Republic	Nakladatelství Orac sro, PRAGUE
France	Editions du Juris-Classeur SA, PARIS
Germany	LexisNexis Deutschland GmbH, FRANKFURT and MUNSTER
Hong Kong	LexisNexis Butterworths, HONG KONG
Hungary	HVG-Orac, BUDAPEST
India	LexisNexis Butterworths, NEW DELHI
Ireland	LexisNexis, DUBLIN
Italy	Giuffrè Editore, MILAN
Malaysia	Malayan Law Journal Sdn Bhd, KUALA LUMPUR
New Zealand	LexisNexis Butterworths, WELLINGTON
Poland	Wydawnictwo Prawnicze LexisNexis, WARSAW
Singapore	LexisNexis Butterworths, SINGAPORE
South Africa	LexisNexis Butterworths, Durban
Switzerland	Stämpfli Verlag AG, BERNE
USA	LexisNexis, DAYTON, Ohio

© Reed Elsevier (UK) Ltd 2003
  Reprinted 2004

Published by LexisNexis UK

A CIP Catalogue record for this book is available from the British Library.

ISBN 0 754 52374 8

Project management by The Partnership Publishing Solutions Ltd, www.the-pps.co.uk

Typeset by Columns Design Ltd, Reading, England
Printed and bound in Great Britain by William Clowes Limited, Beccles and London

Visit LexisNexis UK at www.lexisnexis.co.uk

Foreword

It is a great pleasure for me to write a brief foreword to this excellent handbook on facilities management.

Facilities managment now plays such an important part in the day-to-day running of a business that it is often difficult to keep abreast of all the technicalities of the law, not to mention the financial and practical implications of – for example – rising energy costs. This handbook, which combines practical best practice tips – including, I am pleased to see, business continuity – with advice on complying with the law, offers a veritable encyclopedia on facilities management issues which will undoubtedly be of substantial help to all facilities professionals, from the small businessman right through to those working for large companies.

I am sure readers will find many helpful tips within its pages and I congratulate the authors for making so much information available in such a useful and readable format.

Christopher W Rust
Chairman, Facilities Management Association

Contents

Foreword	iii
About the authors	xv
Acknowledgements	xvii
Introduction	**xviii**

COMPLYING WITH THE LAW
1 Complying with Health and Safety Law

Enforcement	**2**
The HSC and the HSE	2
Regulations	**2**
Health and Safety at Work etc Act 1974 (HSW Act)	2
A successful health and safety policy	4
The 'six-pack'	5
Other key regulations	8
Risk assessment	**12**
Spotting hazards	12
Who might be harmed?	12
Controlling the risks	13
Recording the findings	13
Reviewing and revising	14
'Suitable and sufficient'	14
Criminal sanctions	**14**
Revitalising strategy	16
Directors' responsibilities	16
New legislation expected	17
Civil compensation	**17**
Promoting occupational health	**18**
Avoiding back pain	18
Preventing WRULDs	19
Reducing noise	24
Asbestos-related diseases	25
Legionellosis	27
Improving well-being	30
Towards a safe workplace	**37**
Preventing slips and trips	37
Equipment	38
Vehicles	39
Maintenance and repair	41

Fire safety   **45**
  Fire certificates   45
  Fire risk assessment   46
  Means of escape   51
  Fire notices   53
  Fire equipment   53
  Staff responsibilities   53
  Fire safety: proposed legislative changes   54
Flexible working   **56**
  Homeworking   56
  Hotdesking   56
  Laptops   57
  Driving   58
  Lone working   59
Environmental protection and liability   **60**
  Climate Change Levy   60
  Waste management   61
  Pollution   63
  EU legislation   64
  Corporate social responsibility   64
  Supply chain management   65
Construction work and building management   **65**
  Construction (Design and Management) Regulations 1994 (CDM)   66
  Managing refurbishment works   72
  Building management   73
  Structure and access   73
  Permit to work procedures/safe systems of work   76
  The Building Regulations   77
  Catering facilities   79
Proposed health and safety legislation   **85**

2 Complying with the Law on Staff, Casual and Contract Workers

Flexible working for employees   **87**
  Reforms   87
  Flexible working right of request   87
  The 48-hour week   89
  Part-time workers   92
Leave for parents and carers   **95**
  Maternity leave   95
  Paternity leave   95
  Adoption leave   95
  Parental leave   96
  Time off for dependants   96

Contract and casual workers 97
  Fixed-term contracts 97
  Agency workers 98
TUPE **98**
  The *Süzen* decision 99
  UK case law 99
  Practical implications 101
  Amendments to TUPE 101
Employee consultation **103**
  European Works Councils 104
  Redundancies and transfers 104
  Selection for redundancy 106
  National Works Councils 106
Disability discrimination **107**
  'Reasonable adjustments' 108
  Public access 109
  Building alterations 110
  Complaints and compensation 111
  Contract workers 111
  Disability Rights Commission 112
Unfair dismissal **113**
  Automatic unfair dismissal 113
Workplace surveillance **114**
  Why monitor? 114
  RIP to privacy? 115
  Laws on privacy 116
  Personal data code 117
  Practical considerations 117
  Email and Internet use policies 117
Disciplinary and grievance hearings **118**
Minimum wage **119**
Timetable for new employment/contract legislation **120**

3 Complying with Property Law

Acquisition and disposal **121**
  How is property owned? 121
  Professional advisers – who does what? 122
  Buying property 123
  Completion 123
  Costs involved 124
  Acquisition for own use 125
Business leases **127**
  Parties 127
  Premises let 127
  Fixtures and fittings 127

Rights granted   128
Exceptions and reservations   128
Term   128
Security of tenure   128
Rent   129
Rates and taxes   130
Interest   130
Dealings   130
Use   131
Alterations   131
Repairs   131
New buildings   131
Old buildings   132
Breach of repairing obligations   132
Rights of access   132
Insurance   132
Service charges   133
Options to terminate   134
Landlord's remedies for tenant breaches   135
Planning   **136**
The law   136
When is planning permission required?   136
Understanding planning requirements   139
Applying for planning permission   139
The planning application decision   142
Obligations   143
Appeals   143
When is planning permission not needed?   144
What if planning law is not complied with?   146
Environmental matters   **149**
The law   149
What is contaminated land?   149
Who is liable? – The 'polluter pays' principle   149
Reducing liability for clean-up   150
Occupiers' liability   **150**
Case study   150
Knowing your portfolio and managing costs   **154**
Key knowledge requirements   155
Real estate valuation   **155**
The regulatory framework   156
Procuring valuations   156
The purpose of the valuation   157
Valuations for acquisition/disposal   157
Valuations for incorporation within company accounts   159
Valuation approach   160
Negotiating lease terms   **161**

MANAGING YOUR BUSINESS EFFECTIVELY

4 Financial Management

Background economics   **163**
Universal principles   163
The significance of facilities management costs   164
Systems technology and financial management   165
Best practice financial management   **166**
Budgetary control   166
Cost centres   167
Zero-based budgeting   168
Data   168
Change management   171
Procurement   172
Private investment and partnership   **175**
The PPP process   176
Life cycle cost models   177
Payment mechanisms   178
Benchmarking facilities costs   **179**
Why benchmark?   179
Internal and external benchmarking   181
The process of benchmarking   182
Whole life economics and financial analysis   **188**
Whole life costs   189
Techniques for financial analysis   189
Applying the techniques   193
Property costs   **194**
Rent   194
Rates   194
Service charges   195
Building insurance   196
Sustainable property   197
Principles of facilities finance   **198**
Taxation   198
Capital and revenue expenditure   203
Depreciation   203
Capital allowances   204

5 Risk Management

Three phases of risk management   **207**
Risk analysis   207
Risk assessment   207
Risk mitigation   207
Risk management in business   **208**
Different types of risk   208

Developing a risk management strategy   **210**
   Where to turn for help   210
   Prioritising risk   210
   Outsourcing risk   211
Risk planning and responsibilities   **212**
   Turnbull recommendations   212
   Roles and responsibilities   213
   Risk management plan   213
Digital risk   **214**
   Types of digital risk   214
   How to minimise digital risk   215
Linking risk to the quality process   **215**
Risk management in practice   **216**
   Risk management – the FM workload   216
   Building better at Barclays – case study   218

6 Business Continuity

The Turnbull Report   **220**
Developing a strategy   **221**
   Business vulnerability   221
   An effective strategy   222
   Conducting a business impact analysis BIA   222
Implementing the strategy   **224**
   Drawing up a plan   224
   Roles and responsibilities   225
   Rehearsing the plan   226
Outsourcing disaster recovery   **226**
   Selecting a disaster recovery supplier   227
Dealing with staff   **228**
   Training   229
   Communication   229
   Staff welfare after an event   230
Dealing with the media   **230**
Inventory and restoration   **231**
   Inventory control   231
   Restoration of the business   231
Best practice procedures   **232**

7 Outsourcing

What to outsource   **235**
   Core and non-core activities   236
   Anticipating pitfalls   237
Choosing contractors   **239**
   The tender document   239
   Invitation to tender   239

Final selection   240
Final negotiations   240
The supplier market   242
Service level agreements   **242**
Penalties and incentives   243
Force majeure clauses   243
Contractual arrangements   **244**
The function of the contract   244
What should the contract include?   245
Contract 'management'   246
Key performance indicators   **246**
A balanced scorecard   246
Client satisfaction   247
Building the relationship   **248**
Continuous improvement model   248
Defining added value   249
Good communication   249
Coordinating standards and budgets   250
Anticipating problems   250
Team dynamics   251
Regular reviews   251
Managing the end of the contract   **252**
Key lessons   252
Outsourcing the postroom – case study   253

8 Transport Policies

Travel plans   **255**
Legislation   255
Objectives   256
Guide to effective travel planning   256
Encouraging behavioural change   260
The Transport Energy Best Practice Programme   260
Car park management   **261**
Parking restrictions   261
Planning a car park   261
Floor graphic advertising   262
Lighting and security   263
Fleet management   **263**

9 IT and Communications

The convergence of data and telecom   **265**
Mobile growth   265
Fixed network need   265
Bluetooth   266
Voice becomes data   266
Wi-Fi zones and wireless LANs   267

IT infrastructure management   **268**
   Intelligent buildings   268
   Future-proofing   268
   Cabling categories   269
Voice over IP   **270**
   Features of VoIP   270
   Integration with the data network   271
   Developments in IP telephony   272
Conferencing and presentation technology   **272**
   Conference technology   273
   Projectors   273
Doing business over the web   **274**
   Top-down approach   274
   E-procurement   275
   Negotiating by email   275
   The role of the intranet site   276
   Intranet services   276
Helpdesks   **276**
Digital v paper document systems   **277**
   Paper storage   277
   Establishing an electronic document system   277

THE BUILT ENVIRONMENT

10 Workplace Facilities

Buying gas, electricity and water   **279**
   How to get the best deal   279
   NETA   280
   Combined heat and power   280
   Totally integrated power   281
   Avoiding power failures   283
   Water competition   283
   Checking utility invoices   283
Climate Change Levy   **285**
   Objectives   286
   Reducing emissions and costs   286
Environmental measurement and reporting   **288**
   Measuring energy efficiency   288
   Energy-efficiency improvement programmes   288
   The value of metering data   289
Waste water management   **290**
   Sewerage charges   290
   Preventing water pollution   293
HVAC (heating, ventilation and air conditioning)   **295**
   Indoor air quality   295

Saving energy and improving quality   296
Choosing equipment   297
Air conditioning   298
Promoting cleaner indoor air   300
Waste management   **303**
Disposal   304
Responsibility over profitability   304
A sustainable resource   304
Noise and vibration   **305**
Damage to hearing   306
Sound perception   306
Sound power level   306
Minimising noise through design   307
Control noise at source   308
Sources of advice   308
Furniture   **308**
Selecting furniture   309
Workspace design   309
Workstations   310
Seating   310
Buying furniture   311
Catering   **311**
Drinking water   312
Company restaurant facilities   312
Planning a restaurant   313
Ambience   314
Management   315
Choosing caterers   315
Future prospects   316
Cleaning   **316**
Market dynamics   316
Selecting contractors   316
Costs   317
Lighting   **318**
Energy efficiency   318
Objectives of good lighting   318
Sources of light   319
Standards of lighting   320
Lighting output   320
Lighting quality   321
Computer-controlled lighting systems   322
Emergency lighting   323

11 Space Design and Management

Space planning   **329**
Measuring space   329
Planning grids   330

Bricks and mortar   330
Partitioning   330
Cabling   331
Space per person   332
Workplace options   333
Circulation   335
Adjacencies   336
Group planning   337
Space records   337
Office aesthetics   337
Space-saving tips   338
Third-party planners   339
Relocation and churn   **339**
Benefits and costs   339
Cutting the cost of churn   340
Relocation   340
Hotdesking   341
Computer-aided facilities management (CAFM)   **343**
Infrastructure – buildings, space and asset management   343
Health, safety and environmental management   344
Maintenance, repairs and contract management   344
Helpdesk, service desk and security management   345
Financial, budget and inventory management   345
Specifying CAFM   345
Choosing a CAFM system   346
Choosing a CAFM provider   348
Data entry and protection   348
Planning the transition   349
Implementing the system   349

12 Access, Safety and Security

Closed circuit television (CCTV)   **351**
Threats   351
Security audits   352
Choosing CCTV cameras   352
CCTV operation   353
Remote monitoring   354
Recordings   354
Violence and aggression in the workplace   **355**
At-risk areas   355
The people involved   356
Personal safety – training and counselling   356
Principal strategies for defence   356
Access control, asset protection and guarding   **357**
Access risk analysis   357
Security measures   358

Asset protection   360
Manned guarding   361
Information protection   361
Fire risk   **362**
Causes of fire   362
Statutory requirements   364

13 Maintenance and Repair

Plant and property maintenance   **365**
Statutory requirements   365
Costs   366
Types of maintenance   366
Condition assessments   366
Refurbishment costs   367
Serviceability   367
Managing maintenance contracts   368
Employee safety   369
Preventative maintenance programmes   370
Turnkey service management   **372**
Managing multiple vendors   373
The complete service solution   373
E-business solutions for support   **375**

Appendix
Facilities service cost benchmarking protocol   376
Index   **383**

About the Authors

Amanda Benham has practised in the city as a solicitor for 16 years, specialising in landlord and tenant law and estates' management, and is the leader of the real estate practice in Landwell, the associated law firm of PricewaterhouseCoopers. She is a frequent contributor to property publications and regularly lectures to the property industry.
amanda.benham@uk.landwellglobal.com

Frank Booty is former editor of *Facilities Management* and a contributor to other market-leading titles, books and websites in the fields of business, IT and networking and manufacturing. An award-winning journalist, he has also devised and chaired many conferences in the facilities management market.
fbooty@compuserve.com

Connel Bottom is a facilities management consultant with Bernard Williams Associates, specialising in facilities cost and performance benchmarking/modelling for corporate occupiers and service providers within the UK and Europe.
connel.bottom@bwassoc.co.uk

Nick Croft is a real estate consultant at PricewaterhouseCoopers specialising in valuation advice for both occupiers and investors within the UK and abroad.
nicholas.h.croft@uk.pwcglobal.com

Nick Edwards is a solicitor with Landwell, the associated law firm of Pricewaterhouse Coopers. He coordinates Landwell's real estate publications and advises businesses in the insurance and investment sector on facilities management and premises issues.
nicholas.edwards@uk.landwellglobal.com

Jackie Le Poidevin is a writer and editor on journals specialising in employment law and workplace health and safety. She also compiles the legal section of *Facilities Management*.
jlpoidevin@aol.com

Chris Taylor is a specialist editor and writer on management, and the issues and concerns which affect business today. He is also a member of the Business and Management faculty at the University of Lincoln.
ct@clara.net

Louis Wustemann is a writer and consultant on facilities and employment matters. He is former editor of *Flexible Working* magazine and is general editor of the *IRS Handbook Flexible Working – Policy and Practice.*
lw@sivill.demon.co.uk

Pat Perry is an Environmental Health Consultant and Managing Director of Perry Scott Nash Associates Ltd. She is a recognised expert in the fields of health and safety, food safety and CDM and advises a wide range of clients on legal compliance and best practice. A regular contributor to *Facilities Management* and other industry and trade journals, she has also had books published on CDM and general health and safety topics.

p.perry@perryscottnashassociates.com

Acknowledgements

The publishers wish to express their thanks to:

Pat Anderson
Richard Armitage
Mike Bateman
Jane Bell
Nicola Coote
Ken Coules
Christopher Eskell
Martyn Gilbert
Janice Hunter
Janet Kelly
Maureen Moody
Simon Napper
Lucy Ponting
Phil Roberts
Valerie Taplin
Richard Tinson
Roger Tompsett
Vilnis Vesma
Roger Woodward

Introduction

The world of facilities management has changed dramatically over the past 12 years. From relatively humble beginnings, the job of facilities manager now encompasses a wide range of complex and challenging roles, often across entire estates. In a definition issued by NHS Estates in 1996, facilities management is described as 'the practice of coordinating the physical workplace with the people and work of an organisation'. And that is really just the starting point.

Facilities managers today may well have to run a department responsible for everything from risk assessments to gas supply, from preparing tendering documents to managing IT systems and car parks. They are usually in the unenviable position of having to request funds for functions unconnected to the core business of the company, which are nevertheless essential.

Aims of the book

The goal of this book is to provide information and guidance for facilities managers, allowing readers quick and easy access to the answers to their most pressing questions. Its aim is not to offer a conclusive definition of the role of the facilities manager, which is constantly developing, but to help those working within the facilities function to develop strategies for succeeding in an increasingly high-tech and global marketplace.

Who will find the book helpful?

Individual facilities managers and estate managers in all sizes of companies should benefit from this book. But so, also, will independent suppliers, architects, surveyors, lawyers, space planners, human resources staff and building services engineers who need an insight into the facilities universe.

Keeping abreast of the law

Clearly, not falling foul of the law is a major concern for facilities managers. The main areas of legislation in the sector are health and safety, employment/contract/casual workers and property law, each of which is covered by a separate chapter within this book. The laws and regulations regarding health and safety and employment in particular are fast moving and wide-ranging. Facilities managers need to cope with the needs of office workers for ergonomic workstations, access for the disabled and the demand of TUPE, to name just a few of the areas covered here in the form of practical and actionable advice.

Running a business

Managing the facilities function can be like running a business in itself. Setting and meeting budget targets, cutting costs and making savings have been challenging tasks for facilities managers for some time. The business issues section guides readers through the demands of contract management and the outsourcing process. It also offers up-to-date information on communications and IT, where the combination of a shrinking world and fast-developing technology mean facilities managers need to know exactly what they can – and can afford to – invest in. Private investments and partnerships – with huge implications for facilities managers – are on the increase and there is an ever-pressing need for business continuity arrangements in case of communications breakdown and other disasters. These are also fully explored.

Managing the built environment

Facilities professionals are responsible for an extraordinary array of workplace facilities. The procurement of utilities, the management of waste, the installing of integrated security systems, the purchase of office furniture and the costing of cleaning and catering functions are just some of the challenges facing facilities managers. This section of the handbook offers best practice information and advice on these issues.

Security is a key issue

Companies face potentially devastating litigation from their own staff and the public, if, in the aftermath of a direct terrorist attack, it could be demonstrated they had failed to take measures to identify, assess and mitigate foreseeable risks to human life.

Future challenges

The future workplace will bring with it a number of distinct priorities. More attempts to make flexible working a reality are likely – requiring improved IT and communications infrastructures. The expansion of a 24/7 work culture will necessitate non-stop support facilities – with consequent outsourcing, contract and health and safety considerations needing to be taken into account. PPP (professional/private partnerships) and economic pressures will push facilities professionals towards more benchmarking, more cost benefit analysis and more performance measurement.

Facilities for businesses in the future will have to be more flexible and more streamlined than ever before. Managers will need to exploit growing communication opportunities and facilitate an ever-widening range of support services.

Facilities managers need to become more professional and business-oriented. They must develop a performance profile that is committed to the needs of their organisation. Facilities managers need a variety of skills, as all organisations are different, but all should aim to gain the attention of the board and not just be visible when something goes wrong.

1 Complying with Health and Safety Law

Jackie le Poidevin and Pat Perry

Prosecutions under criminal law and compensation under civil law are the tip of the iceberg when it comes to working out what poor health and safety costs employers. Health and Safety Executive (HSE) studies suggest that for every pound in costs covered by employers' liability insurance, organisations must pay between another £8 to £36 in uninsured costs. The message is that safe, healthy workplaces save money, not only in obvious ways such as reducing absenteeism, but also by making organisations more efficient and productive. By improving workplace design and ensuring workstations are ergonomically suited to the individual worker, for example, facilities managers play a crucial role in this process of improving staff morale and well-being.

The 2001 HSE survey of self-reported work-related illness estimated that 2.3 million employees were made ill by their work that year. Over 1 million people suffered musculo-skeletal disorders, and over 500,000 suffered stress, anxiety or depression. The number of people affected by stress has doubled since 1990. Overall, the total number of working days lost during 2001–02 was reputed to be 32.9 million. The CBI has estimated that the annual cost of absenteeism to UK plc is £10 billion, rising to £20 billion if indirect costs are counted.

As for accidents, 249 people were killed at work in 2001–02, and there were 27,935 major injuries to employees. HSE estimates that injuries cost UK businesses £0.9 billion a year, illnesses £1.6 billion, and non-injury accidents between £1.4 billion and £4.5 billion. The total represents between 4 and 8 per cent of companies' gross trading profits.

Cost of poor health and safety

Costs imposed by ill-health and accidents include:

- sick pay
- lost production
- damaged equipment and materials
- extra administration
- losing skilled staff
- training replacement staff
- increased insurance premiums
- loss of staff morale
- bad publicity (which may put off job candidates and investors)
- compensation, fines and court costs.

Enforcement

The cornerstone of health and safety legislation is the *Health and Safety at Work etc Act 1974 (HSW Act)*. It is an 'enabling' Act, under which detailed regulations on particular work-related risks are made.

These regulations are supported by Approved Codes of Practice (ACoPs) and guidance. ACoPs have a special legal status like the Highway Code. If a court proves an organisation failed to comply with a revelant ACoP, it will be found guilty unless it demonstrates it complied with the law in another way. Following guidance is not compulsory and employers are free to take other action. But by following it, they will usually be doing enough to comply with the law.

The HSC and the HSE

The Health and Safety Commission (HSC) is the agency which has overall responsibility for developing workplace health and safety and deciding on new legislation to lay before Parliament. Its commissioners are drawn from employers' organisations, trade unions and local authorities. Its executive arm is the Health and Safety Executive (HSE). Both agencies are independent of the government, although they are responsible to the Secretary of State for Work and Pensions.

Responsibility for enforcing the law is shared between the HSE and local authorities. The HSE inspects factories, chemical firms and construction sites, while local authority environmental health officers inspect offices, shops, warehouses, hotels and leisure sites. Inspectors may issue an improvement notice if they find a breach of statutory duty, or a prohibition notice stopping an activity which involves a risk of serious injury.

Regulations

Modern health and safety law in the UK is 'goal-setting' rather than prescriptive. The responsibility is on employers actively to apply these broad legal principles to suit their particular organisation, rather than following fixed rules which may not be appropriate to their circumstances.

Health and Safety at Work etc Act 1974 (HSW Act)

The *HSW Act* imposes a duty of care on employers, employees and suppliers.

Employers' duties (s 2)

Employers should, 'so far as is reasonably practicable', ensure the health, safety and welfare at work of all employees by:

- providing safe equipment and working practices
- ensuring safe handling, storage and transportation of goods and substances
- providing information, training and supervision

- providing a safe place of work with safe access and egress
- providing a safe working environment and facilities.

Safety policy (s 2(3))

Organisations with five or more employees must:

- prepare a written health and safety policy, listing the hazards present in the workplace
- provide details of arrangements for carrying out the policy
- make employees aware of the policy and arrangements
- update the policy as necessary.

Duties to non-employees (s 3)

Employers should ensure 'so far as is reasonably practicable' that they do not put anyone not in their employment (such as members of the public, contractors and agency staff) at risk from their activities. This duty can extend to trespassers, so facilities managers need to ensure that high-risk workplaces have adequate security and fencing.

'So far as is reasonably practicable' means that if the cost of removing a risk (in terms of time and trouble as well as financial cost) outweighs the possible benefit to employees and the public, an employer does not have to act. The burden of proof rests with the employer, meaning that, if prosecuted, it has to prove why a safety measure was not reasonably practicable.

Suppliers' duties (s 6)

Those who design, manufacture, import or supply goods or substances for use at work must ensure they are safe when used properly, and provide instructions on how to use them safely.

Employees' duties (s 7)

Employees must:

- take reasonable care for their own health and safety and that of anyone else affected by their work
- cooperate with their employer in ensuring it meets its legal obligations (by wearing personal protective equipment (PPE) or reporting accidents, for example).

Personal liability (s 37)

Company directors and managers may be personally liable for a health and safety offence committed with their consent or connivance. They face being fined and disqualified from being a director for up to two years.

A successful health and safety policy

Under the *HSW Act*, employers must prepare in writing:

- a statement of their general policy on their employees' health and safety at work
- the organisation of the policy
- the arrangements for carrying out the policy.

Policies are normally divided into three sections to meet these three demands.

1. The statement of intent

This involves a general statement of good intent, and a commitment to comply with relevant legislation. Many employers extend their policies to the health and safety of others affected by their activities, such as contractors and the public. To demonstrate commitment from the top, the statement should be signed by the chairperson or chief executive.

2. Organisational responsibilities

This section shows how the organisation will put its good intentions into practice and which responsibilities those at different levels in the management structure will hold. The section might cover:

- making adequate resources available to implement the policy
- setting health and safety objectives
- developing suitable procedures and safe systems
- delegating specific responsibilities
- monitoring people's effectiveness in carrying out their responsibilities
- monitoring workplace standards
- feeding concerns up through the organisation.

3. Arrangements

The policy need not contain all the organisation's health and safety arrangements, but should state where they can be found, such as in a separate health and safety manual or within various procedural documents. Topics which may require detailed arrangements include:

- operational procedures
- training
- personal protective equipment
- inspection programmes
- accident and investigation arrangements

- fire and emergency procedures
- first aid
- occupational health
- control of contractors and visitors
- consultation with employees
- audits of health and safety arrangements.

Employees must be aware of the policy and their own responsibilities. They may be given their own copy, or the policy might be displayed around the workplace. Detailed briefings and induction training may be necessary for some arrangements.

Employers should revise their policies as often 'as may be appropriate'. Larger employers are likely to need to arrange for formal review and, where necessary, for revision to take place on a regular basis (by way of an ISO 9000 procedure, for example). Dating the policy document is an important part of this process.

The 'six-pack'

The 'six-pack' consists of six key sets of regulations introduced together in 1992. Some have, however, since been updated.

Management of Health and Safety at Work Regulations 1999 (Management Regulations)

The *Management Regulations* make explicit many of the duties contained in the *HSW Act*. They require employers to:

- make a 'suitable and sufficient' assessment of the risks to employees (including, specifically, young people and pregnant women) and others affected by their work activities
- plan, organise, control, monitor and review health and safety arrangements
- record the assessment's significant findings and the health and safety arrangements, if five or more people are employed
- appoint 'competent persons' to help apply health and safety law – since 1999, these are preferably to be employees, not outside consultants
- inform employees (and the parents of employed children) of workplace risks, control measures, and procedures in the event of serious and imminent danger
- provide adequate health and safety training
- provide health surveillance where the risk assessment shows it is needed
- arrange contacts with external services where necessary for first aid, emergency medical care and rescue work (a requirement introduced in 1999).

See later in this chapter, **Risk assessment, p 12**, for detailed information on conducting a risk assessment.

Workplace (Health, Safety and Welfare) Regulations 1992 (Workplace Regulations)

Employers and others with any control over the workplace (such as landlords) must ensure the workplace, equipment and devices listed in the regulations are maintained in efficient working order and good repair. These regulations govern much of the responsibility which facilities managers have for ensuring that the work premises are clean, comfortable, well-lit, well-ventilated and well-organised. Specifically, employers must ensure:

- enclosed workplaces are ventilated by sufficient fresh or purified air

- a reasonable temperature is maintained

- there is suitable and sufficient lighting, especially natural light

- workplaces, furniture, furnishings and fittings are clean

- there is sufficient floor area and headroom

- workstations and seating are suitable for the person and the job

- floors are level, not slippery, effectively drained, and kept free from obstruction, and staircases have handrails

- risks from falls or falling objects are removed or controlled, with fences and covers for tanks and pits

- glazing is protected against breakage and marked so it can be seen

- windows and skylights can be cleaned, opened, and left open safely

- traffic routes are marked and organised so that pedestrians and vehicles can circulate safely

- doors, gates, escalators and moving walkways are safely constructed and safe to use

- enough toilets and washing facilities are provided, which are accessible, ventilated, lit and clean

- an adequate supply of wholesome drinking water is provided

- facilities are provided for storing and changing clothes

- facilities for resting and eating meals are provided, with suitable arrangements for non-smokers and pregnant women.

Health and Safety (Display Screen Equipment) Regulations 1992 (DSE Regulations)

Employers must assess the risks to 'habitual' users or operators of computer monitors and other display screens such as video monitors and reduce them to the lowest level reasonably practicable. 'Users' are employees, whereas operators are self-employed people or 'temps'. Habitual monitor users:

- use them continuously for an hour or more a day

- depend on them to do the job

- have no discretion over their use.

Employers must also ensure:

- new workstations meet minimum legal requirements

- users take breaks from their monitor or change activities regularly (a 5–10 minute break every hour is better than 15 minutes every 2 hours)

- on request, employees receive free regular sight tests and corrective glasses

- employees receive adequate training and information.

Manual Handling Operations Regulations 1992

Manual handling is the transporting or supporting of a load by hand or bodily force, including lifting, putting down, pushing, pulling, carrying or moving. Employers' duties are to:

- avoid the manual handling operation if reasonably practicable, by redesigning the task to avoid moving the load or by automating the process

- conduct a further risk assessment, if eliminating the risks is not possible, and reduce the risk of injury to the lowest level reasonably practicable

- provide employees with indications and, where practicable, precise information on the weight of each load and its heaviest side.

Provision and Use of Work Equipment Regulations 1998 (PUWER)

Employers must ensure all work equipment (such as tools, photocopiers, vehicles, manufacturing plant) is:

- suitable for its intended use

- safe to use, maintained in a safe condition and, in some cases, inspected for safety by a competent person

- used only by trained personnel

- accompanied by suitable safety devices (such as guards, warnings, stop buttons)

- used according to a safe system of work (such as maintaining machinery when it is shut down, for example).

Some further points:

- If employees provide their own equipment, or work from home, the employer must ensure it complies with PUWER

- PUWER does not apply to equipment used by members of the public (such as compressed air equipment on garage forecourts), although the HSW Act will apply

- Mobile equipment (such as forklift trucks) meant to carry people must be suitable for the purpose, and employers must minimise the risk of it rolling over

- Power presses and their guard devices must be thoroughly examined at specified intervals, inspected daily for safety, and records kept.

Personal Protective Equipment at Work Regulations 1992 (PPE Regulations)

Employers must:

- assess whether personal protective equipment (PPE) (such as face masks, fall-arresting equipment, gloves etc) is suitable and provide it to employees exposed to risks not adequately controlled by other means

- ensure items of PPE worn together are compatible

- ensure PPE is maintained in efficient working order and good repair

- provide storage for PPE that is not in use – if the PPE is contaminated, this must be separate from ordinary clothing

- provide information and training on the risks the PPE will limit, and how to use and maintain the PPE

- ensure the PPE is properly used.

Other key regulations

Confined Spaces Regulations 1997

The main duties under these regulations are:

- to avoid entry to confined spaces – by having work done from the outside, for example

- if entry to a confined space is unavoidable, to follow a safe system of work

- to put in place adequate emergency arrangements before the work starts.

Construction (Design and Management) Regulations 1994 (CDM Regulations)

The *CDM Regulations* apply to construction work lasting more than 30 days or involving more than 500 person days of work. They require the client to ensure (via its planning supervisor) that its principal contractor is competent to handle the building project safely. It also imposes duties on the project's designer.

- The client must appoint a planning supervisor and principal contractor (it may appoint itself to both roles, provided it is competent); be satisfied they are competent and have adequate resources to fulfil their duties; pass information relevant to health and safety to them; and ensure there is an adequate health and safety plan before construction begins.

- The planning supervisor must notify HSE of the project, and ensure a health and safety file is prepared listing foreseeable risks to contractors.

- The principal contractor must ensure cooperation between contractors, ensure contractors comply with the health and safety plan and promptly provide the planning supervisor with information needed in the health and safety file.

- The designer must ensure its designs prevent at source foreseeable risks to affected persons (builders, cleaners, building occupiers). The *CDM (Amendment) Regulations 2000* ensure the requirements still apply if designers' employees prepare a design on their behalf.

Control of Asbestos at Work Regulations 2002 (CAW Regulations)

The CAW Regulations 2002 came in to force in November 2002. They place an explicit duty on people in control of premises to:

- take reasonable steps to locate materials likely to contain asbestos

- assume that any material contains asbestos unless there is evidence that it does not

- keep an up-to-date written record of the location of these materials

- monitor the condition of these materials

- assess the risk of exposure from asbestos and presumed-asbestos materials

- prepare and implement a management plan to control these risks.

Control of Substances Hazardous to Health Regulations 2002 (COSHH)

Employers must:

- make a suitable and sufficient assessment of health risks to employees exposed to hazardous substances

- in order of preference, prevent exposure, control exposure, or provide PPE

- provide health surveillance for exposed employees

- keep exposed employees' health records for 40 years

- attach safety data sheets to COSHH assessments.

Electricity at Work Regulations 1989

Employers must ensure:

- electrical systems are constructed and maintained to prevent danger

- use and maintenance of systems, and work near systems, is safe

- protective equipment is suitable and properly maintained and used.

Health and Safety (Consultation with Employees) Regulations 1996

Employers must:

- consult employees on the introduction of any measure or new technology which substantially affects their health and safety

- consult employees either directly or through elected representatives

- provide elected representatives with training, paid time off and other facilities reasonably required.

Health and Safety (First Aid) Regulations 1981

Employers must provide:

- adequate and appropriate first aid facilities

- either qualified first aiders (the ACoP suggests one first aider for every 50 employees)

- or, in low-risk or small workplaces, an 'appointed person' to take charge in an emergency.

Health and Safety Information for Employees Regulations 1989

Employers must display an HSE information poster or provide each employee with an HSE leaflet. New versions of both have been in use since 1 July 2000.

Health and Safety (Safety Signs and Signals) Regulations 1996

Employers must:

- provide warning signs if they cannot avoid a risk by other means

- train employees in the meaning of safety signs.

Lifting Operations and Lifting Equipment Regulations 1998 (LOLER)

These regulations supplement PUWER and apply to equipment such as cranes, goods lifts, forklift trucks, mobile elevating work platforms, hoists and ropes. Employers must ensure:

- lifting equipment has adequate strength and stability

- lifting equipment is positioned and installed to make the risk of the equipment or load falling or hitting a person as low as reasonably practicable

- lifting equipment is marked with its safe working load

- equipment for lifting people does not present a risk of them being crushed or trapped or of them falling

- any operation involving lifting equipment is properly planned by a competent person, and properly supervised and executed.

Noise at Work Regulations 1989

Employers must:

- reduce the risk of hearing damage to the lowest level reasonably practicable

- where noise cannot be further reduced, provide ear protection if personal daily noise exposures are 90dB or more (or on request at levels of 85–90dB)

- proposals have been published to amend the regulations so as to reduce the noise levels to 80 dB and 85 dB.

Reporting of Injuries, Diseases and Dangerous Occurrences Regulations 1995 (RIDDOR)

Employers must:

- notify HSE or the local authority (LA) of a death or serious injury immediately

- send a report form within 10 days if a person is absent following a work injury for more than three consecutive days or if there is a 'dangerous occurrence'

- notify HSE or LA if a person suffers a work-related disease (such as carpal tunnel syndrome, hand-arm vibration syndrome, legionellosis, dermatitis, asthma or asbestos-related diseases)

- notify the HSE or LA of specific dangerous occurrences.

Safety Representatives and Safety Committees Regulations 1977

Trade unions may appoint employees as safety representatives with the right to:

- be consulted by the employer on health and safety

- carry out investigations and inspections

- have paid time off to perform their duties and attend training.

Dangerous Substances and Explosive Atmospheres Regulations 2002

These regulations (to be known as DSEAR) came into force in December 2002. They set minimum requirements for the protection of workers from fire and explosions arising from dangerous substances and potentially explosive atmospheres.

Employers must:

- carry out a risk assessment of any work activity involving dangerous substances

- provide technical and organisational measures to eliminate or reduce, as far as is reasonably practicable, the identified risks

- provide equipment and procedures to deal with accidents and emergencies

- provide information and training to employees

- classify places where explosive atmospheres may occur into zones and mark the zones where necessary.

DSEAR Regulations 2002 should compliment existing health and safety management systems.

Risk assessment

HSE has produced an ACoP and guidance to the *Management Regulations*[1], as well as a *Five steps to risk assessment* guide[2]. According to its own definitions:

- 'a **risk assessment** is nothing more than a careful examination of what, in your work, could cause harm to people, so that you can weigh up whether you have taken enough precautions or should do more to prevent harm'

- 'a **hazard** means anything that can cause harm (such as chemicals, electricity, working from ladders)'

- '**risk** is the chance, high or low, that somebody will be harmed by the hazard'.

Spotting hazards

Ways of identifying hazards include asking employees or their safety representatives what risks they have noticed; consulting accident and ill-health records, suppliers' manuals, the trade press, relevant legislation and guidance; or seeking advice from consultants.

Typical hazards to watch for include:

- physical hazards (such as poorly guarded machinery, mezzanine floors, slipping/tripping hazards, vehicles, poor electrical wiring, fire hazards)

- hazardous substances (such as chemicals, dust, fumes)

- a hazardous work environment (such as noise, poor ventilation, bad lighting, hot or cold workplaces)

- psychological hazards (such as stress, long hours, shiftwork)

- ergonomic hazards (such as repetitive work, lifting).

Who might be harmed?

Those at risk might be:

- employees (office, operational and maintenance staff, for example)

- contractors (cleaners and security guards, for example)

- members of the public and volunteers

- young and inexperienced workers
- new and expectant mothers
- staff with disabilities
- home, lone and mobile workers.

Risks may increase at certain times of day, such as after dark or during busy periods.

Controlling the risks

It is important to consider whether existing precautions:

- meet legal requirements
- comply with industry standards
- represent good practice
- reduce risks as far as reasonably practicable.

If not, an action plan will be necessary, categorising remaining risks as high, medium or low risk. Priority should go to those measures which will protect the whole workplace. The aim is to eliminate hazards altogether (by not using a hazardous substance, for example) or, if this is not possible, to control risks, in order of preference, by:

- combating risks at source (for example, if steps are slippery, treating them is better than displaying a warning sign)
- preventing access to the hazard (for example, by installing machine guards, using permits to work which restrict access to authorised staff, isolating a dusty area)
- organising work to reduce exposure to the hazard (by rearranging work patterns to reduce stress, for example)
- issuing personal protective equipment (PPE)
- providing welfare facilities (such as washing facilities to remove contamination).

Taking advantage of technical advances can make work processes safer and more efficient. It is also crucial to provide relevant training and information to staff, and in shared workplaces, to swap information with other firms on site.

Recording the findings

Generally speaking, organisations with five or more employees must write down their risk assessment. The document can make cross-references to the health and safety policy and other relevant paperwork, rather than repeating everything. An inspector or union safety representative may ask to see the risk assessment, or it may provide evidence in the event of a personal injury claim.

Reviewing and revising

Most health and safety legislation requires employers to review the risk assessment, and revise it as necessary, if it is 'no longer valid or there has been a significant change'. Hazardous substance and asbestos assessments must, however, be reviewed 'regularly', and HSE guidance states that this is good practice for any risk assessment. Significant changes which might make the risk assessment out of date could include bringing in new machines, substances or procedures.

'Suitable and sufficient'

The *Management Regulations* require risk assessments to be 'suitable and sufficient'. This means:

- allocating appropriate resources

- making the level of detail proportionate to the risk – overcomplicated assessments of simple hazards are not required

- anticipating 'foreseeable' risks

- ensuring consultants have sufficient understanding of particular work activities

- adapting any 'model' assessment to the actual work situation

- drawing up a timetable for implementing short-, medium- and long-term controls

- reviewing non-routine activities such as maintenance, cleaning, loading and unloading vehicles, changes in production cycles and emergencies

- reviewing off-site activities, such as homeworking

- complying with specific regulations – though repeating assessments is not necessary

- addressing what actually happens in the workplace, not what the works manual says should happen.

HSE's Five steps to risk assessment

1. Look for the hazards.
2. Decide who might be harmed, and how.
3. Weigh up the risks and decide whether existing precautions are adequate or more needs to be done.
4. Record your findings.
5. Review your assessment and revise it if necessary.

Criminal sanctions

Most breaches of health and safety laws are heard in the magistrates' courts, where a maximum fine of £20,000 for breaches of ss 2–6 of the *HSW Act* can be imposed. For most other offences, the maximum is £5,000. Magistrates can, however, refer cases to the Crown Court for a trial by jury, where fines are unlimited. Defendants can also ask for their case to be heard by a jury.

Campaigners have been arguing for many years that many of the fines imposed, especially by magistrates, are inadequate. In the construction industry, for example, where workers are six times more likely to be killed than in any other industry, there were 41 prosecutions in 1999 for fatal accidents. The average fine in these cases (including those heard in the Crown Court) was £15,661, and in 13 cases the fine was less than £1,000. Overall, in the period 2001/02 the average level of fines across all industry sectors rose by 39 per cent. The HSE hope that fines will truly be proportionate to the seriousness of the offence. Total fines in 2001/02 reached £10 million.

Penalties in the Crown Court have, however, been increasing, especially since the Court of Appeal's judgment in the *Howe*[3] case in 1998. This laid out sentencing guidelines, including that:

- the level of fine should reflect the gravity of the offence, the degree of risk, and whether it was an isolated offence

- aggravating factors include whether the defendant failed to heed warnings, deliberately flouted health and safety legislation for financial gain, and whether a fatality occurred

- mitigating factors include a prompt guilty plea, taking steps to remedy health and safety failures, and a good safety record.

Since *Howe*, there have been some well-publicised seven-figure fines, including:

- £1.5 million under s 3(1) of the *HSW Act* against Great Western Trains for the Southall crash, plus £680,000 costs

- a total of £1.2 million against Balfour Beatty Civil Engineering and its tunnelling subcontractor, Geoconsult, following the Heathrow rail link tunnel collapse, plus £100,000 costs each, even though the incident was a 'near miss' and no one was injured

- a total of £1.7 million against Port Ramsgate, two construction and design firms and Lloyds Register of Shipping (which carried out inspection work), plus costs of nearly £250,000, following the collapse of a walkway which killed six people.

Facilities managers should note that even though Balfour Beatty and Port Ramsgate contracted out the work which led to the incidents, they were still held accountable under health and safety law, being fined £700,000 and £500,000 respectively. See elsewhere in this chapter, **Managing contractors, p 41** for more on this issue.

The Crown Court can order imprisonment of up to two years for contravention of an improvement or prohibition notice, and failure to have an asbestos removal licence. The first person to receive a custodial sentence – of three months – was Roy Hill in 1996, followed by a nine-month sentence for Paul Evans. Both men breached the asbestos licensing regime.

Revitalising strategy

In its document *Revitalising Health and Safety*[4], the government laid out an action plan to make health and safety penalties tougher across the board. The plan includes:

- making prison sentences (in Crown Court and magistrates' courts) and maximum £20,000 fines (in magistrates' courts) possible under most health and safety legislation

- considering 'innovative' penalties, such as fines linked to turnover, stopping bonuses, suspending managers without pay or compulsory health and safety training

- publicly naming and shaming companies convicted of offences.

Directors' responsibilities

In July 2001, the HSC introduced new guidance on directors' responsibilities for health and safety[5]. The original proposal for a more formal 'code' was dropped after criticisms that its legal status would be ambiguous.

The first four action points in the guidance are uncontroversial, reflecting existing best practice. They state:

- 'The board needs to accept formally and publicly its collective role in providing health and safety leadership in its organisation.'

- 'Each member of the board needs to accept their individual role in providing health and safety leadership for their organisation.'

- 'The board needs to ensure that all board decisions reflect its health and safety intentions ... it is particularly important that the health and safety ramifications of investment in new plant, premises, processes or products are taken into account.'

- 'The board needs to recognise its role in engaging the active participation of workers in improving health and safety.'

It is the fifth and final action point for which business leaders have reserved their fire. It states: 'The HSC recommends that boards appoint one of their number to be the "health and safety director".' The use of the word 'recommends' suggests some hasty watering down, but business representatives remain concerned at the potential for one individual to become a scapegoat in the event of an accident.

There are two main concerns. First, the government could still use its forthcoming safety bill (see below) to introduce a more onerous, legal requirement to appoint a health and safety director. Second, when the new corporate killing law is passed (again, see below), a health and safety director could face imprisonment in the event of a workplace fatality.

According to a British Safety Council survey, 40 per cent of firms feared directors would leave rather than risk liability for accidents. Others said they would intentionally appoint an easily replaceable 'fall guy' as health and safety director to avoid culpability themselves.

New legislation expected

The new penalties will require legislation, and the government is expected to introduce a wide-ranging safety bill, being hailed as the most significant development since the *HSW Act*.

Corporate killing

Also expected at some stage in the future when parliamentary time permits, is legislation making it easier to convict organisations of corporate killing, provided their conduct falls 'far below what could reasonably be expected'. Under existing legislation, an organisation can only be guilty of manslaughter if a culpable individual can be identified, who acted as its 'directing mind'. This meant that large companies with complex management structures escaped punishment for incidents like the Herald of Free Enterprise ferry disaster, King's Cross fire and Southall rail crash.

Under Home Office proposals for a new law[6], juries would only need evidence of a general management failing that contributed to the death, in order to convict the company of corporate killing. Moreover, directors who 'substantially contribute' to a corporate killing crime could be jailed or temporarily disqualified.

Civil compensation

An employee, contractor or member of the public who has been injured or made ill as a result of a negligent employer's act or omission can bring a claim for compensation. This is based on the common law concept that every member of society owes a duty of care towards others. Employers may also be 'vicariously liable' for an accident caused by one of their employees during the course of their employment.

Civil actions must commence within three years of the claimant finding out about their injury or illness. Claimants can receive damages for a number of losses, including loss of earnings, pain and suffering, medical expenses and disfigurement. Employers, in turn, have a number of defences available. They can argue contributory negligence, which means the injured person contributed to the accident, for example by ignoring safety rules, or they can argue that the injuries were not reasonably foreseeable.

The *Civil Procedure Rules 1998* introduced measures to speed up claims, including a 'fast track' system for claims up to £15,000. In practice, most claims are settled out of court by the employer's insurers. Employers are required to have insurance against such claims under the *Employers' Liability (Compulsory Insurance) Act 1969*.

In 2000, TUC figures show the unions secured £320 million in compensation for members injured or made ill at work – an average of £6,000 for each of the 54,650 cases pursued.

Promoting occupational health

Section 2 of the *HSW Act* provides that employers have a duty of care to ensure the health, safety and welfare at work of all employees. The following sections offer guidance to the facilities manager on how to comply with this duty.

Avoiding back pain

Back pain is the commonest source of workplace ill-health. The causes include poorly-designed workstations which encourage poor posture, and lifting and carrying of loads (manual handling).

More than one third of serious workplace injuries reported each year are manual handling-related, and most of these are back injuries. Employers lose 10 million working days a year to musculoskeletal disorders, half of these to back pain. Many injuries are cumulative, in other words a number of apparently insignificant problems build up over a period of time until the effects become serious.

The best way to prevent injuries is to avoid the need for lifting and carrying in the first place by reorganising the task or automating the handling process. If mechanisation is chosen, facilities managers will need to ensure new risks are not imported. For example, lifting equipment will need to be properly maintained and forklift trucks will need to be kept away from pedestrians.

Low-tech handling aids like trolleys may provide a simple solution. But all aids should be readily accessible or they will not be used, and employees must receive training in their use.

Risk assessment

HSE's manual handling guidance advises employers to assess four problem areas when considering how to make lifting and carrying safer. These are:

- the way the task is done
- the working environment
- the load itself
- the people doing the lifting.

Facilities managers will play a key role in reducing risk in the first two of these areas (see elsewhere in this chapter, **Manual handling checklist, p 20**). Changes to the task and the environment will often also increase efficiency and productivity.

The task

- Change the layout of the task – by storing loads at waist height, for example. Store only lighter loads, or those handled infrequently, higher or lower.
- Eliminate obstacles which the worker has to reach over or into, such as poorly-placed pallets or excessively deep containers.

- Avoid employees having to lift loads from the floor while seated.

- Although a swivel-action seat will reduce the need to twist, bear in mind that a chair on castors might move accidentally.

- Ensure the relative height of seats and work surfaces is well matched.

- Consider using two or more people to handle an awkward load.

- Maintain all handling equipment and personal protective equipment (PPE) (such as gloves or safety footwear) properly.

- Improve the work routine – through self-pacing or job rotation, for example.

The environment

- Remove space constraints, such as narrow gangways, doorways and working areas. Ensure there is enough floorspace and headroom, and think about the positioning of fixtures.

- Ensure floors are flat, well-maintained and properly drained. Clear spillages away promptly, and consider slip-resistant flooring.

- Avoid manual handling activities on more than one level. If this is unavoidable, ensure there is a gentle slope or, failing that, well-positioned and properly maintained steps. Working surfaces should, where possible, be level with each other.

- Provide a comfortable environment, avoiding extremes of temperature, high humidity and poor ventilation.

- Provide sufficient well-directed light.

The load

- Consider making loads lighter, smaller, easier to grasp, more stable or less damaging to hold.

The individual

- Consider whether individuals are at particular risk of injury, because they are pregnant or have a history or back, knee or hip problems, for example.

- Provide information and training on manual handling injury risks and good handling techniques. But remember that training workers is not a substitute for well-designed systems and workplaces.

Preventing WRULDs

Work-related upper limb disorders (WRULDs), sometimes known as RSI (repetitive strain injuries) are injuries to muscles, tendons or nerves, especially in the hands, wrists, elbows or shoulders. Specific WRULDs include tenosynovitis, carpal tunnel syndrome and epicondylitis (tennis elbow). But the courts have also awarded damages to employees suffering from diffuse RSI – that is, a collection of symptoms which do not constitute a medically-recognised injury. Repetitive tasks like keyboard work, assembly line work and packing are common causes.

As with avoiding manual handling injuries, facilities managers have a responsibility to improve equipment and the layout of work areas. But such measures will only be effective if carried out in conjunction with fundamental changes to the way in which work is organised, for example, by allowing workers to take a break from repetitive work.

Manual handling checklist

1. The tasks

Do they involve:

- holding or manipulating loads at distance from trunk?
- unsatisfactory bodily movement or posture, especially:
  - twisting the trunk?
  - stooping?
  - reaching upwards?
- excessive movement of loads, especially:
  - excessive lifting or lowering distances?
  - excessive carrying distances?
  - excessive pushing or pulling of loads?
  - risk of sudden movement of loads?
  - frequent or prolonged physical effort?
  - insufficient rest or recovery periods?
  - a rate of work imposed by a process?

2. The loads

Are they:

- heavy?
- bulky or unwieldy?
- difficult to grasp?
- unstable, or with contents likely to shift?
- sharp, hot or otherwise potentially damaging?

---

3. The working environment

Are there:

- space constraints preventing good posture?
- uneven, slippery or unstable floors?
- variations in level of floors or work surfaces?
- extremes of temperature or humidity?
- poor lighting conditions?

4. Individual capability

Does the job:

- require unusual strength, height, etc?
- create a hazard to those who might reasonably be considered to be pregnant or to have a health problem?
- require special information or training for its safe performance?

5. Other factors

Is movement or posture hindered by personal protective equipment or by clothing?

Source: *Manual Handling Operations Regulations 1992 – Guidance on Regulations* HSE Books.

Risk assessment

Employees may be at risk of developing WRULDs if:

- the work involves:
    - awkward hand, arm, wrist or shoulder movements
    - rapid repetitive movements
    - prolonged physical pressure, such as gripping or squeezing
    - a prolonged uncomfortable position
    - few breaks
    - lack of variety
    - long hours
    - a fast work rate (to keep up with a conveyor, for example).
- tools and equipment are:
    - too heavy
    - an uncomfortable shape
    - vibrating or noisy
    - designed for men but used by women.

- workstations are:
    - the wrong height for the individuals using them
    - not adjustable
    - noisy, cold, or have other adverse conditions
    - badly lit.

Solutions

Ways to reduce the risk of WRULDs occurring include:

- redesigning workstations and equipment, by, for example:
    - reducing the reaching required
    - moving controls
    - making conditions less cramped
    - providing adjustable chairs, footrests, etc
    - improving lighting and cutting out glare, to prevent users sitting awkwardly.
- redesigning tool handles, keeping tools sharp and lubricated, replacing hand tools with power versions, avoiding high vibration tools
- changing the method of work
- allowing self-pacing
- introducing rest breaks and variety of tasks
- training workers, including new staff or those using new equipment or working methods, in warning symptoms of WRULDs, good posture and safe working practices.

Computer workstations

Computer workstations must meet a number of ergonomic standards laid out in the Schedule to the *DSE Regulations* to avoid user strain. In order to comply, HSE has developed a risk assessment checklist in its booklet *VDUs: an easy guide to the Regulations*[7]. This includes the following questions:

- Is the display screen image clear?
    - Are the characters readable?
    - Is the image flicker-free?
    - Are the brightness and contrast adjustable?
    - Does the screen swivel and tilt?
    - Is the screen free from glare and reflections?

- Is the keyboard comfortable?
  - Is the keyboard tiltable?
  - Is there enough space to rest hands in front of the keyboard?
  - Is the keyboard glare-free?
  - Are the characters on the keys easily readable?
- Does the furniture fit the work and the user?
  - Is the work surface large enough?
  - Is the work surface free of glare and reflections?
  - Is the chair stable?
  - Do the adjustment mechanisms work?
  - Is the user comfortable?
- Is the environment around the workstation risk-free?
  - Is there enough room to change position and vary movement?
  - Are the levels of light, heat and noise comfortable?
  - Does the air feel comfortable?
- Is the software user-friendly?

Seating

Adjustable chairs are essential to combat musculoskeletal disorders such as back pain and WRULDs. When choosing or assessing seating, it is important to consider the individual's needs, the type of work and the size of the workstation. HSE guidance, *Seating at work*[8], suggests ensuring:

- the chair is comfortable for the intended period of use
- the back is properly supported
- there is sufficient padding
- the seat and back height are adjustable and the backrest tilts
- armrests (if required) allow enough arm movement and allow the individual to get close enough to the desk
- footrests are supplied if necessary
- the chair meets special user requirements (pregnant women and disabled employees, for example, may have special needs)
- the chair meets special task requirements
- the adjustment mechanisms are well maintained.

Midland Bank: the cost of WRULDs

- In 1999, the Court of Appeal ordered Midland Bank to pay damages of between £8,036 and £15,233 to each of five former data encoders, who it found were suffering from fibro-myalgia despite showing no objective physical symptoms. Interestingly for facilities managers, the court did not uphold the claimants' criticisms of their desk design, apart from uncomfortable keypads, nor did it matter that their chairs were not easily adjustable, because they had found a way around it. In this case, the organisation of the work – particularly speed targets and the lack of any opportunity to stretch or move around – was the main culprit.

- In 1997, the Court of Appeal awarded a Midland Bank secretary, Michelle Mulligan, £155,000 for tenosynovitis, caused by the bank's failure to assess her work posture, provide breaks, or warn her of the risks of WRULDs. It had also increased her work pressure.

- In 1989, the Midland agreed an out-of-court settlement of £45,000 with another secretary, Pauline Bernard, who also had tenosynovitis.

Reducing noise

Under the *Noise at Work Regulations*, employees' daily exposure to noise must not exceed the equivalent of 90dB – roughly equivalent to heavy street traffic – received continuously over eight hours. Engineered solutions are preferable, and ear protectors are a last resort only. Even in workplaces where sound levels are unlikely to reach 90dB, the *Noise at Work Regulations* state that noise should not be distracting or disturb people trying to talk. Although the main concerns are hearing loss and tinnitus (a permanent 'ringing' in the ears), continual noise can also cause stress. Both short bursts of loud noise and long-term exposure to lower noise levels can damage the inner ear. HSE figures suggest that 1.3 million employees in the UK are exposed to dangerous levels of noise. As well as manufacturing environments, call centres and open-plan offices can be unexpectedly noisy. Indeed, HSE found that 41 per cent of call centre operators have to raise their voices when communicating with people at a normal talking distance.

Control measures

HSE recommends controlling noise exposure by:

- designing workplaces for low noise emission – for example, using absorption materials to limit reflected sound; segregating noisy equipment from occupied areas

- engineering controls – for example, cushioning impacts in a yard where unloading takes place by fitting a rubber surface; using damping methods; mounting machines to prevent vibration; fitting silencers; using 'active noise control' to cancel out one sound with another

- modifying noise transmission paths – for example, enclosing machines; providing screens, barriers, walls and noise refuges; increasing the distance between employees and the noise source

- substituting noisy equipment or processes with quieter alternatives – for example, replacing compressed air tools with hydraulic equipment

- maintaining equipment and replacing worn parts

- changing working methods – for example, reducing exposure times through job rotation.

For best practice advice on how to design noise transmission out of the workplace, see **Workplace facilities: minimising noise through design, p 307.**

Asbestos-related diseases

Asbestos kills over 3,000 people in the UK every year, one-quarter of whom have been employed in the building industry. By 2020, 10,000 people a year are predicted to die from asbestos-related diseases, which would make asbestos the biggest single killer of men under 65 years old.

Although all three types of asbestos have now been banned, the substance remains in many buildings constructed between 1950 and 1980, especially those with steel frames or boilers with thermal insulation. Those most at risk of contracting mesothelioma, an incurable and fatal cancer, are those involved in demolition, maintenance and refurbishment work (including plumbers, electricians and carpenters), and other contractors working nearby when asbestos fibres are released into the air. Others who may disturb asbestos are contractors installing computers, fire alarms, window blinds and telecommunications systems. Employees present when the asbestos is disturbed could also be exposed, and they could carry fibres home on their clothes.

There is no safe level of exposure, and repeated low-level exposure can also cause asbestos-related diseases. It takes 15–60 years for the symptoms of mesothelioma, asbestosis of the lungs, or asbestos-related lung cancer to appear.

The most common uses of asbestos, listed in order of how likely they are to release dust if disturbed, are:

- sprayed coatings and asbestos insulation used for fire protection, pipes and boilers, thermal and acoustic insulation

- insulating boards used for fire protection to doors, cladding on walls and ceilings, partitioning and ceiling tiles

- asbestos cement used for roofing, wall panels, pipes and water tanks.

Surveys and logs

The *CAW Regulations 2002* formalise existing good practice. In effect, facilities managers will need to ensure their premises are surveyed for asbestos as a matter of course, rather than waiting until asbestos is accidently exposed.

The regulations include the 'duty to manage asbestos' and place responsibilities on the duty holder to identify, locate and manage asbestos-containing materials. HSE have issued several new *Approved Codes of Practice and Guidance* documents[9]. *ACoP L127* covers the Management of Asbestos in Non-Domestic Premises and sets out ways in which to comply with reg 4. The duty under reg 4 rests with the person in control of the maintenance activities and this is likely to be the Facilities Manager. The ACoP advises duty holders to:

- take reasonable steps to find asbestos materials and check its location

- presume that materials contain asbestos unless there is strong evidence that they do not

- make a written record of the location and condition of asbestos and keep it up to date

- assess the risk of anyone being exposed to asbestos materials is kept in good repair

- provide information to anyone at risk.

Guidance recommends consulting the leaseholder, architects or original building plans to find out if and where asbestos was used. It may be necessary to bring in accredited personnel to analyse samples. If asbestos is present, the risk of fibres being released must be assessed.

Leaving asbestos in place

If asbestos is in good condition and not likely to be either damaged or worked on, HSE recommends:

- leaving it in place and logging where it is (mark it on building plans and/or set up a register)

- warning contractors that some undiscovered asbestos could still be present elsewhere

- making a note of safe materials which could be mistaken for asbestos

- labelling asbestos materials with a warning sign

- ensuring contractors know where asbestos is and its condition

- conducting regular re-inspections.

Repair and removal

Depending on how poor its condition is, asbestos may need to be:

- repaired, sealed or enclosed, then logged following the above steps, or

- removed.

In either case, HSE-licensed contractors must carry out the work. They must double-bag the waste, clearly label it and dispose of it at a licensed site.

Duty to contractors and employees

HSE warns that during asbestos repair or removal work, employers should ensure contractors

Do:

- understand the health risks of asbestos exposure

- keep unnecessary personnel away

- take care not to create dust

- keep the material wet whenever possible

- wear a suitable respirator and protective clothing

- clean up with a vacuum cleaner complying with *BS 5415* (type 'H').

Do not:

- break up large pieces of asbestos materials

- use power tools – this creates dust

- expose workers who are not protected

- take protective clothing home to wash.

Legionellosis

Legionellosis is a group of diseases caused by legionella bacteria found in water. The bacteria occur in natural water supplies, but hot and cold water systems, air conditioning systems and cooling towers offer better breeding grounds. The most serious of the diseases is Legionnaires' disease, a type of pneumonia. HSE figures reveal 200–250 cases of Legionnaires' disease a year, but it believes there is under-reporting. About half these cases are linked to foreign travel.

Legionnaires' disease

Legionnaires' disease:

- kills around 12 per cent of sufferers

- mainly affects people aged between 40 and 70

- affects three times more men than women

- is most likely to affect smokers, alcoholics, people with diabetes, cancer, chronic respiratory or kidney disease, or those on renal dialysis or immuno-suppressant drugs

- is caused by susceptible individuals inhaling water droplets contaminated with legionella bacteria

- is not believed to be transmitted by drinking water containing legionella bacteria, or by person to person transmission

- produces symptoms two to ten days after infection, including chills, high fever, headache or muscle pain followed by a dry cough, and in extreme cases, pneumonia

- has broken out in or near large building complexes such as hotels, hospitals, offices and factories.

Legal duties

Legislation relevant to controlling legionellosis includes *COSHH* and the *Notification of Cooling Towers and Evaporative Condensers Regulations 1992*. The latter require those in control of work premises to notify the local authority or HSE in writing of any cooling towers and evaporative condensers, including any being decommissioned or dismantled. Other places that can harbour bacteria include showers, taps, water softeners, humidifiers, calorifiers and pipework.

HSE's legionella ACoP[10] states that the duty holder 'is required to have access to competent help' to assess whether there is a risk of the disease occurring. The accompanying guidance adds that whether it uses its own personnel, or a consultancy or water treatment company, the duty holder should ensure they are trained and have the necessary equipment. The duty holder should also appoint a manager or director with day-to-day responsibility for controlling the risk of legionellosis – in practice, this may be the facilities manager.

In mid-1999, the British Association for Chemical Specialities (BACS) and the Water Management Society (WMS) formulated a Recommended Code of Conduct for service providers. It offers advice to organisations, individuals or sub-contractors who provide services for controlling legionella bacteria in industrial or commercial premises. It is important for facilities managers to understand the Code so they can measure their current or prospective service provider against its guidelines. They should also ask service providers whether they have signed up to the Code. The Code covers six areas: allocation of responsibilities; training and competence of personnel; control measures; communication and management; record-keeping; and reviews.

Designing out legionellosis

Ideally, health and safety in any environment is designed in at the start. Where facilities managers have input in the design of a new building or a refurbishment, they should ensure the following design criteria are applied to hot and cold water systems:

- ensure storage cisterns and calorifiers are the correct size for their intended use

- do not site cold water tanks in a warm part of the building

- ensure pipework is as short and direct as possible

- ensure adequate insulation of pipes and tanks

- use materials that do not encourage the growth of legionella

- protect against contamination by, for instance, fitting storage tanks with lids.

Risk assessment and control

To minimise the risk of contamination in existing installations, HSE guidance recommends carrying out a site survey of complex premises, including an asset register of plant, pumps, strainers and so on, and an up-to-date diagram of the system. Some factors to consider include:

- the water source (is it mains water?)

- possible sources of contamination before the water reaches the cooling tower or cold water tank

- the system's normal characteristics

- reasonably foreseeable but abnormal operating conditions (such as breakdowns).

Measures to control the risk of disease include:

- controlling the release of water spray (such as the aerosol created by a cooling tower or shower)

- avoiding water temperatures of 20–45°C, which allow bacteria to proliferate

- avoiding water stagnation, which encourages biofilm to grow

- avoiding materials in the system such as sludge, scale, rust, algae and organic matter which harbour or provide nutrients for bacteria

- keeping the system clean to avoid sediments

- using water treatment programmes

- ensuring the system operates correctly and is well-maintained.

Routine monitoring of water systems is necessary, and the guidance suggests this should take place at least weekly. Testing of water quality and monitoring numbers of general bacteria are also important. But HSE suggests testing only for legionella bacteria is technically difficult, and the results difficult to interpret. The guidance states: 'A negative result is no guarantee that legionella bacteria are not present. Conversely, a positive result may not indicate a failure of controls as legionella are present in almost all natural water sources.'

If it is suspected that a user of the building has contracted legionellosis, HSE must be consulted immediately. Facilities managers should then involve senior management and take steps to identify the source of the infection and deal with any contamination as soon as possible.

Improving well-being

Sceptics may still doubt that 'sick' buildings really make people ill. But at the very least, problems like poor air quality, passive smoking, flickering lights and fluctuating temperatures undoubtedly reduce employees' well-being and productivity. Moreover, the *Workplace Regulations* impose a legal duty to look after employees' welfare.

Sick building syndrome

The World Health Organisation (WHO) has recognised sick building syndrome (SBS) since 1982. HSE estimates that 30–50 per cent of new or recently refurbished buildings cause some form of SBS. In the worst cases, 85 per cent of occupants may suffer symptoms.

Symptoms

Symptoms are flu-like and include skin problems, breathing problems (sore throats, coughs, blocked noses, sinusitis), muscle and joint aches (stiff shoulders, backache), and neurological disorders (tiredness, headaches, digestion problems). The symptoms will be much more common than average among workers in a particular building, and will reduce or disappear during weekends and holidays.

At-risk buildings

According to WHO, buildings most at risk of SBS are likely to date from the 1960s or later and have:

- open-plan offices
- a low level of user control over ventilation, heating and lighting
- lighting with high glare or flicker
- air conditioning with cooling capacity
- lots of soft furnishings
- lots of open storage
- synthetic furniture, carpets and paint
- poor maintenance and repair
- insufficient cleaning
- high temperatures or large temperature variations
- very low or high humidity
- indoor air pollutants (ozone from photocopiers and laser printers, chemicals released from carpet adhesive, tobacco smoke)
- airborne dust or fibres
- computers.

Solutions

Bucking the trend for open-plan offices, WHO recommends no more than 10 workstations in any room. Other problems may be resolved through maintaining air conditioning systems, replacing old photocopiers and laser printers, replacing fluorescent lights, and better cleaning. Since cleaning chemicals may themselves cause problems, however, the best solution is redesigning workplaces to be low maintenance.

Photocopiers

Well-maintained, modern photocopiers are rarely a health hazard. But if they are used frequently or there are a number of machines, there could be problems with noise, dry heat, and the release of ozone. The best solution is to place equipment in a separate room with separate ventilation. It is important to follow the manufacturer's recommendations for siting, cleaning and maintaining the machines, as well as following the precautions in the material safety data sheets for toner and other chemicals.

There should also be clear guidance on when it is safe for employees – with the appropriate training and information – to carry out repairs (such as clearing simple paper jams), and when a technician should be called. Modern equipment should turn off automatically when opened, but turning it off at the wall first is a simple safety precaution.

Lighting

Poor lighting can cause eyestrain, headaches, SBS and fatigue, as well as accidents (see elsewhere in this chapter, **Towards a safe workplace: preventing slips and trips, p 37**).

Lighting risk assessment

- Is emergency lighting adequate?
- Are desk lamps provided?
- Are light fittings regularly cleaned?
- Are lamps replaced regularly (after about 7,000 hours' use)?
- Are desks placed at right angles to windows to prevent glare?
- Are fluorescent light strips covered with a diffuser?
- Are windows fitted with blinds or curtains?
- Are walls, ceilings and furniture decorated in light, matt colours (to increase the level of light and reduce glare)?
- Is there a source of natural light?
- Are there any dark, unlit areas?

Source: *Office health and safety – a guide to risk prevention*, UNISON.

The ACoP to the *Workplace Regulations* states that:

- lights should be of a type and so positioned as to avoid glare
- lights should be repaired and cleaned to ensure effectiveness
- windows should be cleaned regularly
- local lighting should be provided as necessary.

The legislation also requires:

- an average illuminance for a whole work area of 200Lx (lux) with a minimum for any individual work position of 100Lx
- the location of lights and associated fittings should not cause a hazard, with employees able to find light switches easily.

In practice, generally accepted levels for offices are 400–500Lx at desk level, rising to 700Lx or more in specialist areas, such as architects' offices, where sharp focus is needed. Where each work task is individually lit and the area around the task is lit to a lower illuminance, as in local lighting in an office, the maximum ratio of illuminances of working area to adjacent area should be 5:1. Ambient lighting in common areas such as stairwells and lobbies may be considerably less powerful than for offices, down to 20Lx or less.

Natural light

Unlike some European countries, the UK has no legal requirement that workers should have access to natural light. But the tradition of placing offices for senior staff round the edges of a floor, making daylight access a privilege of managers and leaving those in open-plan cut off from natural light, is now widely challenged, and the recommended minimum ratio of artificial light to natural light at any long-term work setting is 1:5.

For best practice advice on workplace lighting, see **Workplace facilities: lighting, pp 318–326.**

Air quality

Temperature

The ACoP to the *Workplace Regulations* says that work rooms should normally be at least 16°C, or 13°C for work involving 'severe physical efforts'. There is no legally enforceable maximum temperature, but the ACoP says 'all reasonable steps should be taken to achieve a comfortable temperature'. It is rare for temperatures to be so extreme that they cause serious illness (like heat stroke or hypothermia), but less severe temperature problems can cause discomfort, loss of concentration, tiredness, irritability and SBS.

The Chartered Institution of Building Services Engineers recommends the following temperatures:

- heavy work in factories: 13°C
- light work in factories: 16°C

- hospital wards and shops: 18°C
- offices and dining rooms: 20°C.

The *International standard for office environments ISO 7730–1984* recommends an operative temperature range of 20–24°C with a variation of less than 3°C between head and ankle height. Radiators fitted with thermostats produce least complaint from office occupants of any heating system (probably because it allows for a degree of user control), but many larger office blocks (especially those built in the years following the energy crisis of the 1970s) have sealed windows and centrally-controlled systems.

Uncomfortably hot workplaces can be tackled by:

- providing air conditioning or fans
- ensuring windows can be opened
- shading windows with blinds
- siting workstations away from direct sunlight or hot areas
- insulating hot pipes
- providing a free supply of drinking water
- giving employees breaks to cool down
- introducing more flexible hours to avoid the worst effects of working in exceptionally high temperatures.

Thermometers should also be provided for monitoring temperatures.

In intentionally cold workplaces, such as those preparing food, it will be necessary to provide a warm working station using localised heating, draught exclusion and so on. Catering areas could be particularly hot and humid, and fume extraction and extractor or circulation fans will be necessary. Air inlets must be carefully sited to allow air movement in all parts of the kitchen.

Ventilation

The *Workplace Regulations* require enclosed workplaces to be ventilated by 'a sufficient quantity of fresh or purified air'. The recommended minimum airflow is five litres per second, though eight litres per second is a safer minimum to prevent complaints of airlessness. Care needs to be taken to ensure that ventilation does not cause draughts.

Humidity

The *DSE Regulations*, in s 3(*g*) of the schedule, state that 'an adequate level of humidity shall be established and maintained' in offices where there are visual display unit (VDU) users. To comply with the legislation, employers need to monitor humidity constantly, to ascertain whether adequate levels are being provided. It is also important for employers to recognise any dry heat symptoms being experienced by staff, in order to identify whether any problems need to be addressed to ensure staff health and comfort. For advice on humidity levels and monitoring, see **Workplace facilities: maintaining adequate humidity, p 000.**

Passive smoking

In 1998, a government scientific committee found that long-term passive smoking could increase the risk of lung cancer by 30–40 per cent and cause heart disease. HSE has issued guidance advice on how to deal with passive smoking at work[11]. This requires employers, in order of preference, to:

- ban smoking if reasonably practicable

- permit smoking in designated rooms

- provide smoking and non-smoking areas

- provide adequate ventilation

- reduce the time employees are exposed to smoke.

Particular account must be taken of employees more susceptible to the effects of tobacco smoke, such as those who suffer from asthma, chronic bronchitis and respiratory diseases.

The guidance states that non-smoking should be regarded as the norm in enclosed workplaces, with special provision made for smoking, rather than vice-versa. It also warns employers to consult employees before drawing up a smoking policy, and to give them at least three months before a ban takes effect. It also recommends that employers provide assistance and counselling to employees trying to quit smoking.

Passive smoking case law

Ill-health awards

Two Stockport Metropolitan Borough Council employees have received awards for passive smoking at work:

- In 1995, Beryl Roe received £25,000 after retiring on ill-health grounds, suffering eye, nose, throat and bronchial hypersensitivity. The council had shut down the ventilation system in her office.

- In 1993, Veronica Bland received £15,000 after developing chronic bronchitis.

No right to smoke at work

In the 1992 case of *Dryden v Greater Glasgow Health Board*, Ms Dryden, a smoker, resigned and claimed constructive dismissal three days into a smoking ban. The Employment Appeal Tribunal decided she had no contractual right to smoke at work. It found the employer had introduced the non-smoking policy for a legitimate purpose, consulted employees, given notice of its plans and offered assistance and counselling to give up smoking.

In buildings with mechanical ventilation, HSE says employers should consider discharging air from smoking areas separately rather than allowing it to enter the recirculation system. If this is not reasonably practicable, the recirculated air should be brought up to an appropriate standard by suitable decontamination systems. Tobacco smoke building up in the workplace is a sure sign that the ventilation system is inadequate.

Best practice advice on maintaining good indoor air quality is covered in **Workplace facilities: HVAC, p 295.**

Stress

After carrying out a public consultation exercise, the HSC has shied away from introducing a stress ACoP, fearing that there is currently no clear way to measure employers' management of the issue. Nevertheless, employers have a legal duty under the *HSW Act* to ensure the workplace is healthy, and this applies to psychological as well as physical health.

Employees can also bring a common law claim against a negligent employer, and there have been several well-publicised out-of-court settlements for stress. These include £203,000 to the warden of a travellers' site, and £200,000 to a council employee who had a breakdown after alleged management bullying. In court, claimants have had a harder time, needing to prove that:

- they have a recognised psychiatric disorder

- the risk of psychological injury was reasonably foreseeable

- the employer's negligence caused the injury.

More worrying for employers than a possible court case is the price of stress in terms of absenteeism and under-performance. Stress is second only to musculoskeletal disorders as a reported cause of absence from work in the UK. Research by the TUC shows that over 12 million people complain about stress at work. HSE figures suggest five million people, representing one fifth of workers, suffer from such high work-related stress that it causes them serious mental and physical health problems.

Causes and prevention

The main culprits are work overload, unreasonable targets, poor management habits, bullying and long hours. The causes, in other words, are organisational – staff may have too little control over their work, or work relationships may be poor. The work may be repetitive, there may be too little or too much to do, or staff may be under- or over-qualified. Some staff may have difficulty balancing their work and home lives. Facilities managers can help to tackle these problems in their own staff through:

- taking stress seriously, rather than seeing it as an individual weakness

- allowing staff to plan and organise their own jobs, and contribute ideas

- being supportive, involving staff and communicating well with them

- avoiding bullying, racist or sexist attitudes

- giving staff the opportunity to develop their skills

- changing the way work is done – for example, by introducing job rotation, more variety or responsibility

- giving staff clear objectives

- giving warning of urgent jobs

- increasing flexibility – for example, introducing flexible working hours or working from home.

Personal counselling may have a role to play in mopping up the after-effects of stress, but it should be used in conjunction with improvements in work design which will both attack the root causes of the problem and improve the performance of the organisation.

Stressful buildings

Facilities managers also have a responsibility to ensure that the working environment does not cause stress. Building users often complain about issues such as:

- poor artificial lighting, lack of daylight and glare

- poor temperature control, particularly over-cooling

- draughts, poor ventilation and poor air quality

- windows which must not be opened

- noise and overcrowding

- uncomfortable workstations

- lack of control over their own environment

- poor response from building managers.

These problems can all lead to stress and under-performance. They affect users of both open-plan buildings and buildings divided into large shared rooms. The former may be unhappy that the main circulation route through the building passes through their space. The latter may complain of overcrowding and inequitable distribution of space.

However, facilities managers cannot, on their own, solve their organisation's stress problems. As stated above, the real causes are overwhelmingly working methods and the company's culture. Commitment is needed at all levels of the organisation to resolve these issues.

Violence

Violence to employees encompasses everything from bank robbery, vandalism, hostage-taking and bombing, to the aggression displayed daily by members of the public in places like hospital waiting rooms, job centres and train stations. The risk to staff is two-fold – they may be physically injured, or they may be affected psychologically either following an actual attack or after being threatened. For detailed information about violence in the workplace and measures to combat it, see **Access, safety and security, pp 351–364**.

Towards a safe workplace

Preventing slips and trips

Slips and trips cause one-quarter to one-third of major accidents at work, or about 5,500–6,000 such accidents a year.

HSE has published guidance, *Slips and trips*[12], which contains much useful advice for facilities managers. It recommends:

- getting workplace conditions right in the first place, for example, by selecting the right flooring and lighting, planning routes and avoiding overcrowding

- keeping areas free of obstructions

- checking flooring regularly for holes, cracks, loose mats, and so on

- using the correct cleaning methods to avoid slippery residues building up

- carrying out cleaning and maintenance after hours, or if this is not possible, using signs to warn people about wet floors, providing alternative routes, and avoiding trailing cables

- organising work and machinery to avoid spills, and cleaning up or fencing off any that do occur immediately

- positioning electrical equipment to avoid trailing cables, and using covers to fix cables down

- providing safety footwear free of charge to employees if floors are unavoidably wet or dusty (there are no British Standards for slip resistance, but the HSE guidance includes advice on shoe sole materials)

- keeping lights working, clean and free of obstructions, ensuring they do not dazzle, and providing extra lighting at stairs and slopes

- providing handrails, treads and floor markings on slopes or changes of level, and doormats between wet and dry areas.

Flooring

Cost and appearance should not be the only concerns when choosing flooring. Suitability for the location and the demands that will be made on the surface are also important. The HSE guidance states that 'there is no need to put up with a slippery smooth floor because it is more hygienic or easier to clean'. There are devices for measuring slipperiness, but HSE warns that the resulting 'friction values' must be interpreted with caution because workplaces differ so widely.

There are also floor treatments to reduce slipping – concrete can be abraded or chemically treated, there are coatings containing abrasive particles, and adhesive strips or squares. Some treatments may need regular reapplication.

Flooring needs to be laid by competent people, and kept clean and in good condition to maintain slip-resistance and prevent curling edges or lifting. Different flooring surfaces and certain spills may need different kinds of cleaning.

Employers' liability: case example

An occupational therapist, Alison Hockaday, received a £600,000 negotiated settlement from her employers, Durham Health Authority, in December 1999, after part of her right leg had to be amputated. She injured her knee in 1986, slipping on wet leaves on the entrance steps of the Winterton Hospital. She was left using a walking stick, but returned to work. In March 1990, she slipped on a wet floor at the hospital, fracturing her ankle, and in 1997 her leg had to be amputated below the knee. The health authority was found liable in court for the first accident, and did not contest the second claim.

Equipment

Heavy plant or humble ladder, photocopier or forklift truck, the risk from all work equipment must be as low as possible.

HSE's guidance leaflet, *Using work equipment safely*, advises employers to ensure that:

- new and temporary workers (who may lack experience), people who have changed departments, those with difficulties (such as impaired mobility), and cleaning and maintenance staff are properly trained and supervised

- guards and safety devices are convenient to use, not easily overridden, made from appropriate materials, and allow the machine to be cleaned safely

- control switches are clearly marked and carefully sited

- the type of power supply, (electric, hydraulic or pneumatic) is considered – each has different risks

- hand tools are not worn, the handles are not split, and there are enough tools to avoid employees improvising with something else

- routine checks are made, preventative maintenance is carried out where appropriate, and manufacturers' instructions are followed

- equipment can be safely maintained and repaired:

    o machines should be disconnected and not moving or hot

    o mobile equipment should have the engine off and brake on

    o flammable substances must be cleaned away

○   isolating valves must be locked off

○   equipment which could fall needs support.

Practical examples

The guidance leaflet gives the following examples of risks arising from one of the commonest pieces of workplace equipment, the ladder. Risks include:

- ladders not being securely placed and fixed

- climbing with loads

- overreaching or overbalancing

- ladders being used when other equipment would be safer

- the use of poorly-maintained or faulty ladders.

Many accidents involving ladders happen during work lasting 30 minutes or less. They are often used for short jobs when it would be safer to use other equipment, for example mobile tower scaffolds. If facilities managers maintain equipment well, and ensure employees and contractors use the correct equipment for the job, this can significantly reduce the risk of accidents.

The GMB union has developed health and safety guidance for cleaners, which includes a case study about a group of women using heavy industrial buffing machines to clean floors. The case study demonstrates that work equipment can lead to occupational health problems as well as accidents. The women's union safety representative raised problems such as back and arm pain and numbness in the fingers with their employer, who:

- provided training in safe lifting

- provided thick gloves to minimise the effects of vibration

- increased the amount of manual cleaning

- introduced job rotation.

Using the machines less not only solved the problems the cleaners had raised, it also reduced the number of slip and trip accidents.

Vehicles

Accidents involving vehicles at the workplace kill around 70 people a year and maim 1,000 more. Reversing vehicles are a particular hazard, causing one-quarter of such deaths. The accidents involve cars, vans, trucks and other mobile equipment. People can be injured by being knocked down, falling from vehicles, being struck by a falling load or vehicles overturning.

Under reg 17(1) of the *Workplace Regulations*, every workplace must (so far as is reasonably practicable) be so organised that pedestrians and vehicles can circulate in a safe manner. Under reg 17(2), traffic routes in a workplace must be suitable for the persons or vehicles using them, sufficient in number, in suitable positions and of sufficient size. Under reg 17(3) and (4):

- pedestrians or vehicles must be able to use traffic routes without endangering those at work

- there must be sufficient separation of traffic routes from doors and gates and between vehicle and pedestrian traffic routes

- where vehicles and pedestrians do use the same traffic routes, there must be sufficient space between them

- where necessary, all traffic routes must be suitably indicated.

Work vehicles also count as work equipment for the purposes of PUWER. Regulation 5 says that they must:

- be constructed and adapted to suit their purpose

- be selected so as to avoid risks to the health and safety of persons where the vehicles are to be used

- only be used for the operations specified and under suitable conditions.

Regulation 6 says work equipment, including vehicles, must be maintained in an efficient state, in efficient working order and in good repair. Vehicles must be provided with safety features (a reversing alarm, seat belts, lights, etc). Under the *Management Regulations*, drivers must be trained for the job and supervised if necessary. Contractors also need to know the site rules, so that they can carry out loading and unloading safely.

Safe traffic routes

Facilities managers have a particular responsibility to ensure that the layout of the workplace does not create risks, either from work vehicles or private cars. Safety measures could include:

- creating pedestrian areas, including safe crossings and barriers if necessary

- providing enough designated parking places to avoid stopping in unsafe locations

- ensuring traffic routes are wide enough, well-constructed and maintained, avoid blind bends and are free of obstructions

- increasing visibility for drivers and pedestrians

- providing road markings, signs, road humps and mirrors as required

- redesigning the workplace to remove the need for reversing, by introducing a one-way system, for example

- if reversing cannot be eliminated, ensuring there is enough space for vehicles to reverse and minimising the distance they have to reverse.

HSE guides on vehicle safety provide further information[13].

Maintenance and repair

Facilities managers will generally delegate maintenance and repair work on the premises to outside contractors. They cannot, however, delegate their health and safety duties in the event of death, injury or accidental exposure to asbestos or another hazardous substance.

Contractors have duties too, but if their employees are injured on your premises, or using your equipment, you could be liable. Equally, contractors may import risks onto your normally safe premises, putting your employees at risk and exposing you to possible legal action if you fail to take preventative measures.

Managing contractors

Many large firms keep a list of contractors whom they prefer to use, and who meet their safety criteria. Those who want to make it onto the list may have to undergo an audit on their own premises or while doing work on another site. The qualifications of their sub-contractors are also likely to be checked. Successful bidders for a contract will be asked to draw up a safety plan for the work, which may include targets and a contractual requirement for continuous improvement.

During the work, the employer should monitor the contractors' performance and investigate incidents and near misses. Typically, large firms will expect their contractors to meet the same safety standards as their own employees, to avoid differences across their site. They may set up safety competitions for the various contractors on site, or circulate details of each contractor's performance. Poor performance will, at best, lead to the contractor's removal from the 'preferred' list. At worst, the contractor may be dismissed before the end of the contract and have to pay for a replacement.

Legal duty to contractors

The principle that organisations retain responsibility for the safety of contractors working on their premises was established in the *Associated Octel* case, heard in the House of Lords in November 1996. There have been much higher fines, and much worse incidents, as the figures at the start of this chapter showed. But for facilities managers the lessons are salutary.

The case involved a maintenance job in a confined space, in which a contractor's employee was injured because he used the wrong equipment. The man, Mr Cuthbert, was repairing a tank lining at Octel's Ellesmere Port chemical plant, which was shut for maintenance. He was working by an electric bulb inside the tank, cleaning the lining with acetone. The acetone was in an old paint bucket which he had retrieved from a rubbish bin. The open container allowed the acetone to give off highly flammable fumes. The light bulb broke, and there was a flash fire in which Mr Cuthbert was badly burned.

Octel was prosecuted under s 3(1) of the *HSW Act*. This states:

> 'It shall be the duty of every employer to conduct his undertaking in such a way as to ensure, so far as is reasonably practicable, that persons not in his employment who may be affected thereby are not thereby exposed to risks to their health or safety.'

Five steps to managing contractors' health and safety

1. Planning
- define the job
- identify hazards
- assess risks
- eliminate and reduce risks
- specify health and safety conditions
- discuss with contractor.

2. Choosing a contractor
- check contractor is competent for the job (ask questions, get evidence)
- discuss the job, the site and site rules
- obtain a safety method statement
- decide if sub-contracting is acceptable and will be safe.

3. Managing contractors on site
- ensure contractors sign in and out
- name a site contact
- reinforce health and safety information and site rules.

4. Keeping a check
- assess how much contact with contractors is needed
- is the job going as planned?
- is the contractor working safely and as agreed?
- have there been any incidents?
- have there been changes in personnel?
- are any special arrangements required?

5. Reviewing the work
- how effective was the planning?
- how did the contractor perform?
- record the findings.

Source: *Managing Contractors* HSE Books[14].

Octel claimed Mr Cuthbert's injury was not caused by Octel conducting its undertaking within the meaning of s 3(1). Cleaning the tank was part of the contractor's undertaking, and Octel had no right to control how its independent contractors worked.

Why is the employer liable?

The House of Lords rejected the company's argument. In Lord Hoffman's words: 'The tank was part of Octel's plant. The work formed part of a maintenance programme planned by Octel. The men who did the work, although employed by an independent contractor, were almost permanently integrated into Octel's larger operations. They worked under the "permit to work" system (having to obtain authorisation before every job from Octel's engineers). Octel provided their safety equipment and lighting.'

In this case, he found it was clear that having the tank repaired was part of Associated Octel's undertaking. But he pointed out that in other situations 'there will also be ancillary activities such as obtaining supplies, making deliveries, cleaning, maintenance and repairs which may give rise to more difficulty'.

He gave some useful examples of an employer's duty: 'If he has a repair shop as a part of his plant, that is an ancillary part of his undertaking. Likewise, as in this case, if he has independent contractors to do cleaning or repairs on his own premises, as an activity integrated with the general conduct of his business.' Other activities though, which are completely separate from an employer's business, such as 'the cleaning of the office curtains at the dry cleaners, the repair of the sales manager's car in the garage [and] maintenance work on machinery returned to the manufacturer's factory' would not form part of its undertaking. Thus: 'The place where the activity takes place will in the normal case be very important; possibly decisive.'

Working at a height

One of the biggest risks during maintenance and repair work is falling from a height. Facilities managers need to ensure that contractors have a number of safeguards in place, including:

- edge protection around openings, holes and roofs

- guard rails and toe boards of the right height on scaffolding and work platforms

- base plates on scaffolding uprights, with all ledgers, braces and struts in position and the structure secured to the building

- warnings or barriers to stop people using an unfinished scaffold

- protection from moving equipment and falling materials

- weekly, recorded inspections of scaffolds, hoists, cranes, and so forth

- using trained, competent staff.

Anywhere which has a drop or fall of more than 2m must have guarding and edge protection.

Such guarding and edge protection must be suitable and sufficient. Generally it must be fixed and stable and meet the following requirements:

- top rail at a height of approximately 900–1000mm

- mid rail at approximately 450mm

- toe board of approximately 150mm.

Roof work is particularly hazardous, and additional precautions include:

- avoiding anyone going on the roof – is cleaning just for cosmetic purposes really necessary?

- not allowing your own employees to 'take a quick look' at a problem

- displaying warning signs about fragile roofs and skylights, particularly at access points

- providing barriers or covers for fragile roof materials

- providing safety nets or harnesses if edge protection and secure work platforms are not possible

- excluding people from the area beneath roof work or protecting them from falling debris

- not allowing work in bad weather conditions.

Further information is available in HSE's guides on construction work[15] and roof work[16].

Confined spaces

Fifteen people a year, on average, are killed doing work in a confined space or trying to rescue someone trapped in one.

Regulation 1(2) of the *Confined Spaces Regulations 1997* defines a confined space as 'any place, including any chamber, tank, vat, silo, pit, trench, pipe, sewer, flue, well or other similar space in which, by virtue of its enclosed nature, there arises a reasonably foreseeable specified risk'. Some areas may, for example, become confined during construction or modification work. Risks can arise from lack of oxygen, chemical residues, dangerous gases, leaks, heat, fire, or use of machinery (which may create dust or cause an electric shock).

Under s 2 of the *HSW Act*, employers also owe their employees a duty to provide and maintain safe means of access to and egress from places of work. This duty extends to the workforce of other contractors. Regulation 4 of the *Confined Spaces Regulations* prohibits a person from entering a confined space to carry out work for any purpose where it is reasonably practicable to carry out the work by other means.

In practice, this means that employers should identify another way to do the work, for example by using a remote camera for inspection, or tools that can be used from outside. If entry is necessary, risk control measures include:

- appointing a supervisor

- ensuring workers have suitable training and experience, and are medically fit

- isolating hazardous machinery or pipework

- cleaning chemical residues before entering

- providing ventilation

- testing the air

- providing non-sparking or low-voltage tools and protected lighting as appropriate

- providing breathing apparatus if necessary

- preparing emergency arrangements, including how to raise the alarm

- providing lifelines

- having a safe communication system

- having a 'permit to work' system.

Fire safety

According to Home Office statistics, 55 people died in 2001 and just over 3,300 were injured in fires in commercial premises. Employers or those who have 'control' of a workplace are required to carry out a fire risk assessment. This includes people who through a contract or tenancy have an obligation in relation to the maintenance, repair or safety of a workplace.

The legal requirement to conduct a risk assessment is contained within both the *Management of Health and Safety at Work Regulations 1999* and the *Fire Precautions (Workplace) Regulations 1997* (amended in 1999). Whereas, previously, the enforcing authority inspected the premises, then produced a report detailing what had to be changed or improved, it is now entirely the employer's own responsibility to find out how to comply with the legislation.

It is a criminal offence to place one or more employees at risk of death or serious injury by failing to comply with the *Fire Precautions Regulations*. It is also a criminal offence to fail to comply with an enforcement or prohibition notice.

Fire certificates

In addition, the *Fire Precautions Act 1971* imposes requirements upon occupiers of premises, as distinct from the requirements upon them as employers or persons who 'control' the workplace. The Act requires 'designated' premises to apply for a fire certificate from the local fire authority, which will prescribe in detail what they are required to do to comply. This does not exempt them from also having to carry out a risk assessment.

Designated premises are factories, offices, shops and railway premises in which more than 20 persons are at work at any one time, or more than 10 persons work at any one time higher than the ground floor. Occupiers are required to:

- keep the certificate in the relevant building

- maintain the fire safety provisions in their premises and any other conditions imposed, precisely as detailed in the certificate

- give notice to the fire authority before making any material extensions or structural alteration to the premises

- give notice to the fire authority before making any material alteration to the internal layout of the premises or to the layout of furniture or equipment.

If you are unsure whether or not your proposals constitute 'material' change, it is good practice to consult your local fire safety officer for advice on the matter.

In addition, the *Fire Certificates (Special Premises) Regulations 1976* apply to premises which operate hazardous processes or manufacture or store specified hazardous materials in quantities which pose a significant risk.

Fire risk assessment

It is important to carry out a fire risk assessment appropriate to the particular workplace. It is also good practice to involve staff in the process, as they may have identified a potential fire risk of which people higher up the organisation may not be aware.

The two most important questions to ask are:

- How likely is it for a fire to start in my workplace?

- How easy is it for employees, and other people who may be affected, to escape to a place of safety in the event of a fire?

In larger workplaces, it is good policy to carry out a separate inspection for each significantly different section, area or department. The whole of the workplace should be taken into account, including any outdoor areas and any rooms or parts of buildings which are not currently in use.

If the workplace has been subject to previous approvals by the various enforcing authorities for other fire safety, licensing or building legislation, you are still required to carry out an assessment of your fire precautions under the *Fire Regulations*. However, if there has been no significant change in the workplace, for example, in the number of employees or the activities which they undertake, it is unlikely that any significant additional fire precautions will have to be provided.

If you do propose to make changes to your fire precautions as a result of carrying out a fire risk assessment, these must not conflict with the controls imposed by other legislation. If in any doubt, you are advised to consult a fire safety officer from your local fire service.

If other employers share your premises, your organisation has a responsibility to ensure that they are made aware of any significant risks and any action you have taken to reduce that risk. Under the *Management Regulations*, you are also required to cooperate with other employers who share your workplace to enable them to discharge their responsibilities under the *Fire Regulations*. In addition, you should take all reasonable steps to coordinate your fire safety measures with those of any other employers who may share your workplace.

The 'five steps' approach

The Home Office publication *Fire safety – An employer's guide* advocates extending HSE's five steps approach to risk assessment to fire safety. The five steps are:

1: Identify fire hazards

Potential fire hazards in the workplace will include potential sources of ignition, sources of fuel and any hazards associated with the processes carried out in the workplace.

2: Identify the location of people at significant risk in case of fire

This step needs to take into account not only employees, but other people who may be in the premises, such as customers, members of the public, visitors and contractors. The special needs of any disabled staff and visitors must also be considered. There may be parts of the premises where people are more at risk than others.

3: Evaluate the risks

This step involves deciding whether existing fire precautions are adequate, or whether improvements are required to remove the hazard or to control the risk. It is necessary to look at any existing fire safety measures provided in terms of:

- the control of ignition and fuel sources
- fire detection and fire warning systems
- means of escape
- means of fighting fire
- maintenance and testing of fire precautions
- fire safety training for employees.

The nature of the risk evaluation will depend very much on the nature of the workplace and the work activities carried out.

4: Record findings and action taken

Regulation 3(6) of the *Management Regulations* requires organisations which employ five or more people to record the significant findings of the assessment and any group of employees identified as being especially at risk. Under reg 10, there is a legal requirement to provide employees with 'comprehensive and relevant information'. This means telling employees or their representatives about the risk assessment findings, and perhaps making the formal risk assessment report available to them on request.

5: Keep assessment under review

It is good practice to carry out an annual review of the workplace to ensure that no new risks have developed as a result of, for example, changes to work processes, machinery, substances or the number of people likely to be present in the workplace. There should also be a re-assessment of the workplace if you have carried out alterations or extensions, as they may have affected the fire precautions previously provided.

Fire risk assessment checklist

Escape routes

- Are main and emergency stairways protected by self-closing fire doors?
- Is the emergency route clearly sign posted?
- Are there any 'dead end' conditions where escape is possible in one direction only?
- Are all escape routes clear of obstruction?
- Are all exit doors unobstructed externally?
- Are there enough exits?
- Are exit doors free to open at all times (not locked)?
- Are fire doors fitted with 'fire door – keep shut' signs, and is this instruction followed?

Fire defence equipment

- Is the fire alarm system satisfactory for the risk?
- Will it meet current legal requirements?
- Are the fire alarm, hydrants, fire extinguishers/hose reels, sprinklers and emergency lighting maintained by qualified people? Is maintenance recorded in a log book?
- Is the fire alarm tested weekly?
- Does the fire alarm have automatic fire detectors in corridors, stairways and risk rooms?
- Are routine checks made to ensure equipment has not been obscured, moved or damaged?

Work equipment and furnishings

- Are all items of portable electrical equipment inspected regularly and fitted with correctly rated fuses?
- Is the wiring of electrical installations inspected periodically by a competent electrical engineer?
- Is the use of extension leads and multi-point adapters kept to a minimum?
- Are flexible electrical leads run in safe places where they will not be easily damaged?
- Is upholstery in good condition?

Cleanliness and tidiness

- Are staff encouraged to tidy their personal workplaces?
- Are the premises kept clear of combustible waste?
- Are metal bins with closely fitting lids available for waste such as floor sweepings?
- Are separate, clearly-labelled containers provided for waste and special hazards – such as flammable liquids, paint rags, oily rags?
- Are waste containers removed from the building at the end of each working day or more frequently if necessary?
- Is waste disposal put in a safe place which is not accessible to the public?
- Is the burning of waste on site prohibited?
- Are cupboards, lift shafts, spaces under benches, gratings, conveyor belts and similar places kept free from dust and the accumulation of rubbish?
- Are pipes, beams, trusses, ledges, ducting and electrical fittings regularly cleaned?
- Are areas in and around the building kept free from accumulated packaging materials and pallets?
- Are metal lockers provided for employees' clothing?

Storage

- Are fire doors, exits, fire equipment and fire notices kept unobstructed?
- Are storage areas accessible to fire fighters?
- Are stack sizes kept as small as possible?
- Are there adequate gangways between stacks?
- Are stacks stable?
- Are stocks of material arranged so that sprinkler heads and fire detectors are not impeded and are the required clearances beneath this equipment maintained?
- Are excessive quantities of stock avoided?
- Is access to storage areas restricted to those who need to be there?
- Is stock kept well clear of light fixtures and hot service pipes?

Maintenance of buildings

- Is every point of entry to the site and building secure against intruders?
- After close down of operations are all doors, windows and gates checked and secure?
- Is the building regularly inspected for damage to windows, roof and walls?
- Are the grounds surrounding the premises kept free of combustible vegetation by regular grass cutting and scrub clearance?
- Are all outside contractors supervised while on the premises and their work authorised by 'permit to work' schemes?

Heating and lighting

- Are there restrictions on using unauthorised heaters?
- Are combustible materials at a safe distance from applicances and flues?
- Is care taken that no materials are left on heaters?
- Are portable heaters securely guarded and placed where they cannot be knocked over or ignite combustibles?
- Are goods kept clear of lighting equipment?

Smoking

- Is smoking prohibited in all but designated 'smoking' areas?
- Are non-smoking rules strictly enforced?
- Where smoking is permitted are there enough ashtrays (as distinct from waste bins)?

Staff training

- Are new staff instructed in fire procedures and shown the fire escape routes on their first day at work?
- Are fire action notices posted throughout the workplace?
- Are there trained fire marshals?
- Is there a designated fire assembly point?
- Have staff had the opportunity to operate a fire extinguisher?
- Do staff know how to deal with the disabled, the public and visitors in the event of an evacuation?

Action plan

- Do you have a prioritised action plan for remedial measures following an assessment?

Means of escape

Once people are aware of a fire, they should be able to proceed safely along a recognisable escape route to a place of safety. In order to achieve this, it may be necessary to protect the route by using fire-resisting construction. The means of escape is likely to be satisfactory if your workplace is fairly modern and has had building regulation approval, or if it has been found satisfactory following a recent inspection by the fire authority (and in each case you have not carried out any significant material or structural alterations or made any change to the use of the workplace). However, you should still carry out a risk assessment to ensure that the means of escape remain adequate. If, as a result of the risk assessment, you propose making any changes to the means of escape, you should consult the fire authority (in Scotland you must seek the agreement of the building control authority) before making any changes.

When assessing the adequacy of the means of escape, you will need to take into account:

- the findings of the fire risk assessment

- the size of the workplace, its construction, layout, contents and the number and width of the available escape routes

- the workplace activity, where people may be situated in the workplace and what they may be doing when a fire occurs

- the number of people who may be present, and their familiarity with the workplace

- individuals' ability to escape without assistance.

In some cases, it may be necessary to provide additional means of escape or to improve the fire protection of existing escape routes. If, having carried out your risk assessment, you think this might be the case in your workplace, consult the fire authority and, where necessary, your local building control officer before carrying out any alterations.

Home Office guidance

The Home Office guidance states that:

- Other than in small workplaces, or from some rooms of low or normal fire risk, there should normally be alternative means of escape from all parts of the workplace.

- Routes which provide means of escape in one direction only (from a dead end) should be avoided wherever possible as this could mean that people have to move towards a fire in order to escape.

- Each escape route should be independent of any other and arranged so that people can move away from a fire in order to escape.

- Escape routes should always lead to a place of safety; they should also be wide enough for the number of occupants and should not normally reduce in width.

- Routes and exits should be available for use and kept clear of obstruction at all times.

The time for people to reach a place of safety should include the time it takes them to react to a fire warning. This will depend on a number of factors including:

- what they are likely to be doing when the alarm is raised

- what they may have to do before starting to escape (turn off machinery, help other people)

- their knowledge of the building and the training they have received about the routine to be followed in the event of fire.

Where necessary, these can be checked by carrying out a practice drill.

To ensure that the time available for escape is reasonable, the length of the escape route from any occupied part of the workplace to the exit should not exceed:

- where more than one route is provided, 25m for a high fire-risk area and 60m for a low fire-risk area

- where only a single escape route is provided, 12m for a high fire-risk area and 45m for a low fire-risk area.

The guidance goes on:

- A doorway of no less than 750mm in width is suitable for up to 40 people per minute (where doors are likely to be used by wheelchair users the doorway should be at least 800mm wide).

- A doorway of no less than 1m in width is suitable for up to 80 people per minute.

- Where more than 80 people per minute are expected to use a door, the minimum doorway width should be increased by 75mm for each additional group of 15 people.

- For the purposes of calculating whether the existing exit doorways are suitable for the numbers using them, you should assume that the largest exit door from any part of the workplace may be unavailable for use; the remaining doorways should be capable of providing a satisfactory means of escape for everyone present.

Emergency lighting

Generally, in premises which have a daytime occupancy only, emergency lighting will only be necessary when there is insufficient natural light for people to make their way out of a building safely if the primary lighting should fail. The need for escape lighting is greater in buildings where visitors are present who are unfamiliar with the building.

Emergency escape and fire exit signs are necessary to indicate any emergency exit doors and routes which are not in common use.

Emergency exits

Under reg 5 of the *Fire Regulations*:

- Routes to emergency exits and the exits themselves must be kept clear at all times.

- Emergency doors must open in the direction of escape.

- Sliding or revolving doors must not be used for exits specifically intended as emergency exits.

- Emergency doors must not be so locked or fastened that they cannot be easily and immediately opened by any person who may need to use them in an emergency.

Fire notices

Notices giving clear and concise instructions on the action to be followed in case of fire should be prominently displayed throughout the workplace. It is also important to include a designated assembly point in the notices.

Fire equipment

Where necessary, the *Fire Regulations* require the provision and maintenance of appropriate fire-fighting equipment, fire detectors and alarms. In determining what is appropriate fire-fighting equipment, account must be taken of:

- the dimensions and use of the buildings at the workplace

- the equipment they contain

- the physical and chemical properties of the substances likely to be present

- the maximum number of people present at any one time.

Fire detection and fire warning systems, emergency lighting (including torches) and fire-fighting equipment should be checked weekly. There also needs be an annual full check and test carried out by a competent service engineer.

Staff responsibilities

An effective system for ensuring that the fire safety message is spread throughout an organisation is to cascade the responsibility through all staff levels by appointing floor, department or section fire marshals. The basis of this system is that the fire marshals are given a higher level of fire safety training than the average member of staff in order to look after a designated part of the premises.

The role of the fire marshals should be to check for hazards and potential fire risks within their area. They must check that fire safety equipment is working and in place, and be responsible for organising the evacuation of staff, the public and visitors, in the event of a fire alarm. This should include a final sweep of their designated area to ensure that everyone is out and to report accordingly to the person in charge of the assembly point.

It is not necessary for all staff to receive the same high level of training. This would be inappropriate and unmanageable. It is however necessary to ensure that all staff know:

- the location and use of escape routes

- the location of their assembly point

- how to use fire equipment provided

- how to summon the fire service.

Fire safety: proposed legislative changes

A Consultation Paper was issued in 2002 by the Office of the Deputy Prime Minister outlining proposed changes to the legislative regime for fire safety. The responses to the discussion process are being considered and it is anticipated that in 2004 there will be a new Regulatory Reform (Fire Safety) Order which will set out revised responsibilities for fire safety.

The key points of the Consultation Paper are:

- The *Fire Precautions Act 1971* and the *Fire Safety (Workplace) Regulations 1997* (as amended) will be replaced by one single piece of legislation called the Regulatory Reform (Fire Safety) Order.

- The new legislation will be enforced mainly by fire authorities.

- Occupiers of premises currently designated as requiring a fire certificate under the *Fire Precautions Act 1971* will no longer have to apply for one. None will be issued.

- Fire precautions will not overall be reduced but will be replaced by equal requirements under a new regime.

- Fire authorities will be given a new duty to promote community fire safety.

- The new proposals apply to England and Wales only. Scotland will remain as is until the Scottish Parliament amends its legislation.

- The new Fire Safety Order will be based around a new general duty of fire safety care, with specific requirements that will need to be met to comply with that duty.

- Fire safety will be based on a risk-based approach. Risk assessment will need to be done for all workplaces.

- With the abolition of fire certificates, the risk-based approach will apply to non-employees.

- The existing power for the Secretary of State to make regulations to address key fire safety issues will be retained.

- A 'responsible person' will need to be designated to comply with fire safety legislation.

- Empty buildings would be brought within the order and the owner would be responsible for fire safety.

- People employed to undertake duties that have a bearing on the safety of a building must be competent to do the job. The responsible person must ensure people, including contractors, are competent.

- Legal action would be taken against a contractor if they have been negligent in their duties or if they have failed to complete their duties or misrepresented themselves in any way. Action could also be taken against the responsible person for failing to appoint a competent contractor.

- The new fire safety regime would cover all workplaces and places to which the public has access. Domestic premises would be excluded.

- Voluntary workers operating in premises will be brought into the new regime. They will have to be protected for fire safety.

- The responsible person will have a general duty to ensure fire safety of others.

- Preventative and protective fire safety measures must be implemented by the responsible person.

- Fire safety arrangements must be made by the responsible person.

- Dangerous substances will have special arrangements and requirements.

- Provision must be made for fire fighting and fire detection.

- Emergency exit routes and exits must be designated and maintained.

- Premises and any fire-fighting equipment must be maintained by the responsible person.

- The responsible person must appoint a competent person to assist him in his duties of fire safety.

- Emergency procedures must be put in place for serious and imminent danger, and for danger areas.

- Responsible persons shall ensure that adequate information is available to those who will need it.

- Where there are two or more employers within a building there shall be co-operation and co-ordination to comply with the fire safety regime.

- Information must be given to visiting employees, those working away or in host employer's premises.

- Employees must be given general fire safety training and must be given specific training on risks, changes in responsibilities and so on.

- Employees will have general duties to take reasonable care of themselves and others for fire safety.

Flexible working

An employee's workplace is not always fixed. Some employees may work from home some or all of the time, or hotdesk around the office. Others may visit clients, spend a large amount of time travelling, work alone or work in a remote place. Employers have a duty to assess the risks associated with all these working conditions.

Homeworking

Employers may need to visit – and revisit – homeworkers to check their working conditions. It is important to remember that:

- Not only the employee, but also their children could be harmed – for example by trailing cables or dangerous substances.

- The employer is responsible for maintaining any electrical equipment (normally a computer and printer) which it provides.

- The employee needs training in the safe use of equipment provided (the need to take regular breaks from computer work, for example).

- The employer must ensure the workstation and seating are correctly adjusted, the screen is positioned to avoid reflections, there is suitable lighting, and there is enough space to work comfortably.

- First aid provisions may be necessary.

- New or expectant mothers may be particularly at risk from some types of work.

- Some employees find working alone stressful – regular meetings, support or social events may help.

- Employees may work from home only occasionally, using their home furniture and lighting – if so, they will need advice.

It could be useful to incorporate health and safety into the homeworker's employment contract, requiring them to maintain a separate, designated work area at home. Also, although the employer is responsible for assessing homeworking conditions, it is helpful to give homeworkers their own checklist to display as a good practice reminder.

Hotdesking

To avoid WRULDs, workstations used by more than one person (including part-timers, jobsharers and shiftworkers) will have to be easily adjustable. Employees will also need training on the importance of actually making the adjustments.

Employees may need a mobile cart to store their work, in which case the principles of good manual handling will apply (for example, avoiding the need to wheel the cart further than necessary and avoiding obstacles). Finally, although a recent HSE-funded study found hotdeskers were not more stressed than their 'traditional' colleagues, it found it was important to consult employees before introducing new ways of working.

Laptops

Portable computers are covered by the *DSE Regulations* if they are used for more than an hour at a time. As well as the risks associated with any computer or monitor, there are problems associated with carrying around heavy, valuable equipment, and using cramped keyboards and screens in awkward locations (for example, wedged against the car steering wheel or on the passenger seat during a traffic jam).

An HSE-commissioned study on the safety of portable computers found that fewer than half the organisations contacted had any guidance or policy at all on using laptops, and most of them had started to get complaints from laptop users about health and safety. The researchers, System Concepts, went on to recommend:

- buying laptops with as large a keyboard and screen as possible, while keeping the weight down to 3kg at most

- supplying employees with rucksack-style laptop bags – they distribute the weight better and give away the contents less easily to would-be muggers

- checking the weight of transformers, cables, and so forth

- choosing a machine with long battery life, so transformers and cables can be left behind

- ensuring it is possible to attach a separate monitor, keyboard and/or mouse to a docking station for prolonged use

- encouraging employees to restrict the use of laptops in non-ideal locations, and use docking stations where possible.

Homeworkers' checklist

Eyesight

- Take frequent mini-breaks by looking away from the screen and documents, preferably out of the window.

- Take a 10-minute break at least once an hour and leave the room – a short walk outside to lengthen the optical focus is ideal.

- Get your eyes tested regularly.

- If eyes regularly feel sore seek advice.

- Don't work in poor light or glare.

Strain injuries

- If you change your workstation set-up after it has been health and safety checked, either self-assess it within the company guidelines or ask your supervisor to do another check.

- Take frequent mini-breaks, stretch and gently exercise fingers, wrists, arms, shoulders and neck.

- Take a 10-minute break at least once an hour, leave the room, and carry out another activity.

- Take fresh air and exercise at least once a day.

- Keep work surfaces uncluttered – don't let paperwork and files build up over time, and keep plenty of space for keyboard, mouse and documents.

- Don't store boxes under the desk where they may cramp legs and feet.

- Recognise warning signs such as tiredness, sore eyes, headache or soreness, tension or numbness in hands, arms, neck, back or shoulders. If in doubt seek advice.

Posture

- Always use a good, ergonomic office chair.

- Remember to sit up straight with your back supported by your chair.

- Ensure your screen is close enough to see without leaning forward.

- If you need a footrest, use it.

Electricity

- Don't use multi-socket plugs or extension leads without first consulting your manager.

- Don't put drinks or vases of flowers on computer equipment.

Fire

- Storage of documents and reference material may constitute a fire hazard. Keep a fire extinguisher in the work area and ensure the smoke alarm is in working order.

Driving

The HSE does not, at the moment, treat road accidents as work-related. But a consultation paper by the government's work-related road safety task group proposes making employers liable for crashes caused by employees spending too long at the wheel or trying to meet impossible deadlines. Research suggests 800–1,000 of the 3,500 road deaths each year involve cars driven for work. The government has set itself a target of reducing deaths and accidents on the road by 40 per cent in 10 years.

Research commissioned by the former Department of the Environment, Transport and the Regions in 2000 found that tiredness caused around one in ten road accidents. It advised stopping for 15 minutes after every two hours of driving – but not on the hard shoulder. RoSPA (the Royal Society for the Prevention of Accidents), which has been campaigning on the issue, advises employers to assess the risk of road accidents in the same way as they assess risks on site.

Mobile phones

In 1999, the Highway Code was amended to warn drivers never to use handheld mobile phones or microphones while driving. Hands-free kits, too, are 'likely to distract your attention from the road'. From 1 December 2003, it is illegal to drive while using a hand-held mobile phone. The police can bring prosecutions for causing death by dangerous driving, driving without due care and attention, or failing to have proper control of a vehicle.

A number of drivers have already been imprisoned following accidents involving mobile phone use. RoSPA estimates at least 15 deaths have been caused by drivers using mobile phones, including two using hands-free kits. It wants company health and safety policies to ban employees from using mobile phones while driving, encouraging them to pick up messages when they have stopped the car instead.

Evidence on whether mobile phone emissions are safe, even when using a hands-free kit, remains inconclusive. They do cause a slight warming of the brain, but the long-term effects of this are unknown. One option is to advise employees to make short, essential calls only, and to use land lines whenever possible.

The advantages of mobile phones should not be forgotten. For lone workers, those visiting clients at home or those on the move, they offer invaluable personal protection.

Lone working

Lone workers may include:

- those working outside normal office hours, such as maintenance, cleaning and security staff

- mobile workers, such as sales reps, estate agents, social workers, postal workers, painters and decorators

- homeworkers.

There is no express legislation prohibiting lone working, but the normal rules on risk assessment apply. The assessment may show an activity is too dangerous to be carried out alone (such as lifting a heavy load or visiting a violent client at home), or without supervision (such as working in a confined space). The risk assessment should consider not only normal working conditions but emergencies.

Lone workers may need extra training or experience to cope in an emergency or to deal with aggression. Their employers need to set limits on what they can and cannot do on their own. There needs to be a system for them to report to base and for the employer to take action if they fail to do so. Lone workers need access to first aid facilities, and mobile workers will need their own first aid kit.

Environmental protection and liability

There is, of course, a legal regime for prosecuting firms which accidentally or intentionally pollute the air, water or land during their industrial processes. But for facilities managers, the important new development in environmental law is the scrutiny under which every aspect of every company's environmental performance is starting to come. The regime is subtler – if you forget to turn the lights off at the end of the day, you will not end up in a courtroom, but you will feel the financial effects when your tax bill arrives. So whereas energy efficiency has, until recently, been a matter of choice, it is now starting to be regulated. There is also pressure to report on environmental performance, so that energy wasters will find it harder to conceal their poor record (see **Workplace facilities: environmental measuring and reporting, p 000**).

Climate Change Levy

In 1997, the UK government committed the country to substantially reducing greenhouse gas emissions such as carbon dioxide and methane by 2010.

Non-domestic energy use is one of the government's main targets, and businesses are feeling the effect as the first fuel bills arrive containing the Climate Change Levy (CCL). The levy works by charging businesses and public sector organisations an extra sum on their fuel bills for every kilowatt hour (kWh) of electricity, coal, natural gas and liquid petroleum gas they use. In other words, unlike VAT, which is charged on the cash value of goods and services provided, the CCL is based on the energy value of the fuel supplied. This means that getting a cheaper supply will not reduce the amount of tax payable. Load management – moving energy-thirsty activities to periods of lower cost electricity – will be similarly ineffective at reducing the amount to be paid.

Levy rates

The rates of the CCL for 2001–02 are as follows:

Fuel	Rate
Electricity[17]	£0.0043 per kWh
Gas	£0.0015 per kWh
Liquid Petroleum Gas	£0.0096 per kg
Others (including coal and coke)	£0.0117 per kg

Source: Customs and Excise.

Exemptions

The CCL is not to be applied across the board; for example, the following will be exempt:

- small users and charities who pay VAT on fuel at 5 per cent

- fuels used by the transport sector

- fuels used for energy generation

- oils already subject to excise duty

- electricity generated from new renewable sources such as solar and wind power

- fuels used jointly as a feed-stock and an energy source within the same process, for example coke in steel-making

- electricity used in electrolysis processes, for instance, the chlor-alkali process, or primary aluminium smelting

- fuel used by good quality combined heat and power (CHP) schemes as certified by the Quality Assurance Programme (CHPQA), a voluntary programme which has developed a universal method to assess, monitor and certify the quality of CHP.

Waste management

The UK is subject to numerous European Directives on waste and a key part of the government's strategy on waste reduction is to place recovery and recycling targets on business for a wide range of waste materials.

Producer Responsibility Obligations (Packaging Waste) Regulations 1997

Any business handling more than 50 tonnes of packaging and with financial turnover of more than £2 million is obligated if it is involved in manufacturing raw materials for packaging; converting materials in to packaging; filling packaging; selling packaging to the final consumer; or importing packaging or packaging materials into the UK.

A facilities management company may be asked by a client to assume responsibility for compliance with the regulations.

Any business which is obligated by the regulations must:

- register with the Environment Agency (or other parallel enforcement agencies in the devolved administrations), pay a fee and provide data on packaging handled by the business in the previous year (costs and calculations are always based on the previous year);

- take reasonable steps to recover and recycle packaging waste;

- certify that the necessary recovery and recycling has been carried out;

or

- join a registered compliance scheme in order to have their obligations discharged.

Evidence of recovery and recycling targets being met is demonstrated by the use of Packaging Waste Recovery Notes (PRNs) and Packaging Waste Export Recovery Notes (PERNs). Compliance schemes buy PRNs and PERNs on behalf of all their members and it is their responsibility to show that they have enough PRN/PERNs to cover the recycling and recovery targets. Current targets set by the government are:

- 59 per cent recovery
- 19 per cent recycling.

These targets are due to rise in 2004 once the new European Directive targets have been set. Each PRN required carries a cost – currently between £22 and £30 per tonne.

Minimising waste

The less packaging a business handles the less tonnage there will be to recycle and recover and the lower the cost of regulatory compliance will be. Even for those businesses not affected by the *Packaging Regulations*, waste minimisation is a sound business and environmental strategy. Whether the *Packaging Regulations* apply or not, there are costs associated with waste removal, landfill and special disposal requirements.

Good business practice on waste minimisation suggests an audit of all products, packaging and waste used and produced in the course of the business. Consider what is essential packaging to product safety and what can be eliminated as unnecessary. Review products purchased with suppliers so that they can understand that packaging is superfluous. Set up workshops with key suppliers on waste minimisation. Set targets so that achievements can be quantified.

Facilities managers who have responsibilities for clients' premises which include catering and hospitality facilities may be required to separate food waste from other waste products. Under the EU Landfill Directive, the UK is committed to reducing the amount of biodegradable waste in landfill. Greater emphasis is being placed on composting. Separate containers for refuse may be required at premises and caterers should be encouraged to minimise food/organic waste.

Duty of care in respect of waste

The duty of care is a law which states that all reasonable steps must be taken to keep waste safe, that it is handled by authorised persons and is disposed of legally. Failure to comply with the duty of care requirements is an offence carrying an unlimited fine (under *Environmental Protection Act 1990*).

The duty applies to anyone who produces, imports, keeps, stores, transports, treats or disposes of waste.

Waste can be anything which the business produces.

Waste transfer notes are required to be completed for commercial waste. The facilities manager will probably be responsible for ensuring compliance.

Waste can only be removed by authorised contractors – this is to prevent as far as possible, fly-tipping. Their registration details may be checked with the Environment Agency or from their registration certificate.

When waste is passed from one person to another, the person taking the waste must have a written description of it. The transfer note must be completed and signed by both parties involved in the transaction. One transfer note can cover the same type of waste for up to 12 months, eg weekly trade waste collections.

The transfer note must include:

- what the waste is and how much there is
- what sort of containers it is in
- the time and date the waste was transferred
- where the transfer took place
- the names and addresses of both persons involved in the transfer
- whether the person transferring the waste is an importer or producer of the waste
- details of the authorised persons category for handling waste eg for transport, disposal
- certificate number of the registered waste carrier and the local Environment Agency Office which issued it
- the licence number of the waste management licence and the Environment Agency details
- any reasons for any exemption
- the name and address of any broker if appropriate.

Copies of transfer notes must be kept by both parties for two years. They may need to produce these as evidence if, for instance, they are involved in a prosecution for illegally disposing of waste.

Pollution

Environmental protection addresses pollution to air, land and water and under the *Environmental Protection Act 1990* and the *Environment Act 1995*, plus numerous regulations set down the controls expected to safeguard the environment.

Businesses can pollute the environment by:

- emissions to atmosphere from industrial processes

- effluent discharges to water courses
- contamination of land
- noise.

Environmental compliance is monitored by both the Environment Agency and local authorities and statutory inspections for compliance are undertaken by all enforcing authorities.

A business may be creating a 'statutory nuisance' under the *Environmental Protection Act 1990 (EPA)* by emitting noise which is detrimental to the neighbourhood, eg noisy air conditioning plant keeping residents awake at night, by creating accumulations which are 'noxious', by creating smell nuisances or by emitting atmospheric pollutants.

The enforcing authorities have powers under *EPA* to:

- serve statutory notices requiring remedial works to abate the nuisance
- prohibit the continuation of the nuisance
- undertake remedial measures to abate the nuisance
- prosecute the offender.

Failure to comply with statutory notices can carry an unlimited fine and/or imprisonment. Daily fines can also be levied for each day that the nuisance continues.

Companies can have defences of 'Best practical means not exceeding excessive costs' or 'Best practical option'.

EU legislation

European legislation is setting the agenda for UK standards in environmental compliance. Revised directives and regulations are anticipated on waste management, energy consumption, landfill restrictions, waste minimisation and environmental management systems.

Corporate social responsibility

Corporate social responsibility (CSR) has come to the fore over the last couple of years and is driven, to a large extent, by the many independent reports on corporate governance. 'Stakeholder value' has become a common maxim over the years and CSR requires companies to set out their social policies, corporate governance procedures and stakeholder value initiatives. In particular, *Turnbull* has set the agenda on business risk management and companies know how to address how they effectively manage all risks to the business and how they intend to maximise and protect shareholder/stakeholder value.

Supply chain management

The increasing acceptability of shared responsibility for health and safety, fire safety and environmental protection has led to a new partnership approach in supply chain management.

When contractors, suppliers, consultants and others are appointed it is important to understand the approach they have to their business and compliance issues, and to determine whether they fit in with your own culture and business ethics. Corporate social responsibility requires a more transparent relationship with suppliers and the current expectation is that those companies who have better and more robust policies etc, should be working with their suppliers to help move them towards continuous improvements.

Facilities mangers should play a leading role in developing supply chain management policies and practices.

Construction work and building management

Health and safety and environmental laws apply to construction work no matter who has commissioned it and who is carrying it out. Construction activity is one of the highest health and safety risks and has a poor record for fatalities and major injuries. Fatalities are not just to workers but also to a significantly high proportion of the public.

HSE statistics for 2001–02 for the construction industry are:

79 fatalities to workers/contractors

6 fatalities to members of the public

4,480 major injuries

9,587 over 3-day injuries

382 non-fatal injuries to members of the public.

The greatest cause of fatality and major injury in construction is falls from height.

In addition to physical injuries, there are large numbers of individuals who are affected by occupational diseases caused by working in the construction industry. As an example, it is predicted that over 1,700 people will die from asbestos-related diseases every year until numbers peak in around ten years' time.

Construction safety is enforced by the Health and Safety Executive and the construction division of the HSE is targeting all projects – large and small – to establish compliance with the legislation. During 2002 the 'construction blitz' was carried out across the UK and Inspectors visited an extra 1,113 sites.

Conditions and safety procedures were so poor in 50 per cent of those sites visited that improvement notices and prohibition notices were served. In total 460 prohibition and 97 improvement notices were served.

Key health and safety issues in respect of construction activity are:

- Failure to adequately assess risks.
- Failure to recruit and retain skilled workers.
- Failure to ensure proper site management.
- Poor health and safety systems.
- Inadequate resourcing of site management.
- Poor leadership of front line managers/supervisors.
- Failure to plan work adequately.
- Inappropriate selection of equipment.

Two additional major pieces of legislation apply to construction works:

(i)   Construction (Design and Management) Regulations 1994;

(ii) Construction (Health, Safety and Welfare) Regulations 1996.

Other industry specific regulations cover head protection.

Construction (Design and Management) Regulations 1994 (CDM)

The purpose of the regulations is to improve health and safety in construction by requiring all parties to a project to take responsibility for health and safety standards. The regulations require attention to be paid to better planning, resourcing, design and management of a construction project. They also address the 'competency and resources' of all those involved in a project.

The CDM Regulations apply to all construction work which involves five or more operatives. If the construction activity is to last more than 30 days, or involve more than 500 person days (a person day is calculated for every worker on the site on any one day, eg 50 operatives on site for 10 days will equal 500 person days) then the project must be notified to the local HSE office on a form called F10.

Details of the project and the key appointments have to be declared on an F10, together with a start date and duration of project. Each HSE office will log the F10s received for their area and they will use these for prioritising their statutory site inspections. They will not always prioritise 'high risk' projects but will often single out those projects where, in their view, things do not seem sufficiently 'planned'. This could include, for example, a late notification of the F10 reagarding a project with a start on site date of less than two weeks hence, as the short lead time could lead to poor safety standards.

Projects which require an F10 are known as notifiable projects under reg 7 of the CDM Regulations.

A project must be notified as soon as is practicable after certain appointments have been made under the CDM Regulations.

The regulations also apply to all demolition work (other than the removal of internal partitions and non-load bearing walls etc) because of the high fatality and injury rate of this activity. By applying the CDM Regulations, the HSE believes that demolition works will be better planned and therefore safer.

The definition of construction work is quite wide and generally includes all works to a structure, including term maintenance, work on fixed plant, engineering works, painting and decorating, refurbishment work etc. Any work where there is a potential for operatives to fall more than 2m must be considered as construction work, eg commissioning, installing and testing etc of fixed plant, cleaning works involving high pressure water or where there is a risk of falling more than 2m.

Facilities managers need to be very aware of the CDM Regulations and their applicability to a project. Even if legally the CDM Regulations do not apply, it would be good health and safety management to apply the principles.

The regulations designate key duty holders and all have legal responsibilities and could be fined for failure to comply. Fines are on the usual scales – up to £5,000 in the Magistrates' Court and unlimited in the Crown Court.

The client

A client under the regulations is anyone who commissions a construction project and who is involved in a trade or business. The intent of the regulations is that anyone who embarks on a project which may lead to construction works must consider health and safety through the process, from concept and feasibility onwards.

A facilities management company could well be the client if it is their responsibility to commission new projects, refurbishment works, maintenance and cleaning works.

The HSE believes that clients have tremendous influence over the health and safety culture of a construction project and has allocated them responsibilities accordingly.

Under the *CDM Regulations*, clients must:

- appoint a competent planning supervisor
- appoint a competent principal contractor
- appoint competent designers
- appoint competent contractors
- provide information to the planning supervisor
- ensure adequate resources are available as provided by the duty holders and contractors

- ensure that a suitable construction phase Health and Safety Plan is approved before construction works start

- retain a Health and Safety File for the works and make it available to whoever needs the information.

Facilities management companies may be appointed 'Clients Agent' under CDM. In this situation, the Client (ie the company commissioning the building works), will pass all responsibility for compliance with CDM to the facilities management company. The HSE need to be informed on a form F10. If a facilities manager is appointed Clients Agent it must be done formally and a record kept. It means that the facilities manager assumes all responsibilities for compliance with CDM and must act as if he were the Client.

One of the main responsibilities for the Client is to provide information regarding health and safety as it relates to the site, building, project or proposed works. The information is passed to the Planning Supervisor (see below) and is used to formulate the Health and Safety Plans for the project. Many accidents are caused in construction because contractors are given little information about site hazards and risks (eg whether the building contains asbestos, whether the land is contaminated, what other activities are going on at the same time, residual risks etc).

The *Approved Code of Practice* (HSG 224)[18] which accompanies the CDM Regulations is quite specific about what information the client should provide (proportionate of course to the project).

So, a client must provide the following:

- site details, eg address, ownership

- key appointment details

- environmental information about the site, eg proximity of overhead cables, roads, schools etc.

- site boundary details – who owns what

- condition of the structure – state of dilapidation, structural information

- details of building materials, eg fragile roofs etc.

- details of ground condition and type

- details of underground services, eg gas

- details of any hazardous substances within the proposed site, building, eg asbestos, lead paint

- details of any employers safety rules etc.

The Client will be expected to commission surveys to obtain any information which is unavailable. The ACoP states that it must not be left to contractors to discover hazards. Significant hazards to health and safety must be anticipated before a construction project starts.

The Planning Supervisor

The Client appoints a Planning Supervisor for all CDM-applicable construction projects. The role of the Planning Supervisor is one of co-ordination of the duty holders so that 'joined-up thinking' is achieved regarding the design, planning, management and execution of a construction project.

The Planning Supervisor has certain duties under CDM, namely:

- to ensure that Designers have given adequate regard to health and safety within their designs

- to ensure that Designers co-operate with one another in respect of health and safety matters and design matters

- to ensure that the Pre-Tender Health and Safety Plan is produced before the Contractor makes arrangements to commence the works

- to ensure that a Health and Safety File is produced at the end of the project

- to give advice to the Client when requested

- to notify the project to the HSE on F10.

Planning Supervisors can be an individual or a team of people. The duty holder is a 'function' rather than a person. A facilities management company could appoint themselves Planning Supervisor provided they are competent and have the resources. There are no legal qualifications for the role of the Planning Supervisor and the HSE have always viewed the post as one to be undertaken by existing disciplines and not as a new profession.

The Planning Supervisor should be pro-active in the management of health and safety and should co-ordinate disciplines so that each is aware of the hazards and risks they may be creating for others. Information about site conditions etc should flow from the Planning Supervisor out to the team members.

Being a Planning Supervisor is not about creating mountains of paperwork but is about a pragmatic approach to hazard and risk identification and the implementation of the 'Hierarchy of Risk Control'.

The Designer

Designers under CDM are all those who have some input into the design of a structure, project, concept and include:

- architects

- interior designers

- building services engineers

- anyone who specifies materials, substances, equipment

- temporary works designers and engineers

- design and build contractors

- contractors who design works on site.

Designers have a huge contribution to make to a project and need to consider the health and safety implications for their designs from the concept and feasibility stage onwards. They need to ensure that they have given due consideration to how the structure will be built and how it will be used, occupied, maintained and possibly demolished in the future.

The CDM Regulations require designers to produce Design Risk Assessments for their designs. (See below p72 for more information on **Design Risk Assessments**.) These should highlight the hazards and risks associated with the design and their proposed control measures to minimise the risks. A Design Risk Assessment should focus on significant risks in relation to buildability and future maintenance, and the information contained in the Risk Assessment should enable the Principal Contractor to undertake the works with a full understanding of the residual hazards and risks associated with the design.

A recent HSE 'Designer Blitz' carried out in the Northwest of England and Scotland demonstrated that a significant proportion of the design sector were not fulfilling their responsibilities under reg 13 of CDM (Designer duties). The survey found that many designers lack adequate training or even basic information about their role and some refuse to accept that they have any responsibilities under the CDM Regulations. The survey found that the Design Risk process was rarely applied.

The Principal Contractor

The Principal Contractor has duties under the CDM Regulations for managing the health and safety and construction project once it has progressed to site. Clients must appoint a competent and adequately resourced Principal Contractor who is capable of setting and managing the health and safety of the site.

Principal Contractors must prepare a Construction Phase Health and Safety Plan prior to the commencement of works and must forward this to the Client. The Client is responsible for ensuring that the Plan is adequate and that it meets the requirements of reg 15(4) (see below).

The Principal Contractor is responsible for co-ordinating safety on the site, setting the site rules, induction training, appointing competent sub-contractors, establishing emergency procedures, providing welfare facilities etc.

Information on the hazards and risks of the project, the Design Risk Assessments etc should be assimilated by the Principal Contractor and developed into site safety plans.

The Pre-Tender Health and Safety Plan

The Pre-Tender Health and Safety Plan for the project is usually drafted by the Planning Supervisor but it could be a team effort.

Information gathered during the pre-planning stages of the project needs to be relayed to the tendering or nominated contractors so that they have an understanding of the hazards and risks involved with the project and can plan for them in the tender submission, allowing adequate financial input for such elements as safety equipment, scaffolding and the number of operatives who will be required.

The Pre-Tender Health and Safety Plan should be project specific and proportionate to the job. Volumes of paper are not what are required – effective information is what is most important. Key information to be included in the Pre-Tender Health and Safety Plan will be:

- nature and description of project

- client considerations and management requirements

- existing environment and residual on-site risks

- existing drawings

- significant design principles and residual hazards and risks

- significant construction hazards.

The Construction Phase Health and Safety Plan

CDM Regulations require that a Construction Phase Health and Safety Plan is produced by the Principal Contractor before works on site commence. The Construction Phase Health and Safety Plan must comply with reg 15(4) and must include:

- arrangements for the project which will ensure the health and safety of all persons at work carrying out construction work

- risks involved in the construction work

- site rules

- information about welfare arrangements on the site.

Copies of the Health and Safety Plan must be made available to those who need to know about site safety. The Principal Contractor must manage contractors on the site and must stipulate the site rules to be followed. Copies of the F10 notification must be displayed on site.

The facilities manager may need to approve the Construction Phase Health and Safety Plan on behalf of the Client even if the Planning Supervisor has given advice on it. The ultimate responsibility for ensuring that safety has been pre-planned rests with the Client and it is the Client who would be in breach of reg 10, facing criminal prosecution.

The Health and Safety File

An important requirement of the CDM Regulations is the preparation of a document known as the Health and Safety File. This is a collection of all relevant health and safety information relating to the construction project, covering in particular, the residual hazards and risks associated with the building from the occupiers point of view.

The Health and Safety File should contain information on the design intent of the building and should explain the rationale behind the safe systems of work for maintenance and cleaning of the building. The Planning Supervisor must ensure that the File is compiled but doesn't actually have to write it – often the Principal Contractor provides the information. The Health and Safety File must be handed to the Client at the end of the project and it must be available to whoever needs to access the information, eg contractors for future maintenance, new owners etc.

Design Risk Assessments

These are a contentious issue within the CDM Regulations and should be completed, in some form or other, by Designers undertaking design works. Designers have a significant contribution to make to reducing the hazards and risks associated with construction activity and the intent of CDM is that they address these issues and design out, or reduce, significant hazards.

If working at heights contributes to the greatest fatality rate it is encumbent on a Designer to attempt to design out the need to work at height by sequencing the construction work differently, locating plant elsewhere than on the roof, designing windows which can be cleaned from the insides etc.

There is no legal format for a Design Risk Assessment – the Designer needs to be able to demonstrate that they have:

- taken reasonable steps to ensure that Clients are aware of their duties under CDM before starting design work

- prepared designs with adequate regard to health and safety, and to the information supplied by the Client

- provided adequate information in, or with, the design

- co-operated with the Planning Supervisor and other designers so that everyone can comply with their legal duties.

Design Risk Assessments can be separate risk assessment forms, can include information annotated onto drawings or can be schedules of information. As long as it is clear what residual risk remains from the design then responsibilities under the regulations will have been met.

Managing refurbishment works

Refurbishment works will often fall within the ambit of CDM and should be considered no differently than other construction projects. It could even be argued that refurbishment works are potentially more hazardous because the building will often remain occupied, works may be in restricted areas, other processes may be happening, employees and public may have access etc.

Refurbishment works will fall outside of the CDM Regulations if the following apply:

- the works are not notifiable
- the Local Authority are the enforcing authority
- the works do not disrupt the normal activity of the business
- the works are not separated from usual activity eg by hoardings.

Facilities managers must pay careful attention to refurbishment works, planned and term maintenance projects and must establish whether CDM applies or not. If in any doubt, apply the principles of the regulations. If the facilities management company is competent, it can appoint itself as Planning Supervisor, and if it can be proved that it carries on the business of construction, it can appoint itself Principal Contractor as well.

It is vital to integrate the Employers Health and Safety Policy into any Construction Phase Health and Safety Plan.

Building management

Irrespective of whether CDM Regulations apply, general health and safety applies to all projects undertaken regarding maintenance, refurbishment, repair and development of buildings and structures.

Clients, employers and persons in control of premises are expected to ensure that health and safety management systems are in place and that contractors work safely. It is no longer acceptable for Clients/employers to leave contractors to 'fend for themselves' and anyone who engages a contractor of any sort is expected to guide them on standards of safety.

Employers need to develop robust Contractor Safety Codes of Practice – often known as Employers' Requirements – and ensure that these are followed during all works.

In particular, access to work areas at heights must be especially controlled, as must access into confined spaces, on to fragile materials, using hot works etc. Safe systems of work must be determined with the contractor and employers' requirements for Permit to Work procedures must be clearly stipulated.

Structure and access

The *Health and Safety at Work Etc Act 1974* requires there to be a safe means of access to and egress from a place of work.

- A place of work is anywhere where an employee would carry out job tasks expected by the employer.
- Plant rooms, roofing areas, working platforms, gantries, mezzanine floors are all places of work. Working up a ladder, on a scaffold or tower scaffold is a 'place of work'.

- Access to a place of work must be safe and without risks to health. There must be a 'safe system of work' for the cleaning and maintenance tasks.

- The *Management of Health and Safety at Work Regulations 1999* require Risk Assessments to be completed for all job activities. This will include how you expect someone to get to their place of work.

- The *Provision and Use of Work Equipment Regulations 1998* require that any equipment provided for access to the place of work is safe and properly maintained.

- The *Lifting Operations and Lifting Equipment Regulations 1998* require that any lifting equipment is inspected and tested and maintained in a safe condition.

- The Facilities Manager must consider the safety of all access routes to roofs, plant rooms, gantries etc. Anywhere where equipment is located will need at some stage to be accessed so that the equipment or plant can be cleaned or maintained. Also, parts of the structure may need cleaning, eg gutters need cleaning out, windows need cleaning, roof lights need cleaning.

- The Facilities Manager may be the employer of the persons needing access, or they may be the persons in control of the premises. In any event, health and safety responsibilities are mandatory.

Cleaning windows

Safe means of access for cleaning windows both inside and out is essential. Usually, the common practice is to use a ladder, but a Risk Assessment should be conducted to establish whether a ladder is best. Would a tower scaffold, mobile elevating work platform or 'cherry picker' be better?

How will the window cleaner carry the bucket and cleaning cloths? Will he have to over-reach? What happens in poor weather? Could the ladder be knocked into?

Perhaps a safer method of access to the outside windows is from the inside. Could windows be 360° swivel? (This would be good design under the *CDM Regulations*. For all new buildings, where cleaning of surfaces etc involves heights of 2.0m or more, the Designer must complete a Design Risk Assessment.)

The facilities manager cannot leave the contractor 'to it' and turn a blind eye to the way that windows are cleaned.

The window cleaning contractor must provide you with Risk Assessments and Method Statements. As facilities manager, you must provide adequate information on the hazards in your building eg falls from heights, so as to enable the contractor to plan his job safely.

Using ladders

More accidents are caused by poor use of ladders than any other access equipment.

Ladders should be properly maintained and regularly inspected as they are 'work equipment' (*PUWER 1998*). They should be suitable for the purpose: for example, wooden ladders may not be suitable in some environments.

Ladder safety tips:

- Secure them to prevent slipping, especially at the top.
- Have a second person to 'foot' them (but only if the ladder is less than 5m).
- Extend the top of the ladder to at least 1.0m above the landing space.
- Do not place ladder against fragile surfaces, eg gutters.
- Place ladders on firm and level ground.
- Set ladders to have an incline of 1 in 4.
- Check all rungs for damage.
- Regularly inspect ladders and record findings.

Access for cleaning and maintenance

- Access routes and passageways must be well-lit and properly ventilated.
- There must be no obstructions, disrepair to floors etc.
- Adequate room for access must be provided – and remember, materials, spare parts and plant may need to be brought to the place of work.
- Is the place of work a 'confined space'? If so, a Risk Assessment must be carried out and the *Confined Spaces Regulations 1997* complied with.
- Consider egress from the place of work – can operatives get out the way they got in?
- What emergency procedures have been put in place – fire evacuation, accidents and emergencies etc? How might people be got out if they suffer a severe injury and are not mobile?
- Does anyone have to traverse fragile materials with a risk of falling through them? This would be unacceptable so an alternative method will have to be found or crawling boards used, strengthening the material. As a last resort, fall arrest systems could be used or fall arrest netting.

Consequences of failure to have safe access and egress

- Serious injury to someone.
- Fatalities.
- Prosecution – fines of up to £20,000 or unlimited.
- Statutory Notices – either Improvement or Prohibition Notices under the *Health and Safety at Work Etc Act 1974*.
- Corporate manslaughter.

Top tips for access and safety:

- Assess access routes to all work areas, plant, equipment etc.

- Complete Risk Assessments.

- Devise safe systems of work.

- Work on any level that is 2.0m high must have edge protection.

- Use ladders only as a means of access, not as working locations.

- Ask Architects and Designers what safety provisions they have allowed for access for cleaning and maintenance.

- Check any access equipment, fall arrest systems, eye bolts and lifting equipment regularly and inspect lifting equipment every six months.

- Assess the competency of contractors.

Permit to Work procedures/safe systems of work

There are many instances where a residual hazard exists within work premises and the employer has to put in place procedures and methods for controlling exposure to the risks.

Hazardous environments, such as plant rooms, roof areas, confined spaces, tanks and vats, are all areas where significant hazards can be present and the preferred safety procedure for managing those risks is a Permit to Work or Enter System.

Permits to Work set out the safety procedures to be followed by those undertaking the work and should:

- describe the work being undertaken

   ○ who is doing it

   ○ how long the work will last

   ○ where is it being undertaken

- what are the hazards

   ○ how will these be controlled

- emergency procedures

- requirement for training or competency

- site/employer safety rules

- handback/sign off procedure

- personal protective equipment to be used.

A Permit to Work system is an invaluable safety tool and should be used for all works carried out by external contractors in areas in which they are unfamiliar. A Permit process gives the facilities manager the opportunity to check the safe system of work of the contractor or employee and brings into the open any site safety hazards and their expected controls.

A Permit to Work should be signed by both parties and must be completed at the end of the day or time period specified.

If an accident were to ensue despite the Permit, the Permit would be used as 'due diligence defence', provided of course, it had been drawn up by a competent person and was valid and relevant to the job.

Hot works permits are essential for managing fire safety risks.

Method statements

These are really written safe systems of work and should explain the process, procedures and safe controls to be taken when a job is tackled. Method statements are not legally required but are good practice and a sound safety discipline.

The Building Regulations

The current edition of the *Building Regulations* is 2002, as amended, and the majority of building projects are required to comply with them.

The *Building Regulations* exist to ensure the health and safety of people in and around all types of buildings. They also cover energy conservation and access and facilities for people with disabilities.

Anyone wanting to carry out building work (as defined in the regulations) which is subject to the regulations is required by law to make sure that it complies with the regulations and to use one of two types of Building Control service.

A Building Control service is provided so that all building works can be screened and checked so as to ensure that the works comply. Building Control services are provided either by a local authority or by an approved inspector or firm. There is a charge for either service. The responsibility for complying with the *Building Regulations* rests with the person carrying out building works – the facilities management company if you are using your own employees, or the contractor or builder if using external resources. It is vital to establish at the outset of any contract who is making the *Building Regulations* application.

The owner of the building is the person served with the 'Enforcement Notice' if the buildings works fail to comply with the requirements.

The *Building Regulations* deal with 13 parts – each dealing with individual aspects of building design and construction: structural matters, fire safety, conservation of energy, hygiene, sound insulation, access and facilities for disabled people, ventilation, drainage, resistance to moisture, combustion appliances, glazing, protection from falling and use of toxic substances.

Each part sets out the broad objectives that the individual aspects of building design must achieve. The 'Parts' are accompanied by 'Approved Documents' which contain practical ways on which to comply with the requirements.

The information and guidance contained in the Approved Documents is not a set of statutory requirements and is not mandatory. However, anyone carrying out building works must be able to demonstrate that they have built or are going to build, a structure which meets the requirements in other ways.

Building work is defined as:

- the erection or extension of a building

- the installation or extension of a service or fitting which is controlled under the regulations

- an alteration project which will be relevant to the continue compliance of the building

- the insertion of cavity wall insulation

- underpinning of the foundations.

With a few exceptions, the person undertaking the building works can decide whether to appoint the Local Authority Building Control Service or an Approved Inspector as the 'checking authority'.

Before works can commence either 'full plans' have to be submitted or a Building Notice has to be lodged.

If plans are submitted and they comply with the regulations, a notice is issued to that effect. Building works can then start. If the plans do not comply, modifications can be made and the local authority will advise.

Building notices apply predominantly to small works and avoids the need to submit full plans. Building notices cannot be used for Fire Safety works under Part B. Once a Building Notice is issued, works can commence and the Local Authority will inspect works as they progress.

If *Building Regulations* approval is sought under the 'full plans' principle, a Building Completion Certificate is issued. No such Certificate is issued under a Building Notice approval.

An Approved Inspector will check plans, issue a Plans Certificate, inspect the work as it progresses and if everything complies, issue a Final Certificate. The Approved Inspector will notify the local authority of the intended building work on an 'initial notice'.

Contraventions of the *Building Regulations* are usually dealt with by way of fines – up to £5,000 in the Magistrates' Court and £50 per day for each day the offence continues, or by way of an Enforcement Notice requiring the owner to alter, remove or amend works which contravenes the Regulations. Should an owner not comply, the local authority has the power to 'act in default' and undertake the works themselves and recover the costs. Enforcement Notices normally give 28 days in which to rectify the defects. Appeals can be made against Enforcement Notices to the Magistrates' Court.

Catering facilities

Many facilities management contracts include responsibilities for overseeing the contract or in-house catering service. It is important to be aware of the key aspects of Food Safety and Hygiene legislation as a failure to act on say, premises defects, could result in the prosecution of the Facilities Management Contractor.

Food Safety Act 1990

The Act sets out the standards for the preparation and sale of foods for human consumption. It requires food to be fit for consumption when sold, properly labelled and described, free from foreign objects, free from adulteration and generally non-injurious to health.

The *Food Safety Act 1990* falls into the category of an 'enabling act' and paved the way for a raft of food hygiene and food standards regulations. It is enforced by Environmental Health Departments in the main, with some duties falling to Trading Standards.

The *Food Safety Act 1990* applies to 'food business proprietors' and it is important for contractual agreements to clearly state who is running the food business and on behalf of whom. In addition to the food business proprietor, 'any person' can be prosecuted for an offence involving the selling or rendering of food unfit for consumption.

The powers invested in Environmental Health Officers under the Act can be draconian and Enforcement Officers have the authority to close food businesses if they believe there is an imminent risk to health.

An Authorised Officer of the Food Authority may at all reasonable times inspect food intended for human consumption. It is important to note that there is a presumption under the Act (s 3) that all food usually intended for human consumption is actually for consumption if it is sold, stored, offered or exposed for sale within premises used for the preparation, storage or sale of food stuffs. It is for the person accused of having food unfit for consumption to prove that the 'presumption' was invalid and that the food was not for sale.

Most routine food safety inspections are carried out during normal working hours but inspections can occur at other times, eg during evening functions.

If an Authorised Officer is of the opinion that food is injurious to health and will cause food poisoning, s/he may do one of two things:

- seize the foods and have them dealt with by a Justice of the Peace

- give notice to the person that until permission is given, the food must not be used for human consumption nor removed from the premises.

If a 'delay' or 'do not move' notice is placed on the foods, a decision on their suitability for consumption must be made within 21 days.

Improvement notices

Should food premises be in such a condition that breaches of the *Food Safety (General Food Hygiene) Regulations 1995* are deemed to have taken place, the Authorised Officer can serve an Improvement Notice on the food business proprietor. An Improvement Notice is a legally binding notice served under s 10 of the *Food Safety Act 1990* and requires the food business proprietor to remedy breaches of law within a given timescale.

Improvement Notices must:

- State the officer's grounds for believing that the proprietor is failing to comply with the regulations.

- State the precise reasons why the regulations are being contravened.

- State the measures necessary to rectify the contraventions and a time within which they must be completed.

The time limit for works to be carried out on an Improvement Notice must be at least 14 days as this allows the recipient time to lodge an appeal against the Notice. Appeals are lodged in the Magistrates' Court.

Failure to comply with an Improvement Notice is an offence which carries a maximum fine of £20,000 if proceedings are taken in the Magistrates' Court.

There is a defence of due diligence in respect of any prosecution under the *Food Safety Act 1990*. The food business proprietor or other person charged must show that they took all reasonable precautions to avoid committing the offence, or exercised all due diligence in avoiding an offence. It may be a defence for a person accused of food safety offences to cite that some other person was liable for the offence through their act or default.

The citing of 'another person' could be the facilities management company if the contract caterer believes that the offence was caused by the negligence or inaction of the facilities manager in respect of actioning repairs, maintenance programmes, or pest proofing etc.

Prohibition order

If during an inspection of the food premises, the Environmental Health Officer believes that there is a risk of injury to health, they may apply to the Magistrates'

Court for a Prohibition Order which will prohibit the premises operating a food business. Such orders are made where premises are unsanitary, infested, filthy or where practices are so bad that food is at risk of contamination. The court may grant the application and the premises will close until such time as the defects have been remedied and the order is lifted.

Emergency Prohibition Notice

In certain circumstances, food premises are so unsanitary, defective or filthy that there is 'imminent risk' of injury to health in the opinion of the Officer. In these cases, the Officer can serve an 'Emergency Prohibition Notice' which requires the food business to close immediately. The Emergency Order must be ratified as soon as possible (and within three days) by the Magistrates' Court. Once ratified, the food business must remain closed until such time as the local authority are satisfied that the 'imminent risk' to health has been removed. While the premises are closed, a Statutory Notice advising of the closure must be displayed in a prominent position within the premises for public view.

Direct to court

Finally, in respect of enforcement, Food Authorities can dispense with all service of statutory notices and proceed direct to court with a prosecution for food hygiene offences. Often, when prosecutions are likely, written notice is given prior to the issuing of summonses.

As with all legal issues, if summonses are issued, either the facilities manager or contract caterer or both will need legal advice. Fines per offence can be up to £5,000 in the Magistrates' Court.

The Food Premises Registration Regulations 1991 (amended)

These regulations require that all food businesses register with the local authority, supplying key information on contact details and types of food sold etc. Any significant change in food business ownership for existing food businesses should also be notified. The registration process is to enable the local authority to compile a register of its food businesses so that, in emergencies, such as food scares and product recalls, the Food Safety Team can effectively utilise their resources to safeguard the public's health.

Food Safety (General Food Hygiene) Regulations 1995

These regulations are the mainstay for ensuring that food premises selling food for both immediate or later consumption are hygienic and safe and that contamination of foodstuffs is prevented.

The key elements of the regulations which may affect facilities managers are:

Premises

These must be maintained in good condition so as to ensure that surfaces and structures are easy to clean and free from defects. Surfaces in food rooms must be 'smooth, impervious and easily cleanable' eg tiles, continuous non-porous sheeting or proprietary materials, epoxy resin floors, vinyl sheeting etc. Wood is not recommended as it is porous, harbours bacteria and splinters easily, causing the potential for 'foreign object in food complaints'.

Pest proofing

All food rooms shall be so maintained so as to prevent the ingress of pests, including rodents, cockroaches, flies etc. Proofing strips on the gaps to doors, shutters etc are essential. Mesh screens against windows and openable doors are required. Fill in voids and inaccessible harbourage places. Pests spread diseases on their bodies, in their faeces and urine and can contaminate food and work surfaces.

Services

All food rooms in which open food (ie food not wrapped or placed in containers), is kept or prepared must be equipped with a supply of hot and cold water (or suitably temperature-controlled supply), adequate drainage, sinks and hand wash basins. Food rooms must also be adequately ventilated and have reasonable ambient temperature controls.

Refuse and waste material

Waste must not be allowed to accumulate in food rooms as it is a source of food poisoning contamination and attracts pests. Adequate refuse facilities must be provided and regular refuse collections are essential.

Drainage facilities (including grease traps)

These must be maintained in hygienic conditions and grease traps cleaned and emptied regularly as they can soon become unsanitary.

Equipment

Must be maintained in a safe and hygienic condition. If statutory inspections are necessary, it will usually be the facilities manager who has to arrange them. Do not forget pressure boilers, steam ovens and combi-boilers etc. All will need statutory inspections, as will any service lifts, hoists, and exhaust ventilation systems.

Management systems

A food business proprietor must identify the hazards associated with the food production process and implement suitable controls to reduce the risks. This is commonly known as HACCP (Hazard Analysis Critical Control Points) and the facilities manager should be satisfied that the caterer has addressed these issues.

Food Safety (Temperature Control) Regulations 1995

These regulations require certain foods to be kept at certain temperatures under designated conditions. The responsibility for ensuring compliance with food hygiene standards which involve practices and procedures rests generally with the food business proprietor.

Foods must either be kept hot or cold if food poisoning outbreaks are to be avoided. If foods are to be displayed at ambient temperatures they must be displayed for no more than FOUR hours maximum, otherwise they must be kept chilled at 8°C if intended to be eaten cold, or above 63°C if intended to be eaten hot.

Facilities managers will need to be satisfied that both refrigeration equipment and hot food-holding cabinets are maintained in efficient working order and that the relevant temperatures are consistently achieved. Refrigeration equipment should operate between 1–4°C although up to 8°C would be acceptable for short durations. An effective method of destroying food poisoning organisms is by the application of heat and if foods are cooked above 75°C then most food poisoning bacteria are killed. Hot holding ovens should keep food temperatures above 63°C.

Health and safety in catering units

Health and safety in catering units is also a key priority and a significant percentage of worker accidents and injuries occur in kitchens and food service areas. Slips, trips and falls are common in the catering industry and are often caused by poor maintenance, inadequate cleaning or a failure to clear up spillages.

Kitchen temperatures are often a cause of concern and high temperatures increase food contamination risks (as food may be exposed to temperatures which enable bacteria to multiply) and employee accident rates. Facilities managers must ensure that 'suitable and sufficient' temperatures are maintained in kitchens.

The *Provision and Use of Work Equipment Regulations 1998* require all work equipment to be maintained in a safe condition. Regular maintenance checks will be needed of all catering equipment as well as associated records. Facilities managers should ensure that equipment is inspected by competent persons and must either arrange this or ensure that the caterer does so.

Frequency of inspection is recommended as follows:

As appliances	Every 12 months
Pressure cookers, pressure fryers, steam pans, steam pipes, water boilers etc	According to a written scheme of examination set by a competent person
Electrical appliances in kitchens	Combined inspection and test approximately every 6–12 months
Lifting equipment, hoists etc	Every 12 months if not carrying people
Fire alarm and fire fighting equipment	Minimum of annual maintenance

Finally, facilities managers may be responsible for safety signs in catering areas. These should follow the principles of the *Health and Safety (Safety Signs and Signals) Regulations 1996* and depict residual hazards, prohibition instructions, mandatory procedures, safe areas etc. Ensure that pipes carrying flammable substances are appropriately labelled, eg 'gas pipes'.

The catering facilities provided by any employer, whether directly or in-house or out-sourced to a contract catering company, must be regularly inspected and monitored if good practices are to be maintained and safe food is to be prepared and sold. A major food poisoning outbreak for any company could seriously jeopardise their efficiency and the resulting publicity will be an unacceptable business risk. Where facilities management contractors have catering facilities within their premises, they must ensure a high profile auditing and monitoring regime.

Licensing

Many in-house catering facilities include either a social club or function facility which will be licensed to sell intoxicating liquor and/or provide public entertainment or dancing.

Premises need to be licensed to sell alcohol and it may fall to the facilities manager to make the application to the Licensing Justices. It is an offence to sell alcoholic beverages without a licence unless deemed to be a private members club where there are some exemptions.

The licensing regime is undergoing reform during 2003 and the new *Licensing Act 2003* is expected to come into force in 2004.

Premises will still need to be licensed but so will individuals. Opening hours will be relaxed as will some requirements on Public Entertainment Licenses. All those applying for premises licenses will need to submit an Operating Plan setting out how they propose to control key aspects of running the venue. Licenses will be granted by local authorities and not Licensing Justices. Appeals against refusals will be held in the Magistrates' Court.

Facilities managers will need to ensure that they have both premises and individual licenses if they are intending to sell alcoholic beverages for consumption on or off the premises.

Proposed health and safety legislation

The following pieces of legislation, Approved Code of Practice or Guidance Notes are anticipated within the future:

- New Noise at Work Regulations

- New Working at Height Regulations

- New Fire Safety legislation

- Amendments to the Workplace (Health, Safety and Welfare) Regulations 1992

- Guidance on the Duty to Investigate Accidents

- Guidance/Approved Code of Practice on Vehicle Safety and Driving Whilst at Work

- Legislation on Corporate Manslaughter

- Amendments to the Personal Protective Equipment at Work Regulations 1992

- Revised Food Hygiene legislation especially in relation to Hazard Analysis

Area of Reform	Date of Change	Summary
Noise at Work Regulations	2006	Introduction of new noise exposure limits, requirements for hearing checks, provision of hearing protection etc. Noise exposure limits to be reduced to 80 and 85dB(A) – down from 85 and 90dB(A).
Working at Heights	2004–05	Proposed regulations to cover working at heights, inspections of working platforms, assessment of procedures by a competent person, work on fragile materials, use of ladders, falling objects etc.
Fire Safety	2004	A new Regulatory Reform Order is anticipated to replace the exisiting Fire Precautions Act 1971. Fire risk assessments will become more vital, management and control of fire risks will be expected.
Workplace (Health, Safety and Welfare) Regulations	2004–05	Revisions to numerous parts of the existing regulations to bring them into line with current practices eg traffic routes and vehicle safety, glazing.
Investigating Accidents	2004	Guidance advice is expected on the need to investigate workplace accidents in order to better manage risks etc. An Approved Code of Practice may follow if the guidance does not have the desired effect of reducing workplace accidents.

Vehicle safety and Driving Whilst at Work/Transport Safety	2004–05	Vehicle accidents in the workplace are too high and the HSE intend to issue either an Approved Code of Practice or guidance on how to reduce risks, plan vehicle access routes, separate pedestrians from vehicles etc.
Corporate Manslaughter	2004–06	The Home Office re-affirmed their intention, in May 2003, to introduce legislation to make it easier to prosecute corporate bodies, or company individuals, for reckless killing or killing by gross negligence those who are employed or those affected by their undertaking.
Personal Protective Equipment at Work Regulations	2005–06	Amendments are proposed to the PPE Regulations following a review by the HSE as to their effectiveness.
Food Safety Legislation – especially in respect of Hazard Analysis Critical Control Points (HACCP)	2004–05	EC Legislation has required a revisionof UK regulations so as to reflect stricter controls on businesses in respect of implementing the seven principles of HACCP and keeping a written, documented system of the hazards and control points relating to food safety. At present, food businesses need to identify hazards and implement controls to food safety but do not have to keep a written or documented system.

1 ISBN 0 7176 2488 9.
2 IND(G)132L.
3 *R v Howe & Son (Engineers) Ltd* (6 November 1998, unreported) CA.
4 The *Revitalising Health and Safety* plan is at *www.open.gov.uk/hse/hsehome.htm*
5 *Directors' Responsibilities for Health and Safety*, see *www.hse.gov.uk/pubns/indg343.pdf*
6 The *Involuntary Homicide* consultation paper is at *www.homeoffice.gov.uk/index.htm*
7 HS(G)90.
8 HS(G)57.
9 L27, L28, L127, HS(G) 227.
10 ISBN 0 7176 1772 6.
11 IND(G) 63.
12 HS(G)155.
13 Including HS(G)136, IND(G)199(L) and IND(G)148(L).
14 ISBN 0 7176 1196 5.
15 HS(G)150.
16 HS(G)33 and IND(G)284.
17 Excluding that generated from 'new' renewable sources (except large-scale hydro) and by good quality CHP.
18 HS(G) 224.

2 Complying with the Law on Staff, Casual and Contract Workers

Jackie Le Poidevin and Louis Wustemann

Flexible working for employees

Reforms

The New Labour Government's first one and a half terms have brought sweeping changes to employment rights. Some legislation such as the *Working Time Regulations 1998*, have been introduced as a result of EU legislation. Other changes, like enhanced maternity provisions, were home grown through the government's Fairness at Work proposals.

These reforms are an attempt to enshrine the right to flexible working in law and not just for traditional 'employees'. Section 230 of the *Employment Rights Act 1996* defines a worker as an individual who has entered into a contract of employment or any other contract, whether express or implied, which undertakes to 'perform personally any work or services for another party to the contract whose status is not by virtue of the contract that of a client or customer'. This includes individuals such as IT contractors who are not genuinely self-employed, but who work under a personal service contract. It will also cover some casual or temporary agency workers, and other 'atypical' workers. Facilities managers will need to clarify the employment status of any contract or agency workers to whom they have outsourced work in the light of the ongoing changes in legislation.

Flexible working right of request

The *Employment Act 2002* introduced a right for employees with caring responsibilities for young children to ask to change their working pattern or place of work. The legislation does not give employees the right to work flexibly, but it places the obligation on employers to consider requests seriously.

Parents of children under the age of six (or under the age of 18 where the child is registered disabled) are able to apply to change their work pattern to care for the child.

A parent is defined as anyone with responsibility for raising the child including guardians, adoptive and foster parents, or anyone who is the partner of one of the above and lives with the child.

Eligible employees can ask to change:

- their hours of work (eg part-time working, jobsharing, term-time working)

- their working times (eg variable hours, staggered hours)

- their workplace (eg homeworking or, if available, an office nearer home).

The employee's application has to be made in writing (email and fax are acceptable) and must state the working pattern applied for and when the applicant wants to make the change, the effect, if any, that the applicant believes the new working pattern would have on the employer and how this effect could be offset.

Within 28 days of receiving the application (or of its being sent electronically), the employer must either accept the request and write to the employee notifying them of the variation to their contract and when the change will be effective; or hold a meeting with the employee to discuss the request at a convenient place and time for both the employer and the employee. At the meeting (and at any appeal meeting afterwards) the employee has the right to be accompanied by a colleague or trade union representative. Breaching this provision results in a compensation payment of up to two weeks' pay (limited to £250 per week at present).

Following the meeting, if the employer wishes to refuse the application, they must inform the employee within 14 days in writing, explaining the reasons for the refusal and the procedure for the employee to appeal against the decision.

Reasons for refusal

Employer's can refuse flexible working requests for any of the following reasons:
- the burden of additional costs
- detrimental effect on ability to meet customer demand
- inability to reorganise work among other staff
- inability to recruit extra staff
- detrimental effect on quality
- detrimental effect on performance
- insufficient work during the periods the applicant has requested to work
- planned changes to the business.

The explanation in writing of these reasons to the employee after the first meeting must be 'sufficient'.

Right of appeal

If the employee decides not to accept a refusal of their request, they have the right to appeal the decision within 14 days of receiving the refusal.

The employee must notify the employer in writing giving details of the reasons for the appeal. Within 14 days of receiving notice of the appeal, the employer must either accept the original request and inform the employee in writing, or hold another meeting to discuss the appeal with the employee.

Once a request has been refused or the appeal process is exhausted, an employee must wait for 12 months from the date of the first request before making another application.

If an employee believes the employer did not follow the regulations in dealing with their request or rejected the application on the basis of false information, they can bring a complaint to an Employment Tribunal, within three months of the rejection of the request.

The legislation also protects any employee dismissed because they made an application, appealed against a refusal or brought a complaint because the employer did not follow the correct procedure. Employees in this position may bring complaints for unfair dismissal.

The 48-hour week

The *European Working Time Directive* was officially introduced as a piece of health and safety legislation, to reduce the risk of ill-health caused by overly-long working hours. The Labour Government, however, transposed it into UK law with the promise, in its *Fairness at Work* White Paper, that the legislation 'will enable people to balance better their work and home lives'.

Organisations which allow employees to work flexible hours or from home will need to keep track of their hours to ensure they comply with the working time legislation. Alternatively, they can ask employees to opt out of the minimum requirements, but this could be bad for homeworkers' stress levels and ultimate productivity, since it can be difficult for them to know when to draw a line under their work each day.

The *Working Time Regulations 1998* provide that:

- Workers' maximum working week must average 48 hours, normally calculated over a 'reference period' of 17 weeks.

- Workers can choose to sign a written agreement that they will work more than the 48-hour limit – this is an 'opt-out'.

- Workers who opt out can cancel the agreement provided they give the employer at least seven days' notice, or longer (up to three months) if this has been agreed.

- The regulations define working time as time when an individual is 'working, at his employer's disposal and carrying out his activity or duties' – this includes travel which is part of the job, working lunches and job-related training.

- Working time does not include commuting time, lunch breaks, or non-job-related evening classes or day-release courses.

Rest periods

Workers required to work more than six hours continuously are entitled to a 20-minute rest break. The employer can decide the exact timing, but the break should be during the six-hour period, not at the beginning or end of it. According to the Department for Trade and Industry (DTI), 'employers must make sure that workers can take their rest, but are not required to make sure they do take their rest'.

Young workers are entitled to a rest break of 30 minutes if required to work for any continuous period of more than four and a half hours. This entitlement can be changed in exceptional circumstances, in which case the young worker should receive 'compensatory rest' within three weeks (see elsewhere in this chapter, **Exceptions to the regulations: agreements, p 91**).

Annual leave

The *Working Time Regulations* entitle workers to four weeks' paid annual leave each year. There is no qualifying period for this entitlement.

Workers accrue annual leave during their first year of employment at the rate of one-twelfth of their entitlement per month worked, rounded up to the nearest half day. So if a worker requests leave after three months' service, their entitlement will be three-twelfths (one-quarter) of 20 days; that is, five days

The four-week entitlement includes bank holidays – there is no statutory right for bank holidays to be granted as leave. Employers can specify the times that workers take their leave – for example, over Christmas. Workers must give the employer notice that they want to take leave. When their employment terminates, they have the right to be paid for any leave not taken.

Nightworkers

Facilities managers who employ in-house or external security personnel may need to be aware of the provisions on nightworking (but see elsewhere in this chapter, **Exceptions to the regulations: special circumstances, p 91**). The regulations define a nightworker as someone who works at least three hours a night 'as a normal course'. Such workers should not work more than eight hours daily on average. There has been a court ruling that an individual who worked nights for one third of their working time was a nightworker.

Night time is normally between 11pm and 6am, although workers and employers may agree to vary this. If they do, night must be at least seven hours long and include midnight to 5am.

Where a nightworker's work involves special hazards or heavy physical or mental strain, there is an absolute limit of eight hours on their working time each day – this is not an average.

Exceptions to the regulations

According to DTI guidance[1], there are four types of exceptions where parts of the *Working Time Regulations* may not apply.

1. Agreements

Workers can agree with their employer to vary nightwork limits and the right to rest periods and rest breaks, in return for 'compensatory rest'. They may also agree to extend the reference period for calculating hours worked up to 52 weeks.

The compensatory rest provision allows workers to take their total weekly rest of 90 hours in a different pattern to that set out in the regulations. The principle is that everyone gets their entitlement in the end, although some rest may come slightly later than normal.

These agreements can be made by collective agreement (between the employer and a trade union) or by a workforce agreement, usually made with elected representatives of the workforce. If a worker has any part of their conditions determined by a collective agreement they cannot be subject to a workforce agreement. A workforce agreement can apply to the whole workforce or to a group of workers.

2. Special circumstances

The nightwork limits and the right to rest periods and rest breaks do not apply where:

- workers work far away from where they live and want to work longer hours over fewer days to complete a task more quickly

- workers constantly have to work in different places making it difficult to work to a set pattern

- the work involves security or surveillance to protect property or individuals

- the job requires round-the-clock staffing or there are busy seasonal peak periods

- an emergency occurs.

In these cases, the reference period for the weekly working time limit is extended from 17 to 26 weeks, and workers are entitled to compensatory rest.

3. Unmeasured working time

Apart from the entitlement to paid annual leave, the regulations do not apply if a worker can decide how long they work – for example, a senior manager or director. The regulations state that a worker falls into this category if 'the duration of his working time is not measured or predetermined, or can be determined by the worker himself'.

4. Partly unmeasured working time

This exception refers to workers who have an element of their working time pre-determined, but otherwise decide how long they actually work. The guidance states: 'Additional hours which the worker chooses to do without being required to by his employer do not count as working time; therefore, this exception is restricted to those that have the capacity to choose how long they work. The key factor for this exception is worker choice without detriment.'

This exception does not apply to:

- working time which is hourly paid
- prescribed hours of work
- situations where the worker works under close supervision
- any time where a worker is expressly required to work, eg to attend meetings
- any time which a worker is implicitly required to work, eg because of possible detriment if the worker refuses.

So, if a facilities manager willingly chooses to work longer hours without recompense on their own initiative, they may. But if they feel pressured to work unpaid overtime because the company culture demands it, the company is in breach of the regulations.

Enforcement

Enforcement of the *Working Time Regulations* is split between different authorities. The Health and Safety Executive (HSE) and local authority environmental health departments enforce the weekly limits on working hours. The employment tribunals enforce the entitlement to rest and leave.

Part-time workers

The *Part-time Workers (Prevention of Less Favourable Treatment) Regulations 2000* implement the European framework directive on part-time working. The regulations allow part-time workers to bring a compensation claim if they have been treated less favourably, on a pro-rata basis, than a comparable full-time worker. This right applies both to the terms of the part-timer's contract, and 'to any other detriment by any act, or deliberate failure to act' by the employer. The right applies to workers, not just employees.

Previously, part-timers, 80 per cent of whom in the UK are women, had to prove indirect discrimination under the *Sex Discrimination Act 1975 (SDA)* in order to win damages for unfair treatment.

Comparable full-timers

Part-timers can only prove less-favourable treatment if they can compare themselves to another actual worker (a 'comparator'). Under the SDA and the *Race Relations Act 1976*, the comparator can be hypothetical. A comparable full-time worker must:

- do broadly similar work

- have similar qualifications, skills and experience

- work for the same employer at the same establishment, or if there is no available comparator there, work for the same employer at a different establishment.

The regulations list six different types of contract. The effect is that, for example, a part-time worker on a fixed-term contract may only compare their situation to that of a full-time worker on a fixed-term contract. They may not compare themselves to a full-time employee on a fixed-term contract, nor to a full-time worker on a different kind of contract.

A part-timer who switches to full-time work or returns part time to the same level of job within 12 months – for example, a maternity returnee – can compare their new position to their old one. They can, in other words, be their own comparator.

Pro-rata principle

Part-timers are entitled to the same pay, sickness and maternity pay, access to pensions, training, leave and redundancy selection criteria as full-time workers, calculated on a pro-rata basis. Employers should ignore part-time status when they make promotion decisions or give bonuses, shift allowances or unsociable hours payments. They should ensure that training, assessments etc, are arranged so that part-timers can attend. Excluding part-timers from profit-sharing or share option schemes will normally be unlawful. It will not be enough for employers to argue they could not provide the benefits pro rata. The decision not to provide them must be objectively justified.

The regulations do permit one area of difference between part-timers and full-timers. Part-time workers are not entitled to full-timers' overtime rates until they have exceeded the normal full-time hours.

Justification

The employer can defend less-favourable treatment of part-timers by arguing that it was objectively justified. Drawing from sex, race and disability discrimination case law, this is likely to mean that the employer must have a legitimate business objective for the less favourable treatment, and must have chosen reasonably necessary means of achieving this objective.

Remedies

Part-time staff who believe that their rights have been breached may ask their employer, in writing, why they have been treated less favourably. The employer must respond, again in writing, within 21 days. The aim is to give both parties the chance to resolve their disagreement without having to go to a tribunal.

However, if the employee does bring tribunal proceedings, the employer's written statement may be used as evidence. If the employer fails to provide a written statement, the tribunal is entitled to infer that the individual's rights were infringed.

The worker must bring the complaint within three months of their rights being breached. The tribunal may:

- award unlimited compensation

- make a declaration of each party's rights

- recommend that the employer takes action to remedy the fault within a specified period.

In practice, employees may prefer to bring an indirect sex discrimination claim, because they may receive an award for injury to feelings. This is specifically excluded from the *Part-time Workers Regulations*.

The regulations also protect part-timers from being either dismissed or subjected to a detriment because they sought to use their rights.

Regulatory guidance

The regulations offer protection to individuals after they start to work part-time. They do not require employers to give part-time work to those who ask for it. The government has, however, set up a task force to look at the issue of granting requests for part-time status (see elsewhere in this chapter, **Flexible working: right of request, p 87**). The Guidance to the Part-time Workers Regulations also encourages employers to offer part-time work.

Guidance to the Part-time Workers Regulations

To facilitate requests to work part-time, employers should:

- review whether any vacant posts could be done part-time

- consider, when asked by a potential part-timer, whether part-time arrangements can fulfil that position's requirements

- maximise the range of posts at all levels designated as suitable for part-timers or jobsharers

- take requests to jobshare seriously and, in larger organisations, maintain a database of those interested in jobsharing

- take requests to change to part-time work seriously, and explore with workers, if possible, how to bring about this change

- consider having a procedure to discuss with full-time workers whether they wish to change to part-time work

- review how they advertise their vacancies

- communicate with staff representatives on part-time issues.

Leave for parents and carers

Existing entitlements for parents' paid leave have recently been extended by law and some new enitlements have been introduced. The legal minima are set out below.

Maternity leave

All female employees are entitled to up to 26 weeks' ordinary maternity leave (OML) regardless of their length of service, whether they work part- or full-time and whether they are on temporary or permanent contracts.

An employee's OML cannot begin before the 11th week before their expected week of confinement (EWC) and starts on the earlier of:

- the date she notifies to her employer as the start of her OML

- the first day before the beginning of the fourth week before the EWC, where she is absent for a pregnancy-related reason or

- the day of childbirth.

If an employee has been employed by her employer for at least 26 weeks by the 15th week before the EWC, she qualifies for statutory maternity pay (SMP) during the period of OML at the flat rate set by the government each year.

If the employee satisfies the service requirements to qualify for SMP she is also entitled to a period of additional maternity leave (AML), which is unpaid. The employee can take up to 26 weeks AML (bringing her total maternity leave entitlement up to one year).

Paternity leave

Employees with 26 weeks' continuous service by the 15th week before their partner's EWC may take up to two weeks' paid paternity leave during the two months after the birth (or after the adoption date for adoptive fathers). Statutory paternity pay (SPP) is set at the same rate as SMP.

Adoption leave

Employees who have 26 weeks' continuous service before they receive notification of matching with a child for adoption can take up to 26 weeks ordinary adoption leave (OAL), starting no earlier than 14 days before the expected date of placement of the child. Either adoptive parent can take OAL and the other will then be eligible for two weeks' paid leave at the time of placement on similar terms to paternity leave (see above). During OAL employees receive statutory adoption pay (SAP) paid at the same rate as SMP.

Employees are also entitled to a further period of unpaid additional adoption leave (AAL), lasting 26 weeks (bringing their total adoption leave entitlement up to one year).

Parental leave

Employees qualify for parental leave if they:

- have one year's continuous employment with their existing employer and

- have formal responsibility for a child who was born or adopted on or after 15 December 1999

or

- have one year's continuous employment with their current or previous employer; and

- have formal responsibility for a child who was born or adopted between 15 December 1994 and 14 December 1999.

Provided they have formal responsibility, all mothers qualify for parental leave, as do fathers who were married to the child's mother at the time of the birth or appear as the father on the birth certificate. Adoptive parents, foster parents, step-parents and guardians are also eligible.

Employees may take up to 13 weeks' unpaid leave (18 weeks where the child is disabled) for each child before the child's fifth birthday (18th birthday in the case of a disabled child and fifth anniversary of placement for adopted children).

Employers can change these conditions by collective agreement with employees, as long as the new terms are more generous than the legal minima.

Time off for dependants

The 1999 changes introduced a right to unpaid leave for family emergencies. The entitlement applies in the following situations:

- to provide assistance when a dependant falls ill, gives birth, is injured or is assaulted

- to make care arrangements for a dependant who is ill or injured

- to deal with the death of a dependant

- to deal with unexpected disruption to or the termination of arrangements for a dependant's care

- to deal with an unexpected incident during a son or daughter's education.

Dependants are defined as a spouse, child, parent or person living in the same household (tenants, friends sharing a house, or same-sex couples). The *Parental Leave Directive* allowed member states to limit time off for dependants to a specified number of occasions or length of time, but the UK legislation is silent on this.

Contract and casual workers

The UK has had a reputation for a 'light-touch' approach to regulating the relationship between employers and non-permanent employees. Recent EU-sponsored legislation is introducing more formality into these relationships.

Fixed-term contracts

Around 6 per cent of the UK workforce is employed on fixed-term contracts. *The Fixed Term Employees (Prevention of Less Favourable Treatment) Regulations* came into effect in October 2002 to protect the interest of these workers.

The regulations mirror the similarly-named regulations protecting part-timers. Unlike the *Part-time Workers Regulations*, they apply to the narrower category of 'employees', rather than the more inclusive 'workers'. This means that self-employed and agency workers are not included.

The regulations define a fixed-term contract as being one of the following:

- it is made for a specific term which is fixed in advance

- it ends automatically when a particular task is completed

- it ends with a specified event (which is not reaching the retirement age).

The regulations create a right for employees on fixed-term contracts:

- not to be treated less favourably than a comparable permanent employee

- not to be subjected to detrimental treatment as a result of any act or deliberate failure to act by the employer.

Employees on fixed-term contracts are entitled to the same terms in their employment contract as comparable permanent employees, apart from pay and occupational pension terms. The employer can, however, defend its actions if they were objectively justified. The definition of a comparable employee mirrors that used in the *Part-time Workers Regulations* (see earlier in this chapter, **Part-time workers: comparable full-timers, p 92**).

The same problems will arise in giving certain benefits to fixed-term employees as occur under the pro-rata principle for apportioning part-timers' benefits. Private healthcare and car leases, for example, may only be renewable annually.

The regulations introduced a right for fixed-term employees to receive information about any suitable permanent vacancies at their place of work. They also provide that individuals employed for four or more years on one fixed-term contract or an unbroken series of contracts automatically become permanent employees if they are re-engaged on a further fixed-term contract unless another fixed term can be objectively justified.

Agency workers

The draft *Conduct of Employment Agencies and Employment Businesses Regulations 2002* are due to become law in 2003. Under the *Employment Agencies Act 1973*, an employment business which hires out temporary staff is the employer of those staff. But an employment agency, in contrast, simply finds work for individuals, who go on to be employed by the hirer.

The rules are not, however, operating effectively, and temporary workers have regularly been provided on an agency basis. This means that they work for a succession of different employers, rather than for a single employment business, so that they fail to accrue the year's continuous service upon which many employment rights depend. There has also been confusion about who the employer is in various situations, and whether agency staff are employees or workers for the purposes of employment legislation.

The problems were highlighted in a recent case, *Montgomery v Johnson Underwood*[2]. Mrs Montgomery tried to claim compensation for unfair dismissal when her contract was terminated, only to be told by the Court of Appeal that she was employed by no one, neither her agency nor her hirer, and therefore had no one she could sue.

Agency workers do have some employment rights. The *Employment Relations Act 1999* gives them the right to be accompanied at a disciplinary or grievance hearing. They are protected from discrimination. They are, also, protected under the *National Minimum Wage Act 1998* and the *Working Time Regulations 1998*.

The employment agency regulations aim to clarify the status of agency workers. Agencies will have to make clear whether they are an employment business or an employment agency, and who the worker's employer is. They also limit the ability of employment agencies to charge 'temp to perm' fees for placements who are subsequently taken on as staff by the company they are placed with.

A parallel development is the proposed EU Directive on working conditions for temporary workers. In its current form, the directive would give temporary workers the same rights to equal pay and conditions as permanent staff once they have worked for an employer for longer than six weeks.

TUPE

It is more than two decades since a law was introduced which ensures employees retain their jobs on the same terms and conditions when their business is taken over. The term 'outsourcing' had probably not even been coined, and despite a series of controversial court decisions, the law has failed to keep pace with the trend for contracting out non-core activities to specialist service providers. It remains unclear whether such outsourcing contracts are covered by the legislation.

The key right enshrined in the legislation is that dismissal in connection with a 'relevant' transfer is unfair unless:

- an economic, technical or organisational reason entailing changes in the workforce was the main cause of the dismissal and

- the employer acted reasonably in the circumstances in treating that reason as sufficient to justify dismissal.

What constitutes a relevant transfer has, however, been the subject of much debate in the courts.

The European legislation governing business transfers is contained in the *Acquired Rights Directive*. This was implemented in the UK by the *Transfer of Undertakings (Protection of Employment) Regulations 1981 (TUPE)*. Following pressure from the UK, member states agreed amendments to the directive in 1998.

The changes to the directive, including a new definition of a business transfer, do not, however, clarify the position on outsourcing or address the inconsistencies in the case law. The government's consultation paper on amending *TUPE* and implementing the changes to the *Acquired Rights Directive* was finally published on 10 September 2001 and is set to produce reforms in 2004.

The *Süzen* decision

The case which sparked off the current round of debate over *TUPE* was heard in the European Court of Justice (ECJ) in 1997. Ayse Süzen and seven other cleaners were employed by a company contracted to clean a school premises. The company lost its contract to a rival operation, which did not take on the cleaners.

Prior to the *Süzen* case[3], the ECJ had used a test, established in a previous European case, *Spijkers*, which said that if an economic entity transferred, and maintained its identity in the process, *TUPE* applied (see *Spijkers* test below). In *Süzen*, the ECJ ruled that this test was not met, because there was 'no concomitant transfer from one undertaking to the other of significant tangible or intangible assets or taking over by the new employer of a major part of the workforce, in terms of their numbers and skills'. In other words, contract cleaning was a labour-intensive undertaking, with no other assets apart from its employees. These employees were not taken on, so there was no recognisable economic entity left to which the *Acquired Rights Directive* could apply.

The problem with this logic was that the whole point of the directive is to protect employees from not being taken on, something it clearly failed to do in Ayse Süzen's case. The ECJ has confirmed this stance in subsequent cases, but the UK courts have repeatedly refused to accept the precedent.

UK case law

The first sign of the UK rebellion was the Court of Appeal's decision in *ECM*[4]. The Court of Appeal found that an incoming contractor had deliberately tried to escape its responsibilities under *TUPE* by exploiting the *Süzen* loophole. It had intentionally avoided taking on either assets or the existing workforce, and the Court said it was entitled to take this motivation into account in reaching its decision. The Court ruled that it could not allow a deliberate attempt to evade the law to succeed, and ruled that *TUPE* did apply.

In another noteworthy case, *RCO Support Services*[5], the Employment Appeal Tribunal (EAT) found in favour of a group of cleaners who were dismissed when an NHS trust reorganised its business. The EAT said it was not sorry to have reached this decision. In labour-intensive areas such as cleaning and catering, where there are rarely any assets, contracting-out is common, it found. Any incoming contractor thinks it can avoid *TUPE* simply by not taking on the outgoing contractor's workforce. This not only jeopardises the fundamental objective of *TUPE* – the protection of employees' acquired rights – it jeopardises them in relation to the most vulnerable people, those with simple and commonly-available skills which incoming contractors can easily supply through others.

Spijkers test

In the *Spijkers*[6] case, the ECJ set out a number of factors which the courts should use to decide whether *TUPE* applies. These are:

- the type of undertaking
- whether tangible or intangible assets transferred
- whether employees transferred
- whether customers transferred
- how similar the activities carried on before and after the transfer were
- whether there was any suspension in activities.

These are tough words, and facilities managers (when bringing outsourced services back in-house, for example) will want to avoid being on the receiving end of them in the courtroom.

In its latest decision on 22 June 2001, the Court of Appeal again found that *TUPE* did apply to a labour-intensive service, after the incoming contractor refused to take on the existing workforce. The case[7] is interesting for facilities managers because it concerned a change in security contractors.

ADI lost a contract in which it supplied nine security guards to a shopping centre. The shopping centre made certain facilities available to the guards, including closed-circuit television (CCTV) and a control room. The new contractor was also allowed to use the facilities, but otherwise, no tangible assets transferred.

The new contractor approached the nine security guards with a view to hiring them, but changed its mind following a dispute over terms. It assigned different employees to the shopping centre, gave them different uniforms, and changed their job title to 'customer liaison officers'.

The Court of Appeal found that although no single factor should determine whether there was a *TUPE* transfer, in a labour-intensive undertaking where the service is substantially the same and performed in the same place for the same person, questions about why the incoming contractor failed to take on existing employees could tip the scales in the employees' favour.

It was clear that if the incoming contractor had taken on the nine guards, there would have been a relevant transfer. Consequently, if a court decided an incoming contractor had deliberately avoided *TUPE*, it should treat the case as if the existing employees had actually transferred.

Practical implications

Some legal commentators argue that the *Süzen* line of cases and the *ECM*, *RCO* and *ADI* line of cases are not, in reality, inconsistent. They are simply an application of the law to a different set of facts. But either way, the difficulty of predicting which way the courts will swing in their own particular case is bad news for service companies bidding to retain or take over a contract.

If *TUPE* applies, the new company will have to take on the old contractor's workforce on their existing terms and conditions, which may be different from those of the rest of its employees. The transferred employees' continuity of employment will remain unbroken, and they will be able to sue the new contractor over any disputes they had with their former employer. As long as a potential new contractor knows all of this, however, it can factor these costs into its bid – it is the legal uncertainty which is damaging.

If a contractor believes that *TUPE* does not apply, and that it does not have to take on the existing workforce and the accompanying liabilities, it can put in a lower bid in the hope of undercutting the current contractor and any other competitors. If it succeeds and is right, the former contractor will be left with no contract, all the employees and the associated redundancy costs. If it wins the tendering process but is legally in the wrong, it will face unfair dismissal claims from the sacked employees – and regardless of the ECJ rulings, the sympathies of the UK courts have tended to be with the employees. This means that making a non-*TUPE* bid remains a gamble, despite *Süzen*.

Amendments to TUPE

The government's consultation paper on amending *TUPE* begins by saying: 'The Government considers that the *TUPE Regulations* are based on a positive principle – the coupling of flexibility for business with fairness for employees', but that the regulations need to be made to work as effectively as possible.

It goes on: 'The revised Directive gives for the first time an explicit definition of a transfer of an undertaking, intended to clarify the existing legal position without changing it. The Government proposes essentially to adopt this definition in the new Regulations. This alone, however, may be insufficient to address the problems that have arisen. The Government considers that there may be a case for taking further measures in two particular areas – transfers within public administration, and service provision changes – that have in the past been particularly frequent sources of confusion and dispute.'

The government goes on to propose that:

if:

- a service provision change is to take place and

- prior to the change, there are employees assigned to an organised grouping, the principal purpose of which is to perform the service activities in question specifically on behalf of the client concerned

then:

- the employees assigned to the organised grouping shall be treated in the same way as in cases where *TUPE* normally applies and

- the party with responsibility for provision of the service before the change shall be treated as the transferor and the party with responsibility for provision of the service after the change shall be treated as the transferee.

This would, the government suggests, ensure that 'the Regulations applied comprehensively in relation to such cases, regardless of the particular facts' and 'arguably increase the likelihood that, from the outset, all concerned normally knew where they stood'. The party which takes on the responsibility for providing the service would become automatically responsible for the employees assigned to the organised grouping (whose continuity of employment would be preserved) and for any outstanding liabilities toward them.

Requirement to notify

There would also be a requirement on the transferor to notify the transferee of all such liabilities where they were or ought to be known about at the time of the transfer, and this could then be properly planned for and taken into account. An added advantage, the government believes, is that this would help to ensure that contract bids were made on a comparable basis, and would remove a significant disincentive for potential bidders, particularly smaller firms, to become involved in service contracting.

The new clause is intended to ensure that the extended protection does not normally apply in cases where clients are buying in services 'off the shelf' in the same way as they might buy in goods – for example, the arrangement of conferences, printing work, consultancy advice or plumbing repairs.

The consultation paper goes on: 'In cases where the arrangement between the client and the outside organisation entailed the provision not only of a service but also of goods, the extended protection would apply only where the former was the predominant aspect and the latter an ancillary one. Thus the extended protection would not normally apply where the arrangement entailed, say, the provision of computer equipment with associated IT advice or the provision of photocopiers with on-call maintenance support'. But: 'The extended protection would normally apply, by contrast, where the arrangement entailed, say, the provision of packaging materials in conjunction with a packing service or the provision of food and drink in conjunction with a catering service'.

Drawbacks?

The government then considers the drawbacks of this approach. These include the potential for contractors intentionally to avoid *TUPE* by redesigning services so that the activities are no longer essentially the same following a change of contractor, so that the definition of a 'service provision change' is not met. The government has, it says, 'considered the possibility of introducing a general "anti-avoidance" provision to make such arrangements unlawful, but has decided on balance that this would be inappropriate, in part because the risks of stifling legitimate innovation in the pursuit of efficient and effective service provision outweigh the risks of abuse'.

Further proposals

There are also proposals on:

- better protection of employees' occupational pension rights

- greater flexibility when applying *TUPE* to transfers of insolvent businesses, to make it more attractive for potential buyers to rescue those businesses

- clarifying the 'economic, technical or organisational' defence

- introducing a legal requirement for the transferor to notify the transferee about the rights and obligations being transferred.

The revised regulations are expected to go through a consultation period in the course of 2003 and to be put before Parliament early in 2004.

In February 2003 the government announced that in advance of the larger revisions, from April 2003 new rules would apply to certain public sector transfers. The new Code of Practice on workforce matters in local government provides that following a *TUPE* transfer of local authority staff, contractors will be obliged to apply *TUPE* not only to transferring staff but also those taken on after the start of the contract, ending the so-called 'two-tier workforce'. A mandatory contract clause between the local authority and the contractor will enforce the code.

Employee consultation

At the moment, UK employees have the right to be consulted in a limited number of situations. These are:

- if collective redundancies or a *TUPE* transfer are planned

- if any measure or new technology is introduced which substantially affects employees' health and safety (see **Complying with health and safety law, pp 2–86**)

- if there is a European Works Council.

The UK has, however, agreed to a European directive on information and consultation which will enhance employees' rights in this area.

European Works Councils

The *European Works Council Directive* was implemented in the UK by the *Transnational Information and Consultation of Employees Regulations 1999*. They require undertakings or groups with at least 1,000 employees across the member states and at least 150 employees in each of two or more of those member states to set up European-level information and consultation procedures (usually through a European Works Council agreement).

Redundancies and transfers

The requirement to consult employees before making them redundant is contained in s 188 of the *Trade Union and Labour Relations (Consolidation) Act 1992*. The requirement to consult employees before the transfer of a business is contained in reg 10 of *TUPE*. It is easy to confuse the two sets of requirements, so it is useful to summarise both here, even though *TUPE* is the bigger concern for facilities managers.

Amendments to the requirements came into effect on 28 July 1999. The main changes, according to DTI guidance[8] are:

- If employees who may be affected are represented by a trade union recognised for collective bargaining purposes, that union now has an automatic right to be informed and consulted over collective redundancies and transfers of undertakings; it may no longer be bypassed by the employer in favour of other employee representatives (although these may also be consulted if the employer so chooses).

- Explicit rules have been introduced for electing employee representatives where there is no recognised union (existing employee representatives may be consulted only if their remit and method of election is suitable).

- Where there is no recognised union and affected employees fail to elect representatives, having had a genuine opportunity to do so, the employer may fulfil its obligations by providing information direct to employees.

- Both union officials and non-union representatives have a right to reasonable paid time off for relevant training.

- Employees are protected against being unfairly dismissed or detrimentally treated for participating in an election of employee representatives.

- the amounts of compensation that employers may be required to pay if they fail to inform and consult have been increased and rationalised.

A collective redundancy is one where 20 or more employees are to be made redundant within a 90-day period. Employers are under no legal obligation to inform and consult representatives if fewer employees are to be dismissed. But the DTI warns they may face unfair dismissal claims if they fail to inform and consult individual employees who are to be dismissed.

'Affected' employees are not necessarily only those who face redundancy or a transfer to a new employer. If there is a dispute, it is for an employment tribunal to decide whether any particular employee or group of employees was affected in the light of all the facts.

Consultation about collective redundancies must begin in good time and at least:

- 30 days before the first dismissal if 20–99 employees are to be made redundant

- 90 days before the first dismissal if 100 or more employees are to be made redundant.

Consultation about the transfer of a business must begin 'in sufficient time', but *TUPE* sets out no specific time period.

On collective redundancy, the employer must consult, with a view to reaching agreement, on how to avoid the dismissals, reduce the number of employees affected, and mitigate the consequences of the dismissals. It should disclose:

- the reasons for the proposed dismissals

- the numbers and classes of employees whom it proposes dismissing

- the total number of employees of such description employed

- the proposed criteria for selecting employees for redundancy

- the proposed procedure and timescale for dismissing employees

- the proposed method for calculating redundancy payments.

On the transfer of a business, the employer must inform the union or employee representatives:

- that the transfer is to take place and when

- the reasons for the transfer

- the legal, economic and social implications of the transfer and

- the measures which the employer proposes taking in relation to the employees affected.

Selection for redundancy

The main cause of employees complaining to an employment tribunal is that they believe they were unfairly chosen for redundancy. The most easily understood way of choosing employees for redundancy is to use the 'last-in-first-out' method. But most employers prefer to use a range of criteria against which to 'mark' employees, which might include their attendance record, timekeeping, productivity (quality and quantity of work), their adaptability and the employer's future needs.

If challenged in a tribunal, the employer must be able to show it used a fair, consistent and objective selection procedure. Employers should avoid vague criteria such as 'attitude', which allow room for prejudice, and discriminatory criteria such as part-time working, pregnancy or trade union membership. They should also take care not to discriminate against disabled employees, whose attendance record, for example, might otherwise mark them out for redundancy.

A redundancy dismissal will also be unfair if the employer has failed to consider suitable alternative employment.

National Works Councils

Despite the existing consultation requirements, there have been a number of recent large-scale redundancies where employees have claimed that far from being involved in any debate about the company's problems, they barely received any warning that they were about to be sacked. When Marks & Spencer tried to dismiss 1,700 staff in its French stores in spring 2001, it gave them half an hour's warning before announcing the plans to the stock exchange. The French court successfully ordered Marks & Spencer to suspend the store closures, because it had not allowed employees time to negotiate. However, the 2,000 employees made redundant from Vauxhall in Luton in December 2000, the 6,000 steelworkers dismissed from Corus in Wales and Teeside in February 2001 and the 3,000 employees sacked at Motorola in Scotland in spring 2001 were less fortunate.

The UK will, however, have to comply with a European Framework Directive on informing and consulting employees which the member states agreed on 11 June 2001. The UK has to implement the Directive by March 2005, but because of the lack of existing national framework on consultation, only organisations with over 150 employees will have to comply initially. In March 2007 the threshold will drop to 100 employees, then to 50 employees in March 2008.

The directive gives employees a right to be:

- informed about the economic situation of the undertaking for which they work

- informed and consulted about any planned measures which could pose a threat to employment

- informed and consulted with a view to reaching agreement about decisions likely to lead to substantial changes in work organisation or contractual relations, including redundancies and transfers.

Information and consultation has to take place at an appropriate time and at the relevant level of management. Normally it will be done via employee representatives, defined according to national law and practice. The expectation is that, to avoid having to keep re-electing employee representatives every time there is a substantial change, employers will have to set up permanent national works councils along the lines of the existing European Works Councils.

The directive is without prejudice to existing information and consultation requirements. This means that it does not override the provisions of the *European Works Councils Directive*, which are far more onerous, but affect only a small proportion of employers.

Disability discrimination

The main recent change to the laws on discrimination, and a key concern for facilities managers, was the introduction of the *Disability Discrimination Act 1995 (DDA)*. It works differently from the *Sex Discrimination Act 1975 (SDA)* and the *Race Relations Act 1976 (RRA)*, because it does not include the concept of indirect discrimination or require claimants to compare their treatment to another actual or hypothetical employee (a 'comparator') in order to prove their case.

The *DDA* imposes duties on employers, suppliers of goods and services and landlords. The stages of the Act so far in force require employers to make adjustments to accommodate disabled employees and job seekers and to adjust the way they provide services where their current form makes it difficult for disabled people to access them. The implementation of Part III of the *DDA* means that by October 2004 any business providing a service to members of the public, customers, clients or tenants will have to, where reasonable, remove, alter or avoid any feature of their premises that makes it unreasonably difficult for a disabled person to use a service.

Under the revised *Equal Treatment Directive*, the UK will have to remove the small employer exemption in the *DDA* by 2005. Also, the police and various other public services will no longer be exempt from the *DDA*, although it will not apply to the armed forces. This will bring organisations employing some 7 million workers within the legislation.

The *DDA* defines 'disability' as a physical or mental impairment which has a substantial and long-term adverse effect on a person's ability to carry out normal day-to-day activities. 'Long-term' means the disability must last or be expected to last at least 12 months.

Normal day-to-day activities are those involving:

- mobility, dexterity or coordination
- continence
- ability to lift, carry or move everyday objects
- speech, hearing or eyesight

- memory or ability to concentrate, learn or understand

- perception of risk.

The *Disability Discrimination (Blind and Partially Sighted Persons) Regulations 2003* which came into force on 14 April 2003 mean that the blind or partially sighted are deemed disabled for the purposes of the *DDA*.

An employer discriminates against a disabled person if, for a reason related to their disability, it treats them less favourably than other people, and it cannot show that this treatment is justified. Discrimination also occurs if the employer could make a 'reasonable adjustment' to work arrangements or premises to accommodate a disabled person, and its failure to do so cannot be justified.

Discrimination may be justified in limited circumstances. For example, employers and service providers must not do anything that would endanger health and safety, although they can no longer use 'fire risk' as a blanket excuse for excluding disabled people from buildings. Nor does the DDA require them to do anything which would prevent them from complying with other legislation such as listed building regulations.

'Reasonable adjustments'

Facilities managers will be involved in making reasonable adjustments in so far as they involve changes to the premises and acquiring or modifying equipment. See the box elsewhere in chapter, **How accessible are your premises?, p 112**, for examples of changes which might be necessary to accommodate either employees or members of the public who have a disability.

But facilities managers need to be aware that the responsibility for making adaptations does not rest solely with them. There are also many other adjustments which can be made to accommodate a disabled employee, which involve changing the way the workplace is organised. These include:

- allocating some of the disabled person's duties to someone else

- transferring the person to fill an existing vacancy

- altering the person's working hours

- assigning the person to a different place of work, such as their home

- allowing absences for rehabilitation, assessment or treatment

- giving training

- modifying instructions or reference manuals

- modifying assessment procedures

- providing a reader or interpreter

- providing supervision.

In considering what is 'reasonable', employers are entitled to take into account:

- how far making the adjustment would prevent the effect of the disability
- how practicable it is to make the adjustment
- the financial costs of the adjustment and the scale of the disruption
- their resources
- the availability of financial or other assistance.

The duty to make reasonable adjustments to physical features of premises applies only to your own premises. There is no duty to make adjustments to a disabled worker's own home, even if they work from there, nor to other premises which the person may visit during their work.

Nevertheless, facilities managers are likely to be involved in setting up employees to work at home if this is the adjustment needed to allow a disabled employee to continue working. Test cases in the US relating to the *Americans with Disabilities Act* (which formed the pattern for the *DDA*) suggest that denying an employee the opportunity to telework would be failure to make a reasonable adjustment in many cases. Where employees work from home, their employers have the same duty of care to maintain a healthy and safe working environment there as in their main sites.

There is no qualifying period of time that a disabled person must have worked to be eligible for rights under the *DDA*. Indeed, a number of compensation claims have involved candidates applying for jobs who were not provided with suitable conditions during their interview. But employees of small firms (currently defined as those employing fewer than 15 employees) are presently excluded from protection.

Public access

Those providing a service to members of the public have until 2004 to comply fully with the *DDA*. Specifically:

- Since December 1996, it has been unlawful for service providers to treat disabled people less favourably.
- Since 1 October 1999, service providers have had to make reasonable adjustments for disabled people, such as providing extra help or making changes to the way they provide their services.
- From October 2004, service providers will have to consider making reasonable adjustments to the physical features of their premises to overcome physical barriers to access.

For the purposes of the *DDA*, service providers include public authorities, private companies, charitable organisations and individual suppliers.

Examples of services to the public are:

- use of any place where members of the public are allowed to enter
- communication and information services, eg telecommunications services
- accommodation, such as hotels and boarding houses
- banks financial and insurance services
- places of entertainment, recreation or refreshment
- services of any profession or trade or public or other authority, including schools, hospitals and surgeries
- commercial businesses: shops; broadcasting companies; transport hubs.

Building alterations

Part III of the *DDA* makes it unlawful for those providing goods, facilities or services to the public and those selling, letting or managing premises to discriminate against disabled people in certain circumstances. There is no exemption for small businesses from this provision.

Service providers must identify any physical barriers that would prevent or seriously hamper disabled people from using the service. These barriers include any temporary or permanent feature of the design or construction of premises, fixtures and fittings or anyother physical element of the premises or their approaches and exits.

Once a barrier is identified the organisation has a choice of removing it, altering it so it no longer forms a barrier, or providing a reasonable means of avoiding the feature.

The only circumstances in which failure to make reasonable adjustments is justified are where:

- the adjustment would endanger the health and safety of others
- a disabled person is incapable of entering into a contract or giving informed consent to a legally enforceable agreement
- the adjustment would prevent you from providing the service to the public.

Research in 2001 for the Department for Work and Pensions found that the costs of implementing the provisions of Part III of the *DDA* included an average £1,300 for wheelchair access to over £3,000 for accessible toilets and over £12,000 for hoists or lifts. However, for most kinds of adjustment the average initial cost was between £100 and £1,000. Grants may be available to make adaptations to the workplace or provide special equipment.

Leasing premises

If your organisation rents its premises, the lease may impose conditions which prevent certain alterations. In this case, the *DDA* overrides the terms of the lease. The organisation should write to the landlord asking for permission to make the alteration in order to comply with the duty of reasonable adjustment. You do not have to make the alteration until the landlord has given permission. The landlord must reply within 21 days or within a longer time if reasonable. The landlord cannot unreasonably withhold consent for an alteration, but may attach reasonable conditions. The *DDA* does not state whether landlords can reclaim the cost of any adjustments through increased service charges. This would need to be provided for expressly in the lease. Those selling or renting property do not have to make adjustments to the property to make it accessible – that is the job of the tenant or buyer.

There is no clear ruling in the legislation as to whether a landlord or tenant is responsible for adjustments to the common parts of a building. A tenant in a single let would probably be responsible but in multi-let premises the landlord would probably have responsibility since they are providing services to the public.

If a disabled person brings a discrimination claim, the employer can ask the tribunal to call the landlord as a party to the proceedings. The tribunal will then decide whether the landlord has unreasonably withheld consent for or imposed unreasonable conditions on making alterations. If the tribunal orders the landlord to pay compensation, it cannot require the employer to do so as well. But it can authorise the employer to carry out a specified alteration.

Complaints and compensation

People with disabilities who believe they have been subjected to discrimination may complain to an employment tribunal within three months of the act complained of. The tribunal can:

- make a declaration of each party's rights

- order the employer to pay compensation

- recommend that the employer take action to remedy the problem (by making a reasonable adjustment, for example) within a specified period.

If the employer fails to follow a tribunal recommendation without reasonable justification, the tribunal can award compensation, or increase an existing award. Compensation is unlimited, and ran into six figures even in one of the earliest disability discrimination cases, *British Sugar v Kirker*[9]. The damages can include an award for injury to feelings.

In line with the *SDA* and the *RRA*, the *DDA* makes employers vicariously liable for discriminatory acts by employees carried out in the course of their employment. This is unless the employer can prove it took reasonably practicable steps to prevent the employee doing such acts.

Contract workers

Again like the *SDA* and the *RRA*, the *DDA* outlaws discrimination by those who hire contract workers. Facilities managers who contract work out to a disabled person or someone who becomes disabled must not discriminate:

- in the terms on which they allow the worker to do the work

- by not allowing the worker to do or continue to do the work

- in the way they give the worker access to benefits or by refusing to give access to benefits

- by subjecting the worker to any other detriment.

The hiring organisation must include contract workers in the count of their employees for the purposes of determining whether the small firms' exemption applies under the *DDA*.

Disability Rights Commission

The Disability Rights Commission (DRC) came into operation in April 2000. It has a role similar to that of the Equal Opportunities Commission and the Commission for Racial Equality. The DRC has a duty to review the working of the *DDA* and to propose amendments where necessary. One area under review is the building regulations in Approved Document M relating to access and facilities for disabled people. Any such reviews are likely to raise the requirements for facilities for disabled people. This means that when planning adjustments now, it may be wiser to adopt a best practice approach rather than simple compliance since doing the bare minimum may cost more in the long term if further adjustments are needed later.

How accessible are your premises?

- Are there disabled parking spaces with space for a wheelchair alongside a car?
- Are signs clearly written?
- Is there a ramp to the entrance?
- Are steps provided with a handrail, good lighting and clearly marked edges?
- Are glass doors marked for visibility, and are there handles at the correct height?
- Is there an induction loop in the reception area, and is the reception desk the right height?
- Are walkways free of obstructions?
- Are entrance doors wide enough?
- Is seating height adjustable?
- If telephones are fixed on the wall, can they be reached? Are minicoms provided?
- Are flashing and audible alarms provided? Are personal vibrating alarms provided for disabled employees?

Unfair dismissal

Before the introduction of the *Employment Relations Act 1999*, employees had to have worked continuously for two years for the same employer before they had the right to claim unfair dismissal. The maximum award they could claim was £12,000.

The *Employment Relations Act* reduced the service requirement to one year and raised the maximum compensatory award to £50,000. It also index-linked the award, which now stands at £51,700. The changes mean not only that more people are entitled to bring a claim, but also that it is more worthwhile to bring a claim, especially for higher earners. The government has stated its intention to reduce the qualifying period further, to six months' continuous employment.

The Act also abolished the practice of those employed on fixed-term contracts of a year or more waiving their right to claim unfair dismissal. The waivers had been intended to prevent workers suing their employer for ending their contract when it expired. But the government was concerned that unscrupulous employers were denying individuals their employment rights by forcing them into a series of short-term contracts. Waiving rights to redundancy payments remains lawful, although there are proposals to stop this practice too.

Automatic unfair dismissal

Employment tribunals will rule that a dismissal was automatically unfair if the employee was sacked:

- for exposing poor health and safety (protected under s 100 of the *Employment Rights Act 1996*)

- for maternity-related reasons

- for asserting a statutory right

- as part of a redundancy exercise for any of the above reasons

- for being a member of a trade union, or participating in union activities

- for having a spent conviction or failing to disclose it

- as part of a *TUPE* transfer

- for refusing to work on Sundays (shopworkers only)

- for blowing the whistle on fraud, malpractice or dangerous practices, in breach of the *Public Interest Disclosure Act 1998*

- acting as a companion during a disciplinary or grievance hearing.

The *Employment Relations Act* additionally made it automatically unfair to dismiss an employee for a reason connected with:

- parental leave

- pregnancy and childbirth

- ordinary, compulsory or additional maternity leave

- time off for domestic reasons

- participation in the first eight weeks of industrial action

- acting as a companion during a disciplinary or grievance hearing.

In most of these situations, the employee does not need to have been employed for a year before bringing a claim.

Workplace surveillance

Used properly, email and the Internet are a real asset to businesses, allowing employees to communicate rapidly with clients and carry out research online. Used improperly (eg, to forward gossip and indecent photographs), they can not only affect productivity, but expose the employer to legal action. These problems explain the growing popularity of monitoring employees' email and Internet use, and the introduction of laws aimed at ensuring such surveillance does not infringe employees' right to privacy.

Surveys suggest that more than two-thirds of pornographic sites are viewed during working hours, more than 50 per cent of employees shop online at work, and 90 per cent of economic computer crime is committed by employees.

Nevertheless, employees have a right to privacy when they use telecommunications systems, as the *Halford* case[10] showed in 1997. Ms Halford, a senior police officer, alleged her private work telephone was tapped without her knowledge. The European Court of Human Rights found this breached her right under art 8 of the *European Convention on Human Rights* to respect for private and family life, home and correspondence.

At the end of 2000, the government and regulators introduced various controls that seek to resolve the conflict between employers' need to protect their interests through electronic surveillance and employees' right to privacy. But much of the legislation has been introduced piecemeal and there appear to be inherent legal conflicts.

Why monitor?

There are a number of reasons why employers are keen to monitor email and Internet use. These include the following legal issues and concerns:

- Employees may inadvertently form binding contracts through email – the tone may be chatty, but an email's legal effect is the same as a formal letter (see **IT and Communications: negotiating by email, p 275**).

- Carelessly worded emails could be defamatory or libellous – in a well-publicised case[11], Norwich Union was sued after two of its employees exchanged defamatory emails about Western Provident.

- Downloading or disseminating copyright material (eg, as an email attachment) could lead to intellectual property disputes.

- Employers could face criminal charges if employees download pornography or hack into external computer systems.

- Employers might be vicariously liable for emails or downloads that harass fellow employees. In *Morse v Future Reality*[12], a woman employee who shared a room with men who downloaded explicit material from the Internet resigned and claimed sex discrimination. Her employer was found liable because it was aware of the men's behaviour and failed to prevent it.

- Employees could hack into their employer's confidential database, putting it in breach of the seventh data protection principle (ensuring data remains secure).

- Employers may commit a breach of confidence if an employee forwards on confidential material emailed by a client – or employers may face their own trade secrets or confidential information being disclosed.

- Employers can be liable for unlicensed software on their system, downloaded by employees.

- Monitoring how long employees spend typing may be useful for health and safety purposes, to prevent repetitive strain injury.

RIP to privacy?

In October 2000, the government introduced the *Regulation of Investigatory Powers Act (RIPA)*. This restricts employers from intercepting employees' emails and telephone calls unless they believe both employees and the other party to the communication have agreed. What constitutes reasonable grounds for believing that consent has been given is not, however, entirely clear.

On 24 October 2000, the government tried to clear up the confusion by bringing in extra regulations under the Act. These are the *Telecommunications (Lawful Business Practice) (Interception of Communications) Regulations 2000*. These allow employers more scope to monitor employees' communications, provided they meet each of the following three criteria:

- the communication being monitored must be made in the course of business

- the employer must have taken all reasonable efforts to inform employees about the monitoring (there is no requirement to inform the party with whom they are communicating)

- the monitoring must be for one of the lawful purposes set out in the regulations, including:

  o to establish facts relevant to the business

  o to ascertain employees' compliance with the law and self-regulatory policies or procedures

- o   to ascertain whether employees are meeting the organisation's standards

- o   to prevent or detect crime

- o   to investigate or detect unauthorised use of the telecommunications system

- o   to ensure the system's effective operation.

Organisations may also monitor (but not record) communications without consent in order to:

- determine whether or not communications are business related

- monitor communications to a confidential support helpline.

An employer who routinely monitors email traffic to ensure the system is used for business purposes only will act within the regulations. Employers also do not need to obtain the prior consent of both senders and recipients. They are simply required to make all reasonable efforts to inform them that the messages may be monitored.

Laws on privacy

There is no privacy law as such in the UK. Employers who believe that the regulations give them a green light to snoop on staff may, however, be in for a shock. There is an implied term of mutual trust and confidence in all employment contracts, which controls, to some extent, the behaviour which employees should reasonably have to endure.

In addition, there is the *Human Rights Act 1998*, which took effect on 2 October 2000. This enshrines art 8 of the European Convention on Human Rights (see elsewhere in this chapter, **Workplace surveillance, p 114**) in UK law, and blanket monitoring of phone calls, emails and Internet use could violate this right. The Act is directly enforceable only against public bodies, but private companies are also likely to be affected. This is because the courts are public authorities, and have to interpret any ambiguities in the law in accordance with the Act. So they could declare the *RIPA* incompatible with the European Convention on Human Rights, which would put pressure on (although not oblige) the government to change the legislation.

Private companies might feel the effects of the *Human Rights Act* more directly if they dismiss an employee and, for example, want to use an abusive email to defend their decision before an employment tribunal. If the employee can show the email was obtained in breach of their human rights, the tribunal may not allow the evidence, destroying the employer's justification for the dismissal.

Employers can, however, justify intrusion into private and family life if their reasons were to protect the rights and freedoms of others. So, for example, they can defend surveillance by citing their right not to have employees wasting their time at work, or the right of other employees not to receive offensive emails.

Personal data code

Finally, the Information Commissioner (formerly known as the Data Protection Commissioner) issued a Draft Code of Practice in October 2000 setting down standards in respect of telephone and email monitoring. The Code is still subject to revision and the latest version can be found at the data protection website. In line with the regulations, the Draft Code requires employers to establish a specific business purpose for monitoring, and make all affected staff aware of its operation.

The Code also requires the employer to assess the impact on the privacy, autonomy and legitimate rights of staff. Any adverse impact on the employee must be justified by the benefit to the business and others, and employers should carry out an impact assessment for this purpose. Where the assessment shows monitoring is justified the Code does not require employers to gain consent from the employees.

It is also important to note that the *Data Protection Act 1998* itself requires employers to:

- process data fairly and lawfully (first data protection principle)
- obtain personal data for a lawful purpose and not to process it in a manner incompatible with that purpose (second data protection principle).

These principles apply regardless of the *Telecommunications (Lawful Business Practice) (Interception of Communications) Regulations 2000.*

There is, moreover, the threat of legal challenge against the government. Both the TUC and the civil rights organisation Liberty claim the *Telecommunications (Lawful Business Practice) (Interception of Communications) Regulations* breach the *Human Rights Act.* The European Commission's Information Commissioner is also investigating four possible breaches of European law.

Practical considerations

Whatever the legislation permits employers to do, there are sensible business reasons for avoiding blanket monitoring. Not only will Orwellian surveillance tactics be bad for industrial relations, but the logistics of tracking every employee's every communication are mind-boggling.

Similarly, the simplest policy from a legal viewpoint might be an outright ban on personal calls, emails and Internet use. This may cut down on the employer's areas of vulnerability, but will disillusion existing staff and deter prospective employees. The problem is not, however, entirely new. Employers are used to dealing with personal use of the telephone, and a policy which expands on this, allowing limited and reasonable use of the system, including email and the Internet, is a sensible way forward.

Email and Internet use policies

So rather than waiting for the authorities to sort themselves out, facilities managers should ensure they draw up clear guidelines for employees on using email and the

Internet. In the event of abuse, these will allow the employer to dismiss the employee in accordance with the disciplinary procedure as long as the guidelines have been communicated to employees.

Employers cannot, however, change employees' existing contracts without their agreement. It is therefore important to make changes in a reasonable manner, and to explain why they are necessary. As well as inserting clauses into employment contracts, it is also advisable to use on-screen warning messages when staff log on.

Suggested contents of an email and Internet use policy are:

- Access – covering who within the organisation is authorised to access the Internet and write and receive email and for what broad purposes.

- Acceptable use of the Internet – defining unacceptable downloads (such as unauthorised software), banning inappropriate access to websites or downloading inappropriate images or other material.

- Acceptable use of email, including etiquette for normal use, a ban on transmission of pornography, sexually and racially offensive messages, defamatory material and flame mail, restrictions on forwarding mail inside and outside the organisation.

- Guidance on use of email and the Internet for personal use – for instance a complete ban or limited use during breaks.

- Circumstances where email and Internet use may be monitored.

- Penalties for breach of the policy.

Disciplinary and grievance hearings

On 4 September 2000, a new right came into force for employees to be accompanied at disciplinary and grievance hearings. The right is set out in s 10 of the *Employment Relations Act 1999*. Employers must, if the worker in question makes a 'reasonable' request, permit them to be accompanied by a single companion of their choice.

The companion is allowed to address the disciplinary or grievance hearing, but not to answer questions on the worker's behalf. They may, however, confer with the worker during the hearing.

A person is entitled to accompany the worker if they are:

- a trade union official as defined in ss 1 and 119 of the *Trade Union and Labour Relations (Consolidation) Act 1992*

- a trade union official whom the union has reasonably certified in writing has experience of or training in acting as a worker's companion

- another of the employer's workers.

There is no qualifying period for enjoying the right to be accompanied.

A disciplinary hearing is one which could lead the employer to:

- administer a formal warning

- take some other action in respect of the worker

- confirm a warning issued or some other action taken.

A grievance hearing is one which 'concerns the performance of a duty by an employer in relation to a worker'.

There is no right to be accompanied during an informal interview, although such an interview should be terminated if it becomes clear part-way through that formal action may be needed.

The employer must reschedule the hearing if:

- the chosen companion is not available at the employer's proposed time, and

- the worker proposes a reasonable alternative time within five days of the original date.

A worker may complain to a tribunal if they were not allowed a chosen companion or to reschedule a hearing. The maximum compensation is two weeks' pay, currently capped at £250 a week. More seriously, the worker will almost certainly also claim that any dismissal following the disciplinary hearing was unfair.

Workers who act as companions are also protected from any detriment while seeking to exercise their right to accompany a fellow worker. If they are dismissed, the dismissal will automatically be unfair, regardless of their length of service.

Minimum wage

The *National Minimum Wage Act* was passed in 1998, and has been amended by subsequent secondary legislation. As of 1 October 2001, workers aged 22 and over must be paid at least £4.10 an hour, and workers aged 18–21 must receive a 'development' rate of at least £3.50 an hour. From October 2003, the adult rate will be a minimum of £4.50 per hour, and the development rate will be a minimum of £3.80 per hour.

It is a criminal offence to refuse to pay the national minimum wage, to obstruct compliance officers or not to keep proper records; fines for these offences can be up to £5,000.

Information

Duckworth, S *Disabled Access to Facilities* (2003, LexisNexis Butterworths Tolley)
www.dataprotection.gov.uk

1   See *www.dti.gov.uk*
2   *Montgomery v Johnson Underwood Ltd* [2001] IRLR 269.
3   *Süzen v Zehnacker Gebäudereinigung GmbH Krankenhausservice* [1997] IRLR 255.
4   *ECM (Vehicle Delivery Service) v Cox* [1999] IRLR 559.
5   *RCO Support Services & Aintree Hospital v Unison* [2000] IRLR 624.
6   *Spijkers v Gebroeders Benedik Abbatoir CV* [1986] ECR 1119.
7   *ADI (UK) Ltd v Willer* (22 June 2001, unreported), CA.
8   See the 'employment relations' section of the DTI website at *www.dti.gov.uk*
9   *British Sugar Plc v Kirker* [1998] IRLR 624.
10 *Halford v United Kingdom* [1997] IRLR 471.
11 *Western Provident v Norwich Union* (2000) unreported.
12 *Morse v Future Reality Ltd* (1996) unreported.

Timetable for new employment legislation

Area of reform	Date of change	Summary
Flexible working	April 2003	New right of request to change work patterns for working parents and guardians.
Paternity leave	April 2003	Fathers to receive two weeks' paid paternity leave.
Adoption leave	April 2003	Adoptive parents to receive maternity and paternity leave.
Race discrimination	19 July 2003	Deadline for implementing Directive on race and racial origins.
Working time	August 2003	48-hour week regulations extended to cover most previously excluded sectors.
Sexual orientation discrimination	December 2003	Ban on discrimination by employers against individuals on the basis of sexual preference.
Religious discrimination	December 2003	New ban on discrimination by employers against individuals on the basis of religious belief.
Tribunal reforms	April 2004	Reform to tribunal system introduces minimum disciplinary and grievance procedures for employers.
Disability discrimination	October 2004	Removal of DDA exemption for small employers and requirement to remove barriers to disabled members of the public.
TUPE revisions	2004	Revised rules defining application of TUPE to service operations.
National Works Councils	2005	Employers of more than 150 people must comply with Information and Consultation Directive.
Age discrimination		
National Works Councils	2007	Employers of 101–150 people must comply with Information and Consultation Directive.
National Works Councils	2008	Employers of 51–100 people must comply with Information and Consultation Directive.

3 Complying with Property Law

Amanda Benham

Acquiring, selling and developing property for a company portfolio is a complex process. Company directors are increasingly calling on facilities managers to oversee this process and to report and advise on how to maximise the value of a property and minimise risks. Negotiating lease terms, ensuring any necessary planning permission is secured and procuring valuations all fall within the facilities manager's remit. A knowledge of the legal issues relevant to a company's portfolio is, therefore, a vital tool. It provides the facilities manager with a basis from which to navigate the complex legal processes encompassing property law, from acquisition and disposals, to planning, to liability for environmental clean-up – knowledge which will substantially impact on a company's costs.

Acquisition and disposal

This section is aimed at those wanting to acquire commercial property in England and Wales for their own use. It outlines the procedures involved and highlights particular considerations to be borne in mind. It does not deal with the ways in which an acquisition could be funded or structured.

Scotland and Northern Ireland have different legal systems, and local legal advice should be taken.

How is property owned?

Leasehold and freehold

Property in England and Wales is owned freehold or leasehold.

Freehold ownership is absolute. An owner of a freehold property owns it until disposal.

Leasehold ownership is limited in time. Leasehold is when an owner (a landlord or lessor) enters into a lease with a tenant or lessee to transfer the property to the tenant for a specified period of time (the term) in exchange for payment. The payment will either be a lump sum (a premium) or a periodic payment (rent) or a combination.

The tenant may also, subject again to the provision of the lease, create a further lease interest known as a sub-lease or underlease. This sub-lease must be for a shorter term than the original lease. In turn, further sub-leases can be created provided they are for shorter terms.

The system of land registration

The owner of a freehold or leasehold interest in land must be able to prove ownership or 'title'. Title either consists of documents of ownership (deeds) where title is unregistered, or a 'land certificate' where the title has been registered at the Land Registry. When title has been proved to the satisfaction of the Land Registry, the land is given a title number and a grade. Once title has been registered, a landowner need only show an official copy of the Land Registry entries as evidence of ownership. There are still parts of England and Wales which are unregistered.

Professional advisers — who does what?

The estate agent

When no independent broker is involved, the seller's agent usually acts as the broker. The agent introduces prospective buyers and sellers, will show a prospective buyer around various properties and will often act as the go-between in the negotiations of the price and terms between the parties. In more substantial transactions the buyer may ask an agent to find a suitable property and to negotiate on its behalf. Offers should be made 'subject to contract' and 'subject to survey'. This means that the buyer will not be bound to buy the property if the result of the survey is not satisfactory or until the bargain struck between the parties has been properly and legally recorded and all relevant investigations made.

The surveyor

A surveyor will carry out a physical inspection of the property to check for structural or other physical problems. The survey result is sometimes used by the buyer to renegotiate its offer. A survey is not the same as a valuation. If a buyer obtains finance from a bank or other lending institution in connection with an acquisition, the bank will want to satisfy itself that the amount of the loan is sufficiently covered by the value of the property. It will therefore obtain a valuation. Unlike a survey, a valuation will not contain any detailed comments on the state of repair of the property or on any structural problems.

The solicitor

The buyer's solicitor will:

- negotiate and agree the terms of the contract by which the buyer agrees to buy the property (the first draft of the contract is usually prepared by the seller's solicitor)

- prepare the transfer document transferring the ownership of the property to the buyer

- negotiate and agree the terms of the lease, if a new lease is to be taken by the purchaser (again, the first draft of the lease is usually prepared by the landlord's solicitor)

- make all relevant title and other searches in order to build up a factual picture of the history and present status of the property

- arrange for exchange of contracts – this is when the matter becomes legally binding

- carry out 'completion' or 'closure'

- carry out registration and stamping formalities, following completion.

Buying property

Buying property in England and Wales is a two-stage procedure.

The first stage ends in an exchange of contracts, when the parties enter into a legally-binding agreement for the sale and purchase of the property, but have not paid the price or completed the transaction.

The second stage culminates in the formality of the purchase documents being signed and payment of the purchase price, at which point the transaction is said to have completed.

Exchange of contracts

The stage preceding the exchange of contracts is the most important. All legal issues must be settled and the buyer must be satisfied on all aspects of the transaction before exchange. All the searches and title investigations are done at this stage. Once contracts have been exchanged, the buyer cannot object to the terms of the contract or to anything about the title or the physical condition of the property. The contract is prepared in duplicate, a copy being signed by each party. The copies are then exchanged. It is at this stage that the buyer is committed to buy and the seller is committed to sell a specific property at a specific price. On exchange, a deposit of 10 per cent of the purchase price is usually paid. If a buyer fails to complete through no fault of the seller, it risks losing the deposit.

On exchange of contracts, the 'beneficial' interest in the property is passed to the buyer, so it will need to insure the property from that date.

Completion

Legal title does not pass until completion of the transaction. It is traditional to have some period between exchange and completion, during which the buyer's solicitor will:

- carry out final searches

- make practical arrangements for collection and transmission of purchase monies

- prepare the transfer document which transfers title to the property to the buyer.

The period between exchange and completion is flexible and may be for whatever period the parties agree, but is usually no more than four weeks.

On completion, the balance of the purchase price is paid and thereafter the buyer owns the property. If the transaction needs to be registered at the Land Registry, this is done immediately following completion.

If the property is being purchased with borrowed money, the mortgage documentation is usually completed at the same time as the completion of the purchase.

Costs involved

Apart from the professional fees, the following taxes and statutory fees are payable when acquiring property in England and Wales.

Tax

Stamp duty

Stamp duty is payable on purchases of freehold and existing leasehold. The duty is normally paid by the buyer or the tenant and must be paid within one month of completion. Stamp duty is also payable upon the grant of a new lease and is calculated according to the amount of premium paid (if any), the annual rent and the length of the term. It is possible to mitigate stamp duty in appropriate situations. Advice should be taken early in the transaction. For details of the current UK rates, see **Financial Management, p 202**.

Value added tax

The current full rate of value added tax (VAT) is 17.5 per cent. Where the price or rent is subject to VAT, the seller or landlord must pay it to Customs and Excise, and will normally collect it from the buyer or tenant.

A person selling the freehold of a brand new building will usually need to charge VAT, although this can sometimes be avoided by taking a long lease at a premium instead.

This apart, a sale or lease will usually be subject to VAT only if the seller or landlord has 'opted to tax'. Once a person has opted to tax a building, then in general they are irrevocably obliged to charge VAT on rent received from tenants occupying it and on proceeds of sale from it. The main advantage of a person opting to tax a building is to enable them to reclaim from Customs and Excise the VAT charged on costs relating to the building, such as construction or refurbishment costs.

If VAT is charged on the purchase price or rent, the buyer or tenant may be able to reclaim it from Customs and Excise, depending on the use of the property. If it is used for a business which makes many exempt supplies (for example, as a bank or other financial business) all the VAT paid cannot be reclaimed, and so the VAT charge is a real cost for the buyer or tenant.

Many other businesses (for example, manufacturers and shops) can reclaim all or most of the VAT that they pay on costs. Unless the buyer negotiates to defer payment of

VAT, the buyer or tenant will have a cash flow cost in paying VAT to the seller or landlord before recovering it from Customs and Excise. Where a buyer or tenant is entitled to reclaim, it can usually do so within one to four months. Exempt use of a property by a buyer within 10 years of its acquisition may oblige the buyer to repay to Customs and Excise some of the VAT reclaimed on the purchase price.

For a comprehensive list of these and other supplies liable to VAT, see **Financial Management: Value Added Tax, p 200**.

Other taxes

These include capital allowances (see **Financial Management, p 199**), income tax and corporation tax.

Fees

Local land charges searches

There are various local authorities which maintain registers of planning and other matters affecting local properties. The buyer's solicitor will carry out a search at the local authority, for which a fee of around £150 is payable.

Land registry fees

In cases of dealings with registered land, a registration fee is payable. The fee is calculated on a sliding scale by reference to the acquisition value of the property, and currently runs from £40 for an acquisition of up to £50,000 to £750 for an acquisition of over £1 million. Fees are also payable upon first registration of previously unregistered land.

Other costs

Depending upon the location of the land and whether it is registered or unregistered, additional search fees will be payable. For example, a property may be in an area for which it is necessary to carry out a coal or other mining search. It will also be necessary to have a valuation carried out and often prudent to have a structural survey for which the surveyor will charge. Depending on the nature of the property to be bought, it may also be necessary to have an environmental audit carried out to assess whether the land is contaminated and potential liability for the costs of a clean-up of the land (see **Environmental matters, p 149**, for more on the law relating to contamination).

Acquisition for own use

Freehold or leasehold?

Before deciding whether to buy a freehold or a leasehold property, the buyer should analyse why and for what purpose the property is needed.

Generally speaking, a buyer with out-of-town site requirements needing to install plant and machinery that is not readily moveable will be more attracted to a freehold interest: there are fewer restrictions and the level of initial capital outlay is such that the buyer is looking for a long-term site. By contrast, the buyer requiring town centre office use may be better suited to a leasehold property at a market rent – that is, a lease of 25 years or less for little or no initial premium, but subject to an annual rent based on the market value of the building.

Traditionally, market rent leases were for terms of 20 or 25 years, with five-yearly rent reviews, usually on an upward-only basis (see **Business leases: rent review provisions, p 130**). In recent years, market forces have changed leasehold patterns, and it is now more usual for new leases to be granted for terms of 10 or 15 years and often for as little as five years. If the lease is for business purposes, the buyer as the tenant may have the right to renew the lease when it expires, subject to certain statutory restrictions (see **Business leases: security of tenure, p 128** for more detail).

Leasehold: ongoing liability

A lease is essentially a contract between a landlord and a tenant. For leases granted before 1 January 1996, the rule is that the original tenant and the original landlord remain liable for their respective obligations under the lease for the duration of the lease term. This is the case even where the original tenant has sold its leasehold interest on to a new tenant, or where the original landlord has sold on its reversionary interest to a new landlord. This legal principle is known as 'privity of contract'. In practical terms, it means that where the original tenant has sold its interest to another who in turn fails to pay the rent, the landlord may seek payment of that rent from the original tenant. The original tenant is not free from its obligations even though it has parted with its interest in the property. The landlord is thus cushioned from the effects of tenant default by being able to look to the original tenant to meet the liability.

The *Landlord and Tenant (Covenants) Act 1995* (the *1995 Act*) has abolished original tenant liability in respect of 'new' leases, that is leases granted on or after 1 January 1996. The *1995 Act* provides that where a tenant sells its leasehold interest to the assignee, the selling tenant is automatically released from further liability. There is an exception to this rule. A tenant will not be released if it has sold its lease without obtaining any requisite permission to do so from its landlord. Also, it is possible for a landlord to require a selling tenant to give an 'authorised guarantee agreement' in respect of the buying tenant's obligations under the lease. On a subsequent sale of the lease, this guarantee falls away.

The *1995 Act* means that a landlord loses the safety net that it had under the old principle of privity of contract. Landlords will need to be more concerned at the identity of proposed assignees. The *1995 Act* has given landlords greater power to control assignments, although such controls are in practice limited, not only by the relative bargaining strength of the landlord over that of the tenant, but also by the likely impact of restrictions in the lease on the next rent review. The more restrictive the lease, the lower the rent which can be demanded for a property. Both landlords and tenants favour continuing the recent trend towards much shorter lease terms and are wary of qualifications for assignment which are likely to have an adverse effect on future rent reviews.

The *1995 Act* also has implications for the landlord's liability. Although a tenant is generally automatically released from liability on a sale of the lease, the landlord is not automatically released from its liabilities on a sale of its reversionary interest. A landlord must request a release from the tenant. If the tenant refuses to give a release, the landlord may ask the court to grant one. If the court refuses, the landlord continues to be liable with the new landlord. If and when the new landlord chooses to sell its reversionary interest, the first landlord has a further opportunity to apply for a release.

Business leases

Businesses operate from the following types of premises:

- **freehold** – the occupier owns the premises outright for an unlimited length of time with few restrictions

- **leasehold** – the occupier has use of the premises for rent for a specified length of time

- **on licence** – the premises are used on flexible terms on a short-term basis.

This section sets out the main provisions of a lease of business premises.

Parties

The lease specifies the names and addresses of the landlord, the tenant and any guarantor.

Premises let

The technical term for the premises let is 'demised premises'. Both parties should understand exactly what is being let. A lease sometimes refers to plans which outline the area let. If there are plans, they should be checked for accuracy.

Fixtures and fittings

Ownership of the plant and equipment in the premises is important, as someone has to maintain them. Also, the tenant might want to remove items when the lease expires. Sometimes items fixed to the premises by a tenant can become part of the premises, in which case the tenant is not entitled to remove them at the end of the lease, even though those items belong to it. If, however, the items were put there for the purpose of the tenant's trade and can be removed without causing irreparable damage to the premises, the tenant can remove them.

Rights granted

In order to make full use of the premises, the tenant will need rights over adjoining premises or land. These could include rights to use common parts in a building, such as lifts and car parking areas.

Exceptions and reservations

Just as the tenant requires to have rights over common parts, a landlord will want to be able to enter the tenant's premises in certain circumstances, for example to inspect the premises or to carry out repairs.

Term

This is the length of the lease. Traditionally, leases of business premises were long-term commitments, frequently of 25 years. Recently, much shorter leases have become more common. Sometimes the lease allows the tenant to end it at an earlier date than the contractual expiry. This is an 'option to break' or 'break clause'. If a lease contains such an option, it is important that the relevant date is diarised and a solicitor instructed well in advance of the exercise date so that the notice is dealt with properly and on time.

Security of tenure

Business leases are governed by a statutory code in the *Landlord and Tenant Act 1954* (the *1954 Act*). Some business tenants enjoy 'security of tenure' – that is, the right to have a new lease granted when their current lease expires, subject to the following of a detailed notice and court procedure. The landlord can only deny this request in certain circumstances. It is, therefore, a valuable right. The following paragraphs provide only an introduction to this very complex subject.

The *1954 Act* applies to most leases where the property is occupied for the purposes of a business, unless the parties opt out of the *1954 Act* before the lease starts.

Termination

A lease protected by the *1954 Act* can only be determined by one of the methods prescribed by the *1954 Act*. These include notice given by the landlord or the tenant. A lease which is not determined by one of the methods set down in the *1954 Act* continues to run (despite expiry of the term) on the same terms until terminated by one of these methods.

Landlord's notice

A landlord's notice under the *1954 Act* must be in a special form and must specify a date (not earlier than the lease termination date and not less than six nor more than 12 months ahead) on which the lease is to end. The tenant must then notify the landlord whether or not it is willing to vacate the premises.

If the tenant wants a new lease, it must tell the landlord within two months of the landlord's notice and should make a special court application for a new tenancy, not less than two and not more than four months after the landlord's notice.

The landlord's grounds for opposing a new lease include:

- the tenant's failure to repair or pay rent, or its being in breach of other terms of the lease

- the landlord's intention to demolish or reconstruct the property

- the landlord requires possession for its own purposes.

The time limits specified in the *1954 Act* for service of notices and applications to the court are strict and in general no extension of those limits is permitted.

Tenant's request for a new tenancy

A tenant's request for a new lease must be in a special form and must specify a date (not earlier than the lease termination date and not less than six nor more than 12 months ahead) for the start of the new lease. If the landlord wishes to object, it must tell the tenant within two months, stating on which statutory ground(s) it will rely. The tenant must then apply to the court for a new tenancy not less than two months and not more than four months from the service of its notice.

New lease

Unless the landlord can substantiate its objection to a new lease, a new lease must be granted. Usually this will be on similar terms to the previous one.

Compensation

If the landlord succeeds in obtaining vacant possession, based on a statutory ground which involves no fault on the part of the tenant, the tenant is entitled to compensation. In certain circumstances a tenant of business premises may also be entitled to compensation for improvements it carried out.

Rent

Rent control

There are no statutory limitations on the rent payable.

Payment of rent

The lease will specify the rent payable and when – usually quarterly or monthly. The 'usual quarter days' are 25 March, 24 June, 29 September and 25 December. Different days apply in Scotland. A landlord will generally issue a rent demand several days before rent is actually due and will expect payment to be made punctually and by banker's order. Rent is usually paid in advance, not arrears. For possible action to be taken by the landlord in the case of non-payment of rent, see **p 135**.

Rent review provisions

Many leases contain rent review provisions. It is very common within the UK for leases to have provisions that protect the long-term investment of property from the landlord's point of view by enforcing 'upward only' rent reviews (meaning that the rent cannot fall).

Rent review provisions in leases can be complex. The dates for the reviews and the basis of the review are set out in the lease. Dates should be diarised and a solicitor and surveyor engaged to advise on the conduct of the review. The lease allows the landlord and the tenant to agree the new rent themselves for a certain period before the review date. If they cannot agree, the review can be referred to an independent surveyor to decide.

Rates and taxes

The tenant usually pays the rates and taxes imposed on the premises. A tenant pays VAT on its rent where the landlord has chosen to charge it (see **Value added tax, p 124**).

Interest

Interest at a penal rate is payable on any late payments of rent and other sums due to the landlord under the lease.

Dealings

A lease will contain restrictions on a tenant disposing of its lease outright ('assignment'), sub-letting and sharing or disposing of occupation.

Assignment

A lease will usually say that the landlord's approval must be obtained for any assignment so that the landlord can be sure that the new tenant will be reliable. Usually, the landlord cannot take too long to give this approval and must not be unreasonable about it. The lease can impose conditions which must be met before assignment can take place.

Sub-letting

Similarly, a landlord will want to approve sub-lettings. Again, the landlord cannot take too long and must not be unreasonable.

Sharing occupation

A lease will usually contain restrictions with whom the tenant can share occupation, but it normally automatically permits sharing with companies which are in the same group as the tenant. Other forms of sharing normally require the landlord's prior approval.

Use

The lease will specify how and for what purposes the premises can be used, such as a shop or office. These restrictions can be enforced by an injunction (see also **Planning: contractually permitted use, p 137**).

Alterations

A tenant will often need to carry out alterations to the premises. The lease will set out what tenant's works are permitted or not. Most works will require the landlord's prior approval.

The lease will also allow the landlord to make the tenant 'reinstate' the premises at the end of the lease, undoing any work which it has done during the lease. A document called a 'schedule of dilapidations' is prepared and negotiated by the parties, setting out the work which needs to be done. Sometimes, specialist dilapidations surveyors need to be engaged.

When a landlord gives permission to a tenant to carry out works, the permission is often contained in a legal document called a 'licence for alterations'. It describes the works, attaching plans and specifications.

In certain circumstances, a tenant can claim compensation for improvements it has carried out to the premises during the leases, subject to a complicated notice procedure.

Repairs

The lease should set out clearly who is responsible for carrying out repairs to the premises. The definition of the premises actually let to the tenant is important. A tenant of an entire building will usually repair its entirety, at its expense. A tenant of part only of a building carries out internal repairs to its own premises and would contribute to the cost of repairing the whole building via a service charge.

New buildings

The tenant of a new building can find itself in the unenviable position of being required to make good 'inherent' or 'latent' defects in the design or construction of the building. Accordingly, when negotiating the terms of the lease of such a building, the tenant should:

- seek to shift liability for remedying inherent defects to the landlord

- require a duty of care agreement with the landlord's building contractor and professional team involved in the construction

- have the property surveyed and the plans and specifications reviewed by the tenant's advisers.

Where these proposals are not acceptable to the landlord, it may be possible to agree a compromise – for example, that the landlord will rectify inherent defects which appear during a specified period of time. The landlord should also be prepared to agree to pursue its legal remedies in respect of inherent defects against third parties, wherever it is reasonable to do so.

Old buildings

An old building may not be in a state of complete repair but the lease will generally require the tenant to repair any defects which exist at the time of the lease. The tenant should have a survey to reveal any problems. Ideally, the landlord should remedy existing disrepair or compensate the tenant. Alternatively, it may be possible for the landlord and the tenant to agree a 'schedule of condition' (a detailed description of defects in the property accompanied by a set of photographs). The tenant's obligation could then say that the tenant will not be required to put the premises in any better condition than as evidenced by the schedule of condition.

Breach of repairing obligations

Where a tenant fails to repair, the landlord can either claim damages or, in limited circumstances, 'forfeit' (terminate) the lease. Alternatively, the landlord could enter the premises to carry out the repairs itself and claim the cost from the tenant.

Rights of access

The lease will allow the landlord to enter the premises let to inspect their condition, to carry out repairs where the tenant has failed to repair the premises or to repair other parts of a building where such access is necessary. This is subject to the tenant being given advance notice and the landlord making good any damage caused.

Insurance

The lease will require either the landlord or the tenant (or both) to have various insurances. These relate to the premises, plate glass, plant, loss of rent and public liability. Consideration must be given as to which party should insure, whether the insurance should be in joint names and the sum for which and the risks against which the property should be insured. Where parts of a building are being let separately, the landlord insures the whole building and then seeks reimbursement from the tenants for the premiums.

The insurance should be repair on a full 'reinstatement basis' which means that the insurance cover should be sufficient to repair any damage or to rebuild.

What happens if the premises are damaged?

The tenant will be concerned with the following questions, which should be clearly covered by the terms of the lease:

- Does the rent cease to be payable until the damage is put right?

- Is there an obligation on one of the parties to reinstate?

- Are the costs of reinstatement covered by insurance?

- If reinstatement is prevented by factors which are outside the control of the parties, will the lease terminate and, if so, in what circumstances?

- If reinstatement does not take place and the destruction was caused by an insured risk, which party will own the insurance money?

Other financial considerations relating to insurance payable under the terms of a lease are covered in **Financial Management: insurance, p 196.**

Service charges

Service charges are payments made by a tenant, in addition to rent, to cover the cost of works and services. The amount payable may be fixed or variable according to the costs incurred.

Management arrangements

Either the landlord will carry out the management itself (with or without a managing agent) or pass it to a management company, which may be owned by the landlord, a third party or the tenants themselves.

The services

A tenant will be concerned to see the following services in most cases:

- repairs and maintenance of common areas

- redecoration

- provision of hot water, heating and lighting

- plant and machinery

- cleaning and refuse disposal

- employment of staff.

Apportionment

The share of the landlord's total expenditure that will be reimbursed by a tenant will be a percentage or 'fair or due proportion' calculated by reference to the amount of space occupied or other factor.

Payment

The lease will require the tenant to make payments on account of service charge. There will then be a reconciliation procedure in the lease to deal with any difference between this provisional amount and the actual amount spent by the end of the year. Any shortfall is made up by the tenant and any over-payment is reimbursed or credited against future payments. The service charge accounts should be properly certificated by a suitably qualified surveyor or accountant.

Objections

The tenant will sometimes have the following objections relating to the service charge:

- that items have been included which should not have been

- that there has been a mistake in the calculations

- that the costs are excessive.

The way to challenge the charges depends on the lease. Many leases rule out any challenge at all by providing that the surveyor's or accountant's certificate shall be final.

Reserve and sinking funds

A reserve fund is an 'expenditure equalisation fund' designed to avoid wide fluctuations in the amount of the service charges payable each year on account of relatively expensive and necessarily recurring items. As an alternative to asking tenants to pay every five years for expenditure such as the decoration of the exterior and the common parts of the building, the landlord makes an estimate of the likely costs in advance and collects this sum by five equal instalments over the years preceding the work.

A sinking fund is a replacement fund, by which a landlord aims to build up over many years a fund for the replacement of major items of plant and equipment, such as lifts and heating or air conditioning systems. The drawback for tenants is that these funds can be used to carry out improvements which ought to be carried out at the cost of the landlord rather than of the tenants.

A tenant will be concerned that reserve and sinking funds are kept separate from the landlord's own money to ensure that they do not form part of the landlord's assets on a bankruptcy or liquidation.

Options to terminate

A lease may contain an option for the parties or one of them to terminate the lease at a stated time or times, or on the happening of stated events before the contractual expiry date. This is known as an 'option to break' or 'option to terminate'.

Any matters which are made conditions to the exercise of an option must be very strictly observed. The notice exercising the option must be given within the specified period and any other conditions, such as having paid the rent and complied with the terms of the lease, must be observed. Even the most trifling breach can prevent the tenant from effectively exercising a break option.

Landlord's remedies for tenant breaches

Non-payment of rent

For failure to pay rent, the landlord may carry out the following:

- **Sue the tenant** – (or, if applicable, the tenant's guarantor or any previous tenant). Since 1 January 1996, a landlord can only recover arrears of rent from a previous tenant or guarantor of a previous tenant if it has first served an arrears notice on the previous tenant or guarantor specifying the amount to be claimed. That notice must be served within six months after the rent claimed first became due. Failure to serve the notice means that the rights of the landlord to recover the rent arrears is lost.

- **Seize the tenant's goods** – known as 'distraint'. The landlord may seize goods on the property equal to the value of the rent due (and costs incurred). This process is subject to restrictions and can only be used against goods belonging to the tenant.

- **Take rent from the deposit** – if applicable, the landlord may take the rent due from a tenant's deposit held and then, if necessary, take action in the courts against the tenant for reimbursement of the deposit fund.

- **Forfeit or terminate the lease** – in England and Wales, the tenant has certain statutory protections against forfeiture of its lease. The degree of protection varies depending upon the nature of the tenant's failure. This statutory protection is called 'relief from forfeiture'. Usually, the action is dropped if the tenant rectifies the breach.

Checklist: buying a business lease

A prospective purchaser of a lease of business premises should (in addition to the usual matters to be considered on a purchase) pay careful attention to:

- rent review
- repairing obligations
- service charges
- VAT implications
- whether the existing tenant is in breach of covenant giving the landlord the right to determine the lease
- the likelihood of a lease renewal being opposed by a landlord on other grounds, such as redevelopment
- provisions relating to dealings with the lease
- permitted use.

Other breaches

For other breaches, the landlord may:

- if the lease permits it, remedy the breach itself and charge the tenant for the cost incurred

- forfeit or terminate the lease

- sue

- take action in the courts against the tenant (again, subject to certain statutory restrictions.)

Planning

When companies assess their occupation requirements they rarely give high priority to planning issues. Are these companies running a high-risk strategy? What if a company occupies new premises, only to find that planning restrictions prevent it from operating from that site. Consider, for example, if:

- the planning permission which attaches to the site permits warehouse use but not offices in conjunction with the warehouse

- the company wants to add an extension but local planning policy is such that planning permission for this development will not be given by the local planning authority (LPA).

The company would have wasted capital expenditure on acquiring the site and may have committed to a long-term lease – a situation which will not find favour with the board of directors.

What could the facilities manager have done to protect that company's position before acquiring the property? What development projections should have been made?

This section looks at the key planning issues relating to the use and development of business premises.

The law

The *Town and Country Planning Act 1990* (the *1990 Act*) contains most of current legislation controlling the application of planning laws. The *1990 Act* has been amended by the *Planning and Compensation Act 1991 (PCA 1991)*. The effect of this is that certain amending provisions have been written into the *1990 Act*, whereas other provisions remain as standalone clauses in the *PCA 1991*.

When is planning permission required?

One of the questions most frequently asked by facilities managers is: Do I need planning permission? To determine this it is necessary to establish whether what is proposed (building works or change of use) is classed as 'development' for the purposes of s 55 of the *1990 Act*. If the proposals do amount to development, then planning permission will be required[1].

What is 'development'?

There are two classes of development:

- physical works carried out in, on, over or under land – usually grouped together as 'operational development'

- development relating to how land is used – classed as a 'material change of use'.

Operational development

Any of the following will constitute development:

- **'Building operations'** – as defined in s 336 of the *1990 Act*, this includes 'rebuilding, structural alterations or addition to buildings and other operations normally undertaken by a person carrying on business as a builder'. Demolition works were later brought within the concept of building operations and this is discussed below (see **Demolition works, p 145**).

- **'Engineering operations'** – as defined in s 336 of the *1990 Act*, this is generally interpreted to include operations usually undertaken by or calling for the skills of an engineer.

- **'Mining operations'** – this is not defined in the *1990 Act* but will include the removal of material of any description from a mineral working deposit.

- **'Other operations'** – this is a catch-all category enabling unclassified development works to be brought within the planning permission net. These are judged on a one-off basis and will include such things as installing protective grilles on windows and raising the level of land by the addition of soil or other material. This is, then, a wide and potentially limitless category depending on the facts and circumstances of each case.

Use of land

A facilities manager is expected to deliver premises that operate in an efficient and commercially-effective way. There must be no restriction affecting the use of the building which has a detrimental impact on the business. How then can facilities managers anticipate potential use problems? Firstly, they must understand the distinction between 'contractually permitted use' under a lease or similar arrangement and the 'lawful use' for planning purposes.

Contractually-permitted use

Contractually-permitted use is the use allowed under a contract such as a lease or licence. For example, a lease may permit the premises to be used for the purposes of high-class offices. If the occupier uses the premises to run a shop then it will be in breach of the lease contract, even if the lawful use for planning purposes permits shop use.

Lawful use

Lawful use is the use permitted under planning legislation. The lawful use will override any use permitted under a lease or licence if they are inconsistent. For example, if shop use is prohibited for planning purposes and is permitted under the lease contract, the premises cannot lawfully be used as a shop.

Categories of lawful use are known as 'classes' of use. The classes of use are set out in the *Town and Country Planning (Use Classes) (Amendment) Order 1987 1991, 1992, 1994 & 1995* (the *1987 Order*). It consists of 16 classes of use arranged in four main parts (see **Appendix**).

Mention should also be made of uses which do not fall within the *1987 Order*. It is relatively easy to identify the lawfully permitted use for planning purposes by examining the LPA's records. However, some uses do not fall conveniently within the *1987 Order* and these are referred to as 'sui generis' uses. An example of a sui generis use would be where land is used for the purposes of overnight parking of large distribution lorries.

What is a 'material' change of use?

'Material' changes of use are a question of fact and degree. The change may be material because it constitutes a change in the *type* of use, or because it represents an increase in the *intensification* of a continuing use. The law determining what is a material change of use is not set in stone, although s 55 of the *1990 Act* does give guidance on which changes of use will constitute development:

No change of use

- use of land for agriculture or forestry and
- uses falling within the same use class of the *1987 Order*.

Material changes of use

- deposit of refuse or waste material on land
- use of external parts of the building not normally so used for the display of advertisements
- change of use class within the *1987 Order*.

Does section 55 apply?

The process by which facilities managers can make decisions as to whether or not physical works or anticipated changes of use constitute development within the meaning of s 55 of the *1990 Act* is illustrated in **Table 1** (see below). However, sometimes there will be grey areas, especially where changes of use are concerned. In such cases professional advice from a planning consultant or lawyer should be sought.

Listed buildings and conservation areas

Special controls apply if a property is a listed building or is situated within a conservation area. Listed building consent will be required for virtually all works carried out and a specialist consultant or architect should be involved at an early stage of any application process.

Conservation areas are designated as such to 'conserve' the appearance of the locality. Therefore, works to the exterior of a property in a conservation area will usually require planning permission even if they are of a minor nature. It must also be remembered that trees growing in a conservation area are protected by preservation orders. Any works of lopping, topping or cutting to a protected tree require consent from the LPA.

Understanding planning requirements

Building development projects should be worked around planning requirements so that, in a complex situation, a planning adviser or consultant can be employed at an early stage to advise on compliance and also to instigate and maintain a dialogue between the company and the planning authority.

A facilities manager who understands the planning process will be able to advise the board of directors in respect of any proposed expansion or refurbishment plans. The board can then factor the relevant information into the company's budget and time schedule.

It will also be useful to find out what planning permissions already exist in relation to a property and this can be done by asking the local authority or arranging for a solicitor to carry out a search of the authority's records.

Applying for planning permission

So, if planning permission is required, what is the next step? Is this the time to bring in professional advisers? What role will they play?

Architects/planning consultants

An architect or planning consultant will guide the facilities manager through the application process. Such an adviser is well-placed to advise on local planning policy. They will have experience in interpreting the local development plans[2]. Planning decisions by LPAs are plan-led and it is important to interpret the development plan correctly. A planning application which is not consistent with the policy set out in the development plan is unlikely to succeed. Architects and planning consultants will also have local knowledge and previous dealings with the LPA. They will be able to streamline the application to give it the best chance of succeeding.

Table 1: Do you require planning permission?

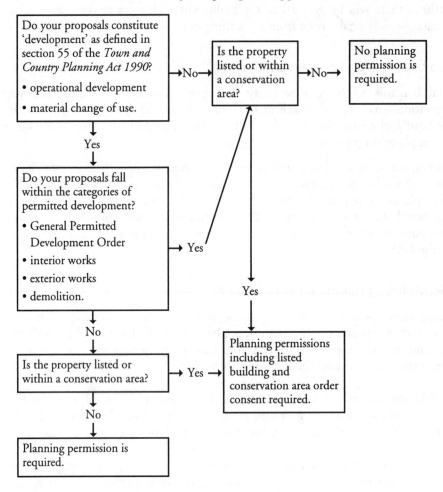

Solicitors

A solicitor can be involved in this process. Due diligence by way of a local search may reveal existing planning restrictions and adverse notices. The solicitor may also have confirmed the use class (see **Lawful use, p 138**). Legal advice will be needed to explain conditions and planning obligations attached to a planning permission.

Formulating the application

The following preliminary steps need to be taken in formulating the planning application:

- Clarify maps, diagrams and plans.

- Obtain copies of the relevant parts of the development plan and any other non-statutory plan which may affect the proposed development.

- Obtain an application form from the LPA, available free of charge. Each LPA produces its own form.

- Consider a pre-application discussion with the appropriate case officer. This is particularly important if the development proposals are not consistent with the development plan or other planning policy statement.

- Decide whether the application will be for full planning permission or 'outline' planning permission. Where the application is to erect a building, the applicant is entitled to apply for outline permission. In this case the application merely has to contain a description of the proposed development indicating its major features. An application for full planning permission will need to include full details of the proposed development. Full plans and elevations will need to be provided together with a considerable amount of detail setting out materials and construction methods.

Making the application

Table 2 illustrates the application process through to the planning decision.

Table 2: Planning application process

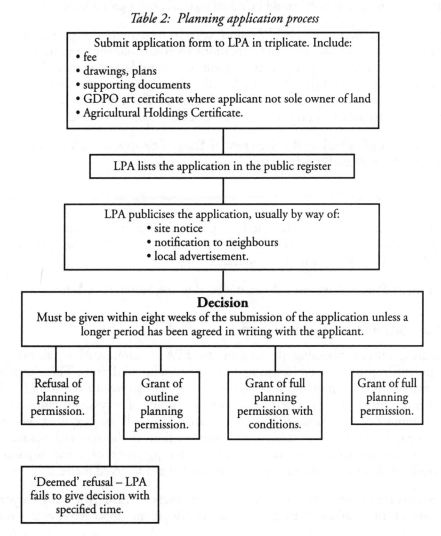

Submit application form to LPA in triplicate. Include:
- fee
- drawings, plans
- supporting documents
- GDPO art certificate where applicant not sole owner of land
- Agricultural Holdings Certificate.

LPA lists the application in the public register

LPA publicises the application, usually by way of:
- site notice
- notification to neighbours
- local advertisement.

Decision
Must be given within eight weeks of the submission of the application unless a longer period has been agreed in writing with the applicant.

| Refusal of planning permission. | Grant of outline planning permission. | Grant of full planning permission with conditions. | Grant of full planning permission. |

'Deemed' refusal – LPA fails to give decision with specified time.

The planning application decision

The planning application will result in one of the following outcomes:

- refusal of planning permission
- failure to give a decision within specified time – a 'deemed' refusal
- grant of outline planning permission
- grant of full planning permission with conditions
- grant of full unconditional planning permission.

Refusal of planning permission

If the LPA refuses planning permission it must state clearly in writing the full reasons for the refusal. If full reasons are not given, this does not necessarily invalidate the decision itself, but it does mean that the decision can be challenged by judicial review and the failure to give reasons could be taken into account upon appeal.

In reaching their decision, the LPA must take into account the provisions of the development plan and also any representations received following publication of the application. Listed building and conservation area considerations will also be taken into account if applicable. The LPA will also consider any other 'material' considerations – meaning considerations relevant to the application; they must be planning considerations and relate to the use and development of land.

There is a right of appeal to the Secretary of State. The appeal must be made within six months of the date of the decision.

A 'deemed' refusal

A deemed refusal is where an LPA fails to give a decision within the specified time. The specified time is eight weeks from the date of submission of the application, or longer if agreed in writing with the applicant.

There is right of appeal against a deemed refusal to the Secretary of State.

Grant of outline planning permission

By granting outline planning permission, an LPA is committed to allowing that development in principal, subject to approval of certain conditions. These conditions are known as 'reserved matters' and require subsequent approval from the LPA. They deal with the siting, design, external appearance, means of access and landscaping of the development. No further planning permission will be required when the development is commenced, subject to determination of the reserved matters. The outline permission cannot be revoked except on payment of compensation and additional conditions cannot be imposed over and above reserved matters.

Applications for approval of the reserved matters must be made within three years of the grant of the outline permission. The development approved by the outline permission must be commenced within five years of the grant of the permission or within two years of the approval of the reserved matters, whichever is the later.

Grant of full planning permission with conditions

The LPA may grant full planning permission but impose conditions. These conditions will relate to the development or use of any land under the control of the applicant, whether or not it is land in respect of which the application was made. The applicant can be required to remove buildings, to carry out additional works, to discontinue a particular use and to carry out subsequent reinstatement works if required. There are judicial restrictions upon the power to impose conditions to prevent these being abused by LPAs. These restrictions are intended to make sure that the conditions are:

- fairly and reasonably related to the development permitted

- not manifestly unreasonable.

There is a right of appeal to the Secretary of State against the grant of planning permissions subject to conditions within six months of the notice of the decision.

Subject to appeal, development work authorised under a grant of full planning permission with conditions must be commenced within five years of the grant of the permission.

Obligations

A mention should also be made of the obligations which can be linked to the grant of planning permission and imposed under s 106 of the *1990 Act*. An LPA can impose additional obligations in return for granting planning permission. Take, for example, an application to develop a new supermarket. An LPA grants planning permission for the supermarket. In return for the LPA's consent, the developer agrees to build a new roundabout in the vicinity. This agreement would be contained in a s 106 agreement.

Grant of full unconditional planning permission

Full planning permission may be granted without conditions. Development works approved by the permission must be commenced within five years from the grant of permission.

Appeals

Only the applicant may appeal against a decision by an LPA, even if the applicant is not the owner of an interest in the land. Third parties, including the owner of an interest in the land who is not party to the application, have no right of appeal. In certain limited cases, a challenge to a planning decision may be brought by way of judicial review.

An appeal can be made in the following circumstances:

- refusal to grant planning permission

- grant of planning permissions subject to conditions to which the applicant objects

- refused approval of reserved matters on an outline permission

- refusal of application or grant of permission subject to conditions under s 73 or s 73(*a*) of the *1990 Act* (these sections allow an application to be made for the implementation of an existing planning permission – before it has expired – where the new applicant is seeking to implement that permission without the conditions originally imposed)

- failure to notify the applicant within the prescribed period – in other words, deemed refusal.

In all these circumstances the applicant has a right of appeal to the Secretary of State within six months of the notice of a decision or failure to determine an application.

Challenging appeals to the Secretary of State

The validity of an appeal decision cannot be challenged in any legal proceedings. However, a 'person aggrieved' (s 288 of the *1990 Act*) may question the decision by appeal to the High Court if the decision was not within the powers of the *1990 Act* or if any relevant procedural requirements have not been complied with. Again, in certain limited cases an application for judicial review may be made.

Human Rights Act 1998

The *Human Rights Act 1998* came into force in the UK on 2 October 2000 and had an immediate impact upon domestic legislation. LPAs are now obliged to consider human rights issues when determining planning applications. In particular, the LPA must take into account the right not to be deprived of property (European Convention on Human Rights, art 1) and the right to respect for private and family life (European Convention on Human Rights, art 8). Facilities managers should remember that this will affect both their company's planning applications and also the ability of the company to object to the applications of third parties. Although a company is a corporate body rather than an individual, it is deemed to have rights protected by the *Human Rights Act 1998*.

When is planning permission not needed?

In certain circumstances planning permission is not required, even where the proposed works or change of use fall within s 55 of the *1990 Act*. These circumstances are usually referred to as 'permitted development'. It must be noted, however, that special rules apply to listed buildings and conservation areas. Professional advice should always be taken in these circumstances.

Permitted development includes:

- certain demolition works
- development permitted by the *Town and Country Planning (General Permitted Development) (Amendment) Order 1995* (as amended)
- internal works
- certain external works.

Demolition works

Demolition of buildings has been brought within the scope of development. Section 13 of the *PCA 1991* introduced a new s 55(1)(*a*) of the *1990 Act*. 'Building operations' now include 'demolition of buildings; rebuilding; structural alteration of or addition to buildings ...'. Nevertheless, certain demolition works do not require planning permission.

Demolition works requiring planning permission

- Demolition of part of a building.

Demolition works not requiring planning permission

- Demolition of a building smaller than 15 m^3.
- Demolition of any building (whatever the size) not being a dwelling house or adjoining a dwelling house.

Town and Country Planning (GPD) Order 1995

The *Town and Country Planning (General Permitted Development) Order 1995 (GPDO)* permits certain types of development which would otherwise require planning permission. There are defined lists of permitted development set out in the schedules to the *GPDO*. Schedule 2 is of primary importance. This has 28 parts setting out descriptions of developments that can be carried out without the need for planning permission. The most important are:

- Part 2 – minor operations.
- Part 3 – certain changes of use.

Internal works

Internal works which are not of a substantial nature involving major structural alterations do not usually require planning permission.

External works

External works which do not materially affect the external appearance of a building do not usually require planning permission. Again, what constitutes 'material' is a question of fact and degree. For the works to require planning permission, the change to the exterior must be capable of being seen by an observer outside the building. It must also materially affect the appearance of the building as a whole and not merely a part. The nature of the building must also be taken into account so that, for example, changes effected to a Georgian façade may have a greater visual impact than changes made to the external appearance of a factory. Special rules apply to signage and advertisements.

What if planning law is not complied with?

The facilities manager will now know that development works as defined in s 55 of the *1990 Act* will require planning permission unless it is permitted development. They will also know that operational development or a material change of use may have been undertaken in contravention of planning controls. If there is a breach of planning control, what action can be taken by an LPA? And what can the facilities manager do to protect the company's position?

The LPA will want to see that operational development and material changes of use have been undertaken within its planning district in a lawful way. In certain circumstances it may only need to view the exterior of the property. In other circumstances a more detailed inspection, including an internal inspection, may be required and it will need to gain entry to do this. Having collected evidence of potential breaches of planning controls the LPA will then want to remedy the contravention. Not surprisingly, LPAs are given wide powers of inspection and enforcement for this purpose.

Power to enter and inspect

LPAs may authorise any person in writing to enter land at any reasonable hour without a warrant where there are 'reasonable grounds' for doing so. Where admission has been refused or if the matter is urgent the LPA may obtain a warrant to enter the property.

The sanction to any owner or occupier in these circumstances is that anyone who wilfully obstructs the person exercising a lawful right of entry is guilty of an offence.

The LPA can also compile evidence of a breach of planning control by using a Planning Contravention Notice (PCN) or a Breach of Condition Notice (BCN). A PCN is used to obtain information about any operations, use or activities being carried on at a property or on land. A BCN will be used primarily to establish whether or not conditions or limitations attached to an existing planning permission have been breached.

Enforcement action

An LPA has three options to enforce against a breach of planning control, namely: injunction, enforcement notices and stop notices.

Injunction

An injunction can be used to prevent an owner or occupier from carrying out activities which are being undertaken in breach of planning controls. Whether or not an injunction is granted is at the discretion of the court.

Enforcement notices

The LPA can also issue an enforcement notice. An enforcement notice must contain the following information:

- a statement of the alleged breach

- steps necessary to wholly or partly remedy the breach

- a statement of the effective date of the notice, being at least 28 days from service of the notice

- a statement of the time within which the steps specified to remedy the breach are to be carried out.

Non-compliance with an enforcement notice makes the owner or occupier liable on summary conviction to a fine of up to £20,000 or, on indictment, an unlimited amount. The LPA also has the power, in addition to prosecuting, to rectify the breach itself and recover reasonable expenses from the owner or occupier.

Stop notice

A stop notice can be issued. As its title suggests, a stop notice requires an immediate halt to the activities causing the breach of planning control. This is a drastic step for an LPA to take and will only be used in very limited circumstances. A breach of a stop notice is subject to the same penalties as a breach of an enforcement notice. However, the LPA will always be aware that if a stop notice has been incorrectly served or is subsequently quashed by legal action or withdrawn, the LPA may become liable to pay substantial compensation. LPAs are often unwilling to expose themselves in this way.

Protection for owners and occupiers

Faced with the impressive armoury of enforcement sanctions available to LPAs, the owner or occupier of the land subject to enforcement proceedings may be able to protect itself by appealing against enforcement proceedings. However, a more attractive and effective option may be for the owner or occupier to 'regularise' its occupation of a property by applying for a certificate of lawful use or development.

Certificates of lawful use or development

Material changes of use and operative development are 'lawful' if no enforcement action can be taken. This will include where the time limit for commencing enforcement action has expired. Enforcement action cannot be taken in the following circumstances:

- where operational development carried out without planning permission has continued for a period of four years from the date on which the operations were substantially complete

- where any material change of use and any breach of condition or limitation attached to a planning permission has continued for a period of 10 years from the date of the change of use or breach.

Facilities managers should remember that LPAs cannot impose further conditions when issuing a certificate of lawfulness. However, if, instead, an application is made for planning permission to regularise the existing use and development rather than an application for a certificate of lawfulness, this gives the LPA an opportunity to impose conditions.

Building regulations

Often, little or no distinction is made between planning permission and building regulations. Although there is a degree of overlap in the sense that they must both be dealt with when carrying out building works, they are separate and distinct concepts. Planning permission deals with the obtaining of consent for the type or nature of work to be carried out. Building regulations are necessary to ensure that the work is carried out with the correct materials and in accordance with appropriate health and safety laws.

The relevant building regulations are the *Building Regulations 2000* (SI 2000/2531), the *Building Standards (Scotland) Regulations 1990* (SSI 1990/2179) also *Building Standards (Scotland) (Amendment) Regulations 1993 & 1994 & 1996 & 1997 & 2001 & 2002*, and the *Building Regulations (Northern Ireland) 1994* also *Building (Amendment) Regulations (Northern Ireland) 1997 no.481*. The 1991 Rules have been amended by the *Building Regulations (Amendment) (No 2) Regulations 1999*. Building regulations are covered in more detail in **Health and Safety Law: building regulations, pp 77–79**.

Complying with these regulations does not represent any form of consent to works and is not a substitute for planning permission. They ensure that the methods and materials used are of an appropriate quality and that they meet all current industry standards.

A buildings regulations officer will be appointed by the local authority to inspect the works at various stages and must be notified before works commence. The officer will liaise with the various contractors to ensure that the works are compliant.

A certificate of satisfaction will be issued when the officer is satisfied that the works meet current industry standards. Conditions can be attached to the certificate and a final certificate will not be issued until these conditions have been met.

A fee is payable to the local authority. The level of the fee is calculated by reference to the cost of the works and the local authority will usually accept an estimated project cost as long as it is realistic. A final certificate will not be issued until the fee has been paid and the works completed to the officer's satisfaction.

Environmental matters

Environmental law – relating primarily to contaminated land – is a complex area of law. Little practical guidance can be given by examining individual statutory provisions. It is an area best dealt with on a case-by-case basis by an experienced environmental specialist, as the potential liabilities and remediation costs can be very high. Nevertheless, there are benefits in being well-informed and facilities managers should be aware of the overall apportionment of responsibility for the clean-up of contaminated land.

The law

It is not easy to follow the relevant statutory enactments that deal with the clean-up of contaminated land. The *Environmental Protection Act 1990 (1990 Act)* was the first serious attempt at introducing detailed statutory provisions controlling this. Further provisions dealing with remediation and apportionment of liability were introduced into the *1990 Act* by the *Environment Act 1995*[4].

The provisions relating to the clean-up of contaminated land came into force on 1 April 2000. Note however, that the regime is retroactive in effect – the regime will apply irrespective of when the land is or was contaminated.

What is contaminated land?

Land is 'contaminated' if, as a result of the substances in, on or under it, there is:

- a resultant significant harm[5]
- a significant possibility of such harm occurring
- pollution or risk of pollution to water.

Who is liable? – The 'polluter pays' principle

The 'polluter pays' principle is a two-tiered system which requires the identification of an 'appropriate person' who will be liable for the remediation of the contaminated land. An appropriate person is either the person who:

(a) caused or knowingly permitted the land to become contaminated (the original polluter) – known as a Class A appropriate person; or

(b) the owner or occupier of the land for the time being – a Class B appropriate person.

The following chart illustrates this:

Local authority	identifies contaminated land
	remediation works enforced against Class A appropriate person: 'polluter pays' principle
	if after reasonable enquiry Class A appropriate person cannot be found
	remediation works enforced against Class B appropriate person.

Reducing liability for clean-up

Clearly, there is an obligation on facilities managers to ensure that no pollution is caused to a site during the period of their company's use of that site. However, they will also want to ensure that the risk of being held liable as a Class B appropriate person is reduced. This means that they will want information about the environmental status of a property *before* that property is acquired for the company's portfolio. There is no public list or register of sites which may be contaminated. How then can the risks be quantified? The following options are available:

Desktop or phase I report

This involves a document-only analysis of the environmental aspects of a given site. Information for a phase I study is likely to be gathered by the following methods:

- specific enquiries of regulatory bodies
- specific enquiries of occupier
- researching planning history
- research title deeds and pre-registration documents.

Physical survey or phase II report

The phase II report is more extensive and requires the taking and analysis of soil, water and other material samples from the site. The phase II survey is expensive. However, where the potential risks of contamination are perceived to be high (if, for example, the site has previously been used for a high risk use, such as storage of solvents or other chemicals), then the cost may well be justified in order to quantify the risks.

Occupiers' liability

Where an occupier acts or fails to act and by doing so creates a dangerous condition which later causes harm to a visitor using the premises, then the occupier may be liable under the provisions of the *Occupiers Liability Act 1957* (the *1957 Act*).

The grounds for making a claim against individuals or companies occupying or controlling premises are wide. They are an easy target, not least because it is widely thought that their insurers will step in to meet the claim. Potential litigants are also aware that it is very difficult for occupiers to show that they have acted as occupiers to the standard required by law.

Case study

Consider the following simple case study:

A company occupies office premises. The facilities manager has a strict cleaning and maintenance programme in operation. This involves polishing the client reception area to a highly polished finish. A client attends the offices, slips on the polished floor and is injured. Is the occupier of the office premises liable for a claim brought by the client because of this accident?

Is the claim valid?

The following key elements will determine the validity of the claim:

- Is the company an occupier?

- Has the accident occurred on 'premises' as defined in the *1957 Act*?

- Does the company owe a duty of care to the client?

- Has the company discharged the duty of care owed to the client?

- Can liability be excluded?

Is the company an occupier?

The rules of common law (determined by case law) define who is an 'occupier'[6]. Exclusive occupation of premises is not necessary. The test is whether a person has some degree of control associated with or arising from their presence and use of or activity in the premises; it is possible to have more than one occupier of premises. Consider the example given above in the following context:

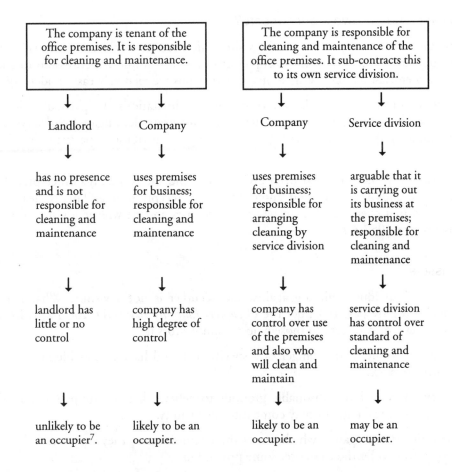

The company is tenant of the office premises. It is responsible for cleaning and maintenance.		The company is responsible for cleaning and maintenance of the office premises. It sub-contracts this to its own service division.	
↓	↓	↓	↓
Landlord	Company	Company	Service division
↓	↓	↓	↓
has no presence and is not responsible for cleaning and maintenance	uses premises for business; responsible for cleaning and maintenance	uses premises for business; responsible for arranging cleaning by service division	arguable that it is carrying out its business at the premises; responsible for cleaning and maintenance
↓	↓	↓	↓
landlord has little or no control	company has high degree of control	company has control over use of the premises and also who will clean and maintain	service division has control over standard of cleaning and maintenance
↓	↓	↓	↓
unlikely to be an occupier[7].	likely to be an occupier.	likely to be an occupier.	may be an occupier.

In the example above, the company uses the premises for its business. It has control of the day-to-day running of the premises and is an occupier for the purposes of the *1957 Act*.

Did the accident occur on 'premises'?

Facilities managers will be forgiven for thinking that premises means only buildings from which a company operates. For the purposes of the *1957 Act*, 'premises' includes:

- any fixed or moveable structure

- any vessel, vehicle or aircraft.

The definition is wide. Examples of what constitutes premises include scaffolding, ladders, grandstands, electric pylons and lifts.

If the *1957 Act* definition of premises is applied to the case study there is no difficulty in establishing that the client reception area falls within the statutory meaning of premises.

Does the company owe a duty of care?

An occupier owes a duty of care to its visitors, licensees and invitees ('visitors'). This will include anyone to whom the occupier gives any invitation or permission to enter or use the premises. Express permissions or invitations are relatively easy to identity.

An occupier must, however, be aware of implied invitations. In particular, it will always be difficult to argue against a claim that, for example, ungated pathways or a long-standing hole in a fence constitutes an implied invitation, particularly where children are concerned[8].

In the case study, the client has been invited to attend the company's office premises. The client attends the office and enters the client reception area. This is clearly an invitation to that client for him to be at the premises and he will be a visitor for the purposes of the *1957 Act*.

Trespassers

What if the individual claiming against the occupier is not a visitor? What if that individual was a trespasser? Under the *Occupiers Liability Act 1984* (the *1984 Act*) an occupier owes a duty of care to those who are not visitors if:

- They are aware of the danger of a specific risk and have reasonable grounds to believe it exists.

- They know or have reasonable grounds to believe that the trespasser is in the vicinity of the danger or may come into the vicinity.

- The risk is one against which, in all the circumstances, they may reasonably be expected to offer the trespasser some protection.

Has the company discharged the duty?

The common duty of care owed by occupiers to visitors is a duty to take such care as is reasonable, taking account of all the circumstances. Visitors must be reasonably safe in using the premises for the purposes for which they were invited or permitted. As with any duty of care-based claims, such as a claim in the tort of negligence, the definition is legalistic and complex.

How then can the facilities manager judge whether or not the common duty of care has been discharged? Examine the case study below under 'Can liability be excluded?'– surely it is sufficient for the facilities manager to have a rigorous cleaning and maintenance programme in place? If a client slips on the highly polished entrance floor, does that client have a claim against the company as occupier under the *1957 Act*? Is this claim supported by case law? In determining whether or not the company has discharged its common duty of care as occupier to the client, the court will consider whether, in light of all the circumstances, the company has failed to achieve the standard of care required by the *1957 Act*. Again this is legalistic and unclear. Facilities managers should consider the following standard of care guidelines developed through case law:

- Children must be expected to show a lesser degree of safety awareness than adults.

- Visitors attending premises to perform their particular skill are expected to be prepared for special risks associated with that skill.

- Where the use of independent contractors gives rise to a claim based on the contractor's negligence, an occupier may satisfy the standard of care if it has acted reasonably in employing that contractor, believing the contractor to be competent.

A lesser standard of care is owed to trespassers under the *1984 Act*. The duty can be discharged if the occupier takes such care as is reasonable in all the circumstances to ensure that the trespasser does not suffer injury on the premises.

Can liability be excluded?

Consider the following in the context of the case study – the facilities manager arranges for the following warning sign to be placed in the reception area of the office premises:

NOTICE

All visitors are asked to take care when entering the reception area. The floors are highly polished and very slippery, particularly when wet.

No liability for personal injury or damage to property is accepted by the company.

Does this warning discharge the company's common duty of care? Once again the legal rules are complicated. If a notice or warning sign is reasonable in all the circumstances and is sufficient to allow the visitor to avoid the danger then the occupier may well have satisfied the required standard of care. To return to the case study: the client is warned of the slippery floor by such a notice. Whilst they know that it is a potential hazard, they have no choice than to cross the floor in order to reach the reception desk. The company has created a danger which cannot be avoided. The notice does not discharge the common duty of care owed to the client.

On the basis that the warning about the slippery floor is insufficient to discharge the common duty of care, can the company rely on the exclusion of liability for loss or damage to personal injury or property contained in the notice? It is possible to limit or exclude liability in certain circumstances – if, for example, a visitor has agreed to such an exclusion, then in so far as loss or damage to property is concerned it would be effective. Such agreement could be formal – by means of signing a disclaimer, for example – but may also be implied. A trespasser, for example, who enters a premises uninvited, implies agreement to exclusion of liability. However, a decision to walk over a slippery floor to reach a reception desk does not constitute agreement on the visitor's part. Therefore, it is not possible to exclude liability for personal injury in these circumstances.

Knowing your portfolio and managing costs

There is no substitute for facilities managers knowing what properties are under their control. It is not enough merely to have details of the address. Building up a detailed set of information about the portfolio is time-consuming and potentially costly. However, the advantages of doing this cannot be overemphasised. Consider how the facilities manager can add value to their role in the company and participate in board decisions in the following scenarios:

- The company's board of directors wants to rationalise that company's premises requirements. A good knowledge of the portfolio will enable the facilities manager to answer questions such as:

  o Which premises are not cost effective?

  o Can leases be terminated early without penalty?

  o Are there title or planning restrictions which may impact on the timing or value of an open market disposal?

- The board is seeking to diversify the company's business. The facilities manager can advise on whether any of the existing premises can be re-developed or undergo a change of use.

- Preliminary discussions are taking place with a potential purchaser of the company. The facilities manager can address issues which may have an impact on the price of the transaction, such as:

  o Can any of the properties be used in the negotiations?

  o Do any of them have unusual or special features?

    o   Do any of them have onerous restrictions which should be brought into the open at an early stage?

- Lawyers or other professional advisers have been instructed to act on a matter relating to a particular premises. The factual details such as the landlord's address and the agent's name are missing. Various deeds and documents are also missing. The lawyers spend a considerable amount of time collecting basic information, which increases their bill. Clearly, it would be more cost effective for a facilities manager to provide factual information to the lawyer or professional advisor rather than to pay the lawyer or professional adviser to collect that information. A transaction is also likely to run more smoothly if the lawyer or professional advisor is provided with all relevant background information at an early stage. A well-informed facilities manager can use their knowledge of the property and the potential problems of a transaction to negotiate a realistic fee structure with the lawyer and professional advisors.

Moreover, knowledge of any occupational and/or use restriction enables the facilities manager to formulate solutions.

Premises requirements are rarely at the core of a company's key business strategy. This is likely to mean that the facilities manager will have little support from the board of directors for any initiatives aimed at scheduling or collating factual information about the property portfolio. Nevertheless, a full knowledge of the portfolio will enable the facilities manager to enhance their position by providing key information at important stages of the negotiations, anticipating problems, offering solutions and achieving costs savings.

Key knowledge requirements

The key information which any facilities manager should know about the premises under his control should include the following:

- identification of property
- planning consents and restrictions
- title matters
- terms of occupation.

Real estate valuation

The valuation of real estate is a broad topic, both in terms of the different categories of property and the methodology involved. It is difficult to envisage efficient real estate management without a clear understanding of the value of the assets and liabilities held. A valuation is an essential tool for considering opportunities to release capital, realise development gains and achieve cost savings.

Valuation theory is best left to the valuer; however, an awareness of valuation procedure is of relevance to the facilities manager. This section provides guidance on procuring valuations, and considers certain practical issues which impact on property value.

The regulatory framework

The provision of valuation advice within the UK is currently regulated by the Royal Institution of Chartered Surveyors' *Appraisal and Valuation Manual*, first published in September 1995 and better known as the 'Red Book'. The *Appraisal and Valuation Manual* has been subject to a major update, with effect from May 2003, to reflect the requirements of the emerging International Financial Reporting Standards.

The 'Red Book'

The stipulations of the red book are mandatory for the majority of valuations, although certain categories of valuation are excluded. These include valuations undertaken in accordance with a statutory code, valuations prepared in the context of negotiations and those undertaken by an in-house valuer solely for use within its own organisation.

As key requirements of any valuation, the red book's specifications include:

- the need to agree the valuer's instructions in writing prior to issue of the valuation report

- the need to adopt the correct 'basis of valuation', appropriate to the purpose of the valuation

- the minimum content of valuation reports.

Procuring valuations

When commissioning a valuation, it is important that both the client and the valuer have a clear understanding of the purpose of the valuation and the level of service required. This is unlikely to be achieved by a letter simply requesting a valuation of a given property for a specified fee, unless standard terms and conditions of engagement have already been agreed.

A more comprehensive definition of the task is normally required and the Red Book specifies the minimum level of detail needed. The main items that need to be agreed in writing before the final valuation report is issued include:

- the purpose of the valuation

- the address of the property and the legal interest to be valued, including the treatment of fixtures and fittings and plant and machinery normally regarded as part of the land and buildings

- the basis or bases of valuation

- any practicable assumptions to be made relative to the basis of valuation (for example, to take into account any change in the value of the property if planning permission for an alternative use is being sought and is likely to be granted)

- the date of valuation (this will have to be either before or at the date of the valuation report)

- any restrictions on how or what the valuer may do in the course of providing the service

- the requirements for obtaining the valuer's consent to publication of the report

- the limits of liability to parties other than the client

- the nature of information to be provided (such as title documentation, lease details, trading accounts, planning permissions) by the client/its advisers and the extent to which the valuer is to rely upon that information

- the treatment of environmental issues, such as land contamination

- the fee basis.

It is always prudent when instructing a valuer to ensure that they have appropriate experience of the nature of the task, the category of property and the geographical location on which to base their opinion of value.

The purpose of the valuation

The purpose of the valuation and the nature of the property will determine the basis of valuation. The Red Book defines the accepted bases of valuation and among those most likely to be encountered in a facilities management context are:

- market value

- existing use value

- depreciated replacement cost

- market rental value.

The purposes and bases are discussed in more detail below.

Valuations for acquisition/disposal

Market value

If a valuation is required prior to acquisition or disposal of a property, the appropriate basis of valuation will normally be 'market value'. This valuation basis is intended to represent the valuer's opinion of the best price at which the sale of a legal interest in the property would have been completed for cash consideration on the date of valuation (the full definition is set out in the Red Book).

As market value supposes completion of a hypothetical sale on the date of valuation, the valuer has to assume that, prior to the date of valuation, there had been a reasonable period to allow for the proper marketing of the property, agreement of the price and terms, exchange of contracts and completion of the legal formalities.

When considering a market valuation, specific factors to be aware of are as follows:

Special purchasers

Market value excludes bids from purchasers with a special interest in the property. A special purchaser might comprise another party holding a legal interest in the same property, such as a tenant, or the owner of a neighbouring property, who might require the property for expansion or to create an access to a nearby development site. In such circumstances, the special purchaser may be justified in submitting a bid in excess of the open market value, although, of course, the amount the special purchaser chooses to offer in excess of the market value will depend on how highly it values the property.

'Hope value'

Market value assumes an unconditional sale. This is particularly important to note in the case of development land. In many instances, development land is sold on a conditional basis, subject to achieving an appropriate planning consent – for example, the disposal of a factory site for residential redevelopment. The market value will reflect the circumstances of the property at the date of valuation. Therefore, if planning permission has not been obtained by that date, it will only reflect the so-called 'hope value' for an alternative use that exceeds the underlying value for the existing use.

The quantum of hope value will be determined by the probability, costs and timescale of obtaining planning permission. If a successful planning permission is unlikely, then the hope value will be limited. Alternatively, if achieving the required planning permission is a virtual certainty, the market value without planning permission may show little, if any, discount relative to the market value had planning permission already been obtained.

If a valuation is required of a property with the benefit of planning permission for an alternative use, before the planning consent has actually been obtained, then it will be necessary to request a 'market value of the property subject to the special assumption that planning permission has been granted'. The details of the planning permission assumed to have been obtained should also be stipulated – for example, the density of development should be specified.

Further investigations

As market value is intended to represent the transaction price, ideally it should take account of all the factors that would be considered as part of the transaction process. This might include a detailed consideration of such matters as:

- the condition of the property
- the possibility of land contamination
- any onerous restrictions in legal title.

Often, for reasons of either cost or timescale, these further investigations are not undertaken when preparing a valuation, and as a result assumptions or caveats are included in the valuation instruction letter and report. Thus, if a property is actually acquired or disposed of and full and detailed enquiries are made, it should be appreciated that the final price may differ from that included in an earlier valuation prepared without the benefit of such investigations (aside from any issues of market movement). In this context, it should also be appreciated that it is difficult or impossible for a valuer to assess the impact of disrepair or land contamination on the value of a property without the costs of making good/remediation having been quantified. This would normally require additional expert advice from, for example, a building surveyor or an environmental consultant.

Net realisation proceeds

Facilities managers should be aware of the difference between market value and net realisation proceeds. While it would normally be the valuer's remit to provide the market value figure, the responsibility for quantifying net realisation proceeds will often lie with the facilities manager. Net realisation proceeds will normally be lower than the market value, reflecting deductions such as professional fees on disposal and holding costs (including rates, security and building insurance), as well as any factors that emerge during detailed enquiries when a sale takes place (see above). In a stable market, clearly the longer a property takes to sell, the greater the reduction in net realisation proceeds, reflecting holding costs over a longer period. When estimating net realisation proceeds, it is therefore useful to obtain details of the disposal period envisaged by the valuer.

Valuations for incorporation within company accounts

Key points to note include:

Existing use value

When valuing for accounts, non-specialised owner-occupied properties are valued on the basis of their 'existing use value', which closely follows the definition of market value, except that it assumes the property can only be used for the existing use and that vacant possession is provided on completion of the sale of all parts of the property occupied by the business. It therefore excludes any hope value for more valuable alternative uses.

Depreciated replacement cost

'Specialised properties', such as an oil refinery, museum or power station, are those which are rarely, if ever, sold on the open market, other than as part of an ongoing business. The appropriate valuation basis for specialised properties is 'depreciated replacement cost', which by definition is not based on a market price.

In practice, the depreciated replacement cost is made up of the existing use value of the underlying land, together with the replacement cost of the buildings and building and site services, suitably depreciated to allow for age, condition, economic or functional obsolescence, environmental and other relevant factors. It is a prerequisite of depreciated replacement cost that every valuation assumes the adequate potential profitability of the business, taking into account the value of the total assets employed and the nature of the operation.

Properties for investment, development or disposal

Properties held as investments, for development or for disposal, are valued on the basis of market value. Thus, owner-occupied properties normally valued on an existing use value or depreciated replacement cost basis, as set out above, will revert to a market-value basis if the properties are declared surplus and are held for disposal.

Financial Reporting Standard 15 (FRS 15)

The procedures to be followed when revaluing properties, other than investment properties, for company accounts are detailed in the *Accounting Standard Board's Financial Reporting Standard 15 (FRS 15)*. Effectively this provides organisations with the choice of either revaluing their properties or holding them at historic cost. If the organisation decides to adopt a policy of revaluation, then it will be required thereafter to revalue the properties according to the specifications of *FRS 15*. The organisation will no longer be permitted to 'cherry pick' – that is, revalue chosen properties only – as either all properties or all properties within a specific category of asset (such as specialised properties) have to be revalued.

For accounting purposes, the value of owner-occupied properties will often need to be allocated between the underlying land value and the value of the buildings, site works and site services. While the value of the land is not depreciated, the portion of value attributable to the buildings, site works and site services is depreciated and reflected in a depreciation charge in the profit and loss account.

FRS 15 does provide opportunities for depreciating individual elements of an asset over different periods – for example, building service installations might be depreciated over a shorter period than the structure of a building.

In the context of International Financial Reporting Standards, *FRS 15* is replaced by *International Accounting Standard 16, (IAS 16)* which relates to property, plant and equipment.

Once a decision to revalue has been made, both *FRS 15* and *IAS 16* require the valuations to be reviewed as frequently as necessary to ensure the carrying value in the accounts does not differ materially from a current valuation.

Valuation approach

Freehold interests

The approach to the valuation of freehold interests will depend upon whether a property is owner-occupied or let as an investment.

The majority of non-specialist owner-occupied properties can be valued by the 'sales comparison approach', which involves obtaining details of sale prices on comparable properties and then making adjustments to reflect physical differences and market circumstances.

Investment properties are normally valued using the 'income approach', which in the simplest case involves capitalising the passing rent to arrive at the capital value.

Long leasehold interests

Leasehold interests fall into two main categories. The first comprises long leasehold interests where the rent payable is normally only a small proportion of the full market rental value and the lease term exceeds 50 years – for example, a 99-year lease at a nominal rent. Long leasehold interests will normally be categorised as assets, although these could be wasting assets as the unexpired lease term diminishes.

Short leasehold interests

The second category comprises short leasehold interests, such as a 10, 15 or 25-year lease, typically with five-yearly upward-only rent reviews. In the late 1980s such leases were often treated as an asset; however, the cyclical nature of property values since then has altered perceptions dramatically. At present, short leasehold interests are often perceived as a liability in value terms, particularly if the supply of a category of property exceeds demand. Often incentives will have to be given to an incoming tenant to take over the leasehold interest. The existence of upward-only rent reviews and a growing awareness that shorter, more flexible leases are available in other countries has resulted in the 25-year lease becoming far less common in the UK, so that today shorter leases and tenant's break clauses (see **Business leases: term, p 128**) are more prevalent. Nonetheless, where a tenant has substantial capital costs, for example, in fitting out a property or installing plant and machinery, a longer lease may be required to ensure an adequate pay-back period on the investment.

The value of a leasehold interest

The value of a leasehold interest is dependent upon the relationship between the market rental value and the rent passing under the lease. If the rent payable is less than the market rent, then a 'profit rent' is created and potentially a positive capital value might arise. This will often be the case with long leases where normally the rent passing is lower than the market rent. However, before reaching a conclusion as to the value of leases it is necessary to consider other factors, such as dilapidation liabilities and, in the case of short leases, what, if any, financial incentives might need to be granted to a new tenant to take on the lease. Such incentives could, for example, take the form of a rent-free period or payment of a reverse premium. With short leases, once these and other factors have been reflected, a positive value derived from a profit rent may in practice become a nil or negative value.

Negotiating lease terms

In the lease negotiation process, the facilities manager will often have a lead role in determining the heads of terms for the occupier (tenant). This will encompass defining the tenant's occupational requirements (such as the floorspace required, the length of lease needed and what level of rent is affordable). Once this has been done, the tenant will in effect have a shopping list of requirements. However, before entering the negotiating process, it is useful to also consider the landlord's motives. In most cases, a landlord will be seeking to maximise the income and capital return upon their investment. This return will be very much dependent upon the lease terms agreed.

The table below sets out some of the main terms of a lease, which will maximise or minimise the value of the landlord's interest. If the tenant has a particular wish to include a term or terms which reduce the capital value for the landlord (from the column on the right), it can in negotiating seek to counter the negative effect of this from the landlord's point of view by proposing the inclusion of a separate term or terms from the left hand column.

Enhances capital value for the landlord	Reduces capital value for the landlord
Maximum lease duration, eg 25 years.	Minimum lease duration, eg five years.
A higher rental value.	A lower rental value.
Maximum security of rental income – ie tenant has strong financial covenant.	Rental income at risk – ie tenant has a weaker financial covenant.
No incentives for the tenant at lease commencement.	Extensive rent-free period and/or capital contribution from the landlord.
More frequent rent reviews.	Less frequent rent reviews.
No tenant's break clauses.	Frequent tenant's break clauses.

In a buoyant property market, when demand exceeds supply, the features in the left-hand column will come to the fore. However, in a bear market, such as existed during the recession of the 1990s, the issues in the right-hand column will prevail. This provides some insight into the cyclical nature of property investment values.

Further reading

Appraisal and Valuation Manual Royal Institution of Chartered Surveyors (RICS).

1 Section 57(1) of the *Town and Country Planning Act 1990*.
2 Outside Greater London and the Metropolitan areas, the development plan consists of the structure plan and the local plan; within Greater London and the Metropolitan area the development plan consists of the unitary development plan.
3 Internal works within listed buildings require listed buildings consent.
4 Part II(*a*), *Environmental Protection Act 1990*. See also *Contaminated Land (England) Regulations 2000* and DETR guidance on contaminated land, dated April 2000. The National Assembly is expected shortly to introduce similar regulations regarding contaminated land in Wales.
5 'Harm' is defined as harm to health of living organisms or other interference with the ecological systems of which they form part and, in the case of man, includes harm to his property.
6 *Occupiers Liability Act 1957*, s 1(2).
7 Duties are imposed on landlords who are under an obligation to repair by the *Defective Premises Act 1972*. The duty is wide and is even extended to trespassers. It is sufficient that the landlord merely has a right to enter to carry out repairs under the terms of the lease.
8 *Cooke v Midland Western Railway of Ireland* [1909] AC 229, HL.

4 Financial Management

Connel Bottom

Financial strategy and management are a core part of any business, supporting the achievement of the organisation's short, medium and long-term goals. For facilities managers, financial management refers specifically to the effective and efficient use of available finance through the use of planning and control mechanisms. This, ideally, is a proactive process which ensures that the right level of financial resource is available at the right times, enabling the required level of service quality to be delivered by a contractor, supplier or staff member.

This chapter aims to provide facilities managers with practical skills for managing finance, focusing on the theory and application of best practice management techniques associated with strategic planning, analysis and/or control of facilities goods, services or projects.

Background economics

Financial management skills may be utilised and supported in different ways, according to the size, function, flexibility and complexity of an organisation. Before looking at the principles of issues such as cost control, benchmarking, procurement and value engineering, it is important to look at the economic structure of the organisation within which those principles will be applied.

Universal principles

Facilities management strategy, structure and scope within an organisation (public or private sector) may take many forms, for example:

- management of a direct labour team

- management through an intelligent client function (ICF) of both in-house and external service providers

- partial management through an ICF and assistance from an external managing agent or partnered provider, such as under the umbrella of TFM (total facilities management), PFI or PPP schemes

- management of facilities as a landlord/institutional investor or agent.

However facilities management is organised, the principles outlined here give basic and practical building blocks which can be replicated by any facilities management function in pursuit of sound, proactive financial management.

The significance of facilities management costs

Typically, the facilities manager is concerned with a wide variety of costs associated with the provision of premises or buildings, business and staff support services. **Figure 1** shows a typical classification of cost centres that might fall within the facilities manager's remit. It also illustrates audited annual costs for a UK portfolio (as an example) and their associated percentage significance to the facilities management team.

		£	
Property costs	Property: rent, rates, insurances, etc	4,028,692	33.12%
Premises costs	Building services maintenance	869,255	7.15%
	Building fabric maintenance	125,595	1.03%
	Grounds maintenance	80,180	0.66%
	Alterations and fitting out	672,835	5.53%
	Cleaning	922,083	7.58%
	Security	602,217	4.95%
	Utilities	1,189,355	9.78%
	Internal décor	55,371	0.46%
Business support	Archiving	18,990	0.16%
	Reprographics	670,450	5.51%
	Stationery	267,746	2.20%
	IT communications	120,855	0.99%
	IT computers	69,719	0.57%
	Post room functions	174,521	1.43%
	Transport and fleet	92,744	0.76%
	Porterage	94,719	0.78%
	Travel management	8,569	0.07%
	Furniture	14,667	0.12%
	Business equipment	22,210	0.18%
Staff support	Catering	1,947,575	16.01%
	Gym	25,324	0.21%
	Occupational health service	49,430	0.41%
	Facilities management helpdesk	39,355	0.32%
		12,162,459	100%

Figure 1: Typical classification of facilities management cost centres

To put these costs into context, **Figure 2** illustrates a typical facilities management budget compared with organisational turnover and profit[1]. While the facilities management budget may appear small in comparison, it is worth considering the impact of facilities services on an organisation. For example, failure of building services due to an inadequate maintenance strategy or the disruption caused by the absence of a disaster recovery plan following a terrorist bomb blast could have a significant effect on the core business financial statistics. Furthermore, staff resources are a significant cost in most organisations and the workplaces that support them, managed by the facilities manager, are known to influence productivity and organisational performance.

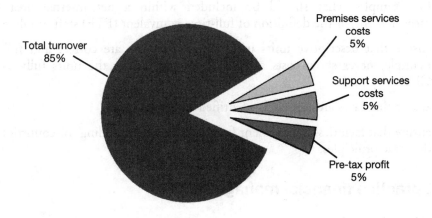

Figure 2: Typical facilities costs compared with organisational turnover

Systems technology and financial management

All too often, an organisation's systems infrastructure is implemented without an understanding of the needs of the facilities management department. In some cases, this has the effect of encouraging individuals to set up or procure separate systems. It is quite common, for example, to see a facilities manager controlling and reporting budgetary performance using the organisation's enterprise resource planning (ERP) system and managing space-recharging or end-of-year benchmarking activities on separate spreadsheet files. However, infrastructure suppliers such as SAP, Oracle and Peregrine Systems now realise the significance and benefit of integrating facilities management information, and more and more facilities managers are turning to these. When setting such systems up, facilities managers should:

- ensure that there is no duplication of data input or storage

- ensure that the system uses meaningful budgetary codes and classifications

- ensure that the classification is sufficient for conducting external benchmarking

- where there are several buildings or clear functional boundaries, ensure that costs can be collated and managed flexibly and logically

- ensure that the system computes costs fairly for recharging purposes

- ensure that direct comparisons can be drawn with contract performance information – remember that financial management is important, but performance information is arguably more important to facilities management customers and their productivity

- ensure that costs can be logically combined with key benchmarking parameters – for example, floor areas and headcount

- ensure that there are adequate measurement definitions for other staff to follow – for example, what should be included within a net internal area (NIA) measurement, or the definition of full-time equivalent (FTE) staff numbers

- ensure that descriptive units in automated reports are correct and full – for example, never show costs as £/sq m, always define the units fully as £/m^2 GIA/p a

- ensure that taxes are separately identified and described

- ensure that facilities management functions in other buildings or countries adopt the same principles.

Best practice financial management

Budgetary control

Budgetary control is concerned with ensuring that the financial management plan that has been agreed with the board of management is achieved. Control is effected through monitoring expenditure before and after commitment to prevent under- or over-expenditure. The principal considerations of budgetary control are:

- planning

- preparation

- coordination

- behavioral effects

- communication

- reporting and reconciliation

- change management

- evaluation.

Planning

The budget-planning process is concerned with the following issues:

- forecasting

- facilities managers' skills

- information on required service levels

- information on the organisation's future business strategy.

Budget planning is carried out in advance of the budget period; it is normal to plan for next year's budget two to three months before the start of a new financial year. In some organisations budgets are prepared on a rolling basis and in these situations planning will be a recurrent activity carried out at pre-defined intervals – say quarterly or half-yearly.

The planning process relies partly on the facilities manager's skills of forecasting, and partly on the quality of information available on previous financial and service quality performance and future business objectives. The facilities manager will normally be able to control the quality of information on the former through an efficient facilities management information system (see elsewhere in this chapter, **Systems technology and financial management, p 165**), and the presence of an intelligent client function ICF or strategic management function with representation on (or at least good links with) the board of management would normally provide enough information on the latter. The absence of a strategic facilities management function in medium to large organisations can hinder the budget-planning phase. If financial planning is not informed and is consequently not proactive then the facilities manager will run the risk of having to react to problems as they arise – 'fire-fighting'. This scenario is clearly an inefficient use of resources in any organisation and is one that can be prevented through effective planning.

Preparation

Budget preparation is concerned with the following issues:

- the use of appropriate cost centres for management and benchmarking
- zero-based budgeting
- provision of data relating to service level quality and cost
- the declaration of all assumptions made
- capital and revenue planning
- treatment of depreciation
- tax planning.

The first three of the above list are discussed immediately below, and the latter four later in this chapter.

Cost centres

The facilities management department should have appropriate cost centres around which forecasts of expenditure and quality can be made. It is advisable to separate facilities services into functional groupings – for example, cleaning, services maintenance, furniture maintenance, security, catering, reprographics, etc. These groupings can sometimes be sub-divided further – catering, for example, can be divided into staff dining, hospitality catering and vending. It is generally accepted that the more detailed the classification the better the forecast, although this depends to some extent on the amount and quality of data available at the preparation stage. The classification adopted by the facilities management department may be more detailed than that required by the organisation's finance department, which is typically more interested in the correct accounting for the needs of the business than in the efficiency and performance of the facilities services. To maximise efficiency and performance, the cost centres must be logical, both in the context of service functions and in terms of retrospective performance appraisal or benchmarking (see elsewhere in this chapter, **Benchmarking facilities costs, p 179**). A suitable classification is effectively a benchmarking protocol, an example of which is given in the **Appendix**.

Zero-based budgeting

The facilities manager normally forecasts the activities necessary, the quality required and the associated cost of each service. It is poor practice to use the previous year's budget figure and add on a percentage for market inflation, as this approach does not always reflect an accurate forecast of future change. Detailed forecasting using a clean sheet of paper is inherently much better practice – particularly where the facilities manager is not experienced or where it is expected that they will leave the organisation within the budget period. The construction of a new budget for each service from basic principles is referred to as zero-based budgeting. This approach has the effect of focusing attention on such issues as waste, unnecessary performance, leasing versus purchasing of equipment, and so on, prompting the facilities manager to ask such questions as 'Why do we do it this way?' and 'Why are we not getting better results?' – questions that are often asked by consultants after undertaking a benchmarking study.

Data

Effective forecasting depends on the availability of good quality data for such issues as:

- business strategy or changes being proposed that affect facilities services
- key dates associated with business change
- service level qualities and costs for supporting the business through any planned changes
- the facilities management market – for example, price increases in labour, equipment and materials
- facilities management staff costs – for example, recruitment, salary and benefit costs associated with new appointments
- stability of budgets/cost predictions on ongoing capital projects – for example, a new building
- the effect of new legislation being enforced – for example, the cost of providing disabled access
- currency or purchasing power parity, if applicable – for example, budgets for a European office portfolio
- flexibility associated with contracts – for example, supply and payment of personnel in disaster recovery circumstances
- travel costs.

A zero-based budgeting approach will effectively accommodate all of these issues, assuming that the facilities manager has completed enough research into the potential for organisational or market change. The zero-based approach is in fact a step-by-step methodology that will ensure accurate forecasting, and the facilities manager should realise that it is important that all assumptions taken in relation to the above issues are well documented. Such information will be of use when reconciling the effect of change or if a new facilities manager is recruited during the budget period.

While zero-based budgeting is considered to be a best practice approach to budget preparation, there are other sources of data that the facilities manager might wish to use. These include the following:

- contract prices from existing or recent agreements

- a schedule of rates for a certain element of the supply chain

- pricing books published within the industry/marketplace.

In addition, contractors can often provide key budgeting information if requested and consultants usually record strategic and detailed cost information for many clients and buildings.

Typically there are three levels at which data may be used for forecasting a budget figure (**Figure 3**). The choice will normally depend both on the accuracy needed in the forecast and on the confidence and extent of the data available.

High level	eg Cleaning £11.00 per m^2 of net internal area p.a.	
Elemental	eg Office areas Toilets Restaurant Windows Pest control	£/m^2 NIA p.a. 6.00 2.00 1.00 1.50 0.50 £11.00
Itemised	eg Wash down partitions, 2,000 m^2 @ £0.25 per m^2 of partition surface area = £500	

Figure 3: Illustration of pricing levels within budget preparation

Coordination

Facilities management budgets need to be coordinated with other departmental forecasts in an organisation, such as marketing and human resources. Furthermore, if the facilities management department is sufficiently large, it is possible that there are individual facilities managers charged with budgeting for the services under their remit. Best practice is for the ICF to prepare an outline budget for the coming year which coordinates with the wider business strategy for the short (annual), medium (next five years), and long term (over 10 years). Individual facilities managers should, within this framework, prepare more detailed budgets relating to their particular areas or 'bundles' (services that can be grouped and managed collectively).

Behavioural effects

The budget should provide tight financial constraints for managers to work within. The constraints must not be too tight or lax, however, as this can influence staff motivation to plan and control costs.

Responsibilities within the facilities management hierarchy must be clearly demarcated. For example, a recent benchmarking study found that a facilities manager could not control a particular budget because another department had management jurisdiction over the contractor. This frequently happens when there is a central procurement team letting contracts without full input from the facilities manager who will be responsible for managing service delivery.

Communication

The budget and its constituent components, including objectives in relation to service level qualities, need to be communicated both to facilities management staff and to any core contract staff who need to understand the business requirements for the budgetary period. Effective communication will ensure that the facilities manager's plans are carried out as required.

Reporting and reconciliation

Reporting and reconciliation are mechanisms for control on a periodic basis – usually monthly. It is important that:

- the format used for reporting is clear, concise, meaningful and useful to the facilities management function

- the information is accurate

- the information is as close to real time as possible to promote proactive management

- the information is, ideally, conveyed in numerical and graphical formats (the latter will improve understanding and identification of potential problem areas)

- there is a written explanation of any numerical and graphical information

- the report is circulated to the staff responsible in advance of any control meetings – timely circulation will ensure that meetings are productive.

The information presented in the report normally includes the following:

- the principal cost centres, and where possible any sub-divisions

- the monthly budget projection for each cost centre

- the actual cost incurred within each cost centre

- total projected and actual costs

- key resource-driver statistics, such as levels of staff resource and volumes associated with the actual costs incurred

- records of service level quality delivered in each main contract/cost centre.

The vast majority of events or services envisaged in the budget preparation period are likely to go according to plan. With this in mind, the facilities manager can concentrate on controlling specific cost centres that are, by their nature, likely to vary. This concept is commonly called 'management by exception'.

Evaluation

The presence of detailed budgets within facilities management provides a means of evaluating the performance of individual facilities managers or demonstrating the value of having an ICF within the organisation. Such a process is considered best practice, particularly where the performance of individuals is linked to skill sets and the facilities management staff training strategy.

The evaluation process can also be considered a useful protocol for financial benchmarking, the procedures for which are discussed elsewhere in this chapter in **Benchmarking facilities costs, p 179**.

Change management

Once authorisation has been granted for a budget, any changes should be resisted – correct preparation and treatment of uncertainty should have eliminated many of the potential areas likely to cause a variation. Particularly dynamic organisations, however, carry an increased degree of uncertainty, and change in planned facilities management services is possible. If this change is significant, and cannot be controlled within the normal reporting regime, then specific reporting within the management hierarchy may be necessary, as well as extra managerial meetings to control the effects of change.

Business change can drive significant expenditure within any facilities operation. Change management is therefore a very important process which should be supported, in organisational terms, with an effective and meaningful policy (normally this is part of an organisation's over-arching facilities management policy). The following principles should be recognised and planned for proactively:

- identify the forms and types of business change affecting the facilities management function

- understand and perhaps quantify the effects of the different types of change unique to the business. For example, will a new building need to be acquired?, will there be an impact upon existing floorspace, its layout, quantity and quality?, will service level quality change?, will there be a legislative dimension that needs to be addressed? etc

- new and existing service provider contracts should be designed to effectively and efficiently cover the potential for change. Change should not provide an opportunity for contractors to over-charge for supplies and services

- a communications plan should be designed to cover both the participants of the change exercise and also the facilities management customers whose expectations need to be satisfied throughout and after the change project

- the identification and quantification process together with clarity of contract agreements will allow effective cost planning for budgeting purposes.

Procurement

Strategic considerations

The procurement of goods and services is a key function within facilities management, ensuring that goods and services are provided competitively and that they add value to the organisation's core business. In this respect, the choice, planning and implementation of procurement activities are a central tenet of efficient financial management.

Any procurement activity must be based around a sound understanding of the overriding strategic considerations. For most organisations these are essentially:

- the extent to which services are to be provided by contractors rather than in-house staff

- the scope/nature of the service that is to be provided

- the capability of the wider facilities management market to satisfy the service requirement.

Contracted-out versus in-house service provision

In deciding whether service provision is to be delivered in-house or by a contractor, the facilities manager should focus on keeping what the organisation considers to be its core business activities in-house, and contracting out non-core business activities (see **Outsourcing: what to outsource, p 235** for more on this topic).

There is a common presumption within British industry that contracted-out service provision is automatically more economical than its in-house equivalent. In fact, there are numerous examples in the facilities management industry where the opposite has been shown to be true. What is certain, however, is that in-house facilities management departments have traditionally been seen as being uncompetitive and inefficient. This perception arises for a number of reasons which include:

- **Poor communication** – facilities managers are notorious for not telling their customers how good they are (and for not having any performance statistics to prove it).

- **Over-provision** – it is easy for the in-house team to be sidetracked into providing more than is required under their service level agreement (SLA), if there is one, thus adding to operating costs.

- **Organic growth** – many facilities management departments have grown organically with the parent organisation. As a result, procedures that worked efficiently in a 100-person environment are struggling to cope when the headcount reaches 500.

Scope of services to be provided

Before initiating any procurement activity, firms should ensure they have a thorough understanding of the scope and nature of the service required (see **Outsourcing: the tender document, p 239**). This will enable an appropriate buying strategy to be put in place. The strategy adopted is likely to vary depending on whether the service required is:

- a single service (cleaning, catering, porterage, etc)

- a group or 'bundle' of services (here the emphasis will be on the mutual compatibility of the services to be provided; thus it is common to find fabric, services and grounds maintenance bundled together)

- a 'total facilities management' package, whereby services across the three main facilities management sub-classifications are supplied by one provider under a single contract.

Facilities management market capability

Within the global marketplace there is a plethora of service providers all advertising themselves as 'facilities management contractors', but in reality offering widely varying types and levels of services to their customers. This can have a significant impact upon efficiency and quality of service provision, the level of support afforded to the core business units and thus the facilities cost/value model.

Any tender shortlist must therefore only be compiled after an exercise has been carried out to check that the core competencies of the prospective bidder companies are compatible with the scope and nature of the overall requirement. For example, there is little point in putting a facilities management contractor on a tender list for a catering contract if the company's core business revolves around the provision of maintenance services (for more on selecting contractors, see **Outsourcing: choosing contractors, pp 239–242**).

It is possible to group facilities management contractors into broad categories which derive from the background of their parent organisation. These initial classifications can help to weed out weaker candidates from the selection process at an early stage. The categories are:

- **General contractors** – typically these organisations have moved into facilities management to take advantage of the improved profit margins (1–2 per cent for contracting compared to 3–5 per cent or greater for facilities management). Their core competencies tend to centre around the building-related disciplines.

- **Single service providers** – this group includes catering contractors, cleaning contractors and the like. In many instances such organisations have been encouraged to offer a broader range of services by their customers. Some have become facilities management contractors in the broadest sense, while others pay only lip service to the concept and may sub-contract these bolt-on services.

- **Management buy-outs** – over the years several of the larger property-owning/occupying corporates have outsourced their property departments. The majority of these ventures have proved extremely successful in a privatised environment; however, this was quickly recognised by the more predatorial elements of the marketplace and only a few of them retain their independence. Typically this type of organisation has strong managerial skills and operates at its best in a fee management/managing agent-type contractual arrangement.

- **Consultancy** – the recession of the late 1980s and early 1990s and the associated drop in the construction industry's workload forced professional consultancy organisations to seek alternative sources of income. Some of them moved into facilities management and again, on the whole, such ventures have proved successful. As is to be expected, such organisations also demonstrate strong managerial skills, but their preference is for the managing agent-type structure (this route is perceived as offering less business risk because the facilities managing agent does not have a direct contractual relationship with the service providers).

- **Consortia** – the advent of PFI and PPP has seen a growth of contracting organisations that have the capability of providing a total package of facilities and services to organisations in a long-term contractual arrangement.

E-procurement

The global facilities management market offers great potential for the use of business-to-consumer and business-to-business e-commerce, not least in terms of the creation of procurement supply chains. Facilities managers in large organisations will undoubtedly be aware of the drive behind the introduction of enterprise management IT systems (See elsewhere in this chapter, **Systems technology and financial management, p 165**) for the effective control of all business information, financial or otherwise. Internet technology is making it possible to integrate office functions with key suppliers of all but the most complex facilities management services.

Growth of e-procurement

The growth of e-procurement within facilities management is being driven by the following factors:

- The pre-qualification process can happen much more quickly, as e-technology enables the rapid transfer of key information.

- The production, copying and distribution of tender documentation can be significantly reduced when e-technology is used for procurement.

- Economies of scale can be created where individual packages of services are procured through the medium of a 'club' e-commerce site. The packages are essentially components of a large contract negotiated on the terms of the buying power of the club as an entity. They create a closed supply chain, linking a defined customer base with selected suppliers. A site would be based on a front-end browser which allows clients access to a global catalogue of business supplies and equipment from approved suppliers, helping them to search for the best value for money in their chosen product category.

- E-technology can support online tendering of commodities such as utilities, where each bidder is allowed to make offers within a certain time frame and can view the result live in the form of a ranked league table.

Drawbacks

There are many problems associated with the movement towards e-commerce. Facilities managers should bear the following factors in mind:

- Portals can only create economies of scale if there are enough consumers and the volume of transactions is high. In other words, greater numbers of participants will bring greater economic benefits.

- Reliability of the technology and the supply chain information is of paramount importance if the system is to function efficiently. For example, service level performance capability information must be realistic and accurate if consumers are to remain confident in the e-procurement system.

- Many businesses or consumers need to streamline their existing purchasing and procurement processes if economies are to be expected. For example, poor business processes are often the cause when an organisation's travel department procures 'competitively' priced tickets that are in reality more costly than when individual staff purchase tickets directly from the airline. In such cases fundamental business processes may need to be re-engineered, and cultural changes must precede them.

- Many procurement departments will want to actually meet and study their potential service providers. In facilities management the 'people factor' is often an important issue when assessing the quality of proposals.

- Usability factors affect even the simplest of websites, not to mention large and complex procurement portals.

- While experts claim that the security of e-commerce transactions is effective, many individuals still remain sceptical.

Private investment and partnership

Private investment and partnership is normally associated with the Private Finance Initiative (PFI), which was launched by the government in 1992 and reviewed in 1997 (The Bates Review)[2]. Now known as PPP, the central objective of the initiative is to involve private sector expertise directly in the procurement of new public sector buildings (or specific assets such as hospital equipment) and the operation of these facilities, including the provision of facilities management services, over a suitable life cycle period. The works and services are paid for over time by means of a single unitary charge. The methodology is equally applicable to the provision of buildings and services to a private sector organisation – sometimes referred to as a 'Private Sector PPP'.

The aims of PPP may be summarised as follows:

- to support the government's aim of reducing the public sector borrowing requirement (PSBR)

- to obtain cost savings (in terms of initial capital and operating expenditure) and efficiency gains by using private sector experts to construct and service buildings

- to enable the transfer of appropriate risks from the public sector to the private sector

- to bring the benefit of using and paying for the asset over time (rather than significant initial expenditure), so that more funds are available for other projects and public services can generally be improved.

Facilities management professionals should have significant input throughout a PFI/PPP project in order to ensure that value for money, particularly over the life cycle of the project, is optimised. The facilities manager should understand the procurment processes involved, how life-cycle economics play a significnat role, the use of performance measurment systems and the application of payment mechanisms.

The PPP process

This normally follows the following steps:

1. **Establishing the business need for change** – issues such as poor building stock condition, lack of functionality and poor service levels are frequently key drivers for change.

2. **Appraisal of options** – eg using techniques for financial analysis.

3. **The preparation of a business case** – establishing if an investment option exists over the life of the project.

4. **Establishment of a procurement team** – the correct level of resource and skills are important factors.

5. **Invitations of 'expressions of interest'** – eg publication in the *Official Journal of the European Communities* (OJEC).

6. **Pre-qualification of bidders** – to identify suitable or competent participants.

7. **Development of tender documents** – normally including contractual terms and conditions, output specifications and pricing shedules for construction, facilities and life cycle replacement costs etc.

8. **Invitation to submit outline solutions (ISOP)** – resulting in a long-list of bidders who are evaluated with more detailed criteria, eg planning, design, construction, decant, property disposals, facilities management.

9. **Invitation to tender (ITT)** – resulting in a short-list of normally three bidders; financial evaluation becomes more heavily weighted at this stage.

10. **Invitation to negotiate (ITN)** – the tender documents are usually well developed at this stage and include a clear scope of work/services, schedule of requirements/output specification, proposed contractual terms covering such aspects as length of contract and performance measurment system.

11. **Receipt and evaluation of the ITN bids** – normally using weighted criteria for contractual and financial criteria.

14. **Best and final offer (BAFO) and revise and confirm (R&C)** – possible extra stages that may be used to elicit further clarification, assurances and evaluation.

15. **Contract award and financial close** – final drafting of all contractual/legal documents/schedules/mechanisms.

16. **Contract management** – throughout the life-cycle of the project; commonly the client forms an ICF for sponsoring of facilities management policy and the monitoring of performance and payment.

Life-cycle cost models

A model, in this case, can be defined as a mathematical representation of the future cash flows associated with life-cycle costs for a given building. Life-cycle cost models can be extremely complex, but all will normally have a common theme – essentially a detailed classification of the elements or components making up the entire building – cross tabulated with each year of the project. The level of detail depends upon the particular objective. For example, it is common for the facilities manager to develop progressively more detailed models throughout the procurement stages outlined above. A good starting point is the classification known as the Standard Form of Cost Analysis, published by the Building Cost Information Service (BCIS) of the Royal Institution of Chartered Surveyors (RICS).

For a basic model the facilities manager will need to be able to write mathematical equations capable of forecasting future cash flows using the following information:

- the current (capital) cost of constructing the item (eg boiler) or element (eg space heating)

- the proportion of replacement (eg 100 per cent)

- the timing of the first and subsequent replacements (eg every 8 years)

- additional on-costs (eg cost of an engineer working out-of-hours, scaffolding etc.)

More detailed models can be developed which incorporate the following information:

- Data which explains the timing of replacements – eg, risk can be represented by a probability distribution of the mean life cycle for normal wear and tear conditions (or not).

- Facilities management service costs – eg, services maintenance, fabric maintenance and cleaning all have inter-relationships that need to be mathematically represented in the models.

- Taxation and financial assumptions – eg, discounting rates, inflation rates etc.

- Facilities management strategies – eg, use of planned preventive maintenance instead of reactive only maintenance.

Further related information can be found elsewhere in this chapter in **Whole life economics and financial analysis: whole life costs, p 189**.

Payment mechanisms

Within PFI/PPP contracts, the unitary payment (paid by the client to the contractor/service provider) represents financial consideration for the provision of buildings/floorspace and the provision of services. The payment mechanism is a mathematical formula for adjusting the unitary payment for issues such as:

- **Unavailability of floor space** – eg, in a hospital the mechanism would normally cover the availability of zones such as a ward or an x-ray room etc.

- **Performance** – the PMS score is normally one of the data inputs in the payment mechanism; a single score may be used or individual/grouped service scores may be weighted and used in the formula.

- **Pass through costs** – where a cost borne by the contractor is passed straight through to the client, eg, commonly utilities costs, postal charges, stationery costs etc.

- **Consistency** – sometimes a mechanism will only make an adjustment based upon past 'performance' or track record over the last 3–6 months.

The formula normally includes weightings which are applied to the measurements listed above. The end result will normally be a financial adjustment figure for a given period – eg, the previous month, which will be deducted from the contractual unitary payment. Payment mechanisms frequently look very complex on paper, but a simple spreadsheet analysis can be undertaken to understand the true effects of the adjustments that might take place in the future. The facilities manager, armed with knowledge of the client's business, the particular building and the potential for service failures, should play a significant role in the practical testing of such systems/mechanisms before they are contractually agreed in the procurement process.

Benchmarking facilities costs

Why benchmark?

In facilities management, benchmarking has been defined as 'a process of comparing a produce, service process – indeed, any activity or object – with other samples from a peer group, with a view to identifying "best buy" or "best practice" and targeting oneself to emulate it'[3]. This definition effectively outlines one of the most important (but often misunderstood) aspects concerning facilities management benchmarking – that is, 'targeting' or taking action in order to release value to the organisation. Facilities managers should fully understand the reasons why they are embarking upon a benchmarking exercise; they are often forced into following a market trend, an organisational mandate, or the potentially dangerous misbelief that at the end of the exercise costs can be cut. Of course benchmarking is about saving costs, where possible, but it is also about performance and value.

The need for benchmarking within organisations can also be linked directly to the competitive environment in which they operate. Globalisation and information and communications technology advances inevitably mean that organisations must be increasingly dynamic in order to stave off the competition. Over the past 10 years there has been a business performance revolution which has been characterised by the introduction of methodologies and techniques such as activity-based costing, the balanced scorecard, the business excellence model, the performance pyramid and shareholder value frameworks, all of which are approaches that many facilities managers will have experienced or even feared!

The techniques discussed above are useful when talking about the value chain that exists within organisations where the facilities management department or its activities could be described as a critical link. The techniques ultimately provide strategic management information through the use of performance measures (in various proportions and mixes) associated with the following issues/themes:

- stakeholders (eg, investors/shareholders, regulators, suppliers, employees) satisfaction/contribution

- leadership (eg, experience, skill)

- company policies and strategies

- processes, skills, policies and procedures (eg, time, quality, safety, waste efficiency)

- cost drivers (eg, resource, productivity, supply chain)

- financial (eg, cost of capital, share earnings, profitability, operating costs)

- capabilities (eg, technology absorption)

- innovation and learning (eg, training and development)

- customer satisfaction, loyalty, profitability.

Misinterpreting the value of benchmarking

It is common for benchmarking to be incorrectly mixed up with performance measurement techniques. The truth, however, is that benchmarking is a systematic process of evaluation; it should be a fluid methodology that *uses* performance criteria (among other measurements) in the search for improvement beyond best practice. Within the facilities management discipline this misconception is prevalent – largely as a result of facilities managers often viewing occupancy costs as their only output, rather than taking the wider view of adding value to the organisation by providing support through accommodation, workplaces and services. In addition, facilities managers always try to rely upon general indicators that are typically available in the public domain. Many published databases provide information which is of questionable value, for example, a facilities manager might try to compare the costs of, say, security services against a published benchmark range of £3.00 to £15.00 m² GIA without any other information being available. Those who understand the nature of facilities management service provision will readily understand that this comparison provides no value at all – different cost levels being driven by individual building/location characteristics and the quality of service provision.

The wider perspective

Facilities managers need to add value to the organisational value chain. There needs to be a realisation that the discipline of facilities management encompasses much more than cost alone. True facilities management benchmarking activities can be largely associated with evaluation of the following aspects:

- assets
- inputs
- processes
- outputs
- systems.

Buildings are significant assets to many organisations and the facilities manager would typically be concerned with such issues as physical, functional and financial performance. In this respect there are many methods of evaluating asset performance and feeding information into the benchmarking process. For example, building condition, post occupancy evaluation, building quality assessment and investment appraisal techniques are all capable of providing data for comparative evaluation. Furthermore the relatively simple analysis of space utilisation is often overlooked – though this in fact influences many of the other issues listed above.

Inputs can be associated with processes and outputs and can relate to many different circumstances within the remit of a facilities manager. For example, the procurement of a new building would be a discrete project with inputs and various activities interacting to make identifiable processes – the final output being the asset or building. The principal inputs in this case would be the labour and materials being used throughout the construction process. The provision of a catering service would normally depend upon various inputs such as catering staff labour and raw food ingredients – the outputs being meals etc. Possible measures that a facilities manager might wish to use during the course of input/process/output benchmarking could relate to (examples given are as applied to security service provision):

- cost (eg, hourly cost of guarding, cost of surveillance activities, total cost of security per annum)

- quality (eg, employee skill/experience level, accuracy of intelligence reports, number of shop-lifters apprehended or customer satisfaction)

- time (eg, surveillance hours per annum, time taken to assimilate intelligence information, time to apprehend thieves)

- risk (eg, health and safety breach by security staff, injury to third parties due to an unplanned activity, excessive loss to the business through theft).

Systems refer to the mechanisms that are in place to assist with the efficiency of processes. In the case of a new building project an example might be a web-based information system for sharing project knowledge. In relation to facilities management service delivery activities a computer aided facilities management (CAFM) system should collect information to assist with the management of processes. Measurements relating to time, cost, quality and risk might equally be applicable in the case of systems.

Internal and external benchmarking

Benchmarking is about comparison with a best practice peer group, where the primary aim is not to copy but to emulate inputs, processes, etc, with a view towards increasing output performance and hence value to the organisation. Peer group information can come from several sources:

- those internal to the organisation

- external to the organisation but similar in terms of business

- external to the organisation but dissimilar (at least in terms of principal business)

- first principles.

In facilities management it is quite common to find organisations operating in different sectors with broadly similar systems, inputs, processes and perhaps outputs. This is largely as a result of few facilities managers challenging the norm or because only a few suppliers routinely develop new and innovative services. This can be a detrimental problem when benchmarking as it is possible that 'peers' are broadly similar. Within the industry there is a growing realisation that the potential value of benchmarking increases as the comparison moves from within the organisation to a level that challenges current practice. Significant innovation can often be achieved by looking at the problem from first principles. However, the facilities manager should understand that this shift in comparative methodology will need to coincide with an increase in the level of commitment needed at all levels in the company hierarchy, the amount of resource dedicated to the project and an increase in skills needed within organisations.

The process of benchmarking

Depending upon business priorities, the facilities manager will decide the nature and extent of the benchmarking process. In practice the objectives may vary widely, for example:

- benchmarking facilities services as part of a buisiness process re-engineering or relocation exercise in order to inform buisness case analyses

- a complete review of all services within the facilities function to prove value for money

- a detailed service function audit covering analysis of costs and performance associated with, say catering to test adequacy of service processes and output performance relative to business group needs

- as part of a formalised contract, commonly called market testing in PFI type contracts.

The paragraphs that follow provide a generic step-by-step guide, illustrated in **Figure 4**, for the facilities manager to implement benchmarking practice and techniques. The methodology is applicable to cost benchmarking and is useful as it indicates the detailed processes involved in ending up with meaningful comparative data on which to base decisions.

The facilities audit

The facilities audit represents a review of the costs of providing office space and services within an organisation. It is important to realise that the audit is not concerned with cost alone, but also includes analysis of the building and organisational characteristics that drive cost (resource drivers) and the associated levels of performance.

Resource drivers

A resource driver is a characteristic that influences the required levels and/or deployment of a resource. It is important for the facilities manager to understand that output performance (eg, how clean a building is) may remain at the same level even though the level of resource required (eg, the number of cleaners and frequency of cleaning operations) varies in different buildings (an otherwise comparable building may, for example, be located beside an area of pollution which increases the amount of dirt accumulating on the glazing).

Figure 4: Methodology for benchmarking facilities management costs

Resource drivers have been classified as[1] :

- **quantitative** – usually relating to characteristics of the building or organisation that can be readily measured – for example, floor area, window area, number of staff and contractors' staff, number of covers served in a restaurant

- **qualitative** – characteristics such as the location of the building or the specific preferences or aspirations of the organisation

- **economic** – for example, interest rates, market conditions

- **operating conditions** – for example, specific lease conditions, organisational aspirations.

Performance data

Performance characteristics are important within benchmarking in order to identify the level of output associated with cost. Unfortunately, many organisations do not record sufficient performance-related information (although this is changing in the advent of developments in computer-aided facilities management (CAFM) and helpdesk software), and in any case it is difficult to make comparisons between organisations which measure performance metrics differently or not at all. In such cases the facilities manager has the difficult and subjective job of comparing and measuring performance. Customer satisfaction surveys can provide a quick means of procuring performance data.

Cost data

The retrieval of cost data will be a relatively simple process for the facilities manager who has developed and maintained facilities service budgets at a detailed level (see elsewhere in this chapter, **Budgetary control, p 166**). It is recommended that facilities costs are audited or collected at the greatest level of detail possible. This will ensure that the facilities manager understands what is included within an overall service cost. For example, from an accountancy point of view, a stationery budget may include reprographics supplies, whereas for the purpose of facilities management benchmarking it is often accounted for under the reprographics cost centre. It is often a lack of such understanding that leads to the failure of many commercial benchmarking groups or partnerships.

A spreadsheet is often the best way of assimilating cost information for analysis checking and ultimately for comparison with peer information. **Figure 5** illustrates such a process for collecting and analysing the raw data.

Invoice description	Cost	Protocol categories	Services maintenance	Catering	Stationery	Mail/ distribution	Reprographics
Xy (lifts)	£7,612.00	Services maintenance	£7,612.00				
supplier → ABC (chillers)	£11,100.00	Services maintenance	£11,100.00				
Dp (sprinklers)	£1,010.00	Services maintenance	£1,010.00				
FG (CB cooler units)	£1,726.00	Services maintenance	£1,726.00				
HIJ (generator controls)	£46,000.00	Services maintenance	£46,000.00				
NOP (lighting controls)	£12,318.00	Services maintenance	£12,318.00				
EFG (kitchen equipment)	£6,840.00	Catering equip		£6,840.00			
P-touch tapes	£177.24	Stationery			£177.24		
stamps	£42.40	Distribution				£42.40	
April stationery	£3,028.25	Stationery			£3,028.25		
Xerox 3050 plan printer	£132.00	Printing & repro					£132.00
May stationery	£931.66	Stationery			£931.66		
July stationery	£782.49	Stationery			£782.49		
Staples for photocopiers (J23456Y)	£37.80	Printing & repro					£37.80
August stationery	£2,201.38	Stationery			£2,201.38		
Photos printed & framed for facilities	£151.00	Printing & repro					£151.00
		TOTALS	**£79,766.00**	**£6,840.00**	**£7,121.02**	**£42.40**	**£320.80**

etc.

Figure 5: Analysis of facilities service costs using a spreadsheet application

Parameters

Parameters are the metrics that are used to express benchmarked costs in a meaningful way. In order to provide useful statistics, it is necessary to establish a direct relationship between the parameter and the cost of service. For example, it is unlikely that vending costs can be related to floor space, whereas there will, under normal circumstances, be a directly proportional relationship with the number of staff or occupants using the building in a 24-hour period. Similarly, it is common to express the costs associated with premises services on a cost per square metre of floor area, and support services such as catering, mail distribution and stationery are commonly expressed as costs per capita.

Parameters must be measured on a comparable basis between the organisation and its peer group. The RICS Code of Measurement Practice provides a standard protocol for floor space measurements that has been readily adopted within the industry. It should be noted that it is common for different countries to have slight deviations from this standard.

Comparing facilities costs using incorrect and incompatible parameters renders the benchmarking process ineffective. Services maintenance costs can be seen to vary significantly (in benchmarking terms) because of the use of gross internal area and net internal area; it is a common error for facilities managers to use the wrong parameter by mistake. All too often, professional and managerial reports relating to premises and facilities are littered with incorrectly described floor area measurements. This is also a common reason for commercial benchmarking partnerships failing.

Obtaining comparable data

Obtaining good quality comparable data is probably the most difficult task that the facilities manager will experience during a benchmarking exercise. The primary sources of information are:

- **Publications** – frequently professional journals publish articles sharing information on facilities costs. However, usually this type of data has been desensitised and/or excludes knowledge concerning specific circumstances, performance characteristics, etc.

- **Questionnaire** – from the very simplest to the most complex, questionnaires can provide good 'average' information. Individual respondents cannot necessarily be relied upon on to adhere to measurement rules, standards of accounting, etc. For these reasons the data may represent a very wide variety of circumstances including resource drivers, performance characteristics and, therefore, costs.

- **Subscription services** – the industry has many subscription ventures, particularly on the Internet. For a fee, facilities managers can obtain data relating to the costs and possibly performance characteristics of peer organisations. However, subscription companies must obtain the raw data in some manner – usually by way of questionnaires, so the quality of the data is constrained by the motivations of individual respondents and their accuracy of description and classification.

- **Benchmarking clubs** – a number of organisations can exchange best practice, cost and performance benchmarks and targets via a club. These are very worthwhile as long as each individual is fully committed and a facilitator is present – that is, someone who can make decisions about measurement standards, accounting methodologies, reporting standards and the implementation of best practice. The absence of a facilitator usually leads to failure.

- **Independent audit** – this is carried out by an independent expert who should understand all the problems and pitfalls associated with collecting and comparing data from different organisations. It is common for such experts to own a consistent database containing service costs, performance measures and resource driver characteristics. Such an approach allows an efficient and informed assembly of true peer-group data.

The facilities protocol

A facilities protocol or standard method of accounting is one of the facilities manager's most important tools. An industry standard is given in the **Appendix**, and illustrates a classification of facilities management services using categories and more detailed sub-divisions of activity – called sections. For novice users, a good protocol also provides definitions or examples of the types of cost that a facilities manager must include, as well as indicating which items should be excluded from the analysis (and where these items should in fact be included).

When conducting benchmarking, the choice of protocol is not as important as ensuring that the rules of what must be included and excluded are standardised – that is, ensuring that what the protocol represents is clear to all those using it. The spreadsheet analysis of an organisation's costs shown in **Figure 5, p 184** illustrates how the facilities manager can label individual invoice costs with protocol category names. The methodology used is then clear to all parties participating in a club benchmarking arrangement.

The importance of clear protocol categories

The following example[1] illustrates the importance of clear protocol categories. One benchmarking club was, on first comparison, misled as to the cost of building services maintenance due to confusion over what should be included within this category. The original figures indicated that the total cost for maintenance was £50/m^2 NIA/p a – although an expert benchmarker would have known that this was too much expenditure for the relatively new facility. Upon further analysis the club realised that this figure incorrectly included costs associated with alterations and churn – a distinct protocol category in its own right. The correct building services maintenance cost was in fact £25/m^2 NIA/p a.

Production of benchmark statistics and graphics

Before interpreting benchmarking results, the raw data from the analysis work must be turned into information ready for comparison. The choice of correct benchmarking parameters will result in meaningful statistics, such as cost/m^2 GIA/p a. However, the computation of statistics at this level is normally called 'first-strike benchmarking' – the most basic level – as opposed to a more detailed study using secondary indicators. These secondary indicators will help the facilities manager understand the occurrence of variance between benchmark statistics such as cost/capita/p a.

The diagnostic indicators used by the analyst (generally in a more detailed study) usually include the following:

- resource driver characteristics – for example:
  - space utilisation/occupancy density
  - ratio of hard to soft landscaping
  - window to floor ratio

- levels of resource – for example, cleaners' hours/m² GIA/p a

- consumption of volume figures – for example:

  ○ kwh/p a

  ○ number of restaurant covers p a

  ○ number of black and white copies p a

  ○ number of mail items p a

- labour rates – for example, cleaning operative cost/hour

- output performance levels – for example:

  ○ percentage of planned maintenance tasks completed on time

  ○ user satisfaction statistics.

Diagnosis and troubleshooting

Statistics are often meaningless when presented in tabular format. Graphical analysis is recommended for revealing the true relationships hidden in the data. An example of graphical analysis showing an organisation's costs compared to those of its peer group is shown in **Figure 6**.

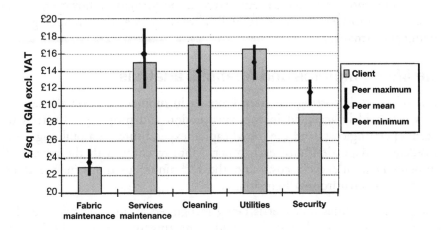

Figure 6: Facilities service cost benchmarking results

A first-strike interpretation of **Figure 6** reveals that cleaning expenditure is high in relation to the peer group.

This should prompt the facilities manager to ask questions such as:

- Is there a mistake in the calculations/analysis?

- Has the peer group reflected all resource driver characteristics?

- Is the peer group comparable in terms of the business performance requirements?

The above three questions would indicate a discrepancy in the benchmarking process. Questions should then be asked relating to the function itself, for example:

- Is the level of resource too high?

- Is the hourly labour rate too high?

All these questions represent examples of the diagnostic process that must be conducted before reporting any benchmark information. At this stage the facilities manager should review all analysis decisions on a 'repeat loop' basis until all variations can be explained confidently without the possibility of error within the process.

Reporting and taking action

Benchmarking is all about learning and doing things better. Just as it is important to understand resource drivers and to use a standard analysis protocol, it is important to communicate the results of the exercise to all concerned. A benchmarking report must always look to the future – it is not good value for money to conduct a fine level of analysis only to report current levels of expenditure and performance. Broadly speaking, a well-run facilities management function will show average levels of expenditure and performance. An 'average' performance, however, should not give rise to complacency, as there will always be ways of reducing cost and improving performance.

Whole life economics and financial analysis

The role of life cycle costing has been growing in momentum over the last 20 years and it is now widely accepted in the construction and property industries that the long-term operating costs and the initial capital expenditure on a building should not be considered independently of each other. More recently, with the advent of PPP-type procurement, life cycle costs and the techniques used to analyse them have dominated many boardroom discussions.

Increasingly the facilities manager is being recognised as an expert who understands the drivers behind life-cycle costs – whether relating to premises, business or staff support costs. Decisions made at the start of a building project, during the design stages, will have most impact upon capital construction cost, but can also influence operating costs. Furthermore, there is an argument that if the design team proactively controls life-cycle costs (with a correspondingly small increase in design cost) then unnecessary costs can be avoided over the life cycle of the building. Knowledge about facilities management markets, processes, business requirements and the interaction of organisations with buildings is of paramount importance when planning the whole life economics associated with a given project.

Whole life costs

Whole life costs comprise:

- **capital expenditure** – the cost of constructing an office building, for example

- **financing costs** – the cost of borrowing money to finance a particular project

- **occupancy costs** – subdivided into the following classification for ease of reference (note that these tie up with the protocol used for budgeting and benchmarking):

    o   *premises costs* – eg, maintenance of building fabric and services, utilities, cleaning and replacement costs

    o   *business support costs* – eg, mail room, reprographics and archiving services

    o   *staff support costs* – eg, catering, crèche and fitness centre

- **taxation** – eg, capital allowances on certain costs associated with new construction

- **residual values and disposal costs.**

What are the techniques typically used in analysing these costs, and what situations are likely to require them?

Techniques for financial analysis

Financial analysis techniques are often considered difficult to apply and understand and are sometimes left to an accountant or financial analyst. They are, however, within the grasp of any facilities manager who can:

- accurately forecast expenditure (see elsewhere in this chapter, **Budgetary control, p 166**)

- decide which method of analysis is appropriate for the type of decision being made

- use spreadsheet software to conduct the analysis and interpret the results (although this is not a pre-requisite).

In practice, the techniques used often centre around the analysis of future cash flows. The techniques are:

- pay-back period

- discounted cash flow

- net present value

- internal rate of return

- cost/benefit analysis.

Pay-back period

This technique is applicable if the underlying question for the facilities manager is how long it will take to pay back the full cost of an acquisition. **Figure 7** illustrates the analysis in simple terms by showing that an initial expense of £10,000 is repaid at the end of year five.

However, the pay-back analysis shown in **Figure 7** does not take into account the cost of borrowing the initial £10,000. Furthermore, the technique does not take account of time and income after the pay-back period – assuming that the equipment does not stop working at the end of year five.

Initial cost of new reprographics equipment £10,000

Period	Income through recharge of occupants	Cumulative total
Year 1	£1,000	£1,000
Year 2	£1,500	£2,500
Year 3	£2,500	£5,000
Year 4	£3,500	£8,500
Year 5	£1,500	**£10,000**
Year 6	£3,000	£13,000

Figure 7: Pay-back analysis for new reprographics equipment

Discounted cash flow

In this technique, the simple pay-back period analysis illustrated above is subjected to a discount rate which takes into account interest or the cost of borrowing the £10,000. It is important to understand what is commonly called the time value of money before using this technique. For example, if the facilities manager decides to buy another piece of equipment in year two, then what amount of money should be set aside or invested now (year zero) in order to match the anticipated expenditure? This can be illustrated as follows:

Year 2 expenditure (in 1 year's time)	£21,000
Real interest rate (net of tax and inflation)	5%
Amount of invest now (year 0)	£20,000
	(ie 20,000 × 1.05 = 21,000)

This example may be extended to allow for subsequent elements of cash flows, such as that created by a planned preventative maintenance contract for the new piece of equipment. The simplest way to deal with this scenario is to work out the discounting factor to be used when analysing each year's expenditure in the cash flow. To calculate the discounting factor, you can use a spreadsheet with the following formula:

$$= 1/((1+i)^y)$$

Where:
i = likely interest rate
y = the year in which a certain cash sum is spent, eg 4 for year 4
(NB ^ = to the power of)

A simple spreadsheet model using this equation to discount the income cash flows derived from the reprographics equipment example (above) is illustrated in **Figure 8**.

The further away a sum of money is planned to be spent, then the lower the present value of that future sum. This does not necessarily mean that expenditure in the future does not matter, rather the technique allows the facilities manager to compare between several options – for example, the technique could be used to good effect for evaluating options that differ in terms of specification quality and subsequent maintenance costs.

Discount rate	5%		
Year	1	2	3
Discounting factor	0.952	0.907	0.864
Net cash income	£ 1,000	£ 1,500	£ 2,500
Discounted income pa	£ 952	£ 1,361	£ 2,160

Figure 8: Example of discounted cash flow analysis

Net present value

The net present value (NPV) technique compares the sum of the discounted cash flows with the initial capital expenditure. Where the sum total of the discounted cash flows exceeds the initial capital expenditure then the NPV is said to be positive and the project can be viewed as economic. When the initial capital expenditure is greater than the total discounted cash flows then the NPV is negative and is deemed uneconomic. Using the reprographics equipment example used above, **Figure 9** illustrates the use of the NPV technique.

Figure 9 uses a formula to calculate the discounting factor for each year and is used in this document purely for clarity, to illustrate all the stages necessary to calculate the NPV. However, most spreadsheet applications have built in functions that calculate the NPV using a single formula, for example:

$$=NPV(5\%, -10,000, 1,000, 1,500, 2,500, 3,500, 1,500, 3,000)$$

In this formula, 10,000 represents the initial capital sum and the following figures represent the yearly net cash income (these figures would normally be substituted by spreadsheet cell references). It is worth noting that each spreadsheet application will have rules regarding the nature of the values being incorporated in the formula – for example, that the net cash income should be at the end of a given period and that each period must be equal. In addition, because of slight differences in approach, the result given by a spreadsheet calculation can be slightly different from the more explicit methodology shown in **Figure 9**.

Discount rate	5%							
Year	0	1	2	3	4	5	6
Discounting factor	1.000	0.952	0.907	0.864	0.823	0.784	0.746
Capital expenditure	£ 10,000							
Net cash income		£ 1,000	£ 1,500	£ 2,500	£ 3,500	£ 1,500	£ 3,000
Discounted income pa	£ –	£ 952	£ 1,361	£ 2,160	£ 2,879	£ 1,175	£ 2,239

£ 10,766   Present value of cash flows (sum of discounted income p.a.)

£ 10,000   Less capital expenditure

£ 766   Net present value

Figure 9: Example of net present value analysis

An important point to note is the fact that the pay-back period, with discounting, has increased to almost six years in this example. The higher the discount rate, the longer the (discounted) pay-back period. In terms of decision-making, the facilities manager is likely to be comparing several options. The key criteria would therefore be that:

- the NPV is positive (discounted income is greater than initial capital expenditure)

- the required rate of return (5 per cent) is exceeded

- the project with the highest ratio of present value to capital expenditure is providing the greatest return (in the above example this profitability index equals 1.08)

- the discounted pay-back period should be the least possible.

It would normally be considered best practice to present these statistics in tabular form, as they will vary with respect to one another according to the characteristics of the project. This will enable conclusions to be drawn easily and the best option for the particular company to be chosen.

Internal rate of return

The internal rate of return (IRR) determines the discount rate at which the present value of the cash flows equals the initial capital expenditure, that is where the NPV equals £0. The IRR percentage should be greater than the company's cost of capital if a project is to be considered as economic. In the spreadsheet example given in **Figure 9**, the facilities manager could use trial and error to find the discount percentage that results in an NPV of £0. However, most spreadsheet applications have an IRR function that automatically determines the correct percentage. The following equation is an example of how this can be set up:

=IRR(-10,000, 1,000, 1,500, 2,500, 3,500, 1,500, 3,000)

Again, the individual cash values in this equation would normally be substituted by spreadsheet cell references.

Cost/benefit analysis

The techniques described above essentially compare initial costs, ongoing revenues and the timing of transactions. The techniques do not necessarily (in their basic application) take account of costs and qualitative benefits that affect the business, third parties or the wider environment. Often these benefits are considered intangible, soft or subjective and difficult to measure – for example, noise, smell, image or even productivity. Cost/benefit analysis is a widely used technique where costs are directly compared with the benefits – usually though the use of a simple two-column table.

Applying the techniques

Because decisions made during the design stages of a building impact on capital occupancy costs, the technique of discounting is particularly relevant for comparing different design options. For these reasons a facilities manager should insist upon the development of a life cycle cost model at the earliest stage of a project. As the design becomes more and more detailed the model will grow and should be capable of assisting with ongoing decision-making.

The methodology followed for the simple examples given above will assist in the development of practical financial analysis models. Indeed, the following are examples of some common uses of discounting future costs in relation to facilities management:

- **Maintenance** – a common example is the comparison of design options where specifications vary in quality, which impacts on the cost of maintenance and the life until replacement. The techniques are very important in this respect as there is a common misconception that high quality specifications will always lead to lower maintenance costs.

- **Energy** – the specification of lamp fittings frequently causes a significant difference in energy consumption and hence utilities costs.

- **Cleaning** – cleaning costs are largely associated with time, degree of mechanisation and type of consumables required. Specification of building finishes, therefore, commonly impacts on overall cleaning costs. The problem may be complicated further by the relationship between the cleaning method and the life cycle of components.

- **Component and material selection** – the above example establishes that material/component specification may impact on cleaning costs. However, the effects are not likely to be limited to cleaning alone and can affect other facilities services, such as utilities, security, churn costs, and so on.

- **Investment appraisal** – it is common for facilities managers to be involved in portfolio or estate management decisions where disposals, acquisitions (both lease and buy), refurbishment and new build options may need comparison. In such circumstances all of the techniques described above can be used.

Property costs

As occupancy in a building rises, premises and support services costs will also rise, whereas property costs will largely remain static (assuming a short time period for the increase in occupancy). For facilities economics, this means that the increase in facilities costs per capita (premises and support services) will be more than outweighed by the corresponding reduction (as staff numbers increase) in property costs per capita.

Facilities managers are, therefore, principally concerned with space (driving property costs) and occupancy (driving facilities costs). In addition, however, the facilities manager should have a working knowledge of costs associated with the provision of property.

Property expenditure is normally associated with payments for rent, rates, insurance and service charges. These costs normally form a significant proportion of the facilities management budget – for instance 33 per cent in the example illustrated elsewhere in this chapter in **Figure 1, p 164**.

Rent

Rent is an amount paid by a tenant in exchange for the use of a building and is usually regulated under the terms of a lease. Mortgage payments to a financial institution (commercial property loan) or 'internal rents' payable to a holding company may be encountered by the organisation if the property is freehold in title. Rent tends to be fixed for long periods of time which means that the facilities manager will only be able to exercise an influence on cost at the agreed rent review date (usually every five years).

Facilities managers are often faced with making the strategic decision of whether to rent/lease or own the freehold title of a particular building. Analysis of the options should be related to the organisation's internal rate of return (IRR) on capital employed (IRR is covered elsewhere in this chapter in **Techniques for financial analysis: internal rate of return, p 192**). The answer to the question relates to whether the organisation can earn more on the capital which is otherwise tied up in the freehold.

For more on the legal issues concerning rent, see **Property law: business leases: rent, p 129**.

Rates

Within the UK, a uniform business rate (UBR) exists as a means of taxation based upon the value of the property. All commercial properties are assessed at prevailing market rent levels by the Inland Revenue Valuation Office, and a rateable value calculated and fixed for a certain period of time (reviewed every five years; values become effective after an additional two years). For occupied property the UBR is added to this value to calculate the total sum payable for rates. The facilities manager should be aware of these rules, together with the following opportunities for effective financial management:

- Unoccupied offices and retail property attract half the calculated total sum.

- Unoccupied industrial properties, warehouses and listed buildings attract the full sum.

- Appeals may be made against rating assessments, for which an expert surveyor's services should be sought.

- Where the property assets have changed materially – through part demolition, for example – then rate liability may be reduced.

- External factors, such as neighbouring road works or building works, can reduce the rateable value.

Service charges

Service charges are normally covered under the terms of the lease and serve as a means for the landlord to recoup the cost of facilities services (such as building maintenance, grounds maintenance, fire protection, cleaning, security, vending, fitness suite, etc) provided to common parts of buildings or estates. From the landlord's point of view, the investment needs to be protected through maintenance and cleaning so that there is no adverse effect on its value over the lease term. Until recently, service charges were largely hidden in so far as tenants did not contest or renegotiate the levels of cost.

In addition to the principles of benchmarking outlined here, the facilities manager should:

- Study the wording of the lease with care, as this will influence the method of remedy as well as interaction with other payments due in connection with dilapidations or costs of reinstatement at the end of the lease term.

- Request copies of supporting documentation relating to the financial calculations for analysis.

- Remember that the landlord's procurement processes and service contracts may influence the competitiveness of the service costs. The facilities manager is likely to have a better understanding than the landlord of what the expected cost of a service should be, and should press for the renegotiation of any uncompetitive contracts.

- Determine if excessive or additional charges are being levied by managing agents.

- Determine if excessive monies are being diverted to sinking funds for large life-cycle replacement costs, such as lifts, air conditioning plant, and so forth.

- Check the measurement of parameters used in the calculation and apportionment of service charges.

- Remember that the common approach for large service charges is for the landlord or agent to budget for the year ahead, recover actual sums periodically and reconcile the balance at the end of the year. In this respect the facilities manager has to rely on the other party's skills of budgeting for facilities management services.

The legal issues relating to service charges are covered in **Property law: service charges, p 133.**

Building insurance

Like service charges, insurances payable under the terms of a lease have also tended to be 'lost' among other charges levied by the landlord and therefore not generally contested or analysed until recently. It is worth considering the following:

- The exact scope (or comprehensiveness) of the policy and whether it is suitable for the business.

- Insurance policies may cover loss arising in connection with buildings (and foundations, but not the site), contents, rent abatement/loss of rent, contracts and loss of profits.

- The insured party should know the exact period of the insurance so that it is not allowed to lapse.

- In cases of indemnification (where the insured party is to be left in the same position after the occurrence as before), the insurance payment will be the cost of works less both depreciation and betterment allowances.

- In cases of reinstatement (where the insured party to be covered for the cost of reconstruction or repairs to restore the property to its original condition), no adjustments are made for depreciation or wear and tear, although a deduction for betterment may be made.

- The effects of inflation may be covered in the insurance policy by way of index-linking. This can have a significant effect if inflation has risen and a claim is made within the insurance period.

- Where statutory requirements have changed, the insured party may not be covered for the additional cost of complying with new standards.

- Insurers of commercial and industrial property are normally protected against under-insurance by an 'average clause' which works by adjusting a claim amount by the same proportion as the difference between the full reinstatement value and the sum insured. The remaining balance is normally paid by the insured.

- Remember that the insurance premium is affected by such issues as specification of materials and fire protection measures, which may be under the control of the facilities manager, therefore compliance with the insurance contract and/or legislation is important.

Flood insurance

While flood insurance has been common in the UK since the 1960s, the risk of flooding in certain parts of UK and Europe appears to be growing. This risk can be translated into rising insurance premiums being passed on to businesses (risk-based pricing) and in some cases the risks are unfortunately deemed uninsurable. The facilities manager should be aware of the following issues that could influence the situation:

- Since the risks of flooding (and associated insurance and remedial costs) are increasing across many parts of the world, this should be one of the criteria used when making portfolio risk or location choice decisions.

- There is a direct relationship between flood insurance premiums and government investment in, or developer-led flood defence initiatives.

- Insurance premiums can also be reduced if the buildings in question are designed to alleviate the risk of flood damage, eg, incorporation basement sump pumps, incorporation of impermeable membranes/tanking.

- It would be prudent to check obligations of any current or prospective lease.

Terrorism insurance

Insurance cover for damage caused by terrorist acts resulting in fire or explosion has been severely curtailed since the early 1990s. Within the UK, costs for damage (eg, fire and explosion, business interruption, loss of rent, etc) are limited to £100,000 in the insurance marketplace, additional insurance cover (eg for biological and nuclear contamination and impact by aircraft) can, however, be purchased which is covered by the government-sponsored mutual insurance fund known as 'Pool Re'. If, for example, there was a shortfall in these funds, then the government would provide the balance of cover (commonly called 'insurer of last resort'). The facilities manager should consider:

- Terrorism may or may not be a specified insured risk in a lease, therefore it is prudent to check the obligations of current or prospective leases.

- The definition of a 'terrorist act' can be important when weighing up the ramifications of a lease.

- Acts of war are excluded and must not be confused with terrorism.

- Pool Re cover must be taken out in respect of all properties in a landlord's portfolio – ie, a landlord cannot target buildings in high risk locations. This will have a direct influence on a tenant's costs.

- Currently cover does not extend to computer hacking or virus damage due to the difficulty in preventing such attacks or proving their origin.

- Changes in legislation are occuring on an annual basis – therefore it is advised that the facilities manager is familiar with current rules and guidelines.

The legal issues relating to insurance are covered in **Property law: business leases: insurance, p 132**.

Sustainable property

The global movement towards companies and individuals becoming more environmentally responsible is witnessed in the abundance of EC directives and regulations published on the subject. Sustainable development of property is founded on the principle that the processes necessary for the construction and operation of buildings do not lead to any environmental deterioration of natural world resources. Some of the primary issues which relate to property and impact upon development and operation costs can be considered as:

- energy sources – striving to use renewable sources, eg, wind turbines

- water – eg, recycling of rain water on-site

- construction materials – using renewable sources, eg, sustainable forests; evaluation of embodied energy characteristics of different materials during design

- energy savings – prevention of energy losses, eg, through sufficient specification of insulation

- waste – recycling of waste material where possible, eg, paper, aluminium, batteries, etc

- pollution – reduction in emissions from building plant and service vehicles.

Distributed workplace strategies

Distributed workplace strategies can be directly related to the issue of sustainable use of resources in the urban environment (See SANE Project[3]). It is a common fact that organisations under-occupy and under-utilise space which they own or rent. The problem is often exacerbated because of relatively short-term changes in the business environment compared to long-term duration of property ownership – eg, the prevalence of the 25-year lease. Organisations can address the situation by developing a formalised distributed workplace strategy which identifies the types of space necessary for supporting individual groups/teams of people. The key consideration will be to decide on the distribution of space and worplaces throughout the city/country/region. For example, staff can be supported at different locations with different facilities services rather than assuming that all staff must be located in a city centre, headquarters office location. The mix of long-term leased buildings, short-term leased offices, serviced offices, professional clubs, business centres, home-working solutions and other options will have a significant impact upon the property and facilities costs described above.

Principles of facilities finance

The facilities manager should have a clear understanding of the background principles of business finance before embarking on any matters relating to the preparation and planning of budgets, the procurement of goods and services, benchmarking facilities costs and the study of occupancy costs and whole-life economics.

Taxation

The facilities manager can contribute significantly to reducing an organisation's overall tax burden. In many organisations, however, there are no processes encouraging the facilities manager to consider the effects of taxation on any particular service or product. Significant investments in facilities should be evaluated carefully through the identification of the correct tax burdens throughout their life cycle, using financial analysis techniques (see elsewhere in this chapter, **Techniques for financial analysis, p 189**). The effect of input and output VAT payments and recovery on cash flow is particularly significant in financial models. The facilities manager should always consult a tax specialist, as rules and regulations are complex and constantly changing. As a general rule, however, the following issues normally affect the availability of tax exemptions, reliefs and concessions:

- the nature of the company or legal entity performing business

- transactions or works being carried out

- location – different countries have different tax/allowance regulations

- the nature of any funding arrangements

- the nature of the industry or business – some organisations may attract significant tax benefits.

The principal types of taxation that the facilities manager should consider when budgeting are discussed below, together with indicative (non-exhaustive) taxation rules.

Corporation tax

Corporation tax is tax payable as a result of income calculated on a trading account. Rates may vary between countries, but additional charges such as social security contributions should be taken into account in financial planning. For the 2003/04 UK accounting period the principal corporation tax rates are:

- 19 per cent for small companies

- 30 per cent main rate.

Income tax

Income tax is payable on the portion of staff wages that are taxable – that is, the salary, adjusted for allowances and benefits. For the 2003/04 UK accounting period income tax rates are:

- 10 per cent starting rate for income between £0 and £1,960

- 22 per cent basic rate for remaining income between £1,961 and £30,500

- 40 per cent higher rate for remaining income over £30,500.

Note that some European Union member states also impose a tax linked to various measures of wealth.

Capital gains tax

Capital gains tax (CGT) is payable upon disposal (sales and/or gifts) of a capital asset (where there is a gain in value), subject to exemptions, allowances and other reliefs.

For the 2003/04 UK accounting period CGT rates are:

- 10 per cent for income below the income tax starting rate limit
- 20 per cent for the portion of income falling within the basic rate bracket
- 40 per cent for the portion of income exceeding the higher rate income tax threshold.

Inheritance and gift taxes are applied to the value of the inheritance or gift. For the 2003/04 UK accounting period the rate is 40 per cent of the value above £255,000.

Value added tax

Value added tax (VAT) is chargeable on the supply or purchase of goods and services. When organisations supply goods or services they will normally be liable to VAT as an output tax. For example, facilities managers should recognise that sales to staff by way of restaurant facilities or vending machines are liable for (output) VAT.

Many goods and services that are bought by an organisation will bear VAT as an input tax. Businesses who make taxable supplies in excess of £56,000 (usually over a 12-month period) must be VAT-registered, which normally means that input taxes can be reclaimed, though not for such items as cars available for private motoring or supplies for business entertainment.

Generally, in the case of public sector organisations, VAT treatment depends first and foremost on whether goods or services are supplied in the course or furtherance of business. If this is not the case (as in the majority of cases), the activities are deemed outside the scope of VAT and there is no tax liability. There are nevertheless grey areas in the application of this rule and HM Customs and Excise provide guidance for public sector organisations.

There are currently three rates of VAT:

- 17.5 per cent (standard rate)
- 5 per cent (reduced rate for domestic fuel and power and the installation of energy-saving materials)
- nil or zero rate (where no tax is payable).

The following are examples of the goods and services liable for VAT.

Standard-rated supplies

- New construction work (other than for houses, flats and buildings for charities)
- repairs and improvements to buildings (except protected buildings)
- professional fees in connection with construction works
- the sale of freehold interests in new buildings (less than three years old since completion) that are neither houses or flats, nor of charitable status

- the sale of freehold interests, lease, tenancy or licences of 'new' holiday accommodation

- where an election to waive exemption (otherwise known as an option to tax) has been made to allow the recovery of some or all of the input tax incurred in supplying the property (for example, where a landlord has waived exemption, VAT will normally be chargeable on the rent and service charge costs – indeed any cost that is consideration for the supply of the property, such as charges for insurance, rates, telephones, reception/switchboard services, recreation facilities, unmetered utilities and management, where clearly supplied by the landlord) (see also **Property law: value added tax, p 124**).

- the provision of car parking facilities and sales of land to be used for car parking, except where related to an exempt supply of a building

- building demolition works

- inducements paid by a landlord to a tenant or by a tenant to a sub-tenant.

Zero-rated supplies

- The sales of new houses or flats by builders and developers (less than three years since completion)

- the granting of long leases (21 years or more) for new houses or flats

- construction of new residential homes, student hostels, etc

- construction of new buildings for charitable organisations

- significant repairs and improvements to protected buildings (listed as Grade I or II or ancient monuments) where use is residential or charitable

- most food (but not meals in restaurants and cafes and hot takeaway food and drink)

- books and newspapers

- young children's clothing and shoes

- prescriptions and many aids for disabled people.

Exempt supplies

(Exempt unless the option to tax has been exercised.)

- Selling, leasing and letting land and buildings (but not lettings of garages, parking spaces or hotel and holiday accommodation)

- sales of freehold buildings over three years of age

- rent and service charges (unless exemption is waived by a landlord)

- betting, gambling and lotteries (but not the takings from gambling machines)

- insurance sales or supplies relating to credit provision

- certain education and training supplies.

Other points of interest to the facilities manager are:

- Where property forms part of the transfer of a business as part of a going concern and the purchaser (who is registered for VAT) intends to carry on the same business, then the supply is outside the scope of VAT. This rule also applies to a landlord who sells a let building to another who has the intention of carrying on the same business.

- Rent-free periods are not seen as a supply for VAT purposes and no tax is payable. However, if the rent-free period is given by the landlord in exchange for something which the tenant agrees to do (such as carrying out refurbishment works that benefit the landlord), then VAT is payable on the amount of rent that the landlord agrees to forego.

- Dilapidation payments are deemed to represent claims for damages by a landlord against a tenant and are considered outside the scope of VAT.

Stamp duty

Stamp duty is usually related to legal documents associated with property transactions or company shares. Current UK rates for stamp duty related to conveyances or land transfers are:

- nil (certified value up to and including £60,000 or £150,000 for residential properties in disadvantaged areas)

- 1 per cent (certified value over £60,000 and not exceeding £250,000)

- 3 per cent (certified value over £250,000 and not exceeding £500,000)

- 4 per cent (certified value over £500,000).

Current UK stamp duty rates payable on average rent associated with a lease term are:

- 1 per cent (where the term does not exceed seven years; only applicable if rent exceeds £5,000 p a)

- 2 per cent (more then seven years but less than 35 years)

- 12 per cent (more then 35 years and less then 100 years)

- 24 per cent (over 100 years).

Current UK stamp duty rates payable on the premium are:

- nil (up to and including £60,000 with an annual rent of £600 or less)

- 1 per cent (over £60,000 and less than £250,000)

- 3 per cent (over £250,000 and less than £500,000)

- 4 per cent (over £500,000).

Landfill tax

Landfill tax applies to waste disposed of at landfill sites in the UK licensed under environmental law. Liability rests with the landfill site operators who in turn pass on the cost to their customers by way of commercial disposal rates. The current UK tax rates are:

- £2/tonne where the waste is certified as inactive or inert (rock, clay, sand, soil, concrete waste, non-contaminated water, brine, and so on)

- £14/tonne for all other taxable waste 1 April 2003 – 31 March 2004. £15/tonne for all other taxable waste from 1 April 2004.

Capital and revenue expenditure

A business commonly has two types of expenditure – capital and revenue expenditure. The traditional (basic) accounting definitions of these are as follows:

- **Revenue expenditure** is associated with purchasing goods and services in the short term, including any associated business input costs – materials, labour, rent, rates, insurance, utilities, maintenance, etc (common facilities management cost centres).

- **Capital expenditure** is the cost associated with acquiring fixed assets which cost a significant amount and usually provide economic benefits in the long term.

It is normal for a finance department to require capital and revenue expenditure to be budgeted and managed on a monthly basis so that the company will understand any peaks and troughs in cash flow. Such forecasting is intended to help financial managers ascertain the impact of capital and revenue expenditure on the working capital of the organisation and on company borrowing.

Revenue expenditure (for example, that associated with maintenance and repair work) is allowable as a deduction from the gross profits of an organisation. In this respect, a full-rate taxpayer who pays 30 per cent corporation tax on taxable income effectively avoids any tax liability for facilities services associated with revenue expenditure (the equivalent of a refund of 30 per cent of the cost of qualifying works).

Depreciation

Fixed assets are normally discounted in the accountancy process in order to show the true (reducing) economic benefit of a capital investment over a period of years (the assets lose value due to use, the passage of time and obsolescence). Another way of looking at the issue is that it would be 'unfair' if expenditure relating to assets purchased in a particular year were included as an expense in the profit and loss account for that year – thus significantly reducing profit levels. In facilities management terms, an effective building services maintenance strategy will normally extend the economic life of assets, which in turn reduces depreciation (thus profits will be higher). Furthermore, capital expenditure associated with improving an asset (for example, life-cycle replacement works) should never be charged as an expense on the profit and loss account. Using alternative accountancy terms, such expenditure should be 'capitalised' and not 'expensed'.

There are two common methodologies for calculating depreciation:

- **The 'straight line' method** – this divides the capital sum (less final salvage value if applicable) by the useful economic life of the asset. The resultant figure is the annual amount of depreciation that reduces the company's profit measurement.

- **The 'reducing installment' method** – this is considered closer to reality in that the asset is treated as if it loses its value more quickly in the early years compared with later years. A fixed percentage is applied to the reducing balance year on year.

Capital allowances

The law and regulations surrounding capital allowances are particularly complex, with the primary difficulty being how to determine 'qualifying expenditure' – that is, capital and revenue expenditure, described above in basic terms.

In most cases an organisation will prefer expenditure to be classified as revenue so that it is deducted in the calculation of profits, and thereby 100 per cent tax relief is obtained (equivalent to a 100 per cent refund of the 30 per cent main rate corporation tax on taxable income). In contrast, there are only a few capital allowances that deliver 100 per cent tax relief (the full refund of 20 per cent or 30 per cent corporation tax). The current rates for applying capital allowances are as follows:

Plant and machinery allowances for the first year

- 100 per cent on expenditure on energy-saving technology (applies to all firms)

- 100 per cent on expenditure on information technology between 1 April 2000 and 31 March 2004 (applies to small firms only)

- 40 per cent on expenditure on most assets (applies to small or medium-sized firms only)

- 25 per cent on expenditure on most assets (applies to large firms only)

- 6 per cent on expenditure on long-life assets (where economic life is deemed greater than or equal to 25 years) (applies to large firms only).

Plant and machinery allowances for subsequent years

- 25 per cent on the reducing balance for most assets

- 6 per cent on the reducing balance for long-life assets.

Buildings

- 4 per cent annually (straight line method) on the cost of agricultural and forestry land

- 4 per cent annually on the cost of new agricultural and industrial buildings or structures excluding land costs – eg, mills, factories, bridges and telecommunications buildings

- 4 per cent annually on the cost of hotels that are permanent, have more than 10 lettable rooms, are open for business for at least four months (between April and October) and support hotel services such as cleaning, laundry and a restaurant

- 100 per cent on qualifying enterprise zone buildings and fixtures expenditure (excludes land costs) in the year in which it is incurred (furthermore, the taxpayer may wish to accept a reduced initial allowance and claim the balance of expenditure over four years)

- 100 per cent on expenditure on buildings and assets that are used primarily for research activities; in addition, enhanced rates (exceeding 100 per cent) are also available for some businesses carrying on research activities as a means of incentivising economic growth.

Facilities managers will normally be interested in plant and machinery assets within buildings which qualify for capital allowances. Typically, qualifying expenditure can range from 15–75 per cent of the overall construction budget for a new building (depending upon specification). While the rules relating to qualification are particularly complex and depend on the precise nature of the business, the following list provides some primary examples:

- air conditioning installations – in some circumstances floors and ceilings used as plenums for air conditioning can also qualify

- heating and hot water systems

- lifts

- security and fire protection/safety systems

- furniture

- demountable partitions (providing you can prove that they are moveable, by showing space plan changes over a number of years, for example)

- carpet tiles

- incidental expenditure relating to the installation of plant and machinery in existing buildings.

Given that significant benefits can be accrued through careful tax planning, the facilities manager should:

- identify allowances as early as possible for new buildings – even at concept design stage

- consider optimal design solutions, such as demountable versus fixed partitions
- identify allowances in connection with potential new acquisitions
- identify allowances associated with beneficial locations, such as enterprise zones
- if applicable, optimise the structuring of tenancy agreements for benefits accruing from fitting-out works
- maintain sufficient information in an asset register for supporting claim calculations.

Further reading

Kelly, J and Male, S *Value Management In Design and Construction, The Economic Management of Projects* (1st edn, 1993) E & FN Spon, London, p 17.

Lucey, T *Costing* (1st edn, 1996) DP Publications, London, p 387.

Robson, W *Strategic Management and Information Systems* (2nd edn, 1997) Pitman Publishing, London, p 226.

1 Williams, B *Facilities Economics in the European Union* (2001) Building Economics Bureau Ltd, London.
2 Sir Malcolm Bates *The first report on the Private Finance Initiative* for HM Government, June 1997.
3 Harrison, A et al *The SANE Space Environment Model* (2003) DEGW, London.

5 Risk Management

Chris Taylor

We learn about risk management as children. As soon as we are old enough to understand that some gains carry accompanying pain, we start to make conscious decisions based on risk. If you take that biscuit, or play with that ball inside the house, and are found out – there'll be trouble. What are the chances of getting found out? And if discovered, is the penalty worth the pleasure?

Growing up, the game continues. Some risks are worth taking; others are not. Whatever the situation, the process is the same. We identify the hazard – the possibility that harm or distress will occur – and assess the risk – the chances of the hazard playing out to our disadvantage. All along, we balance risk and reward.

Managing risk goes somewhat further than simply assessing the risk/reward ratio. It acknowledges the possibility of a situation where you forego the reward because of the risk. Or where, by removing the hazard, you remove, or at least significantly reduce, the risk, as with stopping smoking for instance. And of course there is the middle course whereby, having formed a view about a risk, the likelihood of it occurring, and its potential impact, you may be able to reduce it to an acceptable level. Many of the same principles apply in the business world.

Three phases of risk management

Risk analysis

This is the process of working out the many and various things that can go wrong, the likelihood of it happening, and what the consequences might be. Do not simply focus on the major crises: companies in business or physical areas where such things are appropriate may have coherent plans in place to deal with terrorism, bomb attacks including to nearby buildings etc, but nothing to counter the effect of a fuel strike, an extended national rail strike, and the like. Risk does not only cover major events.

Risk assessment

In this phase, the appropriate action to minimise the probability of the risk occurring is determined, and the cost and resource allocation to manage the impact of the harm, in the event of occurrence, is established.

Risk mitigation

This phase involves the preparation of plans, the identification of management teams, and the assignment of responsibilities for managing the process.

Risk management in business

Business is an inherently risky enterprise, and good managers will seek to minimise risk through removing or reducing hazards – but, in the business as opposed to the domestic context, what exactly does this mean, and how do we set about making it so? The aim of this chapter is to cast light on the subject and, by doing so, to offer facilities managers an understanding of the issues sufficient to understand and recognise hazards which fall within their remit – and to establish, then subsequently minimise, the level of risk through a planned and managed process.

Definitions from the Health and Safety Executive (HSE) tell us that 'hazards' are those things which have the ability to cause harm, while 'risk' is the likelihood that harm will occur. But what is 'harm'? In its purest form, in a business context, 'harm' occurs when an organisation, or any of its constituent parts, has to divert from a predetermined plan to react to unforeseen circumstances. If the goal of business is to make money or create value, anything that interrupts or slows that process could be defined as harm.

Practically speaking, a business can be diverted from its desired course for many reasons, some within our control, some without. Those without our control call for business continuity measures and insurance policies to be in place (see **Business continuity, p 220**). Some within our control are legislated to determine minimum levels of risk management (see **Complying with health and safety law: risk assessment, p 12**), but there is always room for improvement from statutory minima, and there are plenty of situations which are not subject to legislation.

Different types of risk

To consider risk in its proper context, it is important to consider the different types of risk, sometimes called 'pure risk' and 'business risk'.

Pure risk

This includes:

- physical effects of nature, such as fire, storm, flood etc
- technical events such as equipment failure
- personal issues such as sickness or injury
- social deviations from norms of behaviour, including theft, violence, and negligence.

Business risk

The key components of business risk are:

- the impact of new technologies or changes in technology
- social impact, such as changes in customer expectation, or increasing litigiousness

- economic impact, such as inflation or budgetary constraints

- political impact, such as the imposition of government ideology, policy, or philosophy.

For example, consider a self-employed sole trader, who wishes to take an overseas holiday – perhaps a skiing trip. Pure risk here includes everything from flight delays, accidents and injuries. A prudent traveller would carry insurance to reimburse the direct cost of these events. But business risk goes further; what is the business cost to this individual of a week in hospital, or the inability to make that important meeting with a significant prospective customer. Again, key worker insurances and the like can reimburse some of the direct cost, but rarely is this sufficient to account for loss of time, or loss of opportunity.

On a larger company scale, think of a fire destroying (for example) a retail store. Pure risk covers the structural elements – and here we are very much into business continuity areas – but business risk includes loss of business attention while management time is necessarily diverted elsewhere to deal with the business disruption. Insurance covers the simple rebuilding, and loss of earnings but, as the opportunity is almost always taken in such circumstances to bring a building up to a different specification, the costs of this may well not be covered under a straightforward rebuild 'like-for-like' policy. Loss of earnings cover, too, is always an immensely time-consuming negotiation, of which the best that can be said is that if both parties, insurer and insured, are unhappy, that is probably as good as it gets.

The point, however, is that business risk represents the damage that can accrue to a company in these circumstances, both in terms of lost income and lost opportunities. Despite the best insurance cover, many businesses never trade again after such events – that is the real business risk.

There is also business risk in success. A winner of the US Malcolm Baldrige National Quality Award – America's highest and most prestigious business quality award – suffered significant losses in trade after its management team shook hands with the US President who named the company as one of the 'best of the best'. The problem? The directors took their eye off the ball and rested on their laurels for too long. They accepted every invitation to describe at conferences and seminars how they had reached the heady heights of Baldrige but, while this was happening, the company was falling into trouble. Quality – and risk – needs constant attention.

An area of risk of particular interest to facilities managers is the very real risk that can accompany the outsourcing of vital services. Few would argue that the chances of problems are increased when day-to-day control is delegated beyond the immediate structure of the company. The business risk here is a diminishing of productivity – that is, cash loss in real terms – through a variety of reasons. These include loss of reputation through those unversed in company culture delivering poor messages about the organisation; poor service rendering the host company relatively unattractive as an employer; unreliability of the contractor; and even security issues such as theft or industrial espionage. These should all be of concern when placing outsourcing contracts.

Developing a risk management strategy

Awareness of risk in company boardrooms is rising across many areas. In November 2002, a survey by the Institute of Chartered Accountants of England and Wales and the Risk Advisory Group found that directors across the FTSE 500 companies claimed a significant increase in business risk over the preceding 12 months.

This increased risk spread across a wide spectrum. Those surveyed cited as threats accounting issues including the growing detection of financial misstatement; non-compliance with the fast growing number of regulatory and legal frameworks; and criminal and terrorist activity. The risk that caused the greatest concern was damage to corporate reputation. The threats were real, and the concerns high, yet the FTSE directors acknowledged that many companies reviewed risk too infrequently – once every six months or less.

The need for a formal strategy is not an option. It is required by the Turnbull Committee recommendations (see **Risk planning and responsibilities, p 212** below) which places responsibility for risk management squarely on the boardroom table.

A risk management strategy would provide the framework determining an individual company's response to risk, including who would undertake the work involved at a tactical level. It would determine the priority of different risks to the organisation (see **Prioritising risk**, below), state the frequency and scope of reviews, and the trigger levels of risk that would lead to individual areas being upgraded for more frequent, or more stringent review, or to the stage where remedial action needs to be taken in terms of risk mitigation involving investment or other work.

Where to turn for help

A major concern for companies is the question of information security, and a British Standard (BS 7799 Pt 2, or ISO/IEC 17799) now exists to outline best practice in this area. Much information about this standard can be sourced on the Internet.

Most companies are aware of the risks they face – but the task of bringing them all together 'under one roof' may seem daunting at first. There are specialist companies (eg the Risk Advisory Group) or dedicated sections of the major consulting firms (eg, KPMG's Enterprise Risk Management practice) who can offer help, but most professional bodies and functional organisations are now keyed up to offer useful advice, if only to recommend an endorsed supplier of the appropriate advice.

Prioritising risk

A problem for companies when they start to assemble their different and dispersed elements of risk into a single area for attention is that there seem to be so many, they don't know where to start to address the problem. A sound corporate risk strategy will help, in that it should determine exactly what the company aims to achieve through such a strategy, and actions can be measured simply against that yardstick. But there will always be a call for a list of priority elements, and that comes down to someone making decisions.

The key to effective decision making is that it should be a process. There is a right and a wrong way to do it, and often it is too important to work on the lottery basis where you hurl all the alternatives in the air and go with the one which you catch first.

One process for prioritising decisions is described below:

- **Work on the right decision problem.** In this specific situation, are you aiming for finite security, or confidence building, or something else altogether? Pose the right question, and the answers will come more easily.

- **Specify your objectives.** What do you most want to achieve through action? Which of your predetermined concerns are best addressed by any specific action?

- **Create imaginative alternatives.** Brainstorm the options. The more alternatives you have, the better the solution may be. The best answer is not always obvious.

- **Understand the consequences.** Consider all the knock-on effects. Sometimes what seems like the best alternative may, under scrutiny, not work so well.

- **Grapple with your tradeoffs.** You'll need to strike a balance between time, cost, and long-term effectiveness – and maybe other parameters. If you take decision A, will that make B impossible for any reason? Is that acceptable?

- **Working through all the alternatives** and ranking them by their performance in the above criteria will help to prioritise your to-do list effectively. You may use more – for example you may wish to include uncertainty (including, not least, future requirements), and risk tolerance (that of your company, or the individuals involved).

Outsourcing risk

Many companies take the outsourcing route with some elements of their exposure to risk, effectively transferring risk from the company to the contractor. For example, a company may elect to outsource the physical security of its premises and hold the contractors responsible for the safety and compliance of the services they provide.

Transferring risk is a wholly normal manner of dealing with the problem, after all, insurance is little more than transferring the risk from insured to insurer, but companies need to be aware that however stringent the terms and conditions, they cannot transfer the complete business risk through outsourcing, so even these areas need to come under the scrutiny of those responsible for risk monitoring and review.

Contractually, the client company will be likely to have recourse to the supplier in the event of inadequate or improper service provision, and, to a degree, the financial implications of any unsatisfactory work. But as the survey mentioned above describes, corporate reputation is a major cause of concern, and the implications of loss in this area are considerable, as are those of consequential financial loss through unsatisfactory behaviour on the part of a contractor.

So long as the contractor operates on the company site, health and safety law holds the client company responsible for many of the possible risks (see **Complying with health and safety law, pp 2–86**). Risk transfer is a comforting theory, but the trade is more usually between different types of risk, rather than reducing their number or intensity.

Risk planning and responsibilities

Turnbull recommendations

So who, in a company, is responsible for identifying, monitoring, and reviewing risk? The Turnbull Committee on Corporate Governance places risk management squarely on the boardroom table.

Turnbull was given teeth in December 2000, when the London Stock Exchange required that company results from that time would be required to comply with five key recommendations, namely:

- listed companies are expected to have in place a robust system of internal control to protect both the assets of the company and the investments of shareholders

- such controls and their effectiveness should be reviewed at least once a year

- an evaluation of the risks facing the business should be carried out at regular intervals

- risk management is a corporate governance issue, and hence requires the collective responsibility of the board of directors

- the board, while the responsible authority, may delegate aspects of the role.

For the first time, this gave company directors a personal incentive to fulfil their responsibilities as custodians of their company's assets, including its data and other digital assets (see **Digital Risk, p 214** below). Every listed company – the principal but not exclusive target of the *Turnbull* guidelines – is now expected to publish, in its annual report, the processes it has established to protect the shareholders' interests as well as the company's assets. This includes every area of risk management: protection and survival is unequivocally within the shareholder interest.

Furthermore, if the company does not have an internal audit function and the board has not reviewed the need for one, the rules require the board to disclose those facts. The point and purpose of these recommendations is to shame directors into taking responsibility for adequate risk management. If they do not do so, they must disclose the fact to their shareholders, and risk the wrath of the market.

Essentially, this means that the legal case is clear: if a company suffers through failing to manage risk, including digital risk, as best possible, the path is open for shareholders to sue the board of directors individually and personally. It is a move that will surely gain the attention of most people around the boardroom table.

Roles and responsibilities

Practically speaking, who will do the work, and how will the risk management role be structured?

A growing number of companies are finding that there is benefit in co-ordinating risk management under a Chief Risk Officer (CRO). A key driver for this development has been the September 11 attacks, and the war with Iraq, linked with the internal affairs of Enron and others – and the fear that scandals of this scale and scope will cross the Atlantic to the UK. The CRO role first started to appear in US financial services companies, notably GE Capital as far back as 1993, but is now spreading worldwide. The number of CROs is presently estimated at fewer than 500, but this is expected to double within a couple of years, and grow steadily thereafter.

The presumption and rationale for the new role is that risk is a quantifiable factor, and best addressed in an integrated manner across the entire organisation rather than piecemeal. The CRO, then, acts as central co-ordinator.

Whether or not a CRO is in place, someone within the organisation must have overall operating responsibility for risk management. Logically, bearing in mind the weight of responsibility, this should be the CEO, but that may not be practical bearing in mind the other pressures on his/her time and attention. Nevertheless, it is important that the person responsible at a tactical level has the ear of the CEO and can visibly demonstrate support from this quarter; in practical terms, this means the appointment (or additional duties, depending on the situation) must fall no lower than the executive senior management level.

Risk management plan

The Chief Risk Officer should then lead a risk management team, comprising responsible members from the different functional areas of the organisation where significant degrees of risk have been identified. The role of these team members will be to produce an integrated risk management plan to cover the risks of the company as a whole, incorporating elements such as project planning, health and safety requirements, environmental considerations, contracts and general business procedures.

The plan must do more than identify risk, it must prioritise it (see Prioritising Risk, above) and devise plans for implementation in the event of the hazard occurring, and means to minimise the risk exposure. Implicit within this are visible top management support and company-wide communication.

This plan requires regular review in the light of changing concerns, changes to the company exposure for whatever reason, and changing personnel; the team itself may be dynamic, with members changing to reflect the areas of highest priority within the organisation.

Digital risk

How many of us are content that our computer networks are secure against criminal attack, accidental abuse, or the results of flood, fire, or theft? How many of us take it seriously, and view the cost as a corporate requirement as opposed to an expensive option?

But examine the facts. A recent CBI executive briefing was told that one company in five will, over the next five years, suffer major disruption to its business through fire, flood, storm, power failure, terrorism, or hardware or software failure. Following the event, four out of five of those who fail to have a comprehensive business continuity plan in place will be out of business within 13 months. (See **Business Continuity, p 220**.)

There are however risks that fall short of going out of business: consider stock price, corporate reputation, the ability of the company to attract and retain the best staff, and more – and consider how these can be impacted by problems caused within the organisation, often by accident rather than deliberate wrongdoing.

Consider how the following human errors reflect on the host organisations:

- In 2001, an IT consultant accessed credit card details of 7,000 Powergen customers.

- In 2001, a similar occurrence with Barclays Online, following the introduction of a new security infrastructure designed specifically to strengthen the bank's security.

- In 2003, Microsoft stored details of 18 million customers on a public server.

- In 2003, Network Solutions (a US domain name registration company) emailed confidential details of 86,000 websites to its entire customer base.

Such events are not uncommon, and are widely reported.

Types of digital risk

There are different levels, and categories, of risk. Operational risks include staff and human error, a lack of preparedness, and IT security hazards, while those under a data protection heading include the legal responsibilities of the board; the wide risk management responsibility of the board; compliance issues with the UK's *Computer Misuse Act 1990*; internal risks (such as sending the wrong material to the wrong person); and compliance with the *Data Protection Act 1998*.

Other digital hazards include libellous email: the courts have determined that email through a public server is subject to the same legal constraints as any other publicly-available publication. Mistakes can be costly, as Norwich Union found in 1997 to the tune of approximately £500,000. And then there are worms and viruses – 'Slammer' and 'Klez' are current and well-known, and can destroy or steal critical data, not to mention take time and money to resolve. Some victims do not recover.

How to minimise digital risk

The majority of companies make almost no effort to manage their level of digital risk. Four out of five companies with external electronic links do not use any type of firewall protection whatsoever: with microbusinesses (up to 10 employees) one in three have no virus protection. A 2003 InfoSecurity Europe study found that the favourite business computer password was just that – the word 'PASSWORD', followed by the user's first name or child's first name in second place, and a favourite football team in third place.

While many of the solutions are simple and inexpensive, companies with the need to adopt the highest levels of security are looking at biometrics, such as palm prints, ear prints, voice recognition and iris scanning, to manage their digital risk.

Linking risk management to the quality process

Managing risk is inextricably linked to quality. If we understand business risk as the chance that an organisation will have to divert from its chosen path to attend to unforeseen circumstances, the link is even clearer. While quality programmes seek to remove from the process all direct causes of interruption and delay, such as faulty products or components, human error, or inefficient processes, risk management seeks to minimise the interruption due to circumstantial or situational factors including the effects of anything from a rail strike to terrorist action.

Both quality programmes and risk management programmes require continual reassessment in the face of changing parameters inside and outside the company: both require highly visible senior management endorsement and involvement; both require their actions to be communicated and understood across the organisation.

Both quality and risk require a 'champion' within the organisation and neither can be undertaken and then left aside. The review of both risk and quality is continuous, as the business and the environment, both micro and global, in which it operates, are also constantly changing.

It is hard to avoid concluding that risk management and quality are two sides of the same coin. Reduced risk can lead to improved quality, through practical reasons – there will be fewer unexpected diversions from the company's chosen path, so productivity will be higher – and, less quantifiably, because the presence of a risk plan itself will heighten the workforce's ability to spot early warning signals of potential problems. The corollary also holds good: reduced quality can lead to heightened risk.

Risk management in practice

Risk management – the FM workload

Right now, on your desk you have the following: the board wants a report for its next meeting assessing the overall security risk to the company with recommendations for action; the union wants to know what plans exist to counter the perceived and possible threat of biological contamination; the mailroom staff have specific concerns about anthrax; and the chairman is due to fly to the Middle East next month for a conference, then spend a few days as a tourist with his wife, who will be travelling with him. Is it safe to travel, he wants to know, or should he cancel?

Then no one has mentioned it, but you can't get it out of your mind. You occupy a high-rise, high-profile, building close to an international airport. How safe is that? And what about cleaning staff, even security staff, and those others whose work allows them to roam the premises with a high level of autonomy, often at times when few people are around? How much, if anything, do you really know about them? For that matter, how much do their employers, your service providers, know?

Then you start to think of all the other issues that have seemed relatively unimportant for years, but in this atmosphere of heightened security now seem increasingly urgent. Questions of data security, including everything from privacy to disaster recovery, by way of intellectual property theft; questions of travel safety, not just by air, but no less by rail or road; and insurance – do you have enough cover, and are the right things covered? Things like key personnel, for example, and loss or damage as a result of terrorist activity. And how's your business interruption cover looking?

You cannot fix everything overnight, but you do need to identify, and quantify, the risks for the board report, allowing for both time and financial constraints. At the same time, at best it is a matter of employee morale, and at worst, very much worse than that – that clear and visible steps are taken to protect the sense of physical safety perceived by your people, and of the premises in which they work.

Define the problem and make immediate changes

The first step is to define the problem. When faced with many apparently equal and urgent tasks, how does one prioritise between them?

Pick the low-growing fruit first. These are those actions which demonstrate commitment, build confidence, and buy time for the essential planning, talking, and meetings which will be needed before major changes can be made. Examples are those tasks which are low cost and high visibility, for example:

- give the mailroom an unlimited supply of disposable gloves. Make it known that anyone who handles mail can ask for, and rapidly receive, a similar supply.

- ensure the medical centre (or nursing team etc) are up to speed on both the realities and the perceptions of the situation and ensure the workforce understands that this is the case, and that if anyone has concerns, they are to feel free to ask for a check-up, which will be available without delay. Their concerns will all be taken seriously.

- suggest the union liaises with colleagues in neighbouring offices and buildings to share concerns and solutions, and promise senior management attendance at any meetings called to co-ordinate efforts.

- do the same with your own opposite numbers in neighbouring organisations.

- ensure your heating, ventilation and air-conditioning plants have been recently serviced and are in good order. If not, undertake this right away.

- review your outsourcing agreements with companies whose staff enter your premises, and establish whether those companies have an adequate policy regarding security screening. Look at your contracts and SLAs.

- review total site security. Ask colleagues where the weak points are.

You will think of more that can be done in a morning's work and with marginal cost: do them all, and communicate widely that they have been done. While your actions may prove in retrospect to have averted a crisis, even saved life, your principal cause at this stage is to reassure, and to build confidence. To this end, any action taken is a waste of time if it is not widely and effectively communicated.

Tackling the harder issues

For many or most of the other risks you face, or at least want to discount, you need specialist help. Again, it is a decision-making problem, but one which can be addressed by dividing the challenge into bite-sized chunks. Some issues, including insurances, data protection, disaster recovery, and the like, may call for a professional review of the status quo. Reports from the appropriate organisations may be worth commissioning, as they will almost certainly cost a great deal less than the loss of the functionality you seek to protect. Only when the reports come in, and the recommendations and costings for action are compared, will decision-time come – and this may well turn out to be a board matter: the tougher issues are likely to take time and/or cost money.

Risk assessment is in itself a specialist task, and it may be you will want to recommend to the board that you invite a team in to review and undertake a thorough cost-benefit analysis across the entire spectrum of your operations, addressing your specific concerns and any other issues they feel appropriate.

Addressing the internal issues

There will always be issues that you know will benefit the organisation if you undertake them internally, and which need no consultancy report to initiate. In this category, for example, you may wish to review and improve internal computer security, looking to make a start on intellectual property and knowledge management issues. You will almost certainly need help to end up with the optimal system, but there are many ways in which a beneficial start can be made using internal resources.

Or, for example, if air contamination or pollution is a reasonable concern, you may wish to consider the relatively straightforward process of turning your workspace into a positive air pressure zone, through the installation of a fan to blow air into the building, passing through a HEPA (High Efficiency Particulate Airfilter) filter. If a single input, of sufficient capacity, is blown in by fan, every other 'leak' in the building will then leak outwards rather than inwards; appropriate filtering on that input will provide a high level of protection against airborne contamination.

In conclusion

And finally, what to do about your chairman and his wife? It has to be his decision, but he has asked for your views – so give them, highlighting that it is your subjective opinion. What would you do in the circumstances? Would you be willing to travel to that destination? Would you be happy to extend the trip and take your partner? A small amount of time on the phone or by email will give you information you can pass on about any added security arrangements at the airline and the hotel – and the conference organiser will have views too. But the chairman will almost certainly have made his mind up already and you will be unlikely to change it. So do not waste time on this one!

Building better at Barclays – case study

Once viewed as a symbol of corporate power and importance, a company HQ is now often perceived as a target, especially with high profile global operators. One such, Barclays Bank, no stranger to activist action over many decades, is, at the time of writing, building a new 33 storey head office in Canary Wharf, London. The building is planned to be completed in late 2004, and the bank will move in early in 2005. The building has been designed from the ground up to minimise every form of risk, not least from terrorist attack.

The new building has been described as 'one of the most robust buildings in the world, and a blueprint for future tall buildings'. Amongst other elements, the following features have been designed in as part of the company's risk management strategy:

- **Structural redundancy** The design allows two adjacent structural columns to fail without the building collapsing. Floors, too, have been designed so as not to collapse progressively, as seems to have happened in the World Trade Centre towers.

- **Strength** The central core's concrete walls are 30 per cent thicker than standard, and contain additives to reduce fire risk from, for example, aviation fuel.

- **Stairs** The standard two internal flights of staircases have been augmented by two concrete encased stairways at the edge of the building and stairway widths have been increased to boost capacity, hence speed evacuation.

- **Fireproofing** As well as the core concrete (see above), the building has substantially upgraded fireproofing aimed at increasing fire resistance from 1.5 hours to 2 hours.

- **Biological threats** All plants, including intakes for air and water, are on the roof 34 floors above ground.

- **Glass** All glazing in the building will incorporate a laminate layer to prevent damage from flying shards of glass.

Sample checklist for building in risk management:

- give specific consideration to protecting structural elements that are fundamental to the survival of the building

- ensure existing fire protection has not deteriorated or become damaged over time

- ensure existing fire compartments are gas tight

- ensure any modifications to a building or its services have not compromised fire compartments

- make provision for simultaneous evacuation of a building's occupants

- consider the use of lifts to speed simultaneous evacuation

- ensure easy access for fire and rescue teams

- have emergency response plans in place for different scenarios

- train and select staff to manage evacuation

- ensure building services are secure against unauthorised access

- ensure air intakes can be isolated

- ensure vehicles cannot get near to the building

- secure the building against unauthorised entry

- monitor cleaning and support staff and mineral water supply contractors.

---

6 Business Continuity

Frank Booty

Disaster can strike at any time, and often from the least expected source in the least expected area, as was so painfully evident with the New York September 11 2001 terrorist atrocity. Disaster can encompass fire, flood, theft, a crash, a bomb, or any event occurring against the odds which stops a company operating at its expected level. There are over 30,000 commercial building fires each year. IT and telecom – particularly mobile phone – theft increases continually; the Association of British Insurers reckons over £600 million worth of IT equipment is stolen each year in England alone. Natural disasters such as floods are difficult to prepare for and predict. With over 50 active terrorist organisations in the world (*source: security adviser MFD International*), terrorist activity continues to pose real threats and, as any company dealing with commercially sensitive information knows, it need not come from any particular or well-known terrorist organisation. So how does a business continue in the face of such an event?

The Turnbull Report

The Institute of Chartered Accountants of England and Wales published the *Turnbull Report* in October 1999 to the Stock Exchange, recommending all quoted companies should have a risk management strategy in place by 23 December 2000. Some 80 per cent of UK plcs failed to comply.

Companies not planning for interruption stand to lose more than just cash flow, customers and confidence – eight out of 10 companies cease trading after a major incident. Partly because of that, many organisations stipulate that their suppliers must have business continuity plans in place to minimise the knock-on effects any catastrophe would have. In the seven years after 1994, business interruptions affected some 7.5 per cent of businesses, costing the UK some £3 billion each year.

Under 50 per cent of companies who depend on computer systems and other technology have formal business continuity plans, and only 12 per cent of those plans are considered to be effective outside the IT department and across the business. One of the most valuable contributions *Turnbull* has made is to help companies see risk management not just as a means of staying afloat, but as a way of embracing business continuity in order to thrive in the future.

Business continuity demands total commitment at board level, the dedication of key individuals in a company, assistance from business continuity specialists and an enthusiastic and informed staff to carry out all the necessary processes. Remember, even if your building is not the target, it could be impacted by a nearby target.

Developing a strategy

Business continuity management can best be defined as:

'The ongoing process of ensuring the continual operation of critical business processes through the evaluation of risk and resilience, and the implementation of mitigation measures.'[1]

Business continuity management had its roots in disaster recovery planning, but as the market and the players within have matured, so too has the belief that risks to business can be mitigated as well as recovered. Disaster recovery set out with the intention of providing business with protection further to that originally provided by standard maintenance and insurance contracts. Companies have accepted that while an investment in business continuity directly affects the bottom line, and often with no immediate tangible benefits, it is the most important investment they will make. Crucially, companies have woken up to the difference between business continuity and simple insurance, which will at best replenish the value of the equipment lost, and that at a time when it could already be too late.

Business vulnerability

Each business has a different threat portfolio, as no two businesses are exactly alike. In the event of a disaster, at best an organisation can expect to suffer damage to its principal reason for operating. This will mainly be financial, but may also mean damage to reputation, share price, image and customer support. At worst it will result in the damages being irreversible, and the total failure of the business.

There are many statistics published about UK business interruption:

- Power failure accounts for over 10 per cent of all business interruptions
- 57 per cent of disasters are IT-related
- 61 per cent of companies do not publish their business continuity plans throughout their organisation
- 84 per cent of companies do not identify risks in the supply chain.

Average outage times of business interruption in the UK are:

- fire – 28 days
- IT failure – 10 days
- lightning – 22 days
- flood – 10 days
- theft – 26 days
- power failure – 1 day.

Another non-quantifiable aspect is job loss.

Arguments in the business continuity industry suggest that, rather than being the forum for doom-and-gloom merchants to excel, business continuity can be rightly seen as an investment which, rather than just reducing the impact of disaster on business, can also increase employee, investor and shareholder confidence in the company. Note, a good business continuity services provider can be measured by how regularly it is asked to speak to executive boards about the corporate requirement for continuity planning.

An effective strategy

A business continuity strategy has to meet several criteria to be effective:

- It is crucial that the board lead, and are seen to lead; the strategy must be constructed and implemented as an integral part of the company's structure.

- There can be no parts of the organisation that the strategy does not touch. As well as becoming a key and integral part of each department, the strategy has to cross all departmental and functional boundaries.

- The strategy must reflect the way the company interacts with its environment, and it must equally anticipate future demands from that environment and from within the company.

- All necessary resources (vital information such as contact names and numbers) must be available, appropriate to the nature of the company's business.

- Through a greater awareness and better management of risks, the strategy should seek to add value to the company. The reduced uncertainty in the implementation of business strategy will aid this process.

The ultimate aim is for a cost-effective and focused business continuity infrastructure.

An organisation's exposure to operational risk is a measure of its susceptibility to unwanted, unplanned events. The implication is that if the two dimensions of 'unwanted' and 'unplanned' can be managed effectively, the organisation's exposure to risk is *de facto* under control.

Conducting a business impact analysis (BIA)

At the core of continuity planning is an understanding of the organisation's unique threat profile and subsequent exposure to operational risk. Central to this is the BIA. Note, neither management nor the board will ever truly buy into the concept of business continuity until they can see the *quantified* risks of failure associated with serious business interruptions. Unless the board can see risks broken down into £s and $s they are unlikely to appreciate the issues.

A business impact analysis can be defined as 'a management-level analysis which identifies the impacts of losing company resources'; it 'measures the effect of resource loss and escalating losses over time to provide senior management with reliable data on which to base decisions on risk mitigation and continuity planning'[2].

Analysis of potential risk

The first step is to look around you:

- **Study historical data** – what types of emergencies have occurred in the community, at the company's premises and to others in the area?

- **Look at the local environment** – is the site near major transportation routes, airports, flood plains, dams or power plants? Is the company close to other companies which produce, store or transport hazardous materials (which may be a terrorist target)?

- **Analyse the technological risks** – what could result from a process or system failure? What emergencies can be caused by an employee error? Human error is the single biggest cause of workplace emergencies and can result from poor training, poor equipment maintenance, carelessness, misconduct and fatigue.

Analyse each potential emergency from beginning to end. Consider what could happen as a result of:

- prohibited access to the facility
- loss of electrical power
- communication lines going down
- ruptured gas mains, water damage
- smoke damage
- structural damage
- air or water contamination
- explosion
- building collapse
- chemical release.

Once all the risks have been considered, estimate probability and plot the results on a graph. The x-axis should indicate probability and the y-axis should show the amount of probable downtime (the outage) in terms of days. So, for example, while a power failure is highly probable, it causes minimal downtime, while flood is unlikely it will have a serious long-term effect.

Analysis of potential business impact

To assess the potential business impact, consider the loss of market share. Assess the potential impact of:

- employees unable to work
- customers unable to reach the facility
- company violation of contractual agreements

- imposition of fines and penalties or legal costs

- cash flow slowdown

- damaged reputation and image

- job losses

- lack of delivery of critical supplies

- slowed or halted product distribution

- damage to the environment

- drop in shareholder and stakeholder confidence

- compliance with statutory obligations.

Once a company appreciates the impact an interruption could have on its business, it will be in a position to minimise the risks on a priority basis. If it decides reputation is more important than profits, it should first minimise those risks that could affect its reputation.

If the BIA is done objectively, it will have a stimulating effect on the business. Employees will understand how seriously the whole continuity issue is taken. Suppliers – who have to be approached as part of the analysis – will realise they should conduct a similar exercise which in itself will help to protect the company's business. Also, the board will start to take the matter of business continuity seriously.

Implementing the strategy

Drawing up a plan

Planning is the next logical step and procedures need to be in place for staff, recovery of IT and buildings, evacuation procedures, media management and dealing with trauma, as well as any other issue pertinent to the company's operations. A business continuity plan need not be a sprawling document, and if there is confidence in the staff's capabilities, the smaller it is the better. This, together with ongoing training, will also encourage staff at all levels to back the project; any plan is useless unless the people operating it both support it and are capable of implementing it. The plan must be amended with the emergence of new staff, buildings, procedures and any technological upgrades, in conjunction with any third-party disaster recovery supplier.

Plans – operationally oriented – should address or include:

- up-to-date record drawings

- asset registers (addressing those critical to the business)

- how staff or visitors on site will be identified and accounted for

- safety procedures

- mirroring of facilities if these are critical to operations (such as duplicate dealing rooms in the City)

- fall-back communication systems

- essential utility supplies in case of mains failures

- triggers that will initiate the plan or component parts

- prioritisation of action

- any necessary training requirements

- recovery process

- stockpiling of critical supplies – do not forget dependence on single small items which are used 'once in a blue moon' but without which a service folds

- regular updates – remember, staff change, buildings develop, etc.

Plans can be developed by considering exactly what aspects of your operation the business is dependent on. It is important to create a vision of what the business capability will be in the event of an incident – will it be business as usual or will output be reduced?

Roles and responsibilities

Most companies will have a management team to continue running unaffected or undamaged sections of the business, consisting of existing personnel carrying out their normal duties. A second team – the emergency management team – has the task of accomplishing the recovery or continuance of the damaged sections of the business. Such a team is supported by the business continuity manager, business continuity teams and other teams involved in the recovery effort. Mobilisation only occurs in the event of an incident.

The constitution of these teams will have to cover many key areas:

- damage assessment and salvage

- IT recovery

- telecom and data communications recovery and call centre operations

- premises restoration

- procurement of disaster recovery resources (such as sandbags)

- media management (covering corporate communications, public relations and marketing)

- operational/production recovery

- business unit/departmental recovery

- support and coordination for such areas as personnel, transport and administration

- welfare support for staff affected by the disaster

- dealing with insurers.

There needs to be a team leader and a deputy for each business continuity team. All staff must be trained. In the event of a disaster, staff need clear communication informing them of what to do. One way of effecting this is to issue everyone with a telephone number and/or website where up-to-date details of the status of the business can be communicated (if there is a disaster). This system should be tested regularly.

Roles and responsibilities must be assigned and understood. Details must be rolled out to all sites for multi-site operations (an obvious but often overlooked fact). Back-up sites and locations have to be planned. The location of all staff members at work must be known, and full details on home addresses and phone contacts available.

Rehearsing the plan

But the work does not end once the plan has been drawn up and roles and responsibilities recognised. The final and critical step is to carry out rehearsals and maintenance. The Business Continuity Institute reckons only 18 per cent of companies rehearse their plans; but non-rehearsal is the biggest weakness in a business continuity plan. Rehearsal identifies weaknesses in both the plan and the people in the designated crisis management team. The plan has to be kept relevant and up-to-date, and rehearsals should be carried out at least biannually. Testing the plan until it runs smoothly and everyone knows exactly what to do is the only way to stay prepared.

Outsourcing disaster recovery

(See also Outsourcing, chapter 7, pages 235–254.)

Disaster recovery is fast becoming a mission-critical service. Customers need the best the industry has to offer to keep their businesses operational whatever the circumstances. As part of their business-wide disaster recovery policy, businesses almost without exception have chosen to invest in one or a series of third-party disaster recovery agreements. Disaster recovery companies can now help protect almost any vital asset a company may own. This may be a critical server or PC, or may also include standby facilities, buildings or even people.

Disaster recovery companies work by responding to a company's invocation, in a pre-contracted time frame. This is achieved through taking the actual technology and engineering support into the client or recovery site.

Risk management should be central to disaster recovery provision. Companies must first understand what they stand to lose (in real terms) in the event of an interruption to business. This will hopefully have been calculated at the BIA stage of the planning cycle. The investment in the disaster recovery project will only be a valuable one if it is outweighed by the potential loss in the event of an interruption. It is because of this that the industry has only recently seen the small and medium enterprise and public sector markets invest in disaster recovery planning.

Organisations need to make sure their disaster recovery contracts minimise their risk exposure by catering for any eventuality. A thorough understanding of IT and information systems is essential for a disaster recovery company, but business continuity and disaster recovery are primarily risk management tools.

Selecting a disaster recovery supplier

Although a disaster recovery contract is much more sophisticated than an ordinary insurance policy, it is nevertheless based on a similar principle – risk assessment. A dedicated disaster recovery company should have a comprehensive system of risk analysis that considers every type of risk with probable occurrence rates. This system should include site inspectors and a detailed evaluation of the customer's own risk management plans.

Ideally, customers should be grouped in small syndicates based on contrasting risk levels, including geographical location and industrial sector. The risk assessment should also consider factors such as:

- proximity to transport infrastructure
- electricity supplies
- telecom networks.

Each grouping should minimise the risk to individual members and ensure there are adequate resources to cope with multiple invocations.

The supplier of disaster recovery services should sell contracts on a risk, rather than unit numbers, basis. There is no point in buying a contract that covers 200 PCs only to find that when the contract is invoked, the service provider cannot supply 200 computers because it underestimated or miscalculated the risk exposure. The likelihood of invocation, rather than the number of machines covered, should be the key consideration in a disaster recovery contract.

Invest wisely

As more organisations turn their attention to disaster recovery and start investigating the market, it is only natural that some choose to select their supplier on the basis of cost. But disaster recovery, like insurance, is one area where buying on price could prove to be a mistake. Cheap insurance or disaster recovery cover can soon turn out to be expensive if the provider cannot honour its policies.

If a disaster recovery contract is very cheap, there is usually a good reason. The supplier may:

- have failed to make an adequate risk assessment
- have deliberately underestimated risk exposure to keep prices down
- be overselling its PC recovery stock to make a profit.

Demand the best

Today's competitive economic environment dictates that companies must move towards best practices and procedures. They should demand the very best the disaster recovery industry has to offer, including complete risk assessment to highlight areas of vulnerability, dedicated disaster recovery stock in secure storage facilities, and reliable up-to-date equipment. Above all, customers should insist on a disaster recovery company with a successful track record of providing total business continuity solutions for companies of all sizes.

Specifically, a good disaster recovery firm should:

- **Assess and respond to change** – it is important to remember that risk, like all business continuity issues, is not static. It changes as political, economic and social trends develop. Disaster recovery firms must understand these changes and appreciate their impact on risk calculations. This fact makes it essential for a disaster recovery company to review each customer's circumstances regularly and to advise on appropriate changes where necessary. Active response to risk assessment should ensure there are no nasty surprises if a company's disaster recovery cover has to be used in a real emergency.

- **Keep abreast of changes in technology** – not just in terms of staff training but also in their hardware profiles. Dedicated disaster recovery stock should be continually updated to keep pace with technology. As customers regularly update their IT infrastructure with more powerful and efficient equipment, they should expect their disaster recovery provider to do the same.

- **Provide regular testing for recovery plans** – a company should not have to ask for this, the disaster recovery firm should insist on it itself.

Finally, the term 'disaster' should be applied to any incident that prevents businesses operating as usual, from micro-chip theft to computer virus outbreaks, not just to large-scale incidents such as fires, floods or terrorist bombings. Ideally, it should be defined by the client.

Dealing with staff

Care of staff is the final piece of the business continuity jigsaw. A company's people constitute its best (and potentially worst) asset. It is not enough simply to include them in a business continuity plan – they must be at its core.

Remember that human error is the single largest cause of workplace emergencies with, for example, 95 per cent of all commercial building fires started by employees. People also cause disasters without malicious intent if:

- they have not been trained properly

- they have not been adequately communicated with

- they are tired or unhappy

- they are put under extreme pressure.

A company's staff is central to its success. If a whole department were to win the National Lottery as a syndicate and decide to leave, business would undoubtedly be severely disrupted. While IT would still be operational, there would be no one there to use it. Some insurance companies are offering advice and premiums against the possibility of this happening, although this will obviously not cover the potential loss to credibility and image that such an interruption would bring. Planning for such interruptions should be as central to business continuity management as the potential loss of IT.

Training

Key to this must be dedicated training of staff, where politics is discarded, and everyone is suitably prepared for the shock factor an interruption can bring.

Training will:

- raise the awareness of business continuity and its importance within the organisation

- lend ownership of the business continuity plan to employees of the organisation

- ensure the business continuity plan will be effective (even the best-laid plans won't work unless people are aware of their role and how to carry out that role)

- motivate – individuals will feel that the organisation is investing to meet their needs

- help streamline the business continuity plan (in time) as key employees become business continuity experts.

Awareness raising for senior management is often most effective when carried out by an outside agency. Outsiders will not be seen to have any ulterior motive for promoting business continuity, whereas an in-house presentation may be seen as 'empire building'. Outsiders may also be seen to be more credible. They should have had first-hand experience of crisis situations and their repercussions and be able to convince senior managers of the real risks the company faces.

Training the business continuity planner

Practical training for the business continuity planner should also be outsourced from a reputable training supplier. Often, the most effective training course is a bespoke course held on the organisation's own premises. The trainer would normally meet with the business continuity planner, look at existing business continuity plans and procedures, and from there design a course around individual training needs, addressing any information gaps identified.

Communication

Avoiding disaster

Equally important should be an effective channel of communication to ensure staff know how best to avoid causing a potential disaster. This needs to be implemented as early as induction, and continue to be regularly updated and communicated. Failing to communicate clearly and regularly not only threatens recovery should a disaster occur, it also demotivates individuals who interpret a lack of board-level endorsement of business continuity issues as an evaluation of their own personal function at the company as not 'mission-critical'.

Immediate disaster response procedures

After any full-scale interruption, such as fire or flood, management must be confident its staff are suitably prepared to act in a controlled manner and will know exactly what procedures they need to follow.

If a business evacuates its building, it must be to a location that is safe for its staff to group and far enough from any neighbouring businesses that may have been forced to do the same. Typically, businesses should avoid underground car parks, or areas too close to offices. Many people may leave personal belongings in the building and need transportation to return home, for which money should be readily available. There should be enough mobile phones for staff to check others are safe and to reassure them of their own welfare.

Staff welfare after an event

Intense emotions, numbness, flashbacks and severe reactions can be triggered by seemingly unrelated events. Professional trauma counsellors for post traumatic stress disorder (PTSD) argue that an ideal PTSD system should include both an external consultant and system facilitators within the organisation, as well as a debriefing team and occupational health staff, all tailored to the structure and specific nature of the business. A company should immediately issue all personnel with a generic statement in the aftermath of a disaster to let them know the company respects their feelings and actions, and continue to support them long after the event by including trauma counselling as an integral part of its disaster recovery plan.

Businesses cannot cope with this on their own, but must make provision for it in a contingency plan. This is where dedicated business continuity groups are able to offer advice and help, through training, seminars and other similar media. Again, dealing with trauma should not be restricted to company-specific incidents, but should encompass any severe change in mood in an employee.

Dealing with the media

In the event of a disaster, the media will want immediate responses. The crisis management function needs to focus on the media interface: one individual must be appointed through whom all communications will be made or managed, who will report directly to the business continuity management team. No individual member of the company should talk to the media – instead a unified agreed message must be given out. The crux of this vitally important area should be viewed as turning a negative scenario into a positive situation.

Media management does, of course, vary according to the type of business affected. The financial sector, for example, is very coy about releasing information, whereas companies in the retail and distribution sector generally address the situation openly.

It is widely regarded that media relations are bottom of the list where the small- to medium-sized enterprise market is concerned. This is indeed their Achilles heel. Large companies are typically much better prepared.

A unified agreed message

A good example of the success of this strategy is a situation where a fire started at a company in part of its manufacturing facility and administrative complex. The business continuity plan was invoked and the fire was brought under control. The crisis management team agreed a message which was broadcast through a glossy in-house publication with pictures of the fire, key messages and pictures of the facility after the event. The company survived. The publication was then sent to suppliers and customers – not one of them had been aware that there had been a disaster at the company. The continuity plan had ensured it was business as usual.

Inventory and restoration

Business continuity is not a complicated science but to carry it through successfully, it does require:

- dedication from a number of key people in an organisation
- total commitment at board level
- assistance where appropriate of dedicated business continuity specialists
- enthusiasm and understanding of staff
- inventory control.

Inventory control

Inventory control is a key but difficult area. The biggest problem by far is management – and management of assets in particular. Strategy-planning software is recommended to cover suppliers and inventory. Everything is relevant – all IT for example – and the complete asset list must be incorporated into the contingency plan. The software allows companies to run different scenarios of disasters to see what would be lost, what the company would still have, and where the company stands. In a disaster situation, a company might lose 100 PCs but still have 300 or so elsewhere within the company. The plan would be to allow the reallocation of existing resources, as well as having another company ready to be able to supply 100 PCs at short notice.

Restoration of the business

Many business continuity specialists will have relationships with specialist restoration companies. This will cover such reactive services as cleaning and drying, providing advice and counselling services, through to loss adjuster specialists. Environmental crises, which will not be anticipated by most people, may arise as one result of a disaster. Few are aware that in the event of a fire, mixing water with PVC results in the production of hydrochloric acid – as happened once with a chemicals and plastics supplier. The smoke was bad enough, but acid contamination caused widespread environmental damage. Specialist decontamination companies are required to deal with acid spills and damage.

Restoration is not generally the province of disaster recovery providers. It is a specialist service, which is typically outsourced. Disaster recovery providers would usually carry out an environmental survey prior to any incidents to provide a breakdown of what can be covered. Health and safety and environmental issues are key, and are core responsibilities of the facilities department.

Technology restoration

The main restoration challenges facilities managers are likely to face after a disaster relate to the integration of technology. The following are all vulnerable:

- voice over IP (VoIP)
- computer telephony integration (CTI)
- 'smart' telephone switches
- call centres.

Re-establishing matrices across such networks is automated, and in so doing poses problems for the business continuity industry. With data transmitted over voice cables, wide area networks and flexible bandwidth networks spread across Europe, single points of failure are difficult to track.

Call centres are seen as being particularly vulnerable due to the need for re-scripting the complex computerised switches deployed across the IT and communications infrastructures of these sites, should a disaster occur. Companies with one or more centres would usually need to implement a plan involving fall-back or mirroring policies.

Best practice procedures

Business continuity issues are present every day in the working environment. There are a number of procedures that companies can implement at once to improve their plans and help create a business continuity ethic across their organisations:

- Ensure visitor parking is as far from the reception area as possible, reducing the risk of suspect cars containing dangerous devices being left close to the building.

- In a multi-tenancy building, check the evacuation procedures of the other companies.

- Cover all windows in protective film to minimise damage caused by exploding glass.

- Back up all data regularly and store off site in a secure environment.

- Use a password-protected screen saver so no one can use a PC if the building has to be evacuated in a hurry.

- Perform a weekly restore test to check back-ups – restore failure is the most common reason for total data loss.

- Agree with the company's insurers now what the policy is on paying out for bomb and explosion-damaged PCs and servers, as loss assessment is lengthy and often unrewarding.

- Make sure that safe areas are away from windows, stairwells, lift shafts and rooms with suspended ceilings.

- Keep hard hats, goggles etc in every office.

- Ask insurers now for the policy on injury claims, especially if the police advise on evacuation of a building in a disaster and there is a decision not to do so.

- Make a video of the property to help with insurance claims, finding things in a hurry and loss adjusters.

- If answering machines are relied on to take messages during a building evacuation, check how many minutes of recording time there are – it is no good evacuating for four hours if there is not sufficient storage capacity to cover that period.

Simple steps to effective business continuity

- Train all key staff to the criteria already outlined.

- Identify all mission-critical processes, people and applications.

- Perform a risk and business impact analysis (BIA).

- Write the plan, preferably using an experienced third-party consultancy and a recognised software package.

- Take out any necessary additional disaster recovery cover on any mission-critical equipment.

- Ensure the plan is kept current and up-to-date, in accordance with changes in technology, staff and company direction.

Information

British Standard 7799 – UK standard for information security management, section 9 of which deals with business continuity management.

Business Continuity Institute, tel: 0870 6038783, *www.thebci.org*

Centre for Crisis Psychology, tel: 01756 796383, *www.ccpdirect.co.uk*

Cranfield School of Management, tel: 01234 751122, *www.cranfield.ac.uk/som*

Survive, international industry association, tel: 01483 710600, *www.survive.com*

1 Business Continuity Institute.
2 Business Continuity Institute.

7 Outsourcing

Chris Taylor

Outsourcing today is an increasingly common way of doing business. There are sound financial reasons for not employing permanent staff – who must be fully paid regardless of work flows – when you can buy in outside expertise which may be able to do the job better, cheaper and more quickly.

Facilities managers' time is, therefore, increasingly dominated by managing contracts with external suppliers. This has required facilities managers to develop new skills. Whereas before, facilities professionals had to be multi-skilled, multi-functional and good managers of people from a variety of backgrounds, now – on top of all that – comes the responsibility for continuing to motivate those over whom they have no immediate line management authority, while managing outcomes through a third-party employer with their hands tied by legal contracts.

Successfully working with contractors on a strategic level is another challenge facing the facilities manager. Today's outsourced contractors are 'partners' who 'add value' to a company's operations. Command and control, as a management style, would be as self-defeating here as anywhere else. Partners are looking for long-term relationships, where trust means more than mere on-time delivery. It means sharing cost bases, profit ratios and business objectives. To a degree, it also means sharing information you might prefer to keep in-house.

This chapter aims to explain the nuts and bolts of outsourcing, with guidance on the whole process from choosing what to outsource, to writing and managing the contract, to maintaining a dynamic working relationship.

What to outsource

When outsourcing first entered the management arena in the 1980s, it was all about saving money on essentially manual tasks; premises cleaning was a typical and early example. The focus is now on access to skills, with outsourcing expanding to include areas closer and closer to the centre of business; companies are now looking to buy in outside expertise so that they can concentrate on their own core activities, and contract with external suppliers to provide many or most of the tactical elements.

The shift from those early manual tasks has seen us move through other administrative and infrastructure areas, towards innovation: how can the company move further ahead faster than the competition? Outsourcing today, and the expertise that comes with the specialist contractors, has now embraced R&D, design, product management, marketing, communications, even personnel supply and management.

That development has not finished. Already into strategic functions (see **Figure 1**), it is likely that outsourcing of core business areas – even the strategic direction of the company – will follow.

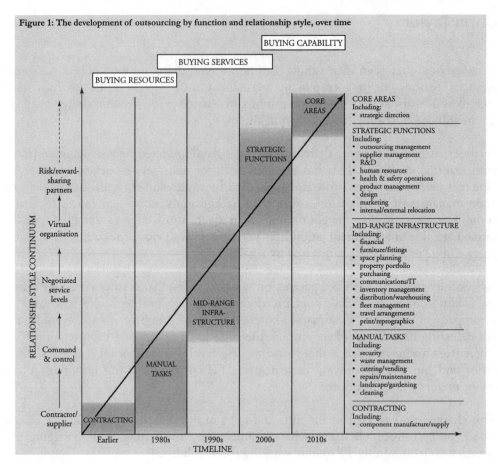

Figure 1: The development of outsourcing by function and relationship style, over time

Outsourcing should no longer be seen as just a money-saving management device or tactic, but considered in terms of the potential value it can bring to a business. It may cost more to outsource, but the job may be better performed, the company image may be enhanced, and it may release expensive management time for core activities.

So what, in your specific business, should you outsource and what should you retain in-house?

Core and non-core activities

A first assessment in considering whether or not to outsource is defining what you consider to be your core business activities. Current practice dictates that companies retain control of these areas – though, as suggested above, this may well change in the future.

The thinking behind this is that organisations should be left to concentrate on their core business activities without the distraction of providing and managing non-core activities. These are better provided by an outsourced commercial organisation whose personnel can be better motivated and rewarded in an environment that recognises their special training and skills.

Of course, what is defined as 'core' will vary significantly from organisation to organisation. A good example here would be the law firm that outsources its conveyancing work on the basis that its core skill is commercial litigation and it is from the latter that it earns the majority of its income.

Consider next the degree to which any selected function is routine and well-defined. If it can be easily defined, then it can be more easily measured, and managed at arm's length – and remember, you are not devolving responsibility, just functionality. So, if a non-core function can be defined and measured, it may be worth considering for outsourcing.

Anticipating pitfalls

Before embarking on any outsourcing initiative, there are a number of potential problems which should be anticipated and evaluated. Many of these are concerned with the people affected by the change in operation, others are to do with changes in the business itself and the manner in which the business is undertaken.

People issues

It is unfortunate that outsourcing is rarely welcomed by a workforce, especially that section responsible for the function being outsourced. Very often it is perceived as downsizing by other means, and strenuous efforts are made to oppose it – diverting business time and energy from development to fire-fighting. Most of the problems that can arise can be pre-empted through intensive discussions and planning. Talk continuously with staff; be certain they understand what is happening, why, how and when – and understand that simply telling them is not the same as being certain they understand.

Before proceeding, ask the following questions:

- Is there a convincing case for outsourcing? People – and unions – will generally accept an argument in which the logic is unassailable, in which all the numbers, from every source, have been reviewed and checked, and where every aspect has been openly examined. Secrecy is not a good strategy here.

- What are the legal requirements? Does *TUPE* apply? (See **Complying with the law on staff, casual and contract workers, p 97.**) How much will it cost to be generous, rather than just to stick to the letter of the law? Is the cost worth it?

- How have the levels of knowledge and skill which exist within the organisation been established, especially within the area to be outsourced? Is the loss of some of these skills acceptable – most probably as a gift to the contractor – or should some or all of these be kept in-house as a supervisory or management resource?

- Is everything possible being done to involve and inform all staff – not just in the affected areas – of the progress towards outsourcing? Be aware, however, that different circumstances apply when an internal bid is on the table alongside external competitive bids; managing information in these circumstances is especially challenging. The function must continue, but one bidder has an effective stranglehold; tell them too much, and external bidders will claim favouritism; too little, and the existing team claim secrecy. The only option here is honesty and openness, supported by a policy, clearly stated, of what is acceptable and what is not, and what information is to be shared and what is not.

Business change

All businesses change. Before entering into an outsourcing contract, you need to consider the following questions so that you are not hampered by a restrictive contract as you pursue your development goals:

- What happens if you are bought out, or buy out another company? They may have a state-of-the-art in-house provision for what you have outsourced – or they may have none, and you need to look at rapid expansion of the service.

- What happens if you have a fundamental shift in business focus – if you decide, for example, to close plant, move headquarters of strategically-important offices, or pursue a new but promising business direction which affects the need for the outsourced service?

- What happens in cases of force majeure – in the case, for example, of a significant market downturn which leaves expensive equipment and facilities underused? What provision has been made to allow for a ratcheting down of the service, and the associated costs?

Process change

The way business is done changes continuously. Think how long you have been using email as a key communications channel. How many standalone fax machines are still used regularly in your business? Do your younger staff even know what a telex machine looks like? Such technological changes can significantly alter the manner in which an outsourcing contract will work over time. For example, if outsourcing had been a significant factor a generation ago, the typing pool would almost certainly have been a prime candidate for it – now typing pools simply do not exist. And it's not just the technology; working and management styles can alter considerably over the duration of a contract.

Consider the following:

- What structural changes could affect the outsourcing agreement? Consider, for example, the effect on the catering service of introducing flexible working; or how devolving autonomy from head office to regional offices could impact on supplier strategies, from transport to telephony or utilities.

- Bearing in mind the growth in power of computing (remember the old axiom which still holds good: every two years double the power/speed and halve the price), what could you be doing for free which used to require specialist input? Think of display media, and how that function has been usurped with presentation software packaged into most laptops, or of the production of newsletters, posters, or other promotional material.

Choosing contractors

The tender document

Time spent preparing the tender document is a requirement, not an option. Although you may feel there is only one logical choice for contractor, it is essential that you approach the tender process with an open mind, and ensure that the process is competitive. Do not rule out the possibility of bids from angles you may not have considered, not least the existing function team, and do not assume you know all the potential bidders.

The process involves three stages:

- detailed specification of requirements

- invitation to tender

- preferred contractor selection.

The first stage, the detailed specification of requirements, is the most time consuming. It involves a microscopically close examination of the function concerned, and a thorough definition of that function. This is necessary because few if any functions of a business can be said to be completely self-contained; all have areas of overlap with other functions, and these must be resolved before you can spell out unequivocally exactly what you are asking a contractor to take on. It may be as simple as defining reporting procedures from company to contractor, or it may involve changing internal processes – between, say, the area being outsourced and the accounts department – to enable an unambiguous command line.

The outcome of this stage should be a lengthy document. It will describe the function in detail, in terms of actions as well as outcomes, and how it dovetails into the organisation. If changes are planned or being considered that will affect the function, they should be spelt out here – but not to a degree that compromises company confidentiality. While the document should state that the contents should be treated as commercially confidential, it is essentially a public document over whose circulation you have less than perfect control.

Invitation to tender

So, to whom should the document be sent? The second stage, the invitation to tender, can be as broad or as narrow as you choose. One option is to advertise in an appropriate trade journal or newspaper, send out multiple copies of the tender document, and accept bids from all and sundry; more than one company has discovered the perfect outsourcing partner in just this manner, from businesses they would not have heard of otherwise. Alternatively, you may prefer to limit the number of bids at the outset through a preselection process, either through advertisements asking for 'expressions of interest', or through a strict invitation-only process where you involve only a shortlist of contractors already known to you, or discovered through advertising or word of mouth recommendation. The 'expressions of interest' route ultimately comes down to a similar selection – all manner of relevant information can be asked of prospective bidders to enable an informed choice of candidates to invite to tender.

Final selection

The next challenge is to draw closer to a final selection. You will have received a wealth of information, and almost certainly business references, from several companies, and three or four will stand out as meriting deeper investigation. A systematic comparison is important, as is involving people close to the function to be outsourced – but clearly, this can be sensitive if the in-house team are among the bidders, whether they have made it past the first 'cut' or not. Be sure to establish what each candidate has to offer. You are not just buying another pair of hands, but a functional expert with a brain. If this is to be the partnership you want and expect, it is reasonable to expect them to bring ideas as well as skills with them, and you should listen carefully to their suggestions as to how the function can be tailored more closely to the objectives spelt out in the tender document.

After discussions, and perhaps more formal interviews, it is likely you will be able to reach 'preferred contractor' status with one candidate. This is the goal of the exercise so far, and, arguably, where the real work begins!

Final negotiations

Next in the process is the interval between the selection of a preferred bidder and the contract signing. This is when 'proceed with caution' is wise advice; this stage can be compared with the period between choosing a new home and exchanging contracts. Both parties have reached an understanding and have a period of time – which their enthusiasm may seek to shorten – to make certain that the decision is the right one; mistakes can be costly.

Sometimes a bidder will fall at this final hurdle. Through a detailed examination of needs and abilities on either side, your goal is to agree a service level agreement which will be your working blueprint for the day-to-day operation of the contract. These final negotiations may reveal incompatibilities, and it is better to discover this before signing contracts than afterwards. Remember that the selection of a contractor is not necessarily a one-off process; you may almost get to the 'altar' and then have to start all over again with a different partner.

Creating a synergy

So what are the areas you should be discussing? It is important for any company to start with questions of its preferred bidder:

- What skills and abilities do both parties have that will provide a synergy, creating added value?

- How will intellectual property and expertise be managed to the benefit of each?

- What cultural factors will make working together easier or more difficult?

Good channels of communication and working towards shared goals are critical from day one, and objectives must be clearly defined. Ensure you discuss:

- the establishment of unequivocal and open lines of communication between named individuals at all levels of operation

- the level of priority that customer satisfaction should hold – the final consumer of your goods or services will notice, and be confused by, conflicting priorities.

Flexibility

Look, above all, for flexibility to adapt to the changes that will come. Think of the future, and look for special skills a partner can bring to the table:

- Can the outsourcing contractor offer a strategic plan?

- Can the outsourcing contractor offer potentially value-adding concepts?

- Can the partner demonstrate commitment to a long-term relationship?

A two-way process

Remember that to turn the supplier into an asset, they need to be part of the organisation, and this means flexibility on both sides. The choice of supplier may come down to how much risk a company is prepared to take. Things will change, and companies should be willing to adapt:

- be willing to change your corporate culture if necessary

- focus on business objectives

- consider making your outsourcing partner a risk-sharing partner – a recent trend is to offer the supplier shares within the client company so they have a direct interest in profits

- establish and agree metrics to reward risk sharing.

And, of course, accept that all parties need to feel that what is offered and received represents value for money.

The specific procurement process particular to PPP projects is outlined in Chapter 4 **Financial Management, pp 163–206.**

The supplier market

When researching possible contractors, it may be useful for client companies to understand that there are four pedigrees within facilities management service providers, each with different experience, priorities, and business focus. They are:

* single service background – these companies started by providing one service and expanded into others to meet client demands. Examples include Drake & Scull.

* construction background – these companies diversified into facilities management during the 1990s recession. Examples include Amec, Jarvis, and Tarmac.

* professional construction background – these are managing agents, quantity surveyors, architects, and engineering companies which have moved into facilities management. Examples include W. S. Atkins.

* client background – many companies have spun off from former employers and expanded to offer the same or expanded services. Examples include FM2, from Allied Dunbar; Johnson Controls (via Procord), from IBM; and CBX, from Xerox.

The well-informed client will consider which approach and background may be most appropriate for its requirements, as each background style will have its own traits, skills and experiences, and not all will suit every market.

Service level agreements

A service level agreement (SLA) is not a summary document, nor is it an outsourcing contract. It is, quite simply, a detailed memorandum specifying the outcomes from many elements of the outsourced function. SLAs need to be defined in detail, as they are an important way of measuring an outsourcing supplier's performance. The most common metrics of quality, speed and accuracy clearly enable each partner to assess the current level of service the buyer is receiving. If performance slides, the SLA may trigger penalties. Putting these metrics in writing provides a legal basis (in the worst case) for contract termination – and gives the client the ability to influence the supplier's performance.

Negotiating an effective SLA that will provide value in the outsourcing relationship need not be – should not be – a one-sided process. The willingness of a preferred bidder to enter into the negotiation of the SLA design speaks volumes for their future acceptance of it, and indeed, they may have as much or more experience in the task as the client. Furthermore, while it is important to specify the desired outcomes in detail, the SLA must not be so prescriptive in the inputs side that it prevents the contractor from seeking ways to do a better job.

An effective SLA:

* identifies certain service levels or performance standards that the outsourcing contractor must meet or exceed

* specifies the consequences for failure to achieve one or more service levels

- includes credits or bonus incentives for performance that exceeds targets

- establishes the level of importance of key service areas by a weighting system.

SLAs are not easy to design or negotiate. But a comprehensive, fair and effective SLA is critical for a successful outsourcing relationship. In the course of negotiation, outsourcing clients and suppliers have the opportunity to learn much about how their future partner will approach important issues in the outsourcing relationship, which can only help in the smooth running of a contract.

Penalties and incentives

The most important factor at this stage is for the outsourcing supplier and client to agree on credible measurements, and establish what would be classed as above and below acceptable levels of service. By weighting the impact on key areas of exceeding or falling short of these measurements, to total 100 per cent, then penalties or payouts can be tailored to fit. If the outsourcing supplier then fails to achieve some of the key service levels, the percentage missed for the month can be applied as a service level credit against a proportion of the invoice.

Often the parties identify a subset of the key service levels as critical. For these elements, the parties will agree that more extreme penalties will apply, even that the outsourcing contract may be terminated if the levels are not reached to the frequency specified. Contract law generally entitles one party to terminate a contract if the other party 'materially breaches' the contract; defining critical service levels and providing specific conditions for termination eliminates ambiguity by determining what is, and what is not, 'material'.

Reasonable clients will avoid over-measuring and trying to include every imaginable service level. They should agree to fair credits for failures in meeting service levels. Suppliers should be willing to understand that the client requires significant protection in the SLA and to acknowledge that there are certain levels of performance that would justify termination of the contract.

Similarly, exceeding the levels may be seen as a potential trigger for bonus payments or other incentives, payable when a quantifiable benefit to the client can be seen, far beyond any expected performance as laid down in the SLA. It is important for the contractor to know they will be properly rewarded for success. If the supplier can add real value to the client's business, clients should be willing to share the value gained as a result of superior performance. In this way, service level objectives become highlighted as a critical parameter for both parties.

Force majeure clauses

Force majeure clauses excuse a party's failure to perform if the failure resulted from a natural disaster. In outsourcing contracts, negotiating the provisions of excused performance in the context of the outsourcing contractor's responsibilities and liabilities can be challenging and time consuming. Examples include:

- failures resulting from the client's non-performance
- failures of third parties
- failures in hardware and software.

Outsourcing suppliers tend to seek a broad definition of force majeure, while clients seek a narrow, tightly-defined provision. Most organisations accept that a fair agreement lies somewhere in the middle, without entirely absolving the supplier from the responsibility of correcting and mitigating the effects of an excused performance failure.

What to include

Every SLA will be different, tailored to the specifics of the contract and its application, but they will usually have several sections in common, including:

- introduction
- definition, boundaries and parameters of the service being outsourced
- minimum acceptable service levels for all aspects of the job
- detailing of improvements from the status quo (if sought)
- agreed cultural norms of (for example) appearance (if contractors are to be perceived as company employees)
- quality criteria (where contractors have to supply materials)
- who reports to whom, how, when, and why
- how service levels are to be monitored, when and by whom
- measures for rewarding exceptional performance, if appropriate
- measures for penalising under-performance, if appropriate
- general payment terms and conditions
- conflict resolution procedures.

Contractual arrangements

Having established an agreement with a single supplier, the next step is to finalise the contract. Only when all the details are agreed is it time to sign. It can take well over a year to reach this stage, and should not be rushed: it is a contract you ideally never want to terminate, so it is important to get it right first time.

The function of the contract

The contract should define both the work itself and the manner in which it is to be undertaken. If the task to be undertaken is ambiguously defined, both in terms of scope (the work to be done) and style (when and to what standard), then there is room for individual interpretation – and one interpretation will almost certainly differ from the next. The contract process is the best system to define unambiguously what is needed and at the same to lay down performance criteria so the execution of the contract can be monitored.

The SLA is arguably the most important document in the tactical day-to-day management of the relationship. It provides the key performance criteria by which success or failure will be assessed. While in industry practice the SLA is a separate addendum to the outsourcing contract, in law it is not a separate agreement, but merely a set of terms and conditions of the substantive contract itself. In other words, the function of the SLA is to specify the goals of the outsourcing relationship, while the contract is the administrative document which outlines all the practical arrangements necessary to ensure these goals are met.

What should the contract include?

As well as terms and conditions, renewal dates and criteria, payment terms, and arrangements for rewards or penalties in the case of over or underperformance (with definitions of these being spelt out), a contract should build in the following considerations:

Flexibility

If you know what's going to happen, you make plans. If you don't know, you make contingency plans. It is inevitable that circumstances – markets, technology, supply chain, and so forth – will change, and that some of those changes are likely to be radical. A contract which allows no flexibility, therefore, is a bad contract.

Unless the contract allows for change, the client may find himself tied down to the letter of the contract by the supplier, even though it may be obvious that a failure to change will be detrimental to the business. That will clearly lead to distress, or worse, dispute.

Disputes and exit strategy

Be aware that there are likely to be disagreements – every relationship has them – and there needs to be an agreed methodology for dealing with them, configured in such a way that the work continues while the disagreement is resolved. This methodology should be written into the contract.

In the worst possible case, disagreement may lead to a complete breakdown of the relationship, so an exit strategy should also be agreed. In many cases contracts are expensive and difficult to terminate prematurely. Without careful management – and the right contract in the first place – the outsourcing contractor can easily gain the upper hand, which can be disastrous for the prospects of a long-term relationship. No client should be obliged to continue with an unsatisfactory contract, simply because the implications of breakdown are worse than maintaining the status quo.

The client should ensure the existence of a reasonable exit route in case the relationship becomes unmanageable. Terminating a contract is the worst case scenario in the relationship: ideally, the contract should define less final consequences for any lack of service or failure to provide to agreed service levels.

Decision-making

Outsourcing relationships should be true partnerships, but one party must take the lead. There are decisions where there may be no right or wrong in qualitative terms, but where someone has to call the shots. It should be made explicit in the contract that while the partnership recognises the expertise brought to the relationship by the supplier, the ultimate call comes from the client.

Contract 'management'

Anyone can sign a contract, but unless it is adhered to, monitored and driven to its optimum, it is simply paperwork. Managing the contract is indisputably the clever bit. It is not the same as managing the same process when handled in-house. Once contracts have been signed and the supplier is providing the service, you have less direct influence on how the job is undertaken, as you have delegated away the tactical element of execution – except in so far as the contract allows. You can no longer hire and fire, or change emphasis or priority; you have a set of rules set down that must be adhered to, no less by you than by the contractor.

Yet at the same time you have a team to inspire and motivate – but this team does not report to you. You have to be seen to be interested and involved, to be monitoring and checking; it is important that the supplier shares your enthusiasm for continuous improvement. Unless you are seen to be involved in the contract – without treading on the toes of the supplier – demotivation will follow, leading to declining standards and ultimate contract failure. These issues are covered in more detail in the section on **Building the relationship, pp 248–252.**

Consequences, positive or negative, can take the form of financial penalties or additional payments for high levels of performance by the supplier (see **Penalties and incentives, p 243**).

Key performance indicators

A balanced scorecard

If an outsourcing relationship is to be successful, clear measurements are needed to manage achievements and expectations on both sides. One of the best ways to establish this is through the balanced scorecard approach.

A balanced scorecard involves goal setting, target setting and an information collection process. It includes a number of categories that represent the most general level of expectations – usually around cost, service and quality. Categories are divided into a number of subsets, known as attributes, defined through a joint buyer-provider process, with the exact composition and number depending on the goals of the relationship and the service in question. Choices are made about an appropriate measure for each attribute.

When establishing the scorecard, some of the key areas to consider are:

- Does the overall scorecard balance long-term and short-term goals, and financial and non-financial goals?

- Do the metrics and measures compensate for each other's blind spots? Consider balancing subjective and objective measures, and qualitative and quantitative measures.

- Are multiple perspectives taken into consideration? Does the scorecard balance the perspectives of the strategic and operation managers, the buyer and the provider, and so forth?

What will a balanced scorecard achieve?

Having balanced scorecards in place during an outsourcing relationship accomplishes at least three things, namely:

- a client-defined, mutually agreed performance management system to reward exemplary service and to discourage sub-par performance

- an established set of metrics by which performance is measured with the opportunity to make ongoing changes in service levels and expectations

- the provision of historical information to help decide the future of the relationship when it comes to contract renewal.

Client satisfaction

Signing an outsourcing arrangement should not mean the abdication of responsibility for a business activity to an outside provider. While one of the true benefits of outsourcing is the transfer of responsibility to an outside expert who is well-equipped to handle the task, clients must put systems in place to ensure their own satisfaction with the service. Below are some guidelines for measurement and evaluation.

- **Measure what you want to manage** – you can only manage what you can measure and you can only measure what you can see. However, it is possible to come up with creative and useful solutions to measuring and managing activities that were previously beyond reach – cost savings and customer satisfaction to name but two.

- **Change what you can control** – not measuring and, in turn, holding providers accountable for things beyond their control is counterproductive and frustrating for all. The activities and measures must be within the service provider's control and having them at the table defining the scorecard is the best way to understand that.

- **Recycle and reuse, don't repeat** – the last thing anybody wants is competing measurement systems; a single 'good enough' system will do – defined as providing the information you need to manage with. The balanced scorecard can absorb earlier measurement systems; don't reinvent the wheel – use the best measures that already exist.

- **Set the systems early** – construct a balanced scorecard as early as possible, customise it once the provider is chosen and then jointly set target levels. A provider's ability and willingness to live up to the criteria set in a balanced scorecard can be a consideration in the selection process.

- **Timely and efficient measurement** – the measurement system to support a balanced scorecard should collect only what is useful and not duplicate material. Unnecessary and overlapping measurement processes are wasteful. Collecting information to support balanced scorecards should also happen as soon after the fact as possible.

- **Measure realistically** – be realistic in what can be inexpensively, quickly, and easily measured. Certain things should not be scorecarded. For example, don't measure the number of failed state inspections – such events do not provide for ongoing management of the relationship, they represent significant and immediate problems.

- **Use all the measurement tools and data sources at your disposal** – there are at least three tools which buyers and providers have at their disposal:

  o **Surveys** – these can be used with external customers, internal customers, and employees of both provider and buyer. Surveys are effective at collecting behavioural information or opinions but the measures tend to be subjective. Relying on this method leaves the process open to serious questions and undercuts the ideal of balance. When they take the form of checklists, surveys provide for more objectivity.

  o **Management information systems** – these can provide valuable information on costs, inventories and other accounting-related data; however they are predominantly financial.

  o **Audits** – these avoid the subjectivity of surveys, while collecting non-financial and other specific information not present in management information systems designed for other purposes.

Building the relationship

Surveys have consistently shown that companies are, in general, dissatisfied with the overall results of their outsourcing agreements. So how can you make the outsourcing relationship one of value, providing ongoing benefit to your business?

Continuous improvement model

To have an outsourcing relationship that works it is important to consider the supplier as a source of value that needs to be constantly realigned if the contract is to succeed. Levels of service need to be continuously improved if they are to result in long-term relationships. This calls for flexibility, which starts in the planning stage and should be the result of candid communication, frankness and a willing approach to working with the aim of creating a 'win-win' situation. With a good plan, there should be flexibility to meet new opportunities and redefine the relationship on an ongoing basis. That means measuring the value and rewarding the supplier on their ability to deliver that value. Then the bar can be raised on a continual basis and the relationships can be moved and aligned with business objectives.

Defining added value

Decide early on how to define added value. Look for one or more of the following:

- the ability of the supplier to come up with the initiatives that reshape the relationship to meet ongoing objectives
- the ability and willingness of the supplier to set and meet concrete and measurable service levels
- the ability of the supplier to commit to and meet specific financial targets.

Clear channels of communication need to be mapped out which encourage the supplier to be proactive and bring ideas to the strategy of your business. The supplier should also be rewarded for ideas and revenue opportunities, with rewards reflecting the benefits brought by the implementation of ideas.

Good communication

Ideally the relationship should start with each organisation appointing an informed and empowered point of contact, to act as contract administrator. These two individuals are responsible for making the relationship work – as opposed to the site managers who will oversee the day-to-day running of the function on site. This is an important first step in implementing a successful outsourcing relationship. Other factors which help to build and sustain the partnership include:

- a strong management team
- a dedicated account manager
- a good working relationship between management on both sides
- a consistent communication chain
- a single point of contact – possibly the administrator (see above) – to resolve queries and remove duplication
- a database of written communication between parties to track commitments.

Trust is essential in developing a successful outsourcing relationship, and communications need to be based on this. An outsourcing contractor should be instrumental in the client's success, therefore they need to have access to the information they need. It is necessary to:

- drive home what the business is all about

- highlight objectives

- be frank in disclosing issues facing the company or its industry – both short and long-term

- give the supplier the tools they need to achieve or maintain status as an industry leader

- be clear about the roles in the relationship.

Coordinating standards and budgets

Relationships need to be developed at multiple levels throughout the organisations involved, to create the trust and understanding required for long-term success. Both parties need to coordinate standards, such as protocols and business processes and perform joint budgeting exercises to understand the key cost driver information inherent in the other's infrastructure. In addition, there needs to be qualitative information associated with the reliability and performance of the outsourced services.

Anticipating problems

Most problems arise because the client underestimates the future work they will require the supplier to undertake. Also, the client often fails to say up front what work is in the scope of the contract and what work is additional. This can lead to a misunderstanding of responsibilities. For example, the manager of a client's data centre is frequently retained in-house to help manage the supplier. That manager is familiar with the way the centre used to be operated in the past but, of course, the supplier may choose to do things differently. This may cause problems all round.

As this example shows, most management problems are not actually 'people' problems, more a result of a lack of clarity over how key objectives are to be implemented. This highlights the importance of the contract. Without a suitable contract the two parties enter their 'marriage' and may go into the honeymoon stage, where everyone is enthusiastic and focused on the objectives of the agreement and the potential benefits that are to follow.

At this stage everyone:

- talks frequently

- gets involved with fine-tuning objectives

- works enthusiastically towards service levels

- has great expectations.

However, too often time erodes this initial flurry of excitement and a sense of anti-climax develops which can lead to exasperation.

At this point:

- communication breaks down

- key people leave

- the original mission is lost

- the client and supplier forget original objectives

- frustrations grow.

Ensuring that the contract is clearly defined, that flexibility is built into it and that there is constant scope for communication and assessment and reassessment of the tasks and responsibilities in hand will help prevent misunderstandings and frustrations.

Team dynamics

Most outsourcing agreements represent long-term, dynamic relationships in which unforeseen opportunities and conditions will appear and will have to be addressed. This means there is a need for flexibility, which should be built in to the first stages of the relationship. However, keeping on an even keel can be fraught with difficulties. Day-to-day decisions have strategic impact while lack of planning and misunderstanding can create difficulties in moving forward. Personality clashes can also cause rifts – managers on both sides need to have good people skills.

Facilities professionals should consider the following guidelines:

- the client should ensure that the supplier's best people are working in the relationship

- there should be contractual terms and conditions spelling out certain processes and disciplines

- the client should have the first right of refusal for members of the supplier's team.

Regular reviews

Many problems can be avoided if the dangers are anticipated and dealt with in the planning process. Communication and incentives for success are key to nurturing long-term relationships, with the company's outsourcing team focusing daily on the mission in hand. Outsourcing specialists often suggest that companies should communicate clearly on a month-to-month basis, discussing performance and anticipating any changes for the next month. These discussions can provide short-term measurement to monitor ongoing behaviour, and benefits expected to be achieved over the length of the contract can be reaffirmed.

> ### Successful contract management
>
> The key messages are:
>
> - avoid relationship deterioration by planning for the pitfalls
> - schedule monthly meetings to reaffirm objectives and measure performance
> - give the supplier financial incentives to succeed.

Managing the end of the contract

A key area, often overlooked at the outset of any contractual relationship, is what happens when the contract comes to an end – it will, eventually. And here we are not necessarily talking about a contract ending in dispute, rather what happens to a contract when its agreed term has run. Few companies can afford to go 'on hold' while they sort themselves out; competitors are waiting to swoop in and take advantage of the gap in the market.

So what then are the alternatives on contract termination? Assuming the function remains necessary, they are limited. You can:

- continue with the same contractor
- find a different contractor
- bring the function back in-house.

Many companies stay with existing providers through inertia – and fear of change. They may be unsatisfied with the existing arrangement, but they suspect that it would be easier to get improved contract terms, and tighter SLAs, from a new contractor, than by renegotiating the existing arrangement. This has dubious logic! The possibility – necessity, even – for change and continuous improvement should have been built in from the start.

Changing contractors can take a year or more to organise, and is fraught with hazards, including the possibility of delaying tactics from the outgoing contractor, removal of key staff and run-down of efficiency, and possible confusion over ownership issues of dedicated equipment. Many of the same reservations apply if attempts are made to bring operations back in-house – key assets, in terms of people, knowledge and equipment, have been relinquished – and you should also ask why you chose to outsource in the first place.

Key lessons

First, too few contracts have adequate provision concerning termination or expiry, and fail to take account of the way business needs will change over the relationship term. Second, usually, it is 'better the devil you know' – that is, it is preferable to stay with the existing provider, who knows your business. If you want new SLAs, renegotiate. Asking incumbents, with others, to re-tender can focus everyone's attention on the key aspects of the task, as well as pinpointing whether there really is a better option out there.

Outsourcing the postroom – case study

Mailroom Management Services (MMS) is a specialist manager of postroom and associated activities, with many blue chip clients. The company is expanding fast in an area increasingly being viewed as a candidate for outsourcing. Why outsource the postroom? It is non-core, and savings are available when the specialists come in. Improvements can always be made to performance criteria, and these are easily measured and monitored, for example:

- delivery-to-desk time of first mail delivery

- final acceptance time for same-day despatch

- speed of internal mail

- accuracy of sorting and delivery

- ability to track items requiring signature

- service/costs from couriers.

Also, the potential for added value is vast. Typically, the postroom is frantic early and late in the day. A well-organised operation, claims MMS, can use the quiet time for other activities, perhaps mail-related (like stuffing envelopes or assisting with bulk mailshots, traditionally operations which leave the building), or for other areas, including taking on responsibility for stationery, archiving, loading bay management, the conference rooms, and more. Postroom staff can tour the building regularly, suggests MMS. They can check safety equipment is present, that light bulbs work, notice boards are up to date, even that water coolers or photocopiers are full and functioning.

In 1997, MMS won Shell International's mailroom contract. Previously, mail services at Shell's London headquarters – housing 3,000 people – were managed in-house, with both employed and contracted staff. The decision to put the service to tender was driven by the need to save money on international couriers (Shell has offices in 158 countries), and a wish to see added value from the service. Some issues also needed attention, including the reliability of the service during staff absences; the need to improve service levels; to introduce a competitive environment for third-party suppliers; and effective billing and re-charging procedures.

MMS was invited to tender along with several other suppliers. First stage was the tender document which outlined the required service provision. At the same time, prospective bidders were invited to a briefing.

MMS submitted its proposal, and was invited (with other suppliers who submitted) to present its proposal to the panel overseeing the tender process. In due course MMS and two other companies progressed to the second stage, when each was asked to identify reference sites with similarities to the service proposed for Shell.

After reviewing the reference sites, the panel determined that MMS was the preferred supplier, but they would need to go through the proposal in detail before being awarded the contract. A series of meetings agreed final costings, mobilisation, issues surrounding *TUPE* etc, and this culminated in the signing of a three-year contract — which has since been extended.

The service has grown to more than 6,000 inbound items from Royal Mail and up to 200 outbound couriers every working day, with 10 per cent fewer staff and reduced costs from when the contract was awarded. Service has improved. New training schemes maximise efficiency through (for example) the ability to move staff between roles to cover for holidays and sickness, through additional internal deliveries, and through improved monitoring procedures which allow a single invoice to be supported by computer analysis, so Shell's accounting department can allocate costs effectively.

Added value has been introduced by operatives taking on additional responsibilities, and through new IT-based track-and-trace technology allowing a complete transit history of items from originator to addressee.

8 Transport Policies

Frank Booty

Transport costs remain one of the biggest factors impacting on the bottom line. For some businesses, it is the second largest cost after personnel. With the government's tax changes now impacting on companies' transport budgets, this situation is unlikely to change. However, with businesses constantly evolving towards a more global working culture, the need for transport is greater than ever before. How can facilities managers seek to resolve this conflict of interests?

Careful travel planning can bring huge benefits to a company. The environmental imperatives remain: transport-derived air pollution, carbon dioxide emissions and traffic congestion still need to be reduced. But the reasons for developing travel plans go beyond environmentalism. Other benefits include time and cost savings, greater flexibility and accessibility for the workforce.

It is easy to overlook the parking issue. The car park represents the largest untapped asset in the property portfolio, with brand names waking up to the potential they offer for floor graphic advertising. But the car park is also becoming the target of both government regulators and taxmen. How can facilities managers ensure they get the most out of their car parks, while taking new government guidance into account?

Travel plans

Legislation

A travel plan is an effective site management tool that also meets the need for continuous improvement in environmental management. When the White Paper *New Deal for Transport: Better for Everyone* was published in July 1998, 'green' transport plans became an explicit component in the new approach to transport. The DTLR (Department for Transport, Local Government and the Regions) now uses a more generic term, 'travel plans', which reflects the department's increasing recognition of the function as a mainstream management tool, rather than as a fringe activity.

Facilities managers must familiarise themselves with the final version of the government's *Planning Policy Guidance Note 13: Transport* (PPG13), issued on 27 March 2001[1]. The guidance pushes environmental points by encouraging all businesses to try their utmost to encourage their staff to take up car sharing, use public transport and work from home wherever practicable. Local councils are expected to consider setting targets for the adoption of travel plans by local businesses.

Planning authorities have to advise local businesses on the impact of this legislation. The squeeze on using the car to get employees to and from the workplace is starting to be felt. Companies contemplating expansion of their sites, relocation, increasing the workforce, or those involved with out-of-town business parks or retail sites will have to draw up different strategies. From now on, travel plans, building databases of potential car sharers, offering company bus/coach travel facilities and/or concessions, bicycle parks, and so on, will all have increasingly important parts to play.

Objectives

Travel plans are designed to reduce the adverse environmental impacts of transport to and from a specific site or building. Travel plans seek to reduce over-dependence on cars, especially when the driver is alone, through encouraging changes in travel behaviour in favour of more environmentally-benign modes, such as public transport, walking and cycling. To complement this, particularly where it is more difficult to provide alternatives to the car, travel plans incorporate measures to reduce the impact of vehicles (for example, through greener fleet management).

Travel plans also seek to reduce the need to travel – both travel undertaken by employees when carrying out their duties, for example when attending meetings, exhibitions, training courses or visiting clients – and travel to and from the workplace. Alternative methods of communication, such as telephone conference calls, are encouraged, as well as vehicle sharing.

Travel plans: a management tool

For facilities managers, the travel plan is a powerful management tool that offers considerable benefits to the company or organisation. Travel plans can help a business to:

- stay operational at a time of expansion
- reduce the costs of car parking provision and/or business travel costs
- improve, or at least maintain, staff journey times to and from work
- contribute to a healthier environment
- enjoy the additional bonus of a healthier workforce.

Guide to effective travel planning

Convincing the CEO

The first step is always to convince the CEO and other senior managers that the travel plan combines resource, facility and site management in one package and that it is essential for the future of the organisation and its site. In other words, the adoption of a travel plan is a strategic issue which needs director-level support.

Establishing the baseline

A survey of staff travel habits needs to be conducted. The questions should be designed to ensure a comprehensive understanding can be gained of how people are currently travelling and what changes they may be willing to make in the future. This should be complemented by a series of audits to obtain a clear picture of current arrangements regarding the following:

- personal security for cyclists and pedestrians on site and along key routes to the site
- business travel – staff travel expenses budget, mileage undertaken and by what method
- car parking arrangements and charges
- traffic counts by vehicle type, time of day and day of week
- access to site by bus, train, on two wheels and on foot
- shift patterns and their impact on staff travel to work.

A package of complementary measures

Possible measures to take include:

- car sharing
- charges for car parking
- encouraging public transport use
- enhanced bus services
- improving cycling facilities
- improving the pedestrian environment (on and off site)
- reduction in the need to travel.

The emphasis placed on different measures varies enormously, according to local circumstances. If, as is the case at a major Liverpool hospital, over two-thirds of staff already travel to work by public transport, then the emphasis will be on helping them to avoid switching to the car. On the other hand, if the site is never going to be well-served by public transport and your staff live in rural areas some distance from it, sharing car journeys to work is likely to be a more important measure. The priorities for action will be determined in part by the baseline assessment and in part by what is judged politically and economically feasible.

Consultation about the plan

A transport working group should be established, which should act as a reference point throughout the development of the travel plan and then assist with its implementation. Membership should comprise:

- facilities manager

- human resources manager

- environmental manager

- staff representatives

- staff willing to champion change

- council officers (on planning, transport, car parking, cycling, local agenda 21).

Because a travel plan involves everyone, it is vital that everyone is on board, so the next stage is to consult all staff about the plan and the changes it envisages. Interest groups can be established (for example, a cycle opportunity group or bus-user group). Also employ the usual methods of raising awareness – an in-house newsletter, team briefings, leaflets accompanying salary slips, or noticeboards.

Adoption of the travel plan

With the results of the consultation process collated and analysed, the plan now needs to be finalised, costed and approved at the appropriate level. A travel plan cuts across traditional disciplinary boundaries and is of strategic importance. So, in most organisations, it is presented formally to the board for endorsement.

Resources for implementation

It is accepted that someone has to drive the travel plan forward. For organisations with many staff on one site, or where there are many employees in an identifiable geographical area, a travel coordinator should be appointed. The coordinator should be:

- a good communicator at all levels

- able to use information and communications technologies

- able to motivate people

- a pragmatic organiser.

This person will need to be fully resourced and supported and will need access to the decision-making process. All of these costs will form part of the business case for the travel plan and are usually offset against savings in staff travel expenses budgets and the reduced need for more car parking, for example.

Project management

As with any strategic plan, the facilities manager's project management skills will be important. By now, the priorities, costings and a timetable have been established and the transport working group should be ensuring coordination across departments and with external bodies. There will be actions that can be taken immediately, for example:

- provision of cycle lockers and better cycle security
- promotion of existing bus services
- telephone conference calls
- improvements to pedestrian routes
- priority parking for car sharers.

Other measures take more time to plan and introduce, such as revising car parking and staff travel policies (severing the link between the pay packet and travel by car), flexible working schemes and improvements to the public transport infrastructure.

Marketing the travel plan

Facilities managers are familiar with energy conservation campaigns. Successful ones have involved all staff in the process and in many instances have produced dramatic efficiency gains. Travel plans also require a constant marketing effort to be made in order to reach every nook and cranny of the organisation and to keep people informed of developments, new incentives for car sharing, walking and cycling, support for public transport users and so on.

Setting targets

Starting with the figures derived from the staff survey, it will be practical to establish desired targets for changes in the way people travel to your site. In the worked example shown in the table below, the emphasis happens to be on more car sharing and public transport.

Mode of transport to work	Actual 2001 (%)	Targets	
		2003 (%)	2005/06 (%)
Car, as driver alone	65	60	55
Car, as passenger	15	17	18
Car, dropped off	9	9	8
Bus	8	9	11
Train	1	1.5	2
Bicycle	0.5	1	2
Motorcycle	0.5	1	1.5
Walk	1	1	2.5

Table 1: Staff travel targets

Assuming there are 3,000 staff in the work premises on any one working day, the 2003 targets outlined in the table represent:

- 90 fewer staff coming by car

- 30 more staff coming by bus

- 15 more coming by train

- 15 more cycling

- 15 more coming by motorbike

- 15 more walking.

Monitoring and evaluating results

Measurable targets need to be established for each element of the travel plan. For example, take-up monitoring will show the number of annual bus passes sold, the number of cycle lockers in use and so forth. Frequent staff surveys will be expensive and are likely to produce diminishing returns. However, conducting a repeat of your survey of staff travel habits every two years will be essential to check whether you are achieving the desired modal shift. Other monitoring methods include checks on key budgets, periodic comparisons of service levels and recording anecdotal and intuitive evidence.

Encouraging behavioural change

Facilities managers will need to employ a range of skills in implementing travel plans. Those more used to building roads and maintaining buildings will find their traditional working methods are needed when it comes to site infrastructure changes, but new skills are required when it comes to encouraging behavioural change. Travel plans have to be handled with sensitivity and care, as reducing over-dependence on the car calls for changes in lifestyle, which is distinctly intimate and personal territory. For this reason, words such as 'consultation' and 'partnership' must not just be part of a new facilities management vocabulary, but must also be translated into meaningful actions, capable of being verified and evaluated.

The Transport Energy Best Practice Programme

The Transport Energy (hitherto the Energy Efficiency) Best Practice Programme provided a service to the road freight transport industry for many years. Covering such topics as energy-efficient fleet management, its impartial and authoritative advice on energy-efficiency techniques and technologies in industry, transport and buildings is widely respected. It now offers an expanded service covering travel plans, which includes free publications on travel planning and access to free expert advice and assistance.

Results from research at the end of 2002 showed the costs of a travel plan varied greatly depending on the type of organisation, location and the input from the local authority and public transport operators. Average running cost was £47 per employee. The highest cost of £431 compares with the average of maintaining a car parking space, typically £300 to £500 per year. For details of how to get hold of a summary of the research and 20 case studies see the information section at the end of this chapter.

Car park management

Parking restrictions

Overly draconian parking measures were feared at one point in the progress of the government's *PPG13* (see earlier in this chapter, **Legislation, p 255**), namely that car parking spaces at hospital developments were to be linked to bed numbers. Now, new hospitals and school developments are all to be planned to maximise accessibility by non-car modes of transport while simultaneously allowing good access for emergency vehicles and those who need to use cars. Office developments should have one car parking space per 30 m^2 – originally it had been 35 m^2 – for all developments above 2,500 m^2. Any threats to new office developments are thus eased.

Parking is, however, going to get tougher. Consider, for example, government plans to raise £2.7 billion a year 'for better transport schemes' by allowing local authorities to charge people who work in towns and cities between £150 and £500 a year to park at their own place of work. These plans will hit the low paid, as employers are likely to pass on charges to the workforce. The answer is to give massive re-location incentives and tax breaks to work-intensive business operations to encourage them to move to accessible locations where people can get to work cheaply and easily or park for free. There is also the issue of congestion charging to consider, something being considered by many local authorities in the wake of the London exercise.

Planning a car park

The first questions to ask when planning a car park are:

- Why do you want a car park?

- How does it fit in with your transport strategy?

- How big does it need to be?

- What other facilities are involved?

- What material will it be built from?

- What buildings will the car park relate to?

The car park may be designed to serve office blocks, in which case it will be predominantly busy for 30 minutes at the start and end of the day, and quiet in between. A shopping centre car park will have more regular patterns of usage, except demand will double or triple in the weeks before Christmas. A multiplex cinema will be busiest at the end of the evening, as all films are timed to finish within a 30-minute window so staff can go home.

When developing a new car parking facility, it is important to:

- identify both the users and the demand

- perform a traffic impact study

- determine the land availability

- aim to provide the maximum number of spaces while maintaining high standards of circulation

- draw up conceptual layouts.

Design

The car park is (or should be) the gateway to the business, town, office, retail centre or facility – it is the first thing a visitor will see. If it is dirty, scruffy, ill-lit and smelly, that is the impression the visitor will have of the facility. If it is clean, well-maintained, well-lit and of pleasant design, the visitor will take that memory away. Given that 2.4m is needed for a car space, the concrete supports need to be spaced at least at 2.4m or multiples of 2.4m intervals.

Aside from an architectural overhaul and/or repainting and cleaning, ensuring car parks are well-maintained can be achieved through outsourcing.

Floor graphic advertising

In the US, outdoor floor advertising is worth over £140 million a year. At present in the UK, the Parkvertising concept allows owners or operators of car parks to tap into a large source of revenue that builds year-on-year. By forming a partnership with Parkvertising, the owner is able to make money from what was previously just a cost centre.

Advertisements of up to 4 x 4m can be produced (subject to local space availability) using a combination of flat line colours. Designed to withstand up to three years' constant use, these advertisements are produced using materials that comply with all current health and safety legislation. The materials used have a luminescence some five times greater than highway cats' eyes, making the messages highly visible at night.

Car park owners and operators, as well as supermarkets and NHS trusts, are all ideal locations as they offer a parking facility for consumers or office workers. Income derived from the advertising can be applied to finance refurbishment costs, or to generate significant incremental revenue, for example.

Lighting and security

Staff working late or hospital visitors, for example, walking to or from their cars in the dark will need good lighting. Under the Chief Police Officers' secure car park scheme, the advice for the design of car parks is to avoid dark corners and corridors. Much emphasis is put on the design and management of the facilities. Now, there are more staff involved in continuous on site surveillance, as well as CCTV (closed circuit television) facilities being deployed (security issues are covered in detail in **Access, Safety and Security, pp 351–364**).

In the UK today there are some 15,000 underground and multi-storey car parks, many hailing from the 1960s. Quick visual improvements can be achieved through improving the lighting and painting using bright colours, but structural difficulties are more awkward to rectify.

Fleet management

A fleet can be a vital part of the company's operational effectiveness, whether that means salespeople arriving punctually for meetings or equipment arriving on site in plenty of time and in suitable condition. Facilities managers should realise that proactive cost management and policy advice from fleet management companies can be useful.

Motorvate, the green fleet certification scheme, can help organisations cut car and van fleet costs while reducing their environmental impact. A typical 200-strong car fleet can save around £33,000 per year through the Motorvate certification scheme (which includes up to two days' free consultancy) (more information can be found by calling 0808 100 9 100 or *www.greenerfleet.org.uk*).

In some quarters, the company car is no longer seen as a 'perk'. The government has long been pursuing a policy of 'greener' motoring, with the overall aim of getting drivers out of big, petrol-thirsty saloons and into more environmentally-friendly vehicles.

Companies may need guidance on aspects of running a fleet, from vehicle acquisition and disposal, to maintenance and accident management – not to mention fuel costs, which in the existing UK climate increasingly form a heavy burden on any business. However, where a fleet management company can be at its most valuable is in providing expertise on the financial, tax-related and environmental issues.

Tax bills for most company car drivers will rise by between 25 and 33 per cent by 2005/06, under scales published by the Chancellor of the Exchequer in 2003. Increases in annual road tax also took effect. Company car drivers pay tax on their car according to how much their car pollutes on a sliding scale of 21 different tax bands. In the year 2005/06, cars producing under 144g of carbon dioxide for every kilometre travelled will be taxed against 15 per cent of the car's list price. Those producing over 240g/km will be taxed against 35 per cent of the list price. Most company car drivers keep their cars for three/four years, so decisions made in 2002 (for example) will affect tax bills for years to come. Changes to the way free fuel is taxed will also leave thousands of drivers worse off.

Information

TransportEnergy Best Practice programme helpline, tel: 0800 585794 or *www.transportenergy.org.uk/bestpractice*; summary of 2002 research from *www.local-transport.dft.gov.uk/travelplans/index.htm*

Motorrate certification scheme, tel: 080 8100 9100 or *www.greenerfleet.org.ukn*

1 See *www.planning.detr.gov.uk/ppg/ppg13/index.htm*

9 IT and Communications

Frank Booty

The past few years have brought accelerating growth in mobile telephony and an equally rapid expansion of Internet use. By 2003 the number of mobile subscribers had exceeded one billion. Yet commentators speculate even that huge number will be insignificant compared to the expected growth in Internet traffic – some five times greater than in 2001. The e-business market is expected to be massive by 2005, with analysts talking of global revenues of $5 trillion. The facilities manager needs to stay on top of this ever-changing market.

The convergence of data and telecom

Facilities managers will need to be prepared for the coming convergence of the data and telecom markets, embracing the fields of IT, telecoms, the Internet and mobile communications. Globally, many carriers are constructing a web of broadband (high capacity) networks to offer companies raw capacity and increasingly sophisticated added-value services. What are the factors driving this market?

Mobile growth

Pre-paid calls, widespread availability, reduced charges for normal mobile calls, free offers and marked increases in wireless data communications are all factors behind the growth in the mobile phone networks.

However, the technologies driving this growth, GPRS and UMTS (general packet radio service and universal mobile telecom system, the name of the third-generation or 3G mobile phone standard) hit the headlines in early 2001 for the wrong reasons. The WAP (wireless application protocol) standard had a notoriously rocky start and while it enables access to the Internet from a mobile phone and the creation of advanced telecom services, its reception, performance and subsequent developments were lacklustre. Improvements are promised.

Fixed network need

The growth curve for voice telephony has levelled, while the already strong growth of data traffic in fixed networks is accelerating, especially in packet-switched networks, which are increasingly based on IP (Internet protocol). Most telecom operator revenues still derive from voice traffic, although already moves to lower call charges are noticeable.

The number of Internet users continues to rise. At present, the figure is about half the 740 million global fixed telephone connections. Average connect times are increasing, but the unbundling of the local loop is still a key concern.

What will convergence mean?

For facilities managers, convergence will mean:

- the ability to run voice traffic over existing data infrastructure, resulting in reduced support overheads and enabling low-cost add-ons, moves and changes

- the delivery of voice, data, video, and so on, through one service, leading to reduced billing costs

- a growth in specialist data centre providers, tele-hotel companies and communications-related outsourcing in general

- increasingly flexible, wireless communication infrastructures, enabling seamless integration between mobile and fixed work, with implications for office space needs.

Bluetooth

Much future communication is expected to be handled between computers. One way for computers to connect to other systems is through a wireless connection. The glue to provide that connection is Bluetooth, an open standard for short-range digital radio – it is not a competing technology for the equally new third-generation mobile phone systems, but a supporting one. It operates in the industrial, scientific and medical (ISM) applications band, which is available almost everywhere globally. It is cheaper than competing technologies and provides up to three voice channels for speech applications. While it is not a replacement for a local area network (LAN), it can provide the final connection to the network through its ports, enabling wireless access from anywhere within the ports' coverage area.

Voice becomes data

The big swing in the future will be the move in the content of traffic carried over networks from voice to data. At present, more voice than data is carried, but by 2005 that situation is expected to change. Note that in digitising voice, the voice patterns become represented as '1's and '0's, which is exactly how data is represented. Networks will be carrying only data – everything (voice, text, video, TV, multimedia, tele- and video-conferences, emails, messages, and so on) will be delivered through one service. The billing will prove a fascinating exercise.

A prospect for the future

Imagine being always online in a wired and wireless world. A manager in their office receives email via the office local area network (LAN). They leave the office for a meeting in the conference room. Email carries on coming via wireless LAN technology, such as Bluetooth. At lunchtime they switch off the PC and leave the office. Email continues to be delivered, this time to their mobile phone or personal digital assistant (PDA) or a hybrid of the two. Back in the office, when the system is next switched on, Bluetooth updates the company server with the PDA/phone's latest information. While this is going on, a phone call comes in from the manager's superior who is travelling over the Atlantic. Access to a video graphic is required during the call, as well as conferencing with colleagues in Australia and Singapore.

- Synchronisation is handled automatically.

- The capability exists of moving seamlessly between data and telecom bearers, no matter how many devices are being used or where they are located.

- Mobile and fixed devices work seamlessly together.

Wi-Fi zones and wireless LANs

The Wi-Fi Alliance, a non-profit organisation formed in 1999 to certify interoperability of IEEE 802.11 products and to promote them as the global, wireless LAN standard across all market segments, has some 250 members offering over 500 products. A global programme under the WiFi Alliance banner promoting the availability of public access terminals in Wi-Fi zones has now been initiated. Hot spots (Wi-Fi zones) are to be found in key European airports, hotels, city centres, coffee shops and increasingly office buildings.

Integrated wireless local area network (WLAN) technology has even been installed in notebook computers used on Lufthansa trans-Atlantic flights, allowing passengers to make wireless broadband Internet connections with their corporate intranets from either airport lounges or while in the air.

Companies involved in early trials of WLAN included BASF, Boehringer Ingelheim, Siemens and Software AG. The results were good, with bandwidth of 3Mbit/s for downloads and 128kbit/s for uploads (expected to increase to 750kbit/s) – even at a cruising altitude of 10,000m and speeds of up to 900km/h. This work offers the opportunity to take the meaning of the mobile office to logical limits.

Few, if any, technologies hold more promise for the enterprise today than wireless. But few, if any, technologies also have more potential security risks. Industry analysts disagree over the successful penetration rates for WLAN into the professional mobile PC-installed base – opinions range from 'it's all over-hyped' to '50% by year-end 2003 to surpassing 90% by 2007'.

IT infrastructure management

Intelligent buildings

There is no universal definition for the term 'intelligent building'. The company GSI consulting services says, 'an intelligent building provides a productive and cost-effective environment because its four basic components – structure, systems, services and management – have been fully integrated, creating the optimum design'.[1]

Intelligent buildings need facilities management to assist in defining requirements, justifying investment, and ensuring the intended benefits are actually delivered. Facilities managers simultaneously require intelligent buildings to control building performance, manage distributed services, adapt rapidly to changing needs, and provide key management information.

Facilities managers have major contributions to make at a building's inception stage – they should be allowed to impart knowledge concerning alterations in previous buildings for incorporation in new designs. There is a vital role for the facilities manager in ensuring the building, the systems and the people work and interact effectively.

Future drivers for intelligent buildings will be: IT, robotics, smart materials, sustainable issues, and the impacts of social change. Besides technological developments, other factors will include climate change, changes in regulations, and how people work and live within these buildings.

Future-proofing

The cost of installing an inadequate IT infrastructure that does not support the company's future requirements is considerable. Whether facilities managers are responsible for IT or whether they work with an IT department, ultimately facilities and IT management converge. If your business is moving or building a new set of premises, make sure you are involved in planning right from the start.

It would have been nearly impossible to future-proof a business 10 years ago against today's IT demands, and it is still difficult for facilities managers to predict what demand will be in the next few years. But continual changes in the way organisations work are generating demand for bandwidth-hungry applications, more efficient data flows and, all-importantly, flexibility.

Any changes to existing systems, or replacement of those systems, should be done with the maximum of forethought. A well-structured infrastructure should build in the flexibility necessary for facilities and IT managers to handle future moves and technological changes.

Resource planning

Infrastructure management or infrastructure resource planning may be a recent concept in facilities management, but taking the principles behind it into account is common sense. It is good practice to assess what you have and how well it is working before moving on to the next step. Consider the following:

- What are your current IT assets – computers, cabling and telephone systems? How old are they – are they nearing the end of their lifetime? Where are they and who is using them?

- What is the gap between their existing value to the company and what company directors and/or employees would like them to deliver?

- Are there ways of maximising the use of existing assets rather than buying new ones?

- Are there ways that your existing system can work 'smarter, not harder' – through better network set-ups which minimise network congestion, for example?

Assessing the market

The facilities management world is full of companies making claims about what their technology can do for you. Each option has its own advantages and disadvantages, and it can be all too easy to be persuaded down a given route without exploring all the options. Assess the products on offer and look carefully at the experience of the companies offering them. When considering a new IT infrastructure, ask the following:

- Is the system easy to deploy and reliable? Is it likely to be overtaken by future developments?

- Will it fit with existing systems?

- Is it based on open standards, allowing flexibility in future?

- What are the cost implications?

As each technology possesses its own particular strength, businesses should always begin by understanding how they differ and what works best for their own networking needs. Before opting for the latest technology, question what value you are looking for over what you already have. Upgrade networks only when it is necessary to incorporate newer technologies, rather than changing investment unnecessarily simply because an older technology is no longer fashionable.

Cabling categories

To a large extent, category 5 twisted pair cabling has replaced coaxial cable in local area network cabling for horizontal distribution, while multi-mode optical fibre has become the main media type for intra-building backbones. Standards are constantly evolving towards new cabling categories with better performance. Such improvements are vital to satisfy the growing demand for more bandwidth and for flexible solutions to changing working environments.

The key factor in choosing the right cabling option is the anticipated demand on network capacity. For office IT, such as word processing and accounts, category 5 offers 100Mb/s, which is commonly regarded as more than enough. However, for data-intensive applications, enhanced category 5 (5e) or category 6 may be required, offering up to 1Gb/s.

Category 5e is an improvement over category 5, but category 6 is already around. The Telecommunications Industry Association (TIA) and the International Standards Organisation (ISO) have collaborated on the technical work associated with the category 6 standard. The aim of the standard is to have a power sum bandwidth of 200MHz, twice that of category 5.

Meanwhile, category 7 has the aim of providing a power sum bandwidth of at least 500MHz. TIA is planning to develop specifications of connecting hardware to ensure backward compatibility and interoperability with category 5 and 5e cabling.

(See **Space design and management, p 331** for more on structured cabling.)

Voice over IP

Facilities managers need to consider the advantages and disadvantages of voice over Internet protocol (VoIP), sometimes referred to as IP telephony. Unlike the conventional phone system, which is a circuit-switched network, VoIP sends calls over the Internet, a packet-switched network. It first converts the voice traffic into data packets. These packets are then routed over the Internet in the same way as other data, reassembled at the point of arrival and then converted back into voice.

While some Internet phone traffic may travel from computer to computer, most VoIP traffic uses the current phone and fax systems. At the network level, this traffic is managed by a VoIP gateway, which converts the call between the Internet and the public telephone service. This gateway may be located at the company's premises, or at the office of a service provider such as an ISP (Internet service provider).

VoIP can offer new applications which can boost productivity. These include:

- integrated voice, email and fax messaging
- computer-telephone integration for call centre representatives
- enhanced network collaboration.

Features of VoIP

- **Unified messaging** – with a conventional system, business employees may phone, fax, email or share files over the company network or the Internet. VoIP combines these into one channel. For example, technology called 'unified messaging' can be used to funnel each employee's voicemail, email, and faxes to a single mailbox, to be retrieved from a single end-station (PC or phone). Calls between offices travel over the existing data network through VoIP. By staying on the company network, these inter-office calls travel free of toll charges.

- **Toll-free telephony features** – IP phones deliver a complete suite of business telephony features, including call-waiting, caller ID, transfer, conference calling, and so on. These features can be deployed across any number of sites that are connected by a company's data network, without incurring toll charges.

- **Remote access via single interface** – VoIP makes it possible to make voicemail, email, fax and video messages remotely accessible through a single interface – PC or phone – at each user's office desktop. This set-up increases productivity for mobile sales and service people and eliminates the cost and hassle of managing separate voicemail, email and fax systems. Employees will have faster access to customer requests from any location.

- **Customer service** – integrated call systems can tie phone and email systems to back-office applications where customer account information is stored. When customers call, call centre agents have instant access to their account history and can deliver a more personalised and timely service. In addition, customers visiting a company's website can use Internet tools to request assistance from a live agent. VoIP enables the agent to deliver voice assistance over the phone while assisting the customer online in real time.

- **Information sharing** – employees can collaborate more easily, sharing documents online in real time, during conversations or during conference calls. VoIP also supports video transmissions over the network, enabling employees to view video-based training modules, product announcements and presentations from their desktops, enhancing productivity, saving time and lowering travel costs.

Integration with the data network

Using VoIP means connecting your voice equipment – phones, fax, machines and private branch exchange (PBX) or key system – to your data network. Users can then be equipped with individual IP handsets which work like traditional phones but plug directly into network LAN switches and deliver enhanced integration with the data network.

Quality

Two main issues affect Internet voice traffic: latency or sound delays and voice quality. Both of these issues are being addressed.

Voice quality is affected by many issues, including how it is compressed and decompressed for delivery over the Internet, and how packets are processed. Often, voice calls sound shaky or robotic – obviously unacceptable for many typical business applications.

Voice quality is often driven by packet loss (data packets failing to arrive, not arriving on time or arriving with errors). To ensure steady quality, experts recommend a packet loss of less than 5 per cent. At 10 per cent voices start to quiver; at 20 per cent they start to sound like robots. In terms of sound delay, a one-way latency of less than 100 milliseconds is acceptable.

The latest round of VoIP products do provide much improved call quality. Increased use of broadband technologies such as DSL (digital subscriber line) and cable modems will also help make VoIP more accessible.

Standards

VoIP standards are not fully established. There is a standard – *H.323* – from the International Telecommunications Union (ITU) for carrying multimedia traffic over IP networks. This defines how delay-sensitive traffic, such as voice and video, is prioritised on LANs and WANs. But many products are not interoperable with competitors' offerings because of the leeway in implementing *H.323*. The answer is to install gateways from a single vendor.

Security

Businesses need to take security measures when implementing VoIP. Traffic must be encrypted as eavesdroppers can listen in on conversations wherever packets pass. The issue is being addressed through the *H.235* standard, which covers authentication, encryption and other security measures.

Developments in IP telephony

IP traffic is increasing exponentially at a time when overall growth in international traffic is slowing. One major carrier estimates it will increase its capacity to carry voice traffic over IP-based networks by 1,300 per cent up to 2006, at a quarter of the cost of doing so over a conventional circuit-switched network.

IP telephony can generally be offered to customers at prices very much below those offered over conventional circuit-switched networks, particularly on long-distance and international calls, because traffic pricing on IP-based networks is largely distance-independent. Comments aired in the US, however, state that VoIP is more about making money than saving money – users should look beyond a chance to cut long-distance costs. Rather, they should think about a new generation of VoIP-based computer telephony integration (CTI) applications which can produce increased turnover and boost a company's productivity.

Conferencing and presentation technology

Technology has made and continues to make enormous strides, but the art of conducting meetings and sharing information has mostly failed to catch up. Now possible are audio-conferences (also known as conference calls or tele-conferences), video-conferencing, data-conferencing and email:

- **Audio-conferencing** – extends the two-way telephone call, allowing multiple parties to interact on a single call.

- **Video-conferencing** – is a fully interactive two-way video and audio communication using specialist equipment, most of which has data-conferencing facilities included.

- **Data-conferencing** – can be used with either conference calls or video-conferencing to allow people to share data files and applications between computers during their meeting.

Email is useful for pre-meeting exchange of information.

Business can use portable, desktop or installed projectors – there are some 300 projectors from over 40 manufacturers (see below, Projectors). Room control systems coordinate lighting, curtains/blinds and audio-visual equipment to create different environments, and to integrate different types of audio-visual equipment to make them work as one. Gas plasma display screens of up to 50 inches diagonally, 130mm in depth and with a 160° viewing angle are available, as are wireless handset controls and TV displays with widescreen and HDTV (high definition television) standards.

Conference technology

Today's managers typically spend up to one third of each business day in meetings. UK executives on average attend six meetings a week, spending 11 hours travelling between them. While new technologies will not replace all face-to-face meetings, they provide less-costly, quicker and more productive ways of communicating. Costs of meetings are not only confined to travel. There are also hidden costs, such as administrative time used for meeting preparations, travel cancellations and the cost of time in transit.

Some meetings are particularly suitable for conferencing, for example:

- meetings that need to take place quickly

- meetings involving lots of people

- international meetings

- briefings to a large number of people.

Of course, many sales meetings, relationship-building meetings with customers or colleagues and introductory meetings will still require the personal contact of a face-to-face meeting.

Projectors

Reliability, projection quality, size and portability are all factors that facilities managers should consider when choosing projectors. Ultimately, choosing the right model comes down to deciding on what best satisfies personal or corporate criteria:

- **Fixed projectors** – any company carrying out regular presentations at a central base where quality of presentation is a critical factor will need a fixed solution –

with maximum flexibility of input options (PC, VCR and DVD). Typical users will be trainers, directors and other senior members of staff, with applications ranging from internal training and demonstrations to product launches and sales pitches. Room costs will range from £4,000 for a basic ceiling-mounted projector to £100,000 for a boardroom incorporating the highest specification products. Features that should be considered are angle, brightness, resolution and maintenance.

- **Desktop projectors** – these are designed for organisations in which different people need access to the system within different areas of the business, in different rooms and even externally, such as conferences and exhibitions. Users could be anyone in the organisation, and ease of set-up and reliability are therefore important. Costs can vary from £2,000 to £8,000 with weight being a major issue (under 7kg is ideal, plus a hard carry case).

- **Fully portable projectors** – models cost between £2,500 and £5,000. Weight needs to be under 4.5kg. These units are typically aimed at those launching products to potential customers, or visiting colleagues in satellite offices.

Doing business over the web

Customer service concerns are seen as the main driver of email for business document distribution, while elsewhere moves to an e-business culture are set to embrace the use of Internet technology, providing there is buy-in at board level. Without the right e-business approach, companies risk losing a significant portion of sales volume and profit margin to companies that have more effectively aligned themselves with their customers' supply chains.

By 2005–06, it is expected that businesses on both sides of the Atlantic will have migrated most of their document distribution to email. A key factor behind increased email deployment is the desire for a more responsive customer service. Email is seen as the key to cutting response times and increasing the quality of customer communications.

Furthermore, e-business enables interactive one-to-one marketing and sales but at practically zero incremental cost, whether the company is trying to reach one customer or thousands.

Top-down approach

The approach to e-business must be sold from the top of the company down, and the facilities manager will have a major role to play as the enabler for the organisation. The emerging electronic marketplace is one which demands anytime, anywhere access (the so-called 24×7×360 model) over a number of devices and converging fixed and mobile networks.

Major stumbling blocks affecting take-up of e-business in earnest are security and trust. The former can be a problem of perception while the latter is a tactical issue that can usually be resolved through discussion and agreement.

E-procurement

An inevitable consequence of e-business business-to-business trading is the closer integration of companies' IT systems with the web to allow linking of accounting applications for orders, invoices and payments. It is not a new idea. Electronic data interchange (EDI) systems have been around for over 20 years but have failed to achieved the expected level of take-up because they require extensive customisation to create common information standards between organisations.

More recently, enterprise management systems have been promoted as a more effective means of controlling business finances, offering improved reporting and management information. But these again rely on consistent information coding using agreed cost centres which often vary significantly between clients and suppliers.

The problem is that many of the new systems and processes cannot make use of legacy data, and then perpetuate the problem by creating a new set of bespoke information. In general, suppliers are not yet well geared up for web-based trading.

There is much potential in the technology, not only to assist in bypassing cumbersome manual processes, but also, if handled correctly, to generate valuable management and benchmarking information. Much expectation surrounds universal communications standards such as XML, a preferred choice by many for future e-business applications. Without common ground on information exchange, Internet trading many never achieve its potential.

For more information relating to the growth and drawbacks of e-procurement, including 'club' e-commerce sites for procurement, see **Financial management, e-procurement, p 174.**

Negotiating by email

It has been estimated that over 610 billion emails are sent each year in the US, with the UK not far behind. Many routine communications between facilities managers and their user group or supply chain are now based on email exchange. However, research at the Harvard Business School has shown people are less inclined to share information when communicating via email than through a face-to-face meeting or voice-to-voice communication. To minimise the negative features of email communication, it is important to create a rapport with the other party, by meeting beforehand, engaging in 'virtual small talk', and avoiding terse statements or shorthand which could create tension or misunderstanding. If the negotiation seems to be getting angry or personal then stop emailing and make a phone call or arrange a meeting.

The role of the intranet site

Many facilities managers are now supporting their operations through a web-based interface with their internal customers. A well-designed interface can make a positive contribution to the climate for virtual negotiation. According to research by Cisco Systems, a successful site has three main features:

- quality of the information architecture
- quality of the graphic design
- readability.

Intranet services

Intranet services currently on offer include knowledge database, room bookings, catering, requests, customer satisfaction monitoring and travel portal. Content management is key – technical issues can be handled through the company's existing network structure, but the facilities manager will need to know information such as who entered what information when. Content management software costs upwards of a few hundred pounds.

Action points

When designing a site, consider the following:

- Base the content of the site on a survey of user/customer feedback.
- Make sure information content is regularly updated.
- Make sure navigation through the site is consistent.
- Field test the usability of the site with a focus group.
- Minimise the graphic content to speed downloading.
- Present the material in a format that the reader can glance through and easily retain the main points of information.

In addition, facilities managers should identify the key stakeholder groups and design specific information resources for their individual needs. Most facilities managers will have three key stakeholder groups:

- interactive customers wanting to access services
- senior management who want to understand the organisation and performance of service delivery
- interactive suppliers who want to access the operation of the supply chain.

Helpdesks

The fundamental purpose of a helpdesk is the speedy restoration of a user to full productivity when that productivity has been impeded by a failure in corporate technology or its use, thus maximising the return on investment in both employee and technology. As well as queries about technology and equipment, helpdesks can also be used to respond to calls and requests such as for room bookings or new services and audio visual aids.

Helpdesks typically adopt call centre practices such as IVR (interactive voice response) and CTI (computer telephony integration) to satisfy customer demands. There are many helpdesk software packages ranging from enterprise-scale customer relationship management systems to entry-level options which can be downloaded from the web.

Digital v paper document systems

Most businesses have long accepted that the much heralded 'paperless' office is a myth. Indeed, the proliferation of PCs in the workplace has actually served to increase the amount of paper printed in most organisations.

This is of course because people find it easier to familiarise themselves with long and/or complicated documents in hard copy format. As a result, paper storage remains a significant facilities issue.

Paper storage

Documents should be kept in the cheapest way possible. If they are no longer current – and unlikely to be needed on a regular basis, they should be transferred to a basement or to off-site storage for whatever length of time is required by statute.

The overall cost of off-site storage is roughly usually about a third of the cost of on-site storage.

Establishing an electronic document system

However information is stored, it makes sense for a document management system to be established. Document management involves the conversion of paper documents into electronic images on a computer: document imaging. The documents are scanned into the system, to be stored on a hard disk drive or optical disk, when they are indexed. To read any document, the imaging system retrieval tools are used, with the process taking seconds to perform.

An EDM system enables an organisation to save space, retrieve documents more quickly and cheaply and to make it easier for operatives to share information.

Under the British Standards Institution's Code of Practice, PD0008, for Legal Admissibility of Information Stored on EDM systems, electronic documents and scanned images may be accepted as evidence in court.

Information

Wi-Fi Alliance: *www.wi-fi.org*

GSI: *www.gsigroup.com*

essentialfm report, 'Intelligent buildings' 12 November/December 2001.

1 *www.gsigroup.com*

10 Workplace Facilities

Frank Booty

The day-to-day running of a building is fundamental to facilities professionals. From procuring the most competitive electricity contract, to selecting the most appropriate air conditioning system, the facilities manager needs to be aware of the market, costs and benefits of all aspects of workplace facilities and equipment.

The increasing impetus on energy efficiency in business operations, health and safety issues and maximum productivity are now among the business objectives that facilities professionals must address. Ensuring that the appropriate services and facilities meet the needs of their users and are functioning efficiently and cost effectively will bring benefits to all aspects of an organisation's operations.

Buying gas, electricity and water

It is becoming an accepted view that facilities managers are kept in the dark over energy costs. Lack of transparency in the existing deregulated gas and electricity markets is costing UK businesses valuable time and money. The sheer number of companies selling gas and electricity in the UK is in itself a headache for facilities managers trying to locate the best deal for their business. There are, for example, some 60 companies in the UK selling natural gas.

Some facilities managers also feel they are taking a gamble when choosing between an established, but potentially more expensive, supplier versus one of the many new but equally viable entrants to the marketplace. The popular view is that the deregulation of energy industries across Europe is likely to intensify the problem further, as foreign suppliers join the market.

How to get the best deal

The solutions to the energy-buying conundrum for facilities managers comprise a much simplified procurement process and more transparency in the market. Some facilities managers utilise the [free] services of reverse auction agencies. Any organisation seeking to obtain the best quote on energy enters a few details about its current set-up on an agency website. All Ofgem-registered gas companies in the UK then 'blind bid' for the organisation's business in a reverse auction to offer the most competitive price. Ofgem (the Office for Gas and Electricity Markets) is the official regulator. Similar arrangements exist for buying electricity. The view promulgated is that only with a truly open market can those in charge of buying commercial and industrial energy be sure they are getting the best deal.

NETA

The new electricity trading arrangements (NETA) went live in late March 2001. The previous pool arrangement was regarded as deeply flawed and seen as 'effectively a means for generators to set a wholesale price which suppliers and large consumers had little choice but to accept'. It was considered to be 'no better than a generators' club'. In contrast, NETA is a genuine market in which, for the first time, generators seek out customers (they have to), giving electricity suppliers and large organisations real choice. Indeed, forward contracts were seen soon after NETA's debut of 30 per cent cuts in real terms compared with wholesale prices in 1998, when the government started the reform process.

Large energy users

Suppliers are expected to focus heavily on the small- to medium-sized enterprises market, where better margins and profits can be made compared to the high volume business. What then can larger users do to improve their position?

When looking at contracts:

- be prepared to be innovative

- look to load-manage

- talk to suppliers about the usage profile

- communicate regularly regarding any changes in consumption habits

- watch the markets and supplier activity and know which suppliers are best suited to match a company's needs

- set budgets in line with an educated view as to where prices might be heading.

Ofgem's advice is to 'shop around to get the best deal'. The role of this government watchdog is to make sure that markets are operating as competitively as possible. What Ofgem has no control over is the Climate Change Levy (CCL) (see below in this chapter, **p 285**). This presents a conundrum. On the one hand electricity prices are lower than they would be otherwise thanks to NETA, while on the other hand the CCL has the effect of raising prices.

Combined heat and power

Combined heat and power (CHP) is a very efficient technology for generating electricity and heat together. A CHP plant is an installation where there is simultaneous generation of usable heat and power (usually electricity) in a single process. The term CHP is synonymous with 'co-generation' and 'total energy', which are terms often used in other European Community member states or in the US. The basic elements of CHP plant consist of one or more prime movers usually driving electrical generators, where the heat generated in the process is utilised via suitable heat recovery equipment for a variety of purposes, including industrial processes, community heating and space heating.

Efficiency

CHP can provide a secure and efficient method of generating electricity and heat at the point of use. Typically, CHP achieves a 35 per cent reduction in primary energy usage when compared with power stations and heat-only boilers. This is because it uses heat from electricity generation and does not suffer any transmission losses, since the electricity is produced on site. So, when there is an optimum balance between heat and power loads, the host company should be able to make economic savings. Today, the existing CHP installed base achieves over 30 per cent reductions in carbon dioxide emissions when compared with coal-fired power station equivalents, and over 10 per cent compared with gas-fired combined cycle gas turbines. Further, the latest CHP installations produce over 50 per cent reductions when compared with power generated by coal-fired complexes.

The total number of CHP schemes in buildings in the UK was approximately 1,500 in mid-2001 (the number of sites increased steadily from 1,220 in 1995 to 1,313 in 1999, with a net increase in electricity capacity of 354MWe). In 1999, the latest available statistics showed 93 per cent of capacity (361 sites) is in the industrial sector and 7 per cent of capacity (952 sites) is in the commercial, public and residential sectors.

The CHP Club

The government is eager to achieve its target of 10GW of CHP capacity by 2010, and has set up the CHP Club to help achieve this. This is particularly targeted at new and potential CHP users, and also aims to help existing users to extend their schemes. It intends to provide members with a one-stop shop – a combination of information, exchange of experience and advice facilities on CHP and related topics, all for free.

The CHP Quality Assurance (CHPQA) programme will enable good quality CHP to earn exemption from the CCL; potential members can visit and register with the CHP Club website. The government issued a consultation paper *CHPQA – A Quality Assurance Programme for Combined Heat and Power* in 2000[1].

The operation of CHPQA will be reviewed in the future. Any changes made will only apply to subsequent CHP developments and will not be applied retrospectively to existing CHP schemes.

Totally integrated power

A lack of a uniform approach to energy monitoring, control and delivery has meant that occupants of industrial and commercial buildings have found it practically impossible to integrate energy supply to the same extent as other critical building services, such as HVAC and security. Heating, lighting, access control and fire and security systems all need to be controlled, along with a building's energy requirements.

Totally integrated power, a concept developed by Siemens, offers integrated power distribution from medium voltage switchgear all the way through to socket outlets on an office wall. The concept covers every aspect of power distribution and electricity management required in an industrial environment. It has been estimated that totally integrated power can bring power use savings of 25 per cent, because it enables electricity users to reduce their total power costs, as well as increasing the efficiency of operation of plant equipment. The market size for totally integrated power has been estimated at €10 billion, and is expected to grow by some 2 per cent per annum. Operators of public buildings, including museums, hospitals and airports, are said to benefit from totally integrated power just as much as industrial and office markets. The theory is that by expanding the capability of data control and management through an entire building, all aspects of energy delivery and consumption can be integrated.

Open systems in building control

The International Alliance for Interoperability (IAI) has the mission 'to provide a universal basis for process improvement and information sharing in the construction and facilities management industries, using industry foundation classes (IFCs)'[2].

IFCs are a practical tool for information sharing, using object technology; they are information-rich, swiftly transmitted and not limited to any one software vendor or system. The IAI's first chapter was set up in the US in 1995 and the second in the UK in 1996. Other chapters now cover German-speaking, French-speaking and Nordic countries, Japan, Singapore, Korea and Australasia.

The IAI has chapters covering facilities management areas such as reactive and preventative maintenance, asset management, move management, change management, helpdesk, energy consumption profiles and performance data, but nothing currently in the signals area. This is the domain of open systems protocols and interoperability, principally involving the use of LONworks, BACnet and EIB. With these systems, the situation is one where central systems increasingly feature distributed intelligence at all outstations.

The LONmark Interoperability Association is a key driving force in the establishment of interoperable guidelines for building, industrial, transportation and residential/utility automation. LONmark membership is open to any manufacturer, end-user and system integrator committed to the development and use of open, interoperable products using multi-vendor LONworks control networks.

BACnet is a data communications protocol for building automation and control networks. Developed by ASHRAE (American Society of Heating, Refrigerating and Air-conditioning Engineers), BACnet is a US standard, a European 'pre-standard' and a potential global standard.

The EIB bus – EIB stands for European Integration Bus but is always referred to as EIB – serves the same function as LONworks and BACnet, offering the sensor-to-sensor and unit-to-unit links of LONworks and the controller-to-controller-level protocol of BACnet.

As yet, there is no 100 per cent open communication. The Building Research Establishment runs an EIB and BACnet training centre. The Energy Systems Trade Association's Building Controls Group is one possible source of information.

Avoiding power failures

Organisations reliant on sensitive electronic and computer-based equipment are vulnerable to even momentary cuts in the electricity supply. Mains failure could bring most workplaces to a standstill. PCs, workstations, network servers, retail point-of-sale systems, medical equipment and telecom systems all depend on a high quality uninterrupted power supply. A distortion of only a few milliseconds can destroy data, disconnect communication links and damage delicate instrumentation.

The best way to limit or prevent potential damage caused by power irregularities is with battery back-ups known as uninterruptible power supplies (UPS) and standby generators. The cost of UPS systems ranges from under £100 to some £150,000 and generators start at £25,000 and can cost hundreds of thousands of pounds. When selecting a UPS, there are several important issues to consider:

- What are the potential consequences of power loss in both the short and long term?

- How much load requires protecting and which pieces of equipment are most critical?

- What is the length of time power needs to be sustained?

- What are the power requirements of critical equipment?

- What is the likelihood and possible duration of power losses or fluctuations?

The use and application of UPS systems needs to be part of a company's disaster recovery policy (see **Business continuity, p 220**). For maintenance of UPS systems, see **Maintenance and repair, pp 365–375**.

Water competition

The government plans to further boost the opportunities for competition in the water industry in England and Wales in order to bring customers more choice, keener prices and better services. The government intends to license new entrants in production (extraction) of water and for retail of water to customers. Companies are to be given clearer rights to enter the water market and incumbent companies will be able to remain vertically-integrated statutory undertakers, retaining their key strategic water resource and environmental duties. In the meantime, the government will continue to ensure that public health, the environment and the quality of drinking water are safeguarded.

Ofwat (the Office of Water Services) is to review its regulatory regime to consider what changes, such as further transparency in incumbents' costing information, are needed to promote competition. Parliamentary information can be found on the DEFRA or Ofwat websites.

Checking utility invoices

It pays to check all utility bills thoroughly – costly mistakes in the supplier's favour can and do occur. Anecdotal evidence suggests major users can expect average refunds of 2–4 per cent from rigorous attention to bill validation. Smaller users are not immune; although errors may affect them less regularly, their effect can be quite disproportionate.

Companies may already have some form of bill-checking procedures in place, supported by specialised software. But it is worthwhile reviewing how effective and efficient the systems are by questioning if the checking process can validate the following items:

- Is it the correct supplier? Ensure, for example, there is no double billing resulting from a previous incumbent overlapping with a new contract.

- Are the prices correct – including transportation of use-of-system charges if separately itemised?

- Is there continuity – for example, no mismatch of 'previous' meter readings, no double-counted or phantom bulk deliveries?

- Is the arithmetic correct?

- Is there proof of delivery – that is, independent verification of meter readings and bulk fuel drops?

- Is there consistency with earlier billing patterns?

The complexity of some utility invoices can make it a daunting task to apply thorough vetting. Bills for contract electricity supplies and effluent charges, for example, can be quite complex. Worse still, much of the proprietary software sold for the purpose is not up to the job and becomes less relevant as non-tariff contract deals proliferate in the deregulated utility marketplace.

One practical approach is to model the invoice for each account with a spreadsheet. The current supplier's details and contract price structure can be built in as constants. When the variable data from a new bill is entered into the appropriate boxes, the grand total should match that shown on the real bill. Changes of supplier, changes of price and even changes of tariff structure can be accommodated by creating a modified version of the model bill.

Meter-reading errors

Experience shows that arithmetic errors are rare. Meter-reading discrepancies, however, do occur. Of course, an incorrect or estimated reading will usually be corrected on the subsequent read and any resulting overcharging will be balanced by a compensating undercharge, but there are important exceptions to this general rule. One is when the estimated reading occurs on the date of a change of supplier or end of contract year, when the price changes. Too much consumption may then be charged at the higher price and too little at the lower price.

More significant is the situation where the meter is changed and the final reading on the outgoing meter is estimated or wrong. Take the case where a refund for 500 m^3 of water was obtained by successfully arguing that a final reading of 13,700 was inconsistent with earlier consumption and appeared to be a misreading for 13,200, which gave a more reasonable result.

Cases of inaccurate billing

- A department store, buying electricity on a maximum demand tariff, had an agreed supply capacity (ASC) of 211kVA, much more than was required to cope with a consistent monthly peak of 110–130kVA. When a year's bills were examined, it was found that the reason for this was one isolated month when demand had apparently peaked at 211kVA. Before that, the ASC had been 160kVA and the increase to 211kVA (a permanent extra monthly charge) had been triggered by that single freak maximum demand. On reviewing the situation, the figure of 211kVA was seen as a clerical error. It was more likely to have been 121kVA. The supplier agreed, repaid the excess, and reduced the ASC to 130kVA to give further long-term savings.

  The case was easily dealt with because it concerned a user supplied by the local electricity company.

- In a similar case, a NORWEB customer in the Southern Electric franchise area, with London Electricity as the meter reader, was concerned about a £2,400 exceptional charge which appeared on a bill, ostensibly to recover unpaid ASC charges arising from the fact that Southern Electric had 'discovered' a previously unregistered peak demand of 415kVA some months earlier. Normal peak demand was 50–90kVA. The 415kVA peak was fiction and fortunately there was half-hourly data for the period concerned to prove it. After some further work, the buck stopped where it belonged – with the electricity supplier – and the spurious charge was cancelled.

- More worrying still is the case of the client whose ASC doubled from 7MW to 14MW when the meter operator changed the half-hourly meters and carelessly added the two meters' records together without allowing for the fact that both were registering simultaneously on the same date.

These are dramatic examples of what has happened in specific cases. Maybe similar things have happened to managers without errors coming to light – yet. It pays to check.

Climate Change Levy

Energy consumption contributes significantly to the UK's carbon dioxide emissions. Business accounts for nearly 70 per cent of these emissions – industry and commerce alone are responsible for nearly 42 per cent. The UK government has set an ambitious target for a 20 per cent cut in the country's carbon dioxide emissions by 2010 (the UK had agreed with the EU to a 12.5 per cent cut on 1990 levels). Initiatives have been launched by the government to assist companies in reducing their energy consumption. However, it is the Climate Change Levy which is expected to provide the push behind getting businesses to think about how they can cut their energy consumption and costs.

The levy is basically a tax on coal, gas and electricity affecting both private and public sectors. Its existence has increased the viability of renewable energy options and combined heat and power (CHP), as these supplies will be exempt. British Gas estimates that the levy will add 10 per cent to electricity bills and 15 per cent to gas bills. Most utilities will, like British Gas, display the levy as a separate subtotal at the bottom of the bill so that you can tell how much you are paying for it and whether you are exempted in that billing period. See **Complying with health and safety law: Climate Change Levy, p 60** for details of levy rates and exemptions.

Objectives

The aim of the levy – which was introduced in April 2001 – is to encourage greater energy efficiency and use of greener power supplies. Reduced levy rates will be accorded to those who demonstrate they have invested in energy efficiency. Any company pursuing an efficiency path will benefit from the levy; the government estimates that most businesses could save 10 per cent of their energy at little cost. Such a reduction would amount to more than just a 10 per cent reduction on the levy – it would also cut the overall fuel bill by a significant sum.

The levy is not aimed at the small- to medium-sized business sector directly, but this group does have a key role to play. According to the Institute of Directors, if every small business in the UK were to cut its energy requirements by 20 per cent, the nation's energy bill would be reduced by £1 billion, and 3 million tonnes of carbon dioxide emissions would be eliminated. Whatever the size of the organisation, every company needs to have an energy management policy. The backing, understanding and support of everyone – from directors to staff – is mandatory.

Reducing emissions and costs

The government has made it clear that the CCL is not a one-off but part of a trend to shift business taxes away from positive activities like job creation and investment to environmental performance. Clearly the levy is not going to go away. An estimated saving of 1.5 million tonnes of carbon a year by 2010 is expected as a result but, in so doing, industry will be paying a bill of £1.75 billion in the first year alone. Most organisations will be looking to the facilities manager to reduce that bill. The government is seeking to reduce carbon dioxide emissions by 60 per cent by 2050, and 15–25 million tonnes of carbon (MtC) by 2020. Energy efficiency is identified as delivering half of the necessary improvements.

Even if long-term levy revenues do get pumped back into business, how is the facilities manager, concerned about short-term rising costs, to ensure that the levy is as small a burden as possible? The short answer is to measure your energy consumption, compare it with industry norms and then manage it down. New ways of doing this are constantly being explored, and nine local or industry-specific pilot initiatives across the country have received funding of £460,000 from the Energy Savings Trust to uncover and set up new ways of improving energy efficiency, and to act as role models. Each project has a target of a 10 per cent reduction in energy usage. Action Energy (formerly the Energy Efficiency Best Practice Programme (EEBPP)) publishes a number of helpful leaflets, has a free helpline and online information. Carbon Trust is a government-backed organisation set up to provide UK businesses and industry with advice on reducing carbon emissions Carbon Trust administers the enhanced capital allowance scheme on behalf of the Department of the Environment, Food and Rural Affairs. More at *www.eca.gov.uk*

Effective January 2003 – and to be implemented by January 2006 – is a statutory requirement through Building Regulations for all new non-residential buildings in England and Wales to be handed over with a log book containing details of the building services installed, enabling owner/occupiers to monitor and control energy consumption. The same applies to refurbished buildings and existing buildings where significant changes have been made. CIBSE has published "Building log books – a guide and standard template for preparing log books for non-domestic buildings" as a key tool to enable design teams and contractors to meet this requirement.

Meanwhile, the utility firm Scottish Power has issued some practical advice:

- Include energy efficiency in buying specifications and for all equipment.

- Get office equipment switched onto standby mode – this can help make energy savings from 25 per cent to over 50 per cent.

- Make staff aware which equipment can be switched off when not in use.

- Inspect and replace worn or damaged refrigeration seals.

- Install motor controllers to reduce fuel consumption of refrigerators and freezers.

- Reduce building heat losses by up to 90 per cent by insulation (while maintaining adequate ventilation).

- Make thorough checks on the building fabric for damp, which reduces insulating qualities.

- Consider reducing the volume of air to be heated by installing suspended ceilings.

- Fit temperature controls, check thermostat settings, draught-proof windows and doors and raise staff awareness – the maximum recommended office heating level is 19°C and for each one degree of overheating, costs rise by about 8 per cent.

- Reduce thermostat settings for storerooms, corridors and where there is a high level of activity – workshops should typically be 16°C and stores 10–12°C.

- Set frost thermostats to optimum levels −4°C internal and 0–1°C external.

- Install seven-day time-switches (about £50 each); check settings are correct and correspond to occupancy patterns.

- Remember that radiators can be switched off before the end of occupancy.

- Check that heating and ventilation operate at the minimum recommended settings when the building is unoccupied.

- Check which rooms regularly overheat and correct.

- Fit thermostatic radiator valves (about £15 each), set them correctly and lock them.

- Have heaters and burners cleaned and serviced at least yearly by a qualified contractor.

- Turn off lights whenever possible, especially in toilets, corridors, storerooms and canteens; make staff aware they can save 15 per cent in this way.

Environmental measuring and reporting

As the government's climate change programme proposals make clear, there will be increasing pressure on users of fuel in business and industry to measure and publish their greenhouse gas emissions.

The Department of the Environment, Transport and the Regions, as it then was, published guidance on how to do this, *Environmental reporting – guidelines for company reporting on greenhouse gas emissions*, in June 1999[3].

Encouragement is given, particularly to larger users, to set demanding targets for the reduction of emissions so that they make a proper contribution to the achievement of national targets.

Measuring energy efficiency

By far the most common yardstick for measuring – and managing – energy is by its cost. For a large number of users, interest does not extend beyond the one line on the expenditure budget for heat, light and power. However, if cost is the only yardstick, interest in energy efficiency depends on whether unit costs of fuel are rising or falling. In recent years, prices have steadily fallen, with a corresponding decline of interest in improving efficiency. The Climate Change Levy (CCL) was intended to help to correct this.

Where energy is used in buildings, a step forward in analysis is cost per unit area. Much information is available on cost standards for offices, schools, hospitals and other types of building, which enable users to compare their performance with best practice. Gas and electricity are sold by the kilowatt-hour (kWh), and this is the most commonly used unit for the analysis. Again, a wide range of information is available, notably through Action Energy, which gives benchmark standards for energy use in various applications.

Energy-efficiency improvement programmes

Programmes of improvement must inevitably consider ways of actually increasing energy efficiency. Sometimes this is done by making major changes to the way requirements are met, for instance by installing a CHP unit, or replacing a centralised steam boiler by smaller units close to the point of use. These are expensive capital projects which have to be carefully assessed and evaluated, with options such as whether to carry through the project in-house or use a contract energy management company.

Far more often, the improvement programme is achieved gradually. Such a programme might typically aim to improve energy efficiency by 2 per cent per year. This is likely to be measured in terms of a performance indicator, which may be in terms of kWh, kWh/sq m², carbon dioxide emissions, and so forth. If it is measured in cost terms, an adjustment for any changes in fuel prices must be made for the results to have any meaning.

The importance of measuring where energy is used should also be emphasised. For instance, many organisations cannot separate their use of electricity for power and for lighting, nor distinguish where steam and hot water are used after they leave the boilerhouse. Measurement enables energy use to be assessed against standards and its costs to be allocated to users. Adequate metering is essential for good energy management.

In practice, there can be all sorts of variations from year to year. The weather has been different, there are more people and more computers in the office, some parts of the building have been enlarged or refurbished. It is, however, possible to apply normalisation adjustments to certain factors – such as heating degree days – and this helps to allow more accurate comparisons. Another option may be to join an accreditation scheme which relies on more than one performance indicator, enabling a better judgment to be made about good management and progressive improvement.

The value of metering data

All organisations with a maximum electrical demand of more than 100kW will already have metering systems that record consumption every half hour, every day of the week. This Code 5 metering is required under the rules covering the operation of the electricity supply market. The data gathered from these meters is primarily intended for use in billing and in balancing supply and demand requirements between generators and suppliers, but also proved useful in combating the extra liability associated with the CCL.

The metering information that is despatched for the purposes of the electricity pool is, however, edited. While this makes balancing supply and demand and billing procedures run more easily, this edited data is of little use for energy management, and it is important to get hold of the raw data. Your data collector should be able to provide this. The supplier's permission should be sought (as, technically, the data belongs to them), but it is now standard practice to allow this.

The figures for consumption will not provide a great deal of information in themselves. Their value lies in comparing them with, for example, trend data, degree day information, and normalised performance indicators. So, the data stream needs to go through some form of analysis.

The results should highlight where energy consumption patterns are exceptional, for example, at night or weekends, or over shutdown periods. They will also indicate any drift from optimum performance and can provide an early warning of serious equipment faults which bring about noticeable drops or increases in consumption over short periods of time.

This information can be made available within a matter of days, rather than the weeks it normally takes the supplier to send a bill. For this reason, it is important to ensure that the contract you make with the data collector provides for the speedy release of this information to you.

Waste water management

Sewerage is an essential service, the exact costs of which are difficult to calculate. There are ways in which businesses can keep track of the amount they pay for waste water. Water charges are tightly regulated and in a constant state of review, with the industry regulator Ofwat protecting customers' interests by setting the overall price limits that govern charges. The 10 sewerage companies in England and Wales are given strict guidelines, but accurately pricing the amount of water the businesses send back into the sewerage system is problematic. Firms can sometimes pay more than they need to.

Sewerage charges

The *Water Industry Act 1991* allows water companies to levy a single charge for sewerage, although Ofwat recommends costs are broken down into three constituent elements:

- foul drainage (including trade effluent)

- highway drainage (run-off from roads and pavements)

- surface drainage (run-off from properties).

The aim is to ensure charges are related to the services provided. This makes it easier for customers to assess whether they are being correctly billed and to check they are getting the services for which they have paid.

Foul drainage

Foul drainage refers to the dirty water discharged from lavatories, sinks, washing machines, etc. Charges are based on the volumes of water supplied to the property with adjustments made for non-return to sewer. It is not possible to measure the exact amount of waste returned and it is the responsibility of each water company to decide how it calculates its own system for payment. However, this does not prevent customers from challenging charges. If a query is made, a representative from the water company visits the site and evaluates the situation according to the evidence supplied regarding the ways in which water is used there. The object is to agree allowances.

Frozen food businesses, which use large amounts of water in production processes, hospitals (where liquids are often disposed of elsewhere) and pharmaceutical companies are examples of organisations which have a relatively low return to sewer and may be eligible for reductions. Even swimming pools can claim a discount for evaporation of water. No foul drainage charges should apply where a property is not connected to the sewerage system. The onus is generally on the consumer to come forward to claim rebates.

Highway drainage

The way water companies charge for highway and surface drainage tends to vary. Some operate a flat fee, others refer to the rateable value of the property or the surface area drained to a public sewer. According to Ofwat's 1998–99 *Report on Tariff Structure and Charges*[4], Ofwat's Director-General believes that as highway drainage benefits all those using roads, directly or indirectly, there is a case for recovering the costs of the service from highway authorities or from users of the highway. Currently, the law prevents this option and costs are recovered from sewerage customers. This situation is unlikely to change in the near future, so it is not currently possible for customers to claim a rebate for highway drainage.

Surface drainage

A charge based on run-off from properties forms a significant part of the total sewerage bill and businesses not using the service, or making only limited use of it, may be able to save money. Again, water companies differ in the way they calculate charges and not all of them differentiate between customers who are connected to the facility and those who are not. Ofwat's Director-General wants water companies to provide a clear explanation of the charges on bills and is encouraging them to reduce those charges if the property concerned does not benefit from surface drainage.

Trade effluent

Trade effluent refers to industrial waste, including that discharged at the end of or during manufacturing processes. This covers such things as waste from food factories, dairy product manufacturers, chemical plants and abattoirs. It is also classed as sewerage, but billed separately. Customers pay according to the strength and volume of the trade effluent discharged, both of which have a bearing on the level of treatment needed for the waste. Public swimming pools, for example, may benefit from lower tariffs because of the lower strength of effluent discharged.

Large-user tariffs have been introduced by most of the water companies. These work primarily through the imposition of a high fixed charge and a lower volumetric rate for water supplied – or alternatively one where the standing charge remains the same, but there is a lower volumetric rate for all consumption over an agreed level. The aim is to provide attractive water charges for high users without presenting an incentive to waste water.

Allowances

Water companies may make allowances for customers who can prove that rain water, for example, is drained and taken away by means other than the public sewer. The water may go to a soak-away or watercourse using the customer's own arrangements, or even a trade effluent meter. If significant volumes of water are not returned to the sewer, or if only a small volume of surface water is discharged, it may be worth diverting all the water so that none returns to the public sewer – which is one way to cut charges. Ofwat considers that some businesses may be underpaying for this particular service.

Metering

Some 20 per cent of non-household users, normally small businesses, remain unmetered, and in some areas this figure rises to nearly 30 per cent. Since most sewerage charges are based on the volume of water supplied to a property, meters are the best way of ensuring costs relate to usage. The regulator is keen to encourage the use of meters and believes it is the sensible option where economically viable.

Remote reading

Remote reading of meters is gaining favour. Accessing each water meter to take a direct reading is not always easy, and manual readings have to be keyed into the energy management system by hand. To combat such problems, manufacturers have developed remote-reading systems, the main technologies of interest being electronic meter reading and radio reading. For electronic approaches, the meter requires an in-built encoder linked to a touch-pad which passes data to a handheld interrogator. The data is subsequently downloaded to the energy management system. No access to premises is required to take readings. With radio, the meter reader does not have to touch the meter at all. Most remote reading systems can be retrofitted if required.

Individual water companies will have advisers on commercial and industrial metering issues. Accurate, timely information on consumption patterns can help managers keep water costs under control. If there are cost savings to be made, the water meter could be the key.

EC directives

Meeting EC directives is a requirement for water quality and compliance adds to the cost of treating sewerage and effluent. So how can reduced tariffs be justified? Ofwat considers that reduced charges are based on customers making less use of the reception and conveyance part of the service, consistent with the way tariffs for large users have developed on the water side. The way sewerage companies calculate charges is far from straightforward and structures differ from company to company. General advice from sewerage companies is to contact them if you believe you are not making full use of their services or can prove you are being overcharged.

Preventing water pollution

Point-source pollution – from sewage and industrial effluents, for example – is easily regulated. However, pollution from diffuse sources such as surface water run-off from urban areas is not. Diffuse pollution – from silt and solids in particular – is the most significant pollution being faced today. Surface water can be contaminated by oil, silt, leaves, dog or cat mess, carbon and a mixture of pollutants from the air, roads, industrial yards, car parks and other hard surfaces, such as drives and pavements. Discharges from surface water outfalls have been found with average concentrations of suspended solids over 200mg/litre – almost the same as raw sewage. Discharges have also been found contaminated with sewage debris and high levels of dangerous bacteria.

Main causes of contamination

There are five main causes of contamination:

- contaminants deposited on drained surfaces, such as oil, rubber, chemicals, pesticides and mud

- wrong connections of foul water to surface water drains, by accident or ignorance

- public ignorance of where drains ultimately lead

- spills and deliberate disposal, particularly oil, flushed into surface water drainage systems

- sudden flushing of contaminated water into drains, leading to flooding and subsequent groundwater pollution.

Heavy rainfall accelerates run-off, producing a mixture of pollutants flushing rapidly into drains, then into rivers, causing contamination and flooding. Because the natural settling-out process is bypassed, the common result is widespread contamination of natural watercourses and the public water supply.

Best management practices

The introduction of best management practices (BMPs) means non-point-source pollution and flooding can be effectively and economically prevented and/or controlled. BMPs are ways of minimising diffuse pollution. Two techniques have been developed – procedural and structural – which aim to:

- slow the speed of run-off to allow settlement, filtering and infiltration

- reduce the quantity of run-off collected

- provide natural ways of treating collected surface water before it is either discharged to a watercourse or infiltrated into land.

BMP options

A range of BMP options exist from which designers, developers, planners, drainage specialists and civil engineers may choose. These include grass swales and filter strips, infiltration basins, extended detention ponds, retention ponds, wetlands, porous surfaces, and procedural BMPs (aimed particularly at agricultural areas).

- **Swales** – these can utilise the common green space alongside roads or other open areas. Basically a much-improved ditch with a broad bottom and gently sloping sides, a swale gives a low sheet flow, slowing the water and enabling pollutants to settle out. Swales obviate the need for expensive roadside kerbs and gullies. Maintenance costs are much lower and drainage of the road surface is guaranteed.

- **Detention ponds** – these are designed to collect storm run-off, holding it for a few hours to let sediment settle out. Outside of storm periods, most ponds will be dry. The main function is to remove solids – removal rates of 80 per cent are possible. Rates for nutrient and trace metal removal are more modest, however – a retention pond or wetland will improve this performance.

- **Retention ponds** – these retain a significant volume of water all the time. The design can allow for substantial variation in the retained water level and the pond can become an attractive local amenity – as well as an effective filter for nutrients, trace metals, bacteria and organic matter.

- **Storm water wetlands** – these are enhanced wet ponds with shallow areas incorporating a variety of marsh and wetland plants covered in up to 0.15–0.3m of water. The algae and plant material filter and remove nutrients to a much greater degree than ponds alone. Storm water wetlands must always be purpose built. Leading surface water into an existing natural wetland can harm aquatic life and is not an acceptable practice.

- **Porous pavements** – these are an alternative to conventional paving and allow water to permeate through, rather than run off, the paving. Rainwater can filter directly into the subsoil or can drain into a reservoir (about 1m deep) before soaking slowly away, discharging to the watercourse or being stored for landscape watering. Porous surfaces are appropriate where run-off is lightly contaminated and close to source. They have been shown to remove up to 80 per cent of sediment, 60 per cent of phosphorus, 80 per cent of nitrogen and substantial levels of trace metals and organic matter.

- **Infiltration trenches** – these are shallow, excavated trenches, backfilled with stone to create an underground reservoir. From this, the water filters into the subsoil, and can help replenish groundwater resources.

- **French drains** – these are below-ground systems comprising a trench filled with gravel wrapped in a geotextile membrane. Run-off water is led to them directly from the surface or through a system of pipes. French drains are less costly than kerbs and gullies, and are useful where only small watercourses are available to receive run-off water.

Key facts about BMPs

- BMPs are mostly always cheaper than conventional systems, usually by up to 50 per cent.

- Maintenance requirements are generally less than those for conventional drainage systems. BMPs trap pollutants at one point, sparing managers the task of having to clean out many small structures.

- Research conducted in the US shows that pollutants cannot be considered to be hazardous or toxic material.

- Storm water ponds can be designed to be safer for children by adjusting the geometry; slopes to ponds should be gentle, minimising the risk of a child falling into one.

- With sensitive planting and landscaping, BMPs such as swales, ponds and wetlands can be attractive features, as can porous surfaces for car parks and pedestrian areas.

- Benefits include:

  o increases in property values

  o increased wildlife and conservation value

  o sustainable development

  o a cleaner water environment.

BMPs in action

Examples of BMP sites in the UK include: porous car parks at Nottingham Trent University; infiltration trenches at Shire Hall, Reading; storm water retention ponds at Lexmark's site, Rosyth; and grass swales at Freeport Leisure, West Calder.

Information on groundwater protection can be obtained from the Environment Agency.

HVAC (heating, ventilation and air conditioning)

Indoor air quality

It is estimated that the average person spends up to 90 per cent of their time inside a building. Maintaining air quality is vital to ensure health and well-being, as well as maximum productivity in the workplace. Yet, despite recent air quality initiatives relating to external air pollution and the reduction of emissions, there is currently no legislation and there are no EU directives related specifically to indoor air quality.

When defining air quality, it is important to consider everything from temperature and humidity to air flow and cleanliness, as well as the maintenance of any air conditioning or ventilation equipment used. The Heating, Ventilating and Air Conditioning Manufacturers Association (HEVAC) has set up an initiative specifically on indoor air quality. It is evaluating research on the subject and is keen to create a greater understanding about the problems that may occur if air quality is poor (see later in this chapter, **Promoting cleaner indoor air, p 300**).

Health problems (such as asthma, eye irritations and nausea) are known symptoms of poor air. There have even been cases of legionnaire's disease spread by bacteria in HVAC systems. Poor air quality also impacts on productivity in the workplace.

The effect of equipment on air quality

Factors influencing indoor air quality include furniture, carpets, fixtures and fittings, process plant and equipment and general office apparatus such as computers, photocopiers and fax machines, as well as HVAC equipment.

Temperatures increase with the amount of electrical equipment used, small quantities of toxic ozone can be produced by printers and fax machines, for example, and emissions of volatile organic compounds (VOCs) are possible by-products of soft furnishings, carpets and some furniture. Assessing the equipment and furnishings in a space and choosing equipment with minimum impact on indoor air quality is advisable and can mean smaller and less expensive HVAC equipment is needed as a result.

Saving energy and improving quality

To save energy and improve indoor air quality, HEVAC suggests:

- choosing electrical equipment with a sleep mode where possible to reduce power consumption during inactive periods

- fitting ozone filters to equipment where appropriate

- fitting carpets and furnishings with low emissions of VOCs

- having dedicated extraction equipment to control fumes and emissions

- using solvent-free inks where possible

- checking how easily equipment can be cleaned and following manufacturers' recommendations on cleaning and maintenance.

Indoor air quality can be improved simply by removing or limiting as many pollutants as possible, providing a good quality environmental control system (which includes the removal of pollutants) and ensuring adequate ventilation (natural, where possible).

The Chartered Institution of Building Services Engineers (CIBSE) recommends[5]:

- eliminating contaminants at source

- substituting with sources that produce non-toxic or less malodorous contaminants

- reducing the emission rate of substances

- segregating occupants from potential sources of toxic or malodorous substances

- improving ventilation (by local exhaust, displacement or dilution, for example)

- providing personal protection.

Choosing equipment

Choosing the correct HVAC equipment is essential. It needs to be appropriate for the space in which it is installed and maintained properly thereafter, otherwise it could have the effect of reducing air quality. Plant today is smaller and more efficient than it used to be and likewise (new) buildings are becoming more energy efficient. The Federation of Environmental Trade Associations (FETA) emphasises the importance of maintaining equipment and stresses that using top-of-the-range equipment in the wrong place can be just as damaging as older equipment, especially if it is not maintained and cleaned regularly.

Air conditioning which brings fresh air inside may be an excellent idea, but if the unit is sited in the wrong place it could actually be counterproductive, dragging more pollution indoors in the form of traffic fumes, especially if filters are not changed regularly. According to CIBSE, the grade of filtration needed varies according to several factors, including the level of external pollution and the exposure limits set to protect occupants and the amount of protection required for the internal surfaces of the building, air handling plant and air distribution system.

A voluntary system run by Eurovent, the European testing body for HVAC equipment, certifies products. Eurovent tests the equipment's performance and power rating – which ensures that the manufacturers' claims about the amount of energy the product uses are correct. The CCL encourages the use of energy-efficient systems.

Bacteria attack on HVAC systems

Experts first brought bacterial attacks on HVAC systems to London property owners' attention in 1998. In 2001, an increasing number of cases were discovered throughout the UK. The bacteria in question – pseudonomas – attack the inside of systems and ultimately turn them into sprinkler systems. Pseudonomas attack anything that will corrode. London-based systems appear to be well-covered but increasing numbers are being discovered elsewhere. It is crucial to assess risk at the testing stage of HVAC systems as problems start as soon as the pipes get wet and are then left with stagnant water. Pseudonomas – which are harmless to humans – can be spread through using dirty hoses for filling systems and unscrupulous companies selling products claiming to eradicate the problem, or giving incorrect or inappropriate advice.

A nine-point plan has been drawn up and facilities managers should check consultants and installers are complying[6]:

1.   The quality of water for filling systems should be monitored and controlled.
2.   Biocide and dispersant should be considered for use with initial fill.
3.   Dose with an appropriate biocide prior to the clean.
4.   Always test water by sampling in the cleaning process.
5.   Ensure all temporary hoses and equipment are chlorinated before use.
6.   Consider the type of filtration to be used carefully.
7.   Consider the type of biocide carefully – its longevity, for example.
8.   Consider the type of inhibitor carefully (nitrite-based units provide bacteria nutrients).
9.   Regularly monitor the micro-biological condition of the water.

Air conditioning

The view of air conditioning as a luxury product is generally being abandoned. Indeed, in a range of locations encompassing offices, shops, restaurants, bars and cars, it has become essential to have an air conditioned environment. The international marketing consulting company Frost & Sullivan believes the rising awareness of the effectiveness of air conditioning systems, linked with their ease of use and low installation costs, is adding momentum to overall market growth. Sales of commercial air conditioning systems in Europe are predicted to reach $4.4 billion by 2006, a doubling in size over the previous six years.

The need for air conditioning

Trends toward open-plan offices have led to increased demands for air conditioning systems, as the space allocated per employee is more restrictive in an open-plan area than in a conventional office. Add to this the massive amounts of heat generated by the many electronic systems in today's offices and the need for cooling becomes obvious. Opening windows is not always the answer, as in many cases the windows will be sealed units. Where the windows do open wide, the outside environment may be a busy, noisy and dirt-polluted thoroughfare.

A small office with two people and a typical range of office equipment can generate 3,000W of heat per hour, which is more than a two-bar electric fire. Poor air quality is known to reduce or inhibit productivity. The increasing drive towards air quality is expected to spur growth in the air conditioning market, certainly up to 2006. Market research shows that the office segment accounts for 59 per cent of sales.

Types of systems

Fixed

The packaged air conditioning market, which consists of packaged split systems and packaged multi-split systems, is expected to increase its share of the total market from 39.7 per cent in 1999 to 47.5 per cent in 2006.

The central-based air conditioning market, which includes the fan coil, air handling unit and chiller segments, is expected to decline from 60.3 per cent to 52.5 per cent during the same period.

There are said to be over 250 manufacturers capable of supplying air conditioning systems. Key players are Toshiba/Carrier, Daikin, Mitsubishi, York and Climaventa-De'Longhi, who between them have 38 per cent of the market. The other 62 per cent includes such names as Sharp, Sanyo, Hitachi, Fujitsu, Biddle, Airwell, Galletti and Jucker Clima. Many companies will sell systems through distributors, specialist dealers or facilities management companies. Central-based systems tend to be distributed directly by the manufacturer because they are fitted to a building's requirements.

Portable

It is possible to hire portable air conditioners with solutions ranging from small mobile temporary air conditioning units for short-term or emergency use to permanently installed heat pump units – supplying both cool and warm air – suitable for offices of any size which need cooling in the summer and heating in the winter.

Many customers for portable units are facilities managers in end-user companies or facilities management companies or heating and ventilation personnel. The market exists all year round. If a computer complex's systems go down, the facilities manager can make one call to bring in suitable equipment. The ranges on offer handle offices up to server rooms, with rental hires from £30 per week for the smallest system to £220 per week for an 8kW unit. Domestic customers – a small market – would need to spend £800 per room to acquire suitable portable systems.

Business is typically split 60 per cent for cooling in office environments to 40 per cent for emergency failures of fixed systems – and '80 per cent of the market is London'. Typical scenarios have been setting up new offices in buildings which are not air conditioned and relocations within an existing building. Listed buildings figure prominently too, as planning consent to install fixed systems is difficult to obtain.

Close control

The close control air conditioning market comprises data centres, web server farms, Internet service provider (ISP) computer rooms and centres for telecom switch gear and computer network management apparatus, where key requirements are for temperature control, humidity and filtration. This segment is valued at some £30.7 million, according to BSRIA (Building Services Research and Information Association).

The telecom market generally needs electrical energy and air conditioning (cooling) in equal measures. Combined cool and power (CCP) claims to eliminate most of the air conditioning power needs, reducing overall energy demand of a 'telehouse', typically by 22–25 per cent. The ratio of cooling and power produced by CCP closely matches the needs of a typical telehouse. Carbon dioxide emissions are reduced by over 20 per cent, securing a number of tax advantages including CCL exemption and enhanced capital allowances (see earlier in this chapter, **Reducing emissions and costs, p 286**).

Temperature control

Whatever type of air conditioning system is used, the key objective is temperature control, ideally – for office workers – a pleasantly cool, clean atmosphere with adequate levels of humidity (see earlier in this chapter, **Maintaining adequate humidity, p 301**). With web server farms however, there has to be a positive pressure in the room so that when a door is opened there is no ingress of dirt or other contaminants. Temperature has to be maintained at 21°C, plus or minus 2°C, while the relative humidity needs to be maintained at 50 per cent plus or minus 5 per cent.

The machines in these environments (computers, disk drives, network switching equipment, telecom systems, and so on) are particularly sensitive to these two drivers and cannot tolerate any rate of change. While staff in an office might tolerate variations of 10 per cent fluctuations, the machines in server farms and network switching centres cannot.

Refrigerant policy

Since usage of the R22 refrigerant has been banned in all new systems sold, most systems marketed today will be equipped with R407C refrigerants. Advice on CFC (chlorofluorocarbon) and HCFC (hydro CFC) phase-out is available from DEFRA and DTI which reflects the *EC Regulation 2037/2000* on ozone-depleting substances[7]. Two temporary exemptions are 1 July 2002 for fixed systems with cooling capacity of less than 100kW and 1 January 2004 for reversible air conditioning or heat pump systems. No one will be permitted to use virgin HCFCs from 1 January 2010 and all HCFCs, including recycled materials, will be banned from 1 January 2015.

Recovered CFCs must now be destroyed by an environmentally acceptable technology. Recovered HCFCs can either be destroyed or reused until 2015. There are some rogue companies still marketing equipment with the wrong refrigerant.

Promoting cleaner indoor air

Improving outdoor air quality in terms of lower emissions is a key objective – but what is being done to promote cleaner air indoors?

CIBSE guidelines

While legislation and guidelines on the subject are lacking in the UK, there are standards for indoor air quality set by CIBSE. These are mainly based on comfort levels. In its *Guide A on Environmental Design*[8], CIBSE states that indoor air quality 'may be said to be acceptable' if:

- not more than 50 per cent of the occupants can detect any odour

- not more than 20 per cent experience discomfort

- not more than 10 per cent suffer from mucosal irritation

- not more than 5 per cent experience annoyance, for less than 2 per cent of the time.

CIBSE also points out this does not take into account contaminants such as radon gas, which may have serious health effects, but is nevertheless odourless and difficult to detect. Workplaces should therefore be comfortable and ventilated by a sufficient quantity of fresh or purified air.

Getting the balance right is more complex than it sounds. The BRE recommends that natural ventilation is used where possible, but accepts there is a trade-off for many managers. Keeping windows tight, for example, prevents energy from escaping and thus cuts down on energy wastage. It also stops outdoor pollutants such as traffic fumes from coming in. However, with windows sealed, the risk is that temperatures will rise and indoor pollutants increase as a result.

Main pollutants

Air can become polluted in a number of ways, some of which are more obvious than others. HEVAC's indoor air quality (IAQ) initiative cites the following as the main sources of pollution:

- industrial processes producing fumes and air borne contaminants

- bacteria and dust spread by inadequately filtered and poorly maintained HVAC systems

- emissions from building materials, furnishings and equipment

- carbon monoxide produced from gas and paraffin heaters

- tobacco smoke

- pesticides sprayed on potted plants

- mould in damp areas and rotting food, both sources of bacteria

- an excessively humid atmosphere which can help the growth of bacteria.

In addition, certain types of rock can release radon gas into buildings through the foundations and air intakes. Domestic pets, dust mites, cockroaches and household plants can release irritants that result in allergic reactions.

Maintaining adequate humidity

The *Health and Safety (Display Screen Equipment) Regulations 1992* provide that employers are to ensure that 'an adequate level of humidity shall be established and maintained' in offices where there are visual display unit (VDU) users[9]. Exact levels of 'adequate humidity' are not specified, but there is a duty of care to ensure reasonable conditions are maintained. For staff health and comfort, the optimum adequate level of relative humidity is normally considered to be about 50%rH (relative humidity) and certainly not less than 40 per cent. Several optometric organisations (Association of Optometrists, College of Optometrists and EyeCare Information Service) agree with this level, as do professional bodies such as CIBSE, BSRIA, BRE and HEVAC's Humidity Group. The HSE says it is generally considered to be in the interests of worker efficiency that humidity be maintained in the range of 40–70%rH and that in warm offices the relative humidity should ebb towards the lower end of this range. *British Standard 29241* (from 7179) recommends 40–60%rH for office terminals[10].

(For more information, see the chapter on **Complying with health and safety law, pp 1–86.**)

Employers' duties

Employers are under a duty to comply with this legislation. This means monitoring humidity constantly to ascertain whether adequate levels are being provided. It is also important for employers to recognise any dry heat symptoms being experienced by staff, in order to identify whether any problems need to be addressed to ensure staff health and comfort. If such problems are not addressed by the facilities manager, the normal course of action would be for employees to complain to their employers, who would take steps to remedy the problem. If the problem continued, the next step would be to involve Environmental Health Officers and, in some cases, the unions. Eventually it could lead to prosecution as with cases of RSI (repetitive strain injury).

Recognising symptoms

Employers are now under an obligation to identify symptoms of low humidity and recognise they have a duty to take corrective measures for staff health and comfort. VDUs produce dry heat and this can cause discomfort to staff who work with computer monitors. Dry air acts like a sponge and absorbs moisture from all surrounding surfaces, such as operators' eyes, nose, throat and skin. Typical resultant dry air symptoms include headaches, dry eyes (particularly for contact lens wearers), dry throats, dry skin, frequent cold and flu-type conditions, and tiredness and lethargy. People with dry skin conditions such as eczema or psoriasis and respiratory or breathing problems such as asthma are often worst affected by the dryness. Static electricity is a conclusive indicator that humidity is too low.

Stress

Stress levels can be affected too. A nationwide research study in 2000 by stress expert Dr David Lewis of over 100 workplaces investigated the links between overly dry workplace air and employee stress. Readings showed that the environments of one in five subjects had only 25%rH, making them as dry as the Sahara desert. One in 10 had only 23%rH – as dry as California's Death Valley. In these excessively dry surroundings, employees suffer a rapid loss of water, affecting their physical and mental well-being while increasing vulnerability to workplace stress. Nationally, 83 per cent of workplaces with 35%rH or less were rated as high stress environments by their employees.

Staff discomfort

Although essential for comfort of workers, central heating and air conditioning also dry the air considerably. In addition, lighting and solar gain contribute to the problem.

As early as 1980, the World Health Organisation (WHO) recognised that air conditioning, computers, photocopiers and dust were the scourge of office life. Statistics also show that 6 per cent of staff sickness and absenteeism is due to sick building syndrome (SBS), costing the UK economy between £300 million and £650 million a year (estimated by WHO and a House of Commons environment committee). See **Complying with health and safety law: Improving well-being: sick**

building syndrome, p 30 for details of buildings at risk of SBS and WHO-recommended solutions.

However, it is possible to monitor and maintain humidity at comfort levels, resulting in a healthier, happier workforce with less sickness absence and increased productivity. This has to be good news for long-suffering employees and employers alike. It makes economic sense too, as the cost of a free-standing retrofit humidifier which plugs into a 13-amp socket is less than two to three days' staff absence due to sickness.

Measuring humidity levels

Free surveys and impartial advice are provided by the Air Improvement Centre. Since 1993, the organisation has carried out numerous humidity and air quality surveys at computerised offices in the London area. In most cases the air was too dry. Feedback from facilities managers led the organisation to design a low-cost, simple to use humidity recording kit.

When workstation risk assessments are carried out, humidity levels should be measured and recorded to ascertain whether there is an adequate level of humidity. The Centre's humidity recording kit comprises a digital thermo-hygrometer with built-in memory, a year's supply of charts showing the adequate humidity band, plus information on the legislation and what practical steps to take if the humidity is too low.

The Centre recommends taking readings in the same location at the same time each day, for example, beside the workstation in mid-afternoon when computer screens have been running for several hours and the worst (driest) conditions are being experienced. On day one, simply read off the relative humidity, record the readings and repeat daily. If readings are below 40 per cent, the air is too dry. In computerised offices, it is most unlikely humidity will be too high. By mid-afternoon humidity can frequently fall to as low as 20–25%rH, which is well below the adequate band.

Managing humidity levels

If humidity is too low, causing staff discomfort, humidity needs to be raised to adequate levels. If the air is too dry, the simple solution is to put just the right amount of moisture back into the air to restore a more healthy and comfortable atmosphere. This usually means aiming for about 50%rH for a normal indoor temperature of about 20°C. It is important to seek specialist impartial advice on the right type of humidifier, and its output rating, for the size of area. Aspects such as hygiene, noise levels and running costs must also be taken into consideration. Some units also combine air cleaning functions and will help filter out dust, traffic exhaust and tobacco smoke, as well as ozone from copiers and printers. The end result will be a healthier – and standards-compliant – workplace.

Waste management

Waste management is an ethical problem that no one can bury. Defined as the unwanted residue of an organisation's activities, waste can include anything from toxic liquids and solids, pallets and packaging, expired light bulbs and printer cartridges, to the contents of the waste paper basket.

Disposal

Three options exist for waste disposal:

- the strict reduction of waste generation – through adjustment, redesign of processes and cooperation with suppliers

- the internal – and responsible – recycling of waste materials to provide new or different products

- getting rid of the waste to someone else and making it their problem.

The third option is the most commonly deployed for business; it is an attractive option, particularly as specialist companies move into the waste management field. In the past companies had to pay the local authority or a dedicated contractor to take away unwanted rubbish (to the nearest landfill site or incinerator). Now someone may collect waste for free and use the output as their raw material.

Responsibility over profitability

Of the many millions of tonnes of solid materials, and many more tonnes of consumed water, only 25 per cent is converted into products physically consumed by customers. The balance is the national waste problem. The waste handling industry is understandably booming, worth something like £6 billion in 2001–02, according to research by the Chartered Institution of Wastes Management[11].

The public wants to see that companies are behaving responsibly. Awareness of the impact of waste is at an all-time high. Legislation is following public concern too. Company and product liability is extending into every aspect of the production process from inception to final disposal. The issue embraces a growing emotional draw to environmentalism and the pragmatism of economics. Landfill sites have become a scarce resource and there is not enough space to bury rubbish as has been the practice in the past.

Companies have to implement a coherent waste management strategy, argues DEFRA. The Environmental Protection Agency obliges directors to ensure the waste generated by their businesses is stored, moved and disposed of by approved means (or they face fines of up to £20,000 or six months in prison per offence).

A sustainable resource

The concept of waste as a sustainable resource has been around for a long time. The idea has been given a boost and recognition through the introduction of European and UK legislation. A recent guide produced by the Environment Council, *A stakeholder's guide to sustainable waste management*, is most useful. The Environment Council firmly believes 'environmental problems can be solved by involving, listening to and working with people' and indeed applied that principle in developing the guide[12].

How do companies turn waste disposal into waste management? The first step is to understand the problem, and the starting point for this is a waste audit. This identifies the materials existing as waste within the company and provides data for subsequent comparison to monitor improvement. A further benefit could be the introduction to a specialist company with which to work in implementing improvements. Kick off with the relevant local authority and/or existing waste contractor.

Savings

Responsible environmental management is logically consistent with low costs. Savings can accrue through careful housekeeping, but longer-term savings follow investment in research technology or process design.

Waste is set to be the next frontier of competitive advantage. By looking in their dustbins, companies can find new ways to improve internal business performance.

Noise and vibration

The Association of British Insurers says some 80 per cent of claims for occupational disease against employers' liability insurance relate to deafness. This compares with 6 per cent for lung diseases and 4 per cent for upper limb disorders. Hazards of high noise levels at work include:

- incurable hearing damage
- disturbance to work
- interference with communication
- stress.

Disablement benefit is paid by the Department of Social Security to people who suffer at least 50 decibels (dB) of noise-induced hearing loss in both ears (that's like trying to listen to the television through a brick wall). Any claimant must have been employed for at least 10 years in a specified noisy occupation.

Statutory requirements relating to noise at work generally are contained in the *Noise at Work Regulations 1989* (see **Complying with health and safety law: Noise at Work Regulations 1989, p 11**). Employers are required to take reasonably practicable measures on a long-term ongoing basis to reduce employees' exposure to noise at work to the lowest possible level, and to lower noise exposure where employees are exposed to levels of 90dB or above. For HSE guidance on controlling noise exposure, see **Complying with health and safety law: Reducing noise, p 24**.

There are currently no specific provisions relating to vibration other than those contained in the *Social Security (Industrial Injuries) (Prescribed Diseases) Regulations 1985* and the *Reporting of Injuries, Diseases and Dangerous Occurrences Regulations 1995*.

Damage to hearing

It is natural to lose hearing acuity with age. Loud noises cause permanent damage to the nerve cells of the inner ear in such a way that a hearing aid is ineffective. With prolonged exposure, the region of damage moves to both higher and lower frequencies. Damage begins to extend into the speech range, making it difficult to distinguish consonants, so words start to sound the same. Eventually, speech becomes a muffled jumble of sounds.

Some people are much more susceptible to hearing damage than others. There is the condition of tinnitus (ringing or whistling in the ears and a temporary dullness of hearing), experienced when a person leaves a noisy location. Care should be taken to avoid further exposure (symptoms disappearing with continued exposure actually indicate that the ear is losing the ability to respond to the noise). Medical advice should be sought.

The risk of hearing loss is dependent on the noise dose received and on the cumulative effect over time (except from catastrophic circumstances, as with explosions). A procedure for estimating the risk of handicap due to noise exposure is provided in *British Standard BS 5330*. Here, a hearing loss of 30dB is defined as a handicap (understanding of conversations and appreciation of music impaired). But note, to be entitled for DSS disability benefit, a person must suffer a loss of 50dB[13].

Sound perception

Typically, the quietest sound that can be heard (in other words, the threshold of hearing) is zero decibels (0dB) and the sound becomes painful at 120dB. It should be noted that zero decibels is not zero sound.

Depending on the method of presentation of two sounds, the human ear may detect differences as small as 0.5dB. But for general environmental noise the detectable difference is usually taken to be between 1–3dB, depending on how quickly the change occurs. A 10dB change in sound pressure level (SPL) corresponds, subjectively, to an approximate doubling/halving in loudness.

The SPL of industrial and environmental sound fluctuates continuously. It is possible to measure the physical characteristics of sound with much accuracy and to predict the physical human response to characteristics such as loudness, pitch and audibility. But it is not possible to predict subjective characteristics, such as annoyance, with certainty. A meter can only measure sound and not noise, which is defined as sound unwanted by the recipient. But in practice the terms are often interchangeable.

Sound power level

Sound output of an item of plant or equipment is often specified in terms of its sound power level, measured in decibels relative to a reference power of 1pW (pico-watt). It must not be confused with SPL, which at a particular position can be calculated from a knowledge of the sound power level of the source, provided the acoustical characteristics of the surrounding and intervening space are known. Thus, to provide a picture of the SPL-sound power level relationship, for a noise source which is emitting sound uniformly in all directions close above a hard surface in an open space, the SPL 10m from the source would be 28dB below its sound power level.

Minimising noise through design

Sound travels either via transmission or reflection. Noise transmission is the main problem in cellular offices – especially conversational noise leaking from adjoining cells. This can be especially distracting since there is less background sound in the enclosure to mask it.

In modern offices most cellular space is created by combinations of demountable full-height partitions rather than brick or block walls. The acoustic performance and fit of these partitions is crucial to good sound insulation. Manufacturers' specifications for the noise reduction coefficient of demountable partitions will be for optimum performance.

It is up to facilities managers to get as close as possible to this by ensuring that the partitions are well-fitted (special mastics and packing materials can help seal gaps where panels meet uneven floorplates).

Where there is a suspended ceiling and the panels do not pass through and stop at the upper slab, then sound will travel through the ceiling void and compromise the insulation offered by even the best partitioning. Air vents between cells and holes for piping and electrical cabling will also channel noise.

Manufacturers of suspended ceilings should be able to provide a statement of the material's noise reduction coefficient and speech frequency sound absorption.

In open-plan space, noise reflection is more of an issue than transmission. All office surfaces – flooring, wall coverings, ceilings and furnishings – can combine to reduce or increase noise reflection. Hard, flat surfaces will obviously bounce noise around a space. Soft carpeting with in-built cushioning or combined with underlay will contribute strongly to deadening ambient noise reflection as well as footfalls.

Noise reduction through screening in open-plan space is problematic. The recommended screen height to deaden sound transmission between workstations is 1.65m, but this creates the kind of cellular warren in open space that has become increasingly unfashionable over the last 10 years. Even the most absorbent low-profile screens have little effect on sound transmission.

HSE guidance warns that barriers and screens can provide a limited solution on their own. Near the noise source, most sound is received by direct transmission. A brick or steel sheet barrier can stop this, but even when it is lined with sound absorbing materials, problems with reflected sound further away will remain.

Control noise at source

One of the best ways to cut out noise is to control it at source. Modifying existing equipment to make its mechanisms quieter, for example, will cost only one-fifth of building a box around the piece of equipment.

An even better solution to noisy equipment is not to buy it in the first place. According to HSE guidance *Reducing noise at work*[14]: 'Often the single most cost-effective, long-term measure you can take to reduce noise at work is to introduce a purchasing policy for choosing quieter machinery'. This avoids the need for 'expensive retrofitting of noise control measures'.

Another example of controlling noise at source is those call centres which have abandoned the traditional rows of booths in favour of low-screened workstations. Large numbers of employees work in close proximity, avoiding excessive noise by moderating their voices (with the help of sensitive telephone headsets).

Sources of advice

HSE figures have suggested 1.3 million employees in the UK are exposed to noise levels above 85dB. Both short bursts of loud noise and long-term exposure to high noise levels can gradually, but relentlessly, damage the inner ear, according to the Royal National Institute for the Deaf (RNID). Employees may only realise their hearing has been damaged years later.

The BRE says noise is one of the most emotive issues in today's built environment, with the potential to impair health and productivity in the workplace. Once any facilities manager has acknowledged noise reduction is an issue in their workplace, BRE may represent a valuable source of help. Services include:

* accredited measurement of field and laboratory sounds transmission

* product development

* advice on best construction practice

* innovative measurement of building element performance with sound intensity

* environmental noise measurement and assessment.

Furniture

There is significant investment in new desks and office furniture. On average, new furniture is acquired every 10 years at a cost of some £1,000 per workstation. It is sobering to realise that office workers constitute nearly 50 per cent of the working population and many of their waking hours are spent at their desks. The functionality, appearance and general cleanliness of the workspace will influence how efficiently staff work, how they interrelate with colleagues and within their teams and how they view the office environment and its ambience.

Selecting furniture

Facilities managers may need to replace existing stock – desks, chairs, storage and office desk accessories. The process of selecting the right products, supplier and manufacturer need not be complex. Most suppliers will agree to lend samples of their furniture for trials. There are many consultants and facilities management contractors willing to take on any aspect of space planning. Some furniture suppliers offer free or low-cost space planning services. Whatever the decision, always seek references or testimonials.

There is also an emerging market for rental furniture. Points in its favour include:

- no capital expenditure
- no cash flow disruptions
- instant flexibility to changing work patterns
- no storage costs relating to redundant furniture
- 'free' space planning services
- immediate disaster recovery.

Workspace design

Furniture and storage options integral to a more cost-efficient and flexible workspace design include:

- **Standard workstation** – as with the principle of the universal footprint, the closer you can get to a single desk size and type for all staff, the less likely you are to have to move any desk. Where individuals need larger work surfaces or more storage than the average or are allocated meeting tables, try and provide these through modular extensions to the standard workstations, so that only these extras have to be relocated, leaving the desk undisturbed.

- **Mobile furniture** – if you are likely to have to move complete workstations, choose a system that is robust enough to stand relocation (not all are!) and is ready to move after a minimum of disassembly. Most manufacturers offer desking and filing pedestals with built-in lockable castors to facilitate movement. Check that the wheels are up to the job (again, not all are).

- **Centralised storage** – the more localised the bulk storage, the greater the chance it will have to follow staff in intra-departmental moves. Centralised filing areas on each floor mean moves around the floor shouldn't necessitate moving anything but a small amount of local filing. There may be some trade off with individual efficiency, though, if staff have to walk any distance to refer to documents.

- **Shared worksettings** – the idea that most office space was taken up by desks, each allocated to one employee who would work there all day, went unchallenged until the 1990s. Although this pattern is still dominant, an increasing number of organisations have experimented with alternative models over the past decade, such as reducing personal workspace or removing it altogether and replacing it with a variety of shared worksettings.

The thinking behind shared worksettings was that many white-collar employees were in jobs that took them away from the office for a majority of the time. These workers still claimed permanent desk space which was seldom used. Even those tied to the office were often engaged in types of work which were inadequately catered for by the traditional desk. The latter point has been reinforced by the growing emphasis on knowledge management and teamworking among white-collar workers. Traditional, rigid layouts cannot support collaborative group work or the regular forming and disbanding of project teams. These drivers have produced a variety of new office configurations, all of which have elements in common:

- **teamspace** – in which groups of employees retain a small 'home' desk each and the rest of their space is recycled for shared worksettings such as meeting space and break-out areas.

- **hotdesking** – where employees who spend a large minority of their time out of the office have no allocated space but use non-allocated workstations, either on a first-come, first-served basis or by booking in advance.

- **hotelling** – where all workspace is bookable by the hour.

The most common of these configurations, hotdesking, is covered in more detail in **Space design and management, pp 329–350.**

Workstations

Existing workstations can be easily recycled as shared desking. For hotdesking, an 1,800mm-wide desktop is unnecessary and takes up space that could be better used. A surface deep enough to hold a computer monitor – for a shared PC or docking facilities for laptops – and wide enough to spread papers is all that is needed.

Height-adjustable desking

Height-adjustable desking is now more common and should be specified where possible to allow users maximum comfort, however short the stay. When choosing workstations for hotdesking, work surfaces and edgings should be checked for durability. Also ask for references from other users to ensure the products will stand up to more intensive use from multiple users.

Seating

Workstation chairs need to be easily adjustable for height, back support and preferably seat tilt. If more than one person is going to use a chair, the configuration controls need to be easily located and robust. To alert staff to hotdesking chairs, one idea is to colour-code them with vivid fabrics and designs.

Soft seating for break-out areas gives an opportunity to add a splash of colour to the office layout. Sofas and tub chairs should be simply styled and firmly upholstered, designed for comfort but not for curling up on in front of the fire. Fabrics should be hard-wearing and easily removed for cleaning, especially if they are located near catering or vending points.

Aiding correct posture

The type of chair should fit both the task and length of time doing it. Chairs should have a forward tilt mechanism to open the pelvis – similar to the position in standing – and allow the correct concave curve to be maintained in the lumbar spine while sitting. This consequently leads to correct positioning of the other spinal curves. Seating should support the body in a suitable posture – in other words, the 'S' form of the spinal column should be maintained. The purpose of the backrest is to support the whole spinal column effectively, no matter what seating position is adopted.

The user should be able to move and change postures regularly and freely without any constraints from the chair. Cushioning and covering should allow for air circulation over the skin and the surface material must provide sufficient friction to prevent sliding. For details of HSE guidance on seating, see **Complying with health and safety law: seating, p 23**.

The cost of back problems

Back problems are the greatest cause of illness among people of working age. Most people spend over 70 per cent of their waking day sitting, and this is cited as one of the major factors responsible for back pain and associated injuries. Each year there are 30,000 work-related back injuries, 33,000 work-related back accidents and 500,000 work-related back illnesses. The cost to industry has been estimated at 117 million days of certified sick leave, resulting in at least £5.5 billion in lost production each year. Given all these statistics (even allowing for margins of numerical error) it obviously pays to get the seating right.

Buying furniture

The Office Furniture Advisory Service (OFAS) provides full information on standards and what to look for in purchasing furniture. There are about 350 office furniture and seating manufacturers in the UK, and many more suppliers.

Catering

Why should a company have a restaurant? Many large organisations do not, arguing that nearby local restaurants, cafes, coffee shops, sandwich bars and fast-food outlets provide all the resources required. This philosophy can have an adverse effect: long off-site lunch breaks and stress caused by having to hurry back to the office are two potential pitfalls, and a lack of control over the staff's diet is another – a healthy diet produces a healthy workforce, which means less absenteeism. Furthermore, a company with no restaurant is less likely to be able to attract staff because of the lack of quality food and subsidised prices, and has nowhere to provide hospitality for customers.

Staff have to be well-watered and fed to be content. In research undertaken by Zenith International in 2001, 85 per cent of sample respondents said they worked more effectively in a smarter workplace and the two items workers considered most essential to a productive day were natural daylight (93 per cent) and chilled water (83 per cent).

Drinking water

Workers do not drink enough water. Indeed, nearly 70 per cent said the amount of water they drink is directly related to where the water cooler is kept, and 80 per cent of these people were frustrated at coolers being too far away. Lack of water leads to poor concentration, fatigue, irritability and headaches. It would thus appear that a key factor in keeping productivity to a maximum is ensuring staff have access to a water cooler which is integrated into the design of the workplace. Not everyone wants to eat at work, but everyone needs water.

Company restaurant facilities

Sitting down to eat together at lunch or for a snack is one of the best ways to break down barriers, discuss problems, thrash out misunderstandings or share company gossip. To do this, staff typically adjourn to the restaurant, coffee bar or similar facility. Company size will dictate the type of restaurant or cafe facilities and levels of services offered. But the driver behind all these plans is to get staff into a mood where they not only want to come to work, but enjoy it as well, with eating and drinking central to that enjoyment.

What do the staff want?

Where company catering and restaurants are concerned, facilities managers must try to understand their customers' needs. Easy-to-organise staff surveys of what foods and drinks are preferred, what times of day staff would like them served, reaction to special menus and themed eating days, for example, can produce extra usage of the restaurant facility.

A focal point

Making the restaurant an attractive, comfortable and interesting place to eat and socialise, as well as promoting it as a centre for networking, meeting visitors or prospective clients and holding impromptu and scheduled meetings, will pay dividends for the company – and, in so doing, for the facilities manager. To that end, the restaurant should be easily accessible from all parts of the building and as equally visible.

Fast food

While only operating a fast food-type operation is not recognised as common sense, it may be prudent to offer staff the opportunity to have access to a 'fast' service. The staff survey can help here. Making eating a worthy experience within the company will help boost staff morale and retention.

Vending machines

Many facilities managers eschew vending machines because of the quality of the beverages produced and the image that has built up around them. However, there is still a market for these machines. It is unlikely that the 'tea lady', complete with trolley, buns of dubious freshness and a steaming urn, will ever make a full-scale reappearance. The future of the vending machine would seem assured. But canny facilities managers will approach the area sensitively and provide the staff with what they want. Assuming the board can be convinced, this will help the staff work better, aid staff retention and help percolate money through to the bottom line.

Times

A restaurant should offer a full range of meals and general refreshments – at times the staff want them. Moves to more global trading have resulted in offices being open at what were hitherto deemed antisocial hours. The concept of facilities being offered at practically all hours is not as ridiculous as it used to sound. It is a fact that food still being served fresh at 2.30 pm will both encourage a wider spread of diners sitting down for a meal and increase the numbers of staff utilising the restaurant.

Menu

Some people will want to bring in their own food and drink. This should not be discouraged, and space should be made available. Others will increasingly want organic food, or gluten-free products – again the level of demand can be gauged through a staff survey. It is a misnomer to label food 'home-cooked' when it isn't. But this is an expression that has crept into the vernacular and now sits alongside such culinary delights as seasonal specials, cordon bleu cooking, chicken tikka masala, regional speciality days and low-fat cuisine.

Planning a restaurant

Design

The company must select a design strategy (embracing appearance, space planning, lighting, utilities and acoustics) to reflect its culture and image. The physical appearance of a restaurant is important and care will have to be taken to differentiate it from any offerings in the local surroundings. Decisions will have to be taken on whether to provide Internet access points, so that staff can plug in their laptops while having a break or talking to customers.

Siting and layout

Siting of the restaurant facility is determined by the availability of utility services and the fact that cooking smells wafting into the reception atrium might not be a good idea for customers waiting there. The restaurant needs to be welcoming and designed so that people can flow freely without obstruction. Key to restaurant layout is throughput, trying to avoid or alleviate queuing problems (one suggestion is to provide a flexible paypoint arrangement, to avoid what is typically the biggest bottleneck). Food should always be on display, tables cleaned regularly and dirty dishes removed efficiently. Clear notices and signs should guide customers through the facility.

Space and costs

If a company opts to serve ready-prepared meals with supporting beverages, sandwiches and soup, its kitchen space requirements will be much less than for an operation providing a gastronomic experience starting from raw ingredients. The amount of space required for food production areas is dictated by the type and range of food offered. Specialist help is needed to design a catering kitchen. If the restaurant is to offer a single-sitting hot meal service only, there needs to be a ratio of three restaurant spaces (that is, areas that can earn money) to every kitchen space (the food preparation area, stores and servery). For two or three sittings this ratio reduces to two restaurant space areas.

The operating costs per employee per year average at about £400 but will increase if the company provides a subsidy.

Ambience

Food is always associated with a feel-good factor. Conducting business, meeting friends, or discussing issues with work colleagues can be carried out more enjoyably over a meal, snack or drink. What adds to the enjoyment is the ambience of the surroundings. This is aided by the décor, sounds, lighting and building infrastructure.

- **Décor** – this concerns colour schemes, furniture, wall and floor coverings, crockery and cutlery design, plants/flowers/foliage and paintings, sculpture and murals, and so on. A good designer is necessary to ensure optimum results. Too garish a colour scheme makes diners feel ill while minimalist white walls call for sensitive incorporation of pictures and plants. Likewise with soft furnishings and furniture generally – too wild a pattern and the diners will be turned off. The type of soft furnishings also impacts on sound absorption and thermal barriers, as well as being decorative. Restaurant staff should wear uniforms of a suitably restrained colour.

- **Sounds** – piped 'muzak' is not to everyone's taste but designers consider noise a pre-requisite. Noise mostly comes from the diners themselves. Noise creates an atmosphere of being busy. Quiet(er) areas need to be supplied – also with 'muzak', such as water features or wind chimes, to mask extraneous noise. What diners do not want to hear is kitchen noise.

- **Lighting** – daylight plays a major part in the restaurant. Lights are used to create atmosphere and good lighting designers are worth employing. The range and type of lamps available means most moods can be catered for and created.

- **Building infrastructure** – the restaurant facility needs to be serviced regularly, with food supplies delivery and waste removal, for example, taken care of. It must also be well-served by water, electricity and gas supplies. Heating and ventilation are key requirements, as is humidity control and air temperature. Air filtration to remove particles above 5 microns is mandatory.

Management

Some catering facilities will be staffed and managed in-house, but most will be run by a catering contractor under the management of the facilities manager.

Costing

How to cost a catering facility is difficult. What should be included? All vending machines, for example? Is the service costed per user or per member of staff? Some companies provide a space – a shell – within the building and request a caterer to provide a defined level of service. The caterer pays no rent but must provide the right quality of service to recoup costs. With some of these deals, the company will fit out the kitchens and furnish the restaurant areas, while the caterer provides the staff, meals and beverages. To make a return, it is generally accepted that at least 50 per cent of the staff should utilise the restaurants regularly. Prices should be kept below those of outlets in the local High Street and the ambience, as noted, must be acceptable.

Subsidies

Staff restaurants can be run with or without subsidies. A typical form of subsidy occurs where an employer pays the overheads of the facility – premises and staff, say – and the cost of the food and other items is obtained from the restaurant users. There are subsidies which involve a fixed cash payment from the employer. Average food cost per meal in 2002 was 81.9p, the same as in 1999 (according to the British Hospitality Association survey).

Choosing caterers

Few companies have the resources to run a catering facility in-house. This means most outsource. Nevertheless, the company still needs to set the pace and define what is wanted of its catering supplier. Facilities managers have pivotal roles to play. The choice of caterer will involve setting up a project team whose members must cover all the points already discussed here. The process of selection of caterer must involve food tasting, layout, menu content and discussions with caterers, their employees and existing customers (including site visits). Will the two companies be able to work together, or is there likely to be some culture clash?

Practical advice on how to go about selecting a catering contractor on the basis of best value for money is contained in a booklet from the Chartered Institute of Purchasing and Supply (CIPS), *How to buy catering services*. Each year the British Hospitality Association surveys the contract catering market in the UK, based on responses from the 16 main companies in the food service management industry. Various statistics are produced by this report, such as average food cost per meal, salary expectations, turnover, number of PPP projects in which contractors have an interest, and types of contract.

Future prospects

More change is expected in the catering sector. Food will become a more potent weapon to attract key workers, with free breakfasts (full English or continental) being offered to entice staff into the office early and beat traffic hold-ups – and to make the workforce more productive. More food options will be available throughout the day, reducing pressure on the restaurant and meaning that a smaller-sized facility is all that is needed.

Cleaning

Cleaning is one of the most outsourced functions. While it is arguably one of the least glamorous, people will always notice if it is not done. It is also a thankless task – a facilities manager might expend an inordinate amount of resources and budget ensuring the wards and corridors of a hospital are clean, for example, only to be judged on how quickly and efficiently they put up a shelf in a sister's office. Cleaning is also an antisocial occupation, most workers in that sector having to work after offices have closed for the day. Late and nightshift working is normal.

Market dynamics

The market comprises everything to do with industrial and commercial cleaning – interior cleaning of office space, leisure facilities, retail units, factories, non-domestic buildings generally, local authority units, and so forth, and exterior cleaning (such as of windows, metal cladding), as well as vehicles, industrial equipment – and pest control services. Of late, however, the sector has seen many companies hitherto totally dedicated to cleaning diversifying into offering facilities management services as well as janitorial and portering services, linen, washroom and workwear hire and equipment hire.

With the introduction of the Private Finance Initiative (PFI) and Public Private Partnership (PPP) contracts it has not been uncommon for contracts of 30 years (and more in some cases) to be agreed. But according to the CSSA, which acts as a marker for the industry, contracts have traditionally been from a few months to five years, and sometimes seven, in duration.

Selecting contractors

Service level agreements (SLAs) need to be marketed carefully. The main objectives are:

- establishing the project objectives
- identifying key players
- securing commitment
- agreeing the scope of services within review.

Cleaning in the office environment will be broken down into general cleaning, janitorial services, window cleaning and deep cleans.

When selecting contractors, useful documentation for the facilities organisation includes:

- customer satisfaction surveys
- service utilisation statistics
- job descriptions of services delivery staff
- number and type of complaints
- service specifications
- menu of call-off services
- budgetary information
- contractors' performance information.

Once SLAs have been established, they have to be periodically reviewed to ensure they continue to deliver the right services to support the activities of customers. Annual budget preparation should include a review of service levels. The initiation of an SLA project often increases the need to demonstrate the consistency of service delivery. Customers expect the facilities manager to market the services offered, track performance of the services over time and report regularly. This expectation will require the facilities manager to develop better documentation about each service and develop systems that will track the volume of call-offs, frequency of service failures and rectifying measures. Creating an audit trail is part of the overall communications process, but key documents that need to be developed include:

- facilities management services policy
- service directory
- service specifications
- operating procedures
- customer feedback records.

SLAs and managing contractors are covered in greater detail in **Outsourcing, pp 235–254**.

Costs

How do you cost a cleaning contract? There is no magic formula, although generally, labour, National Insurance contributions, holidays, supervision, materials and equipment would need to be included.

The national minimum wage hourly rate is £4.50 (October 2003) and, economic conditions allowing, expected to rise to £4.85 in October 2004. It is understood that over half the cleaning workforce was paid less than £3.60 before the national minimum wage was introduced. According to CSSA, 35 per cent of its members are paid at the national minimum wage rate, 65 per cent above this. Cleaners employed in the public sector tend to be full-time employees whereas in the private sector the work is traditionally part-time.

When the *Working Time Regulations 1998* (see **Complying with law on staff, casual and contract workers: working time, p 89**) were introduced, the cleaning sector suffered a double whammy, as to make up income streams to pay the workers at the proper levels, SLAs had to be adjusted and in many cases the frequency with which cleaning was carried out had to be curtailed. The impacts of that were keenly felt in certain quarters, most notably the health service. There are no known statistics which might indicate how the total contract cleaning workforce might have been reduced as a result of these initiatives, although the diversification mentioned earlier by some of the key players in the industry could have helped to alleviate any difficulties.

Lighting

Energy efficiency

Lighting accounts for some 20 per cent of total electricity consumption in the UK. The 0.43p per kW/h CCL levy on electricity used affects all sectors, including industry, utilities, transport and local government. Introducing energy-efficiency lighting schemes is one way of mitigating the effects of the levy, as well as following the Action Energy initiative of cutting carbon dioxide emissions. Replacing obsolete installations with more efficient light sources and introducing high frequency control gear and lighting controls are also steps that can be taken. It is often the case that lighting efficiency savings exceed the cost of the levy.

A survey by Frost & Sullivan in 2000 reported how the surge in demand for lighting controls across Europe was attributable to end-users' rising awareness of energy-saving issues and the benefits associated with high quality lighting and effects. The study cited levies of fossil fuel-generated energy as being a principal driver behind growth in the European market for lighting controls.

The market is set to change with the wider use of electronic gear, especially involving digital addressable lighting interface (DALI). According to Frost & Sullivan, the new interface will effectively merge all the superior aspects of the light management systems and control gear markets, allowing complete lighting control and improved light output. How DALI integrates with open systems protocols BACnet, EIB or LONworks remains to be seen (see earlier in chapter, **Open systems in building control, p 282**).

Objectives of good lighting

Good lighting should vouchsafe employee safety, acceptable job performance, and good workplace atmosphere, comfort and appearance – a task that is not limited to maintaining correct lighting levels. Of ergonomic relevance are:

- horizontal illuminance
- uniformity of illuminance over the job area
- colour appearance
- colour rendering, glare and discomfort
- ceiling, wall and floor reflectances
- job to environment illuminance ratios
- job and environment reflectances
- vertical illuminance.

Sources of light

Natural lighting

The cheapest form of lighting is the most natural – daylight. There is only limited application where production is needed beyond the hours of daylight, at all seasons, and where daytime visibility is restricted by climatic conditions. Windows alone, however, cannot always provide adequate lighting for the interior of large floor areas. The most common source of daylight is through side windows. But large areas of glass can cause uncomfortable thermal conditions in summer within the building.

To maximise the benefits of natural light, low screens and glazed partitions can help allow clear sightlines to windows. Also, 'owned' desks should be closest to the windows, with areas of occasional use, such as meeting spaces, placed further away. Proximity to daylight does bring with it the problem of glare, especially for DSE users. The easiest solution is to introduce blinds, preferably of a venetian or similarly adjustable type, to allow local control. The value of anti-glare filters placed in front of computer screens is debatable and these should only be used if all else fails.

Natural lighting has to be supplemented, most of the time, with artificial lighting, for which the most common source is electric lighting. The recommended minimum ratio of artificial light to natural light at any long-term worksetting is 1:5.

Electric lighting

The selection of the sources of electric lighting for particular applications are most often driven by factors such as capital costs, running costs and replacement costs. These costs are as important as the size, heat and colour effects called for from the lighting units. Any lamp's efficiency is measured as light output in lumens per watt of electricity. A lumen is the unit of luminous flux, describing the amount of light received by a surface or emitted by a source of light. Typical values for various lamp types are:

Type of lamp	Lumens per watt
Incandescent lamps	10–18
Tungsten halogen	22
High pressure mercury	25–55
Tubular fluorescent	30–80 (depending on colour)
Mercury halide	60–80
High pressure sodium	100

Common incandescent lamps (that is, coiled filament lamps where the temperature is raised to white heat by the passage of current, so emitting light) are generally inexpensive to install but suffer from relatively expensive running costs. A discharge or fluorescent lighting scheme (where electric current passes through certain gases and in so doing produces an emission of light) has higher capital costs but higher running efficiency, lower running costs and longer lamp life. In larger workplaces, there is often a choice between discharge and fluorescent lamps. The normal mercury discharge lamp and the low-pressure sodium discharge lamp possess restricted colour performance, although recent developments in high-pressure sodium discharge lamps and colour-corrected mercury lamps do not suffer from this disadvantage.

Standards of lighting

The amount of light (standard of illuminance) needed for a given location or activity depends on many variables, such as general comfort considerations and the visual efficiency called for. The unit of illuminance is the lux (Lx), which equals one lumen per square metre. The unit of foot candle is not used – this unit referred to the number of lumens per square foot. To measure the degree of illuminance at a specific workplace, a reliable measuring instrument is called for, such as a pocket light meter, which incorporates a photoelectric cell.

HSE Guidance Note *Lighting at work* (1997)[15] relates illuminance levels to the degree or extent of detail which needs to be seen in a specific task or situation. For example, for work requiring perception of detail in an office, the average illuminance should be 200Lx and the minimum measured illuminance should be 100Lx.

See **Complying with health and safety law: lighting, p 31,** for more on the statutory requirements and health and safety issues relating to lighting.

Lighting output

The lighting output of a given lamp will reduce gradually in the course of its life, but improvements can be obtained by regular cleaning and maintenance – not only of the lamp itself but also of the reflectors, diffusers and other parts of the luminaire. A good, economical lamp replacement policy could include, for example, changing batches of lamps, rather than deal with them singly as they wear out.

Lighting quality

While the quantity (or amount) of lighting assigned to a location or task in terms of standard service illuminance is a key feature of lighting design, it is equally necessary to take in the qualitative aspects of lighting. These have direct and indirect effects on the manner in which people view their work activities and any dangers that could be posed. Quality of lighting is affected by:

- **Glare** – this is the effect of light causing impaired vision or discomfort experienced when parts of the visual field are very bright, compared with the surroundings. It can be experienced in three different forms:

  - *Disability glare* – caused by bright lamps directly in the line of vision, this is visually disabling.

  - *Discomfort glare* – caused by too much contrast of brightness between an object and its background, this is often associated with poor lighting design. Discomfort often occurs without a person's ability to see detail necessarily being impaired.

  - *Reflected glare* – this the bright light reflected off shiny or wet work surfaces, where detail may be completely hidden.

- **Distribution** – this relates to the way light is spread. A standard to classify light fittings has been drawn up called the British Zonal Method which classifies the luminaires according to the way they distribute light, from BZ1 (light passes downwards in a narrow column) to BZ10 (light spreads in all directions). It is important to note that a fitting with a low BZ number does not mean it offers less glare. The shape of the room, reflective surfaces and position are all equally relevant.

- **Brightness** – also known as luminosity, is very subjective and difficult to measured. Nevertheless, a good brightness ratio (the ratio of apparent luminosity between a task object and the surroundings) can be computed by making sure the reflectance of all surfaces in the working area is well-maintained. Interior design should take account of reflectance values. If the recommended illuminance level for a particular task (or task illuminance factor) is 1, the effective reflectance values ought to be 0.6 for ceilings, 0.3–0.8 for walls, and 0.2–0.3 for floors.

- **Diffusion** – this is the projection of light in all directions with no particular priority. Diffused lighting is popular, and reduces the amount of glare emanating from bare luminaires. Drawbacks stem from the density of shadows caused – these can affect safety standards or even reduce lighting efficiency.

- **Colour rendition** – this refers to an object's appearance under a particular light source, compared to its colour under natural light (a reference illuminant, for example). The colour-rendering properties of luminaires should not clash with those of natural light. They should also be as effective at night, when there is no natural light contributing to the working area's total illumination.

Fluorescent light strips are the cheapest and most common form of lighting in workplaces, but can cause glare and (often imperceptible) flickering. Indirect light sources such as uplighters (using more powerful halogen or sodium bulbs) provide a warmer, flicker-free light and are popular with building users. Unfortunately, the flat surfaces (on suspended ceilings, for example) required to reflect light to desk level may not be easy to combine with good acoustic absorption.

Computer-controlled lighting systems

The Energy Saving Trust (EST) launched its 'Lightswitch' initiative in 2002 to provide funding to small and medium-sized UK businesses and individuals to adopt energy-saving measures. As a result there are now a number of consultancies and suppliers who recommend the application of local automatic switching devices, such as standalone presence detectors, as a means of reducing lighting energy costs within the working environment. UK building regulations have also recognised the importance of local control in achieving energy savings. It has been stipulated that no switch should be more than 8m from the light fittings it controls.

Lighting specialists, however, believe a more holistic approach, involving the centralised control of all lighting within the working environment, provides a much more powerful solution. Such schemes allow total control of each open-plan area, both from a central control point and locally by staff themselves. They offer a number of ways to achieve high energy savings while simultaneously offering flexible control of lighting schemes to reduce other building operational costs. Automatic control interfaces with the building management system (BMS) can provide energy-saving benefits which go far beyond lighting alone.

Even a simple local management system combining a manual switch-on facility with a 'staff absent' switch-off feature can effectively double energy efficiency. Getting staff to switch on lighting themselves ensures that lighting is only turned on when staff actually need it, and it can then be switched off automatically once staff have left their work area. With a computer-controlled system, the switch-on operation can be achieved in a number of ways, for example by personal infra-red transmitter, desk telephone or an icon on each individual PC screen.

Studies have shown that where staff are able to dim personal lighting, they typically set their lights at a comfort level below traditional guidelines. They thereby accrue additional energy savings while working in their own optimum lighting conditions.

Lighting management systems

Lighting management systems (LMSs) provide flexibility through the independent monitoring and control of every luminaire in a building. The key to effectiveness here is the flexibility of the hardware and graphics software which monitors the installation on screen. The system utilises virtual wiring, where light fittings are 'linked' to switches on other local control devices through software, and where essential and non-essential lighting 'distributions' exist in software only. In a virtual wiring system, changes to light-switching arrangements associated with staff or office layout changes are carried out from the PC.

Such systems combine digital dimming technology with LonWorks interoperability. LonWorks provides a platform for implementing distributed, open, multi-vendor, interoperable control network systems enabling various systems from different manufacturers to communicate and interoperate. Using LonWorks, the integration of a building's lighting control system within the BMS can be achieved. This ensures facilities managers are able to control energy-saving routines which are triggered by factors such as occupancy, external temperatures, solar-heating effects and light levels.

Staff entering offices can be detected by LMS presence detectors, which broadcast an 'occupation message' over the LonWorks control network. Messages received by the BMS then boost the speed of the heating/cooling unit in the occupied area. Staff who want their lighting on can set the desired dimming level from their desktop.

Motorised window blinds can be centrally controlled (for reducing solar gain), with local control in occupied areas. Once areas are vacated by staff, lighting will be automatically switched off or dimmed to a reduced level and local environmental controls switched to a non-occupancy mode.

LonWorks and LonTalk protocols can be used throughout systems for transmission of data on both vertical and horizontal buses. Systems claim to be able to receive and transmit data to and from other LonWorks systems from any point on the lighting management network.

Emergency lighting

Emergency lighting provides a lower than normal level of light and illuminates exit signs to assist in the evacuation of a building. It also provides light on safety equipment, such as fire extinguishers, call points and hose reels.

Emergency lighting luminaires

Emergency lighting luminaires fall into three main types:

- **Self-contained** – the luminaire contains the battery, a control circuit for charging the battery and an inverter for operating the lamp in case of supply failure.

- **Conversions** – almost any type of mains luminaire can be converted for emergency use by the addition of either a self-contained conversion kit (conversion module plus battery) or a slave inverter conversion module.

- **Slave** – the luminaire is powered from a remote central battery cabinet and is interconnected via fire-resistant cable, which should ensure that, if fire affects the wiring, the salve luminaire would continue to operate. The emergency supply can be DC or AC.

Categories of emergency lighting

The different categories or modes of emergency lighting can be described as follows:

- **Non-maintained** – the luminaire only operates when the electrical mains supply fails or there is local circuit failure.

- **Maintained** – the luminaire operates when the supply fails but also operates in a mains-healthy condition using a separate switched mains supply.

- **Sustained (combined)** – the luminaire contains two or more lamps, one being for normal mains operation and the other only for emergency use.

Standards

An emergency lighting scheme must comply with the requirements of the statutory authority and the appropriate standard. The duration of an emergency lighting system is a minimum of one hour. However, most applications in the UK stipulate three hours. In the UK, the latest addition has been the publication of *BS5266 Part 7:1999* (hereafter known as Part 7) which is the UK's adoption of the European Standard *EN1838:1999*. Part 7 forms the standard for emergency lighting applications and replaces the Code of Practice *BS5266 Part 1:1988*. The important changes in the requirements are noted later[16].

Emergency lighting systems within buildings are required to be verified to the new requirements. The best way to ensure compliance is to seek a product approved by the Industry Committee for Emergency Lighting (ICEL), part of the Lighting Industry Federation, (LIF).

Illuminating escape routes

Part 7 states a minimum level of 1Lx is required on the centre line of the emergency escape route (formerly 0.2Lx). However a deviation is listed – applicable in the UK – for a minimum level of 0.2Lx but is only for 'routes which are permanently unobstructed'. In practice such criteria would be difficult to guarantee. Points of emphasis, whether on an escape route or in an open area, should be provided with the appropriate illuminance. These points include a change of level, stairs, change of direction, fire-fighting equipment, call points and first aid posts. The ratio between the minimum and maximum level should be no greater than 40:1. In addition, a clause has been added for the limiting of disability glare within the field of view.

Part 7 states the minimum level of illuminance at floor level should be 0.5Lx. Originally it had been an average of 1Lx. The effect of this may result in the requirement for additional luminaires. Similar to the escape routes, the ratio between the minimum and maximum level should be no greater than 40:1.

All these minimum levels must be obtained, even at the end of discharges from aged components, while ignoring the effects of reflections from surfaces such as walls. So with a new installation, in practice, the light output measured should be two or three times the minimum to ensure that the standard is met throughout the full life of the installation.

Illuminating safety signs

Part 7 specifies that the safety signs used to indicate emergency escape routes and first aid areas have to be illuminated and be capable of being seen in all relevant viewing directions. In addition, viewing distances are specified for internally and externally illuminated signs, based on the height of the pictogram on the signs. The European Safety Signs Directorate enforced in the UK by the *Health and Safety (Safety Signs and Signals) Regulations 1996* stipulates a common European pictogram for means of escape from buildings. All worded-only 'exit' signs should have been replaced by December 1998.

Maintenance

Taking care to install reliable emergency lighting is commendable, but the lighting needs to be regularly inspected and maintained. Facilities managers should not fall into the trap of leaving it to the next time a fire officer is expected – by then it could be too late. Batteries fail, chargers can stop working and lamps can be faulty. For users, that means an expensive refurbishment and premises closure while remedial work is undertaken.

Testing equipment

Manual testing today is viewed as labour-intensive and expensive. Self-testing systems complying with relevant standards and European directives are available from reputable manufacturers and, despite the higher capital cost, they are efficient and reliable. A key advantage for users is the ability to produce records to the fire authorities which demonstrate that the lighting has been tested and proven to be functional.

Testing of emergency lighting comprises two areas:

- automatic self-testing emergency lights suitable for smaller installations
- centrally controlled test and report systems for large-scale installations.

Timers within standalone self-testing systems can carry out tests at weekly, monthly, six-monthly and annual intervals with system failure indicated either visually or audibly. For buildings with more complex emergency lighting, testing units exist which can provide detailed information on fault detection. On these, the exact location of faulty luminaires will be shown and tests can be carried out at times to suit the user.

Some basics, applying equally to manual and automated systems, need to be observed when testing emergency lighting systems. Although automatic systems offer many advantages in saving labour and providing consistency of test format, they must have facilities that are appropriate for the site they are to be used for. The main considerations are to ensure:

- the test duplicates the emergency operation

- the faults indication is clear and retained until rectified

- the tests minimise the risks of the building being inadequately protected while batteries are being recharged.

The function test is of short duration and checks that the lamp operates satisfactorily from the battery and that the circuit is healthy. For manual systems this should be done monthly; for automatic systems, weekly. The full discharge test checks battery capacity in addition to circuit operation. The British Standard Code of Practice allows this to be performed twice a year for one third of rated duration, for the first three years of self-contained battery life. Thereafter an annual full-rated test is needed. Revised draft application standards simplify this, calling for systems to just have the annual full discharge. Whatever system is installed, all tests must be logged and made available at any time.

1 CHP quality assurance information *www.chpqa.com*
2 International Alliance for Interoperability (IAI), *www.iai-international.org*
3 Environmental reporting – see *www.defra.gov.uk/environment/envrp/gas/index.htm*
4 Ofwat, *www.ofwat.gov.uk* and list of reports at *www.waterview.org.uk/aptrix/ofwat*
5 CIBSE, tel: 020 8675 5211, *www.cibse.org*
6 For more information visit *www.fhp.uk.com*
7 EC regulations are available through London office of The Stationery Office, tel: 020 7873 8372, *www.tso.co.uk*
8 CIBSE, tel: 020 8675 5211, *www.cibse.org*
9 Copies of HSE guidance on the DSE Regulations 1992, ISBN 0 11 886331 2, are available from the Stationery Office.
10 British Standards BS 29241, see *www.bsi-global.com*
11 Chartered Institution of Wastes Management, tel: 01604 620426, *www.iwm.co.uk*
12 Environment Council, tel: 020 7836 2626, *www.wasteguide.org.uk*
13 British Standards BS 5330, see *www.bsi-global.com*
14 ISBN 0 7176 1511 1.
15 HS(G)38.
16 British Standards BS 5266 Part 7:1999 and EN 1838:1999, see *www.bsi-global.com*, *www.icel.co.uk*, and *www.tso.co.uk*

Information

General

Action Energy *www.actionenergy.org.uk*

Action Energy helpline 0800 58 57 94

BSRIA (Building Services Research and Information Association), tel: 01344 426511, *www.bsria.co.uk*

British Institute of Facilities Management (BIFM), tel: 01799 508608, *www.bifm.org.uk*

Building Research Establishment (BRE), tel: 01923 664000, *www.bre.co.uk*

Carbon Trust: *www.eca.gov.uk*

Chartered Institute of Building Services Engineers (CIBSE), tel: 020 8675 5211, *www.cibse.org*

Facilities Management Association (FMA), tel: 020 7727 5238, *www.fmassoc.org*

HSE, tel: 0870 154 5500, *www.hse.gov.uk*

The Stationery Office, tel: 0870 600 5522, *www.clicktso.com*

Gas and electricity

BACnet, *www.bacnet.org*

CHP Association, tel: 020 7828 4077, *www.chpa.co.uk*

CHP Club website, *www.chpclub.com*

The EIB bus, *www.eiba.com*

The Energy Systems Trade Association's Building Controls Group, *www.esta.org.uk/bcg*

International Alliance for Interoperability (IAI), tel: 020 8660 1631, *www.iai.org.uk*

LONmark Interoperability Association, *www.lonmark.org*

Ofgem, tel: 020 7901 7000, *www.ofgem.gov.uk*

Siemens, *www.siemens-industry.co.uk*

Water management

Parliamentary information relating to water management, *www.defra.gov.uk/environment/water/index.htm*

Ofwat, tel: 0121 625 1300, *www.ofwat.gov.uk*

Water pollution

Environment Agency general enquiry line (for information on groundwater protection), tel: *08459 333111*

HVAC

Air Improvement Centre, tel: 020 7834 2834, *www.air-improvement.co.uk*

Eurovent (European testing body for HVAC equipment), tel: +33 1 4996 6980

Federation of Environmental Trade Associations (FETA), tel: 01491 578674, www.feta.co.uk

Heating, Ventilation and Air Conditioning Manufacturers Association (HEVAC), *www.hevac.com*

Waste management

The Environment Council, tel: 020 7836 2626, *www.wasteguide.org.uk*

The Chartered Institution of Wastes Management, tel: 01604 620426, *www.iwm.co.uk*

Noise

Association of Noise Consultants, tel: 01763 852958, *www.association-of-noise-consultants.co.uk*

Royal National Institute for the Deaf (RNID), tel: 0808 8080123, *www.rnid.org.uk*

Furniture

Chartered Institute of Purchasing and Supply (CIPS), tel: 01780 756777, *www.cips.org*

Office Furniture Advisory Service (OFAS), tel: 01344 779438, *www.ofas.org.uk*

Catering

Automatic Vending Association of Britain (AVAB), tel: 020 8661 1112, *www.ava-vending.org*

British Hospitality Association (BHA), tel: 020 7404 7744, *www.bha-online.org.uk*

European Point-of-use Drinking Water Association (EPDWA), tel: 01923 833660

Cleaning

Cleaning and Support Services Association (CSSA), tel: 020 7481 0881, *www.cleaningassoc.org*

Lighting

Energy Savings Trust, see Action Energy

Industry Committee for Emergency Lighting (ICEL), *www.icel.co.uk*

Lighting Industry Federation (LIF), *www.lif.co.uk*

11 Space Design and Management

Louis Wustemann

While most of a facilities manager's functions are carried out behind the scenes, space planning and management is the most conspicuous part of the job. The way that an organisation's workspace is laid out and maintained is a vital part of its corporate image, giving an important message to visiting customers, potential recruits and existing employees.

More fundamentally, a comfortable, safe and efficient working environment is essential to enable employees to perform at their best, and to ensure that good use is made of the space available so that facilities managers bring added value to an organisation.

An essential consideration for space planners is the effect the layout and worksettings have on communications and productivity. The chance interaction between staff that generates valuable ideas cannot be made to happen, but research shows that poorly thought-out layouts and the wrong adjacencies make it much less likely.

How can facilities managers plan the workspace to serve its users safely and comfortably and to ensure maximum productivity? This chapter gives advice on successful space planning and the effective management of space changes and office moves ('churn'), setting out both practical design considerations as well as the technological support available for planners in the form of computer-aided facilities management (CAFM) systems.

Space planning

Measuring space

Before beginning to plan or re-plan people into any given space, you first need to know the size of that space. Area is usually estimated in one of the following ways:

- **gross internal area** – the whole internal area of the building measured from wall to wall.

- **net internal area** – the gross internal area minus service cores, toilets, lift lobbies and stairways.

- **net usable area** – the net internal area minus any areas that cannot be used for the purposes of space planning, such as areas behind doors and narrow gaps between columns and walls.

- **net lettable area** – the area on which an organisation pays rent in a leased building – usually somewhere between the net internal and the net usable area.

Planning grids

The planning grid is a means of imposing a notional structure to help plan the occupants into the floor space. The most common grid sizes are based on modules of:

- 90 × 90cm
- 120 × 120cm
- 135 × 135cm
- 150 × 150cm.

The 90cm module (creating blocks of $0.8m^2$) was the common standard in the office buildings of the 1960s and 1970s, but grids based on 150cm ($2.25m^2$) sections have become more common, as the larger grid square allows more flexibility of planning and is more compatible with common distribution patterns of cabling and other services.

Bricks and mortar

Much of the building infrastructure is likely to be handed to the space planner as a fait accompli in many cases. Nevertheless, an understanding of the properties of the fixed elements is useful to make the best use of the space.

While small offices built before the 1920s are likely to have upper stories floored with the boards over timber joists, most space planners will be faced with a concrete floor slab, probably with a raised floor through which cabling is run.

When replacing a raised floor or commissioning one from scratch it is worth considering if the services can be fitted under a low-profile floor that sits as little as 10cm above the structural floor, rather than the traditional systems that may be up to 50cm above it. The extra height gained will help reduce claustrophobia caused by low floor to ceiling depth and create more airy offices.

Suspended ceilings feature in most mid- to late-twentieth century offices. Hung from the bottom of the floorplate above, they provide a simple distribution system for services such as ventilation, heating and lighting. Modular systems are easiest to match up to planning grids and partitioning systems and best support reconfiguration of the space below. Carefully specified ceiling materials and coatings can also improve the acoustics in any space.

Partitioning

Interior partitioning in offices ranges from blockwork, through plasterboard and stud walls, to aluminium and monobloc partitions. Which is used depends on various factors, including how long the interior configuration is expected to last. Changing the first two means messy small-scale demolition, while the second two are often demountable and offer the opportunity to reconfigure the workplace.

Factors to consider when choosing a partitioning system include:

- compatibility with other structural elements (suspended ceilings, raised floors, etc)

- fire resistance

- acoustic properties

- load-bearing capacity, if you are likely to want to use it to hang shelving

- ease of relocation – some systems are more demountable than others.

Cabling

No building over 15 years old was built to cope with the volume of cabling now needed to handle information and communications demands at desk level.

In small spaces, cabling is handled adequately by perimeter trunking with wall outlets, but on most larger floorplates it is run through a raised floor. In cases where such floors cannot be used, a suspended ceiling is often used for distribution with wiring run down structural pillars or specially installed power poles.

Structured cabling offers a unified alternative to the mess of different wiring types that grew up to serve telephone and data systems. It provides a single system that can be configured to offer telephone, ethernet, multimedia and even CCTV connectivity all at once. The floor void is usually flooded with wiring and outlets provided at every 2–3m throughout the floor grid. This means that wherever the workstations are located or relocated they can simply be plugged into the nearest outlet.

Structured cabling systems comprise two basic components:

- **Backbone cabling** – this begins where transmissions enter the building from outside and are routed to a series of telecom rooms serving an individual floor or discrete area of the building.

- **Horizontal cabling** – this is pulled from each room to the individual workstations or outlets on that floor.

The choice of cable – fibre optic, copper or wireless – is crucial and will have an impact on the design, installation and performance of the system.

Structured cabling must be considered as early as possible in the process of planning changes to a building's systems or planning a new building. Combining structured cable planning with heating, ventilation, air conditioning, plumbing and electrical systems can prevent problems of cables interfering with ductwork, electrical wires, or ceiling and flooring grids. When cabling projects are completed, all details of cable routes, types, connections and associated hardware and software, along with documentation of standards and testing procedures, must at least be filed with easy access, and at best incorporated into the company's computer-aided facilities management (CAFM) system (see below, **p 343** for more on CAFM systems).

When user requirements alter, the change is enabled by changing the patching configuration in the equipment room without having to touch the horizontal cabling to the floor outlets.

The most common means of connecting equipment to sub-floor cabling is via one of the following:

*   **Floor boxes** – these are recesses in the raised floor with standard phone sockets for voice and data plus power sockets, usually covered by hinged lids, which are flush to the floor when closed. These provide easy access for plugging and unplugging equipment, but need effort to relocate when layouts change.

*   **Grommets** – these are essentially apertures through which cables are passed to connections in the floor void. They look neater and can be easily relocated, but once in place make it more difficult to access the plug-in points below.

Cable management

If a cabling infrastructure is what you have behind the scenes, cable management is the art of dealing with cabling between outlets and equipment. Bad cable management leads to unsightly runs of wiring across the office and, at worst, trip hazards. The simple rule is that the more outlets you have, the closer any workstation will be to one and the less cable you have to manage.

One way to run cables into open space where no local outlets are available is to use screen-based furniture where the cables are run through the screens that hold up adjacent workstations. This makes reconfiguring the layouts very time consuming.

Where cabling has to be run in open space at floor level for short runs, cable bridges that cover and protect the wires forming a shallow bump on the floor are an option, but these should never be run across circulation space.

(See **IT and communications, pp 265–278** for more on cabling.)

Space per person

UK health and safety law specifies $11m^3$ minimum workspace per person. This suggests a minimum space allocation of $4.2m^2$, while architects and planners have traditionally used an average of $10m^2$ per person when calculating maximum occupancy of the net internal area. This figure attributes a proportion of all support and ancillary space (such as circulation and catering areas) to the individual, not just their work area. The British Council for Offices suggests a good practice range of $12–17m^2$.

These averages give you a rule-of-thumb idea of how many people you can fit into a given net internal area. How you actually fit them into the net usable space depends on the shape of the space and your organisation's space standards. A space standard is the number of square metres allotted to each employee in the organisation as workspace, taking in their desk, chair, local storage and immediate access to the workstation. These can be used as a minimum allocation per person, an ideal to aim for where space permits or as a rigid model for planning large numbers of people into a given area. Space standards vary enormously between organisations, as do the principles for determining them. The most common strategies are:

- **Single standard** – also known as a universal footprint, where every member of staff receives the same space allocation and/or furniture. This makes for very simple space planning and churn management, but only the most deliberately non-hierarchical organisations carry the principle through to the most senior management.

- **Space by seniority** – the most common form of space planning since the mid-20th century. The size – and often type – of the individual's space is dictated by their rank. For example, in an organisation where non-managerial staff receive $5m^2$ in open space, supervisors might be allocated $7m^2$ also in open-plan, while managers would have a $10m^2$ cellular office.

- **Space by need** – space is allocated based on an assessment of each individual's job needs. Those who can prove they need a lot of personal storage are allotted more room and those whose work is highly sensitive or confidential are placed in cellular space rather than open plan.

- **Space budgeting** – space is allocated to departments or teams based on a total of their individual notional space, but they are then free to arrange this space as suits them. A team of 10 people with a combined entitlement of $60m^2$ could use small workstations and limited personal space to free up more of their team area for shared meeting and break-out space.

Simple standards

For simplicity of planning and managing churn it is best to stick to the smallest set of space standards possible and to make them multiples of each other. For instance, in a status-based system, if the basic standard for staff in open-plan is $4m^2$, junior managers and those with extra space needs might be allocated $6m^2$ and middle managers $8m^2$ (in partitioned cells where necessary).

Except in the smallest footprints, the space standard does not dictate the orientation or the arrangement of the workstation. Combining the space allocation of a team it is possible to produce regimented bays of desks that can be planned straight across an open floor, variations on a single theme, or, especially using the newer workstation shapes (such as 120° radial desks) seemingly random groupings, all keeping strictly to the relevant space standard.

Workplace options

Occupants of open-plan space frequently complain about lack of privacy and environmental control, but a return to highly cellular accommodation is unlikely to come soon. The cost of churn and the new emphasis on knowledge-sharing, face-to-face as well as electronically, means that segregation is not yet on the cards again.

Apart from support and ancillary areas (computer rooms, catering areas and so on) the two most common types of cellular space found in offices are 'owned' offices for one or two people and meeting rooms.

Where individual contained office space is still an entitlement (because of rank or the need for a high degree of privacy or security), such offices are usually planned in blocks, making economic use of shared partition walls, easing the provision of power and voice connections and making planning of the surrounding open-plan areas less complicated.

Open-plan

The principle of offering people different types of workspace in addition to their standard workstations, to suit different types of work, has spread in recent years. (See elsewhere in this chapter, **Space saving tips, p 338**.) These facilities include:

- **Break-out areas** – providing break-out areas with soft seating and coffee tables, or even formal meeting furniture, beside inter-circulation in open layouts or beside vending or catering points both creates these nodes and increases local meeting space. If they are located near to workstations, break-out areas should be at least partially screened to avoid distracting those nearby (see below, **Quiet areas,** for more on this).

- **Touchdown space** – this started as one of the types of workspace offered in hotdesking offices, but the recognition that all office users need ad hoc work surfaces when they are away from their desks has led to their adoption in more conventional offices. The cheapest touchdown space is simply any spare desk placed in the corner of an office or reception area. The most space-efficient option is a counter fixed to a wall to cater for short stops by employees who need a surface to lean on or spread documents briefly. Wall-mounted touchdown surfaces – which need be no deeper than 450–600mm in most cases – are best placed at the entrances to office floors to maximise their use by staff and visitors. Touchdown surfaces should not have sharp edges or corners. No seating is needed, though bar stools are provided by some organisations. These must be easy to move in and out and adjustable. Power and data connections will allow people to plug in laptops.

- **Quiet areas** – quiet areas or meeting cells should ideally be placed in dead areas of the floorplate (against windowless walls, for example, as they are not designed for long-term use). Where areas of open desking are designated as quiet areas, it seems common sense to put them as far away from the noisier break-out areas as possible. In practice, as long as the two are not next door to each other and there are enough acoustically absorbent surfaces in the workspace, they can be in reasonable proximity (say 10–15m apart) without significant sound leakage. Paradoxically, the lower the screening around quiet areas, the less people will make noise around them because they can see others concentrating.

- **Carrels** – also known as study booths, carrels are hotdesks with some form of screening to provide enclosure for concentrated work in open space. They vary from rows of small 800 × 800mm library-style booths to free-standing desks surrounded by 1,800mm free-standing screens on three sides, and are a flexible alternative to permanent enclosures.

Meeting rooms

Dedicated meeting rooms are often an underused part of the office space, simply because they are over-proportioned. Research by Alexi Marmot Associates found that two-thirds of meetings in a typical organisation involve six people or less, and almost half involve four people or less. This suggests that organisations need very few large meeting rooms. That said, small-scale cellular space, for two to six people, is likely to be well used, especially in organisations where most staff work in open-plan space and may need enclosed space for interviews, important phone calls and short periods of work requiring heavy concentration. The late 1990s vogue for tiny one-person cells as small as $2m^2$ has now passed after experience showed they were little used, presumably because they induced claustrophobia.

For an administrative department, one small meeting space in the work area for two or three people might be sufficient for every 40 staff. In a consultancy this would rise to one for every 16 staff. Meeting rooms should always be accessible by main circulation routes and, where they are expected to be heavily used by visitors, should be located near lavatories and coat storage if possible.

Using structural glass for doors or walls of cells creates a less blocky appearance and gives passers-by an immediate indication of whether or not the room is occupied. But if more than one wall is fully glazed, etched glass is recommended for some of the expanse to avoid occupants feeling as if they are in a fishbowl.

Circulation

Circulation includes stairs, corridors and routes through open floor space. The first two are usually fixed, but the third needs careful planning. The primary consideration is the legal requirement for 'escape distance' – see **Complying with health and safety law: fire safety: means of escape, p 51** for details of maximum escape routes. Beyond the necessity of quick access to fire escapes, it is necessary to consider whether each route will simply be used for getting to individual workspace or to encourage ad hoc communication and how much traffic they might need to cope with in peak periods.

Circulation can be divided into two types:

- **primary circulation**, including stairs, lift lobbies and corridors
- **secondary circulation**, providing access within the open floors.

The latter can be sub-divided into two types: inter-circulation that takes people from the primary routes through open floors to team areas, vending or storage points; and intra-circulation, which gives immediate access to each workstation off the inter-circulation and is often accounted for partly in the individual space standard.

The recommended width for inter-circulation is 1.5m, which allows three people, or one person and another in a wheelchair, to pass comfortably. The minimum clearance for one person without turning sideways is around 55cm. Where lifts open straight into offices the recommended minimum circulation space in front of the doors is 3m.

Inter-circulation is usually planned through the middle of the workspace, so that access to workstations is equal on both sides. In cases where a shallow floorplate (under 10m) is wrapped round a large service core, circulation can follow the outside of the core.

With the vogue for less regimented-looking layouts, routes that wind through offset groups of workstations have become more common. These give the office a more pleasant appearance but the designer has to make sure they do not take the travel distance to fire escapes over the legal limit.

Adjacencies

Co-locating team members and staff in the same department is an obvious priority, but co-locating different teams and departments is a more subtle business. Unless you are sure that existing arrangements make for maximum interactivity between parts of the organisation whose work is interdependent, this should form part of your research before planning new space (see elsewhere in this chapter, **Relocation and churn, p 339**).

Research by BT found that employees interact with those in the same work area as themselves for 10 per cent of their working time, but this drops to 0.4 per cent of their time for employees on different floors. Nevertheless, two departments which need constant interaction may be better served if they are placed on the same end of separate floors near a staircase, than if they are at remote ends of the same floorplate.

Detailed planning

Once you have set your space standards and taken into account the size of the space you have to plan and the desired adjacencies, in the detailed planning your decisions will be affected by a mix of the following factors:

- open-plan v cellular space
- team v individual space
- incorporating room for expansion
- flexibility and ease of churn
- aesthetics and staff comfort
- the planning grid.

Group planning

When laying out multiples of workstations with similar space standards in open-plan space, it is time consuming and inconvenient to work in single units. Most planners group workstations together in clusters of four or six or more, combining the space standards of the workstations into a larger unit, preferably fitted to the planning grid. These units, often arranged as bays to create some sense of team identity in the open space, can then be replicated across the floor, simplifying the planning. There is no need for this form of cluster planning to produce a monotonous and rigid layout. Once the size and access requirements of a cluster have been set, variations on the theme will break up the appearance of the layout without complicating the plan.

Space records

As the planning process progresses, space planners will need to assemble different types of plan to record information on the proposed layouts, either on paper or on a CAD (computer-aided design) system (see **Computer-aided facilities management: space usage, p 343**). They include:

- **Block and stack plans** – block plans can be prepared early on to map the desired adjacencies on a single floor. Where more than one floor is involved, stack plans group all the floors together to show vertical adjacencies as well.

- **Sketches, 3D renderings and mock-ups** – impressions of the planned décor and layouts give the opportunity to try out colour schemes and furniture arrangements and to bring flatplans to life for non-specialists.

- **Detailed space plans** – the final plans will be the blueprint for the new layouts, with all services, circulation routes, storage and workstations marked with details of which teams are based where. These must be updated as soon as and as often as there is any churn.

Office aesthetics

Beyond the essential environmental hygiene factors, space planners need to account for other more subtle environmental issues.

Coloured wall and furniture finishes have become popular. Before deciding on a colour scheme for your workspace, consider the impression and atmosphere you want to create. Reds, oranges and yellows encourage activity and energy but can also cause fatigue, while blues and greens promote contemplation, concentration and creativity. Light colours produce the impression of coolness and spaciousness, while dark colours create a closed-in feeling.

Even in an interior where walls must stay monotone or pale, say to maintain required light levels, bright accent colours can be introduced via chair coverings and storage cabinets – now available from most suppliers in a bewildering choice of hues.

Other ways of softening an office environment are by hanging artworks or indoor planting. Plants are high maintenance, particularly in deep office space where natural light levels are low, but are also highly valued by office users. Studies also suggest the proximity of greenery helps reduce stress levels.

Space-saving tips

Every facilities manager wishes to reduce property costs. Making better use of existing space is the easiest way to put off property expansion. One of the most obvious means of space saving is by moving staff who spend a high proportion of their time away from the office to some form of hotdesking or desk-sharing arrangement. Another is to invest in flat-panel computer monitors. The cost differential between flat LCD screens and the traditional bulky cathode ray tube (CRT) monitors has almost vanished in recent years. Switching to flat panel displays can allow you to cut the depth of a standard workstation by 300mm which adds up to a substantial space saving on a large office floor.

Other ways of reclaiming space include rationalising storage and cutting the number of meeting rooms.

Rationalising storage

Much paper filing is unnecessary or kept in the wrong place. Documents accumulate in piles around workstations through inattention, suggesting the need for more storage cabinets, which are then duly provided. Migrating filing from floor-based units to shelving above desk level on load-bearing walls and partitions where possible will release space.

An increasing number of organisations are now setting a fixed filing allocation (commonly one or two linear metres) for all members of staff except those who can make a strong case for more.

Another option, especially useful for organisations which need to keep a lot of paper records, for regulatory reasons for instance, is off-site storage. All non-essential records can be archived at cheap, secure warehousing space, freeing up as much as 25 per cent of the prime square metrage on office floors.

The ultimate in space-free records storage is through the use of document image processing (DIP) systems, which allow all incoming documentation to be scanned and stored electronically. DIP systems may one day be the norm, but they are currently expensive to install and suffer from the popular lack of confidence in IT systems as the sole repository of important information.

Fewer meeting rooms

Meeting space in most organisations is usually oversized (see elsewhere in this chapter, **Meetings rooms, p 335**) and underused. Dedicated meeting rooms can be downsized. There are usually plenty of underused spaces that can be recycled as meeting space. Company restaurants are the obvious example. Chairs and tables in catering areas remain unoccupied for most of the working day and the simple provision of a couple of mobile whiteboards to be wheeled in outside mealtimes will allow a cafeteria to double as non-bookable meeting space. Corners of reception spaces and lobbies are other candidates for touchdown tables.

Third-party planners

For those who feel they lack the expertise or time to carry out space planning, consultants and facilities management contractors offer external assistance with anything from individual moves to the whole property management operation.

Independent specialists or the planning services offered by larger architects, surveyors and even removal companies, will almost certainly bring experience and ideas for space efficiency that most facilities managers would not have access to otherwise. More specifically they may be able to provide benchmarking data to help managers compare standards with other organisations.

When choosing a contractor, look for someone who understands your organisation, can provide references from other satisfied clients, will keep your plans secure and will commit themselves to a detailed service level agreement (for more detailed information on procuring and managing contractors, see **Outsourcing, pp 235–254**).

Relocation and churn

Churn is defined as the number of people who relocate within a workspace in a year, divided by the total number of occupants and multiplied by 100 to give a percentage figure. If 20 per cent of your staff move once, you have a churn rate of 20 per cent for that year, but if 10 per cent of the staff move twice your churn rate is still 20 per cent.

Benefits and costs

In fact, 20 per cent would be an enviable rate for many facilities managers, who have to cope with levels well in excess of 50 per cent, giving the impression of perpetual motion in the workspace. But the rate of churn – which seems to be rising in most industries – is not necessarily a cause for concern. As more organisations adopt project management principles, high churn that reflects the grouping and regrouping of staff to deal with time-limited tasks and projects is a sign of dynamism and a healthy response to constant change in the wider world.

What facilities managers should concentrate on is making churn less disruptive and, above all, less costly. A study by Cornell University in the US found that office moves cost an average £119 (at 1998 prices) for a simple 'briefcase' move with no disturbance to the layout, rising to over £430 where furniture and storage is shifted, and jumping to £1,270 where any alterations (such as moving partitions or reconfiguring wiring) are needed. Cutting the cost of churn is a matter of building as much flexibility as possible into space plans, building services and fixtures, in order to maximise the number of briefcase moves.

Cutting the cost of churn

Where managers have any influence over the fit-out of a space, the specification of some of the following features will add to the initial cost but generate savings in churn expense year after year:

- **Open-plan** – the fewer fixed partitions there are in the space, the more easy it is to move people round and the lower the risk of structural alterations when people do move. Where partitioning is used, take care to choose a system that is truly demountable.

- **Structured cabling** – the flood distribution of wiring through a floor (see elsewhere in this chapter, **Cabling, p 331**) and the 'plug and play' facility offered by structured cabling systems means that ICT (information and communications technology) needs a minimum of reconfiguration.

- **User-configurable phones** – a telecoms set-up (available for all but the oldest systems) that allows users to relocate their extension number to any handset makes moves easy, especially short-term relocations of days or weeks.

- **Space standards** – the closer you can get to a single standard or universal footprint (see elsewhere in this chapter, **Space per person, p 332**), with the same space allocation for most employees, the less often you will have to rearrange a layout or move furniture to accommodate individual or group moves.

All the above will cut churn costs, but the single most effective way to manage down the price of moves is to plan ahead. Strategic facilities planning, carried out two or three years ahead in conjunction with property and HR functions will give you a much better idea of the moves that will definitely have to be scheduled and a chance to avoid the wasted effort that comes from moving the same employees twice in a matter of months.

Relocation

Moving from one set of premises to another is churn on a grand scale. Space planning for a work group due to relocate should start at the earliest stage while the new premises are being chosen. Space planners should work with property managers or agents to check that any proposed new location has the right type of space as well as simply the right square metrage.

Relocation often brings a chance for a more fundamental change to space use and/or working practices. This sort of change needs serious planning and sound project management. Space audits of existing offices will offer up metrics that should help facilities managers decide if changes to space standards or new patterns such as hotdesking are possible. You may have to work out adjacencies and basic layouts many months in advance of a move to allow for internal partitioning of the new space, so the earlier a rough idea of new arrangements is available, the better.

The months leading up to the move should be spent communicating the planned changes to staff and carrying out trials of new furniture, layouts or workstyles in the old location to iron out any obvious problems.

At the move-in date, make sure there is support on hand for any features of the new space that are unfamiliar to its occupants as this will reduce the 'downtime' associated with the move.

Hotdesking

In a hotdesking office workspace is not parcelled out to individual employees but shared between a department or team. Employees sit wherever they can find convenient space. The arguments in its favour are compelling on paper. Although most organisations accept the costs of maintaining and servicing buildings that are only open around one third of the available hours in the year (allowing for nights and weekends), occupancy rates can be reduced to as little as 10 per cent of the available time due to the needs of many nominally office-based staff to leave the office on research, client or supplier visits, and with homeworking on the increase.

Making it work

But simply taking away 'owned' workstations and replacing them with fewer, shared desks is not likely to be greeted with any enthusiasm by those affected by the change; they simply lose the status of fixed workspace and gain a new set of responsibilities, including tidying up after themselves. Where hotdesking has succeeded it has been accompanied by a wider change to working practices that brings benefits to the hotdeskers themselves.

The most common quid pro quo for employees giving up their desks is to offer them more pleasant workspace for the times that they are in the office. Some of the space saved from removing 'owned' desks is commonly recycled for new types of worksettings (see elsewhere in this chapter, **Workspace options: open plan, p 333**), such as touchdown points, soft-seating areas and study booths, as well as standard desks. Even with these provisos, hotdesking schemes commonly generate space savings of 30 per cent or more.

How many hotdesks?

There is no rule of thumb for the correct ratio of desks to employees in hotdesking arrangements. Ratios in existing schemes vary from 3:4 (hotdesks:employees) to 1:10. The level of provision will depend on several factors, including:

- the proportion of an average week staff spend in the office
- whether they are equipped to carry out desk work elsewhere (at home, for instance)
- whether it will be appropriate for employees to use empty desks in other departments if hotdesks are all full.

The best pointer to a correct ratio is an occupancy study, carried out over several days, probably spread over a fortnight or more, to gather data on how many of the existing desks are used by peripatetic staff on an average day and at peak usage.

The perennial question about hotdesking is how to cope with the eventuality of all the employees wanting to come in on the same day. Though this overload almost never occurs in practice, providing a range of space-efficient worksettings (touchdown counters and so on, see elsewhere in this chapter, **Workspace options: open plan, p 333**) can make it possible to cope with unexpected spikes in demand for workspace.

Efficient hotdesking

The aim of introducing hotdesking is to save space, but not at the expense of staff productivity. If employees have to spend much more time finding a desk, configuring their phones or connecting to the company network, any gains will be wiped out. The following points will help ensure a smooth operation, though some may be unnecessary for small hotdesking schemes.

Layout

Place the worksettings designed for the shortest stops nearest the entrance to the hotdesking space, with desks for longer, concentrated periods of work nearer the back. By the same token, any 'owned' workstations for staff who are not hotdesking should be furthest from the entrance, away from the comings and goings of the hotdeskers.

Managing shared space

Although there should be adequate provision for employees dropping in and out without notice, hotdesks and meeting rooms should be bookable by telephone, in person and, ideally, over an intranet. Staff should be discouraged from booking the same space for weeks at a time and other territorial habits, such as leaving material at workstations. A clean desk policy is essential for success. A dedicated concierge or receptionist may be useful to take bookings, maintain facilities (replenish stationery, log IT faults and so on) and, located near the entrance to the hotdesking area, can provide added security in a space with a transient population.

Communications and IT

Telephones must be configured so that hotdeskers can receive calls wherever they are sitting. Most PABXs allow temporary reassignment of extension numbers already. The more expensive addition of a 'follow-me' phone facility is the best solution. Access to sockets for voice, power and data must be easy for laptop users. Desktop power pods will avoid making visitors scrabble under workstations. Desks earmarked for longer stays should be equipped with screens and keyboards to which users can hook up to their laptops, since portable computers are unsuitable for prolonged use. (See also **IT and communications, p 265**.)

Furniture and storage

Standard workstations, mobile furniture and centralised storage are all-important features of an adaptable workspace and are covered in more detail in **Workplace facilities: furniture, p 308**.

Though permanent storage at hotdesks is inappropriate, as built-in storage at desk level encourages people to territorialise them by leaving things in the drawers, employees must have some means of moving files between bulk storage and their workspace. Most furniture systems now include wheeled storage pedestals which can be pushed or pulled round.

Chairs may have multiple users every day and must be quickly and easily adjustable.

Stationery

Stationery supplies, which should be easily accessible and sited somewhere near the common areas, are best located near communal printers and photocopiers and pigeon holes/post boxes – another feature facilities managers need to allow for where employees do not have post delivered to a desk.

Computer-aided facilities management (CAFM)

The rise of the networked PC has coincided with the establishment of facilities management as a recognised profession and has led to a rush by software companies to provide tools designed to make paper plans redundant and to help managers keep track of an organisation's assets and model changes with ease.

The programs available range from the simplest space-planning software, available free from many office furniture suppliers, which can be used for planning small spaces, to full-blown CAFM systems that support any or all aspects of the facilities manager's job. For the purposes of this chapter, computer-aided systems have been divided into five basic types. However, any one package may contain some of the functions and tools listed under each category.

Infrastructure – buildings, space and asset management

Property-based CAFM holds the data needed to ensure property and its contents are properly catalogued and monitored. Property databases hold details of all topics associated with construction, ownership, lease and occupancy and can aid routine tasks by, for example, flagging up lease renewal and refurbishment dates or calculating multiple occupancy costs so they can be re-charged to groups of occupants.

Space usage

Space usage is a prime function of this type of CAFM system. Object-oriented databases link to CAD space-plan drawings to provide a complete picture of space usage down to workstation level. Detailed information, both textual and graphic, can be produced on current space usage, and space needs can be planned for. Churn decisions regarding structural alterations and moving equipment and people can be made online, resulting in work orders being issued and CAD drawings being updated automatically.

Networks and cabling

CAFM systems allow you to manage telecoms and cable infrastructure effectively. Network connectivity can be tracked, an electronic inventory can be created of the physical cabling and telecom network connections and network plans drawn up.

Health, safety and environmental management

Health and safety CAFM

Health and safety CAFM helps the facilities manager ensure a safe working environment and demonstrate compliance with legislation and best practice. Systems come ready loaded with health and safety legislation guidance on topics such as the European 'six pack', *RIDDOR* and The *Control of Substances Hazardous to Health Regulations 1999*. These can link to the asset register or a human resource database, and suggest and diary appropriate actions such as checking first aid provision or organising manual handling training. Hazard registers can be compiled and maintained on topics such as asbestos, actions can be scheduled and worksheets created. Relevant health and safety data can be appended to work orders, and the resulting health and safety-related actions recorded. Many health and safety CAFM systems include DSE (display screen equipment) workstation self-assessment software.

Environmental CAFM

Environmental CAFM allows you to monitor, compare and manage the consumption of energy, and to monitor emissions and flag up hazard levels by integrating all energy-related data from existing building control systems and meters across sites and existing energy-related databases, plus all entered data. Energy usage is recorded and compared with pre-entered industry norms. The facilities manager can then identify areas for improvement, and once energy-saving measures are in place, continue monitoring. Reports can then be produced to demonstrate energy saving.

Pollution levels can be monitored across sites and over time, and staff can be alerted automatically if levels exceed pre-set values. Similarly, indoor air quality can be monitored for inadequate ventilation, improper temperature and humidity or excessive carbon monoxide.

Maintenance, repairs and contract management

With a maintenance CAFM system you can keep a full maintenance history of every piece of equipment or plant held on all sites, and the entire fabric of every building. Users can establish total downtimes and ongoing cost of ownership, which subsequently helps in assessing performance and planning replacements and refurbishments. Maintenance CAFM also enables a preventive maintenance schedule to be planned and implemented, so that essential services are maintained and equipment is ready when needed. Equipment such as heating systems can be interfaced so they can flag up their own faults, or trigger maintenance works orders after an optimum number of operating hours. And day-to-day maintenance repairs can be requested and recorded.

Online purchase requisitions, material requests and work requests can be submitted directly to internal departments or external partners. Scheduling, work assignments, shop assignments, work weeks, personnel histories, department assignments and relocation histories can all be stored and interrogated.

Helpdesk, service desk and security management

Help and service desk CAFM

Helpdesk CAFM helps the facilities management team to provide a responsive fault reporting and resolution service to building occupiers, and to fulfil occupiers' requests for routine services. Data can be collated to show which equipment or parts of a building generate the most faults or complaints. CAFM allows you to automate some of the helpdesk functions within service desk CAFM by allowing occupiers to access services such as room bookings, vehicle servicing or catering online.

Security CAFM

Security CAFM enables the facilities manager to monitor all the physical, personnel and electronic aspects of security – access control, CCTV, movement detectors, intruder systems, security staff routines – and manage them as an integrated system from a single control room. Access control systems can be interfaced, enabling the online issuing and cancellation of tokens and photo-ID visitor passes, and alterations to access times and levels, while if necessary occupants can be located within a site on screen. Alarms can be monitored remotely and fire safety can also be integrated, with heat and smoke detection and break-glass call points automatically alerting staff to the location of any suspected fire. These in turn can activate fire alarms and automatic voice evacuation messages.

Financial, budget and inventory management

Financial and inventory CAFM allows you to track and manage costs associated with capital assets, operations, consumables, work orders, training – anything in fact which impinges on facilities management work. At strategic level, these systems enable accurate measurement and forecasting of the cost of all activities undertaken by the facilities management function, and the control of its budgets.

Facilities staff can requisition spares from inventory or order them directly from suppliers according to pre-set agreements and price structures. This enables the close management of facilities management-specific inventory of equipment, spares and consumables, such as cleaning materials.

Specifying CAFM

It is essential to specify the 'owner' of the CAFM project. Who has ultimate responsibility for ensuring the system meets the objectives set? And who therefore has the authority to make sure necessary resources and support are available when required? Primary contacts within individual departments or divisions need to be pinpointed, as they will be the people who you will ultimately rely on to feed through information on any changes, whether it be a layout modification or change of occupancy.

Choosing a CAFM system

With so many CAFM products on the market, how do you ensure you are choosing the best system for your needs? Be rigorous in studying a CAFM system portfolio and take up references from existing users.

In planning a CAFM system, the best place to start is probably the space management aspect, since space is the second largest business cost after salaries. As most CAFM systems take a modular approach, it therefore makes sense to plan the first phases of the project to incorporate the space management requirements, and bolt on other applications later.

Ask the right questions

To select the right CAFM product, you will need to ask the right questions. Some examples of questions, and the reasoning behind them, are listed below.

Is the system standalone or are there any extra software packages to buy?

Does the system need additional database software, or is this integral to the CAFM system and not, therefore, an extra expense? Recommended add-on databases are typically Oracle, Sybase or SQL, but these require licences. Check compatibility as well; many systems have to be mounted on a CAD system.

What is the scope of the CAFM system?

Check that the CAFM portfolio will deliver on all requirements. For example:

- For **management information** there should be information on publishing on the web, planning, benchmarking and performance measurement.

- For **business support** there should be data on finance and contract management.

- For **property management** there needs to be information on property portfolio control, estate diary and real estate development.

- For **space and asset management** there needs to be information available on design, costs and inventory, recharge, moves and changes and visualisation of space usage. Can the system be used to place assets, and then list them and data points by space ID, floor, building and so forth? Can the CAFM system also contain scanned or typed contract information regarding buildings, floors or equipment? Can it be used to create zones for cleaning, security, occupancy, etc?

- For **call handling** the information must relate to the helpdesk, vendor tracking, maintenance procedures, purchasing and vendor invoicing.

- For **building management**, information needs to be available on environmental monitoring, HVAC, plant management, energy inventory, and reports and actions.

- For **security** there needs to be information on access control, alarm monitoring, fire monitoring and incident reporting and tracking.

Will it be difficult to integrate existing data into the new system?

Any package must interface with existing systems to avoid expensive data re-entry. Check that the system has an open architecture that can complement, integrate and/or support existing systems. For example:

- Can you import and export between databases?

- Does the system support open database connectivity (ODBC) with, for example, dBASE, Microsoft Access and Paradox?

How can I access the information?

Depending on your needs, on-site access may not be sufficient. You may wish to access the data remotely, via an Internet browser or 'thin-client' scenario, whereby you can run small programs running on your PDA (personal digital assistant) or laptop to access the CAFM system remotely.

Will an off-the-shelf package do?

Off-the-shelf products will be cheaper than customised ones. Check, however, that the product really will be able to meet your needs, and be aware that project-scope creep and sales pressure can change the boundaries.

Is it future-proof?

There is always a worry that existing technology will soon become obsolete. Be clear about your current and future specifications from the outset, to ensure that the product will be able to grow with your business needs. Ensure also that the system has developing procedures and continual development in place so that databases can be upgraded easily as technology changes.

How are graphic images handled?

Facilities management automation will often involve linking some kind of graphic image with a database. Check what types of image files can be accommodated and whether the system can scan and digitise existing paper images.

How is the information presented?

- Is the database information available in both tabular and graphical formats?

- Can you change between view formats easily and are changes entered into one format automatically updated in another, or do you have to go back to the master database?

- Can reports integrate data and graphics for professional-looking reports?

Are there any user groups?

Hopefully you will have talked to other purchasers of the CAFM system when going through the selection process. But contact should not end here – keep in touch with them. If your provider has a user group, join it.

Choosing a CAFM provider

Once the system has been shortlisted, careful attention should be paid to choosing the right provider to implement it.

Suppliers should be able to offer all of the following services:

- project management consultancy

- software installation and customisation

- data management and capture

- software support and training.

Consultants worth their salt should offer to perform an information audit and needs analysis prior to any implementation. They should agree with you exactly what is required to be input into the system, what outputs are required, and what, how many and how often reports are required.

Data entry and protection

Accuracy is crucial in the setting up of original databases and where banks of data are to be transferred across from current legacy systems. If you engage temporary clerical staff to enter raw data, take the time to explain the context of what they are doing, and check their work thoroughly, especially in the early stages.

Thought should be given to exactly what needs to be captured in order to achieve the desired results. What will the resultant data analysis be used for and how much depth is required? Who is the target audience and what kind of reports will they expect to see? It is important to identify your exact needs for the initial phase, as it is complicated to insert or delete columns into the database design once data entry has begun.

Where data already exists, do not transfer it to the CAFM database until you have cleansed it, otherwise errors and miscounts will be replicated. For instance, a desktop copier which has been moved to three different offices may end up appearing three times on a paper-based asset register.

Accuracy is also needed when entering ongoing data. Free-form text is useful for informative notes shared by users, but if data is to be sorted and collated, events must be described in the same words every time. This means having only relevant fields on screen, and pick-lists for which the choice of entry is unambiguous.

Early in the project explore with your provider the levels of security offered by the CAFM system. Firewalls and encryption are essential where data is available to third parties. Internally you need to set up appropriate user access levels, good password practice and clean screen policies. Be aware also of your responsibilities under the *Data Protection Act 1998*. If your system holds details of identifiable individuals, such as staff, within a space plan or access control system, you need to register with the Data Protection Registrar.

Planning the transition

In the run up to switching to CAFM, the following will help ensure a successful transition:

- Identify exactly what needs to be achieved with CAFM to justify the investment. Take time to develop a series of measurables – and also a process for tracking them to ensure the project is on target. These could range from the logistics of a particular process to quality of data. The project plan should also have a time frame with target dates to ensure everyone involved has clear objectives to focus on.

- Plan and make provision for the ongoing management and maintenance of the system. From the moment CAFM is up and running, you will need to keep the system updated with every change that takes place on the ground.

- Check that you have people available in-house who are willing to train on the computer system. Who will be in overall charge of maintaining the database?

- Do you have the appropriate hardware and software to run the system? Check if current terminals are powerful enough and what, if any, modifications to other programs or the network will be needed to share data.

Implementing the system

By the time it comes to implementation, the project plan should be fairly well advanced. You will have defined your data capture requirements, and the processes developed for ongoing maintenance should include a change management methodology to capture changes during the initial implementation period. The next steps are:

- Obtain existing CAD plans and ensure their format is compatible for linkage to the database. Take some time to verify the floor plans are accurate and up to date before commencement of the data entry. Although established processes should deal with changes as they occur, it is worthwhile kicking off the project with pristine data.

- Identify common space and allocate ambiguous space to the relevant departments or cost centres.

- Commence data entry and CAD updates, whilst adhering to the agreed standards.

- Submit individual building reports and floor plans to the relevant contact for verification.

- Produce your first set of reports for your target audience, using the agreed data requirements and reporting format.

Review your measurables and the original cost-benefit analysis at the end of the initial implementation phase. Can you prove the CAFM system's financial viability by showing that actual savings have reached what was originally estimated? Is it providing the data that was expected? Before making it your default system, are there processes that can be tightened up or improved?

The first implementation of CAFM may be complete, but new uses for this powerful resource will quickly become apparent. You will most likely find that a continual stream of requests will require the addition of several more modules in the system.

12 Access, Safety and Security

Frank Booty

Statistics from the Home Office and Metropolitan Police show that the incidence of armed raids increased during the 1990s with perpetrators more willing than in previous years to threaten or use violence for limited gain. And, of course, all organisations are aware of the need to act to pretect themselves against terrorism. (See **Business Continuity chapter, pp 220–234.**)

So what options are available to the facilities manager seeking to maximise security? Closed circuit television, access control, and staff training are among the practical measures which can be taken.

Closed circuit television (CCTV)

The purpose of a closed circuit television (CCTV) system is to deter and detect crime and unauthorised actions involving threats to property and people and to aid with the identification of aggressors before, during and at the end of an incident.

There are also other applications for CCTV that many people are not aware of, such as monitoring a premises' environment to meet health and safety requirements for public and staff, staff training, and site traffic control.

Threats

Threats can affect both premises and their contents and those who work in them. Threats to premises, particularly external areas, are reasonably easy to identify (exits, entrances, perimeters, etc). Internal threats are more subtle and are often influenced by the function of the space – shoplifting and staff pilfering are two examples.

Identifying threats is a pre-requisite when planning a CCTV project. Past experience is seen as the best guide, with the best people to consult being staff, as they are most likely to have spotted potential security breaches or suffered threats. Areas which will need surveillance are: areas where valuable items are stored, including cashiers departments where money is kept or handled; areas where staff may face dangerous situations; and all public areas.

The guiding principle is to achieve a balance between crime prevention and protecting personal privacy. It is therefore important to ascertain not only that CCTV is necessary, but also exactly what its purpose and key objectives are.

Security audits

For most CCTV projects it is advisable to conduct a security audit. Such an audit should assess:

- who, what and where needs monitoring or protecting

- procedures for cash movement and tills

- the location of sensitive or valuable equipment

- types of cameras and other security systems, such as alarms, access control and facial recognition

- siting the cameras to cover designated areas and avoid blind spots

- on-site and remote monitoring

- evacuation procedures.

Security consultants can play an important role in planning a CCTV project. Aside from being independent, they should have experience and knowledge of security issues and situations. Indeed, one of the many major factors to consider when choosing a security consultant is the background and expertise of their team. Another criterion should be membership of industry or professional associations (such as the British Security Industry Association), although not all reputable consultants and suppliers are necessarily members (it is not mandatory to join such a body).

Overall security measures and systems should be audited once or twice a year, paying close attention to reported incidents and the response. All employees must be made aware that, whatever their job or status, they have collective and individual responsibility for security in their workplace.

Choosing CCTV cameras

The choice of cameras and accessories depends largely on the application and location for which they are intended. External cameras may need supporting lighting for night-time use, and weatherproof housing. The choice of lens is vital to cater for such factors as focal length, depth of view and variable lighting levels. For internal locations, less obtrusive cameras might be required, to avoid affecting the interior décor. This type of demand has led to the development of cameras such as dome models.

Every site and building is unique and facilities managers will need to translate the purpose and key objectives of the project into a technical specification to arrive at the best CCTV installation. The following factors should be borne in mind when identifying objectives and technical needs:

- Colour is appropriate for indoor surveillance, since colour aids identification, but externally the level of lighting present will dictate whether black and white or colour cameras are appropriate.

- If the budget is limited, a smaller number of higher resolution cameras will be more effective than a large number of low specification devices.

- Various levels of control over cameras are possible: pan, tilt and zoom can cover a far larger area. Dome cameras conceal the direction in which the camera is pointing, making it impossible for individuals to tell whether actions are being surveyed.

- Criminals will eventually find out whether a camera is dummy or operational and the cost differential is usually minimal, making dummies an unwise purchase.

- External cameras need weatherproof, robust housings and may need demisters, washers and wipers.

- When specifying equipment, consider how future demand might change and try to make expandability and upgrade possible.

Cameras should be sited carefully and mounted low enough to give a clear picture, but high enough to prevent vandalism. CCTV can be integrated with other elements of company security – cameras can be triggered by alarms from intruder or access control systems, for example.

CCTV Operation

For layout and operation of the CCTV control room, refer to *British Standards 7499* and *5979* (a security consultant will be able to advise the level of control and sophistication necessary). Do consider the following:

- Do not overspend on unnecessarily sophisticated equipment – it should be easily operable by the minimum number of staff in the control room.

- Multiplexers enable continuous images to be viewed and recorded from up to 16 cameras.

- Images from several cameras can be shown sequentially, or on a split screen simultaneously.

- Restrict access to the control room to authorised personnel.

If live surveillance is considered necessary, be aware that a person's typical concentration span when viewing monitors is only 20 minutes. Sufficient staff will be necessary to build in breaks and constant rotation. Cameras can be triggered by movement detectors in normally quiet areas, with an alarm to prompt a guard to monitor the screen. Alternatively, remote monitoring is available by an alarm-receiving centre.

The integrity and success of any scheme is only as good as the staff who operate it. Staff should understand the purpose and objectives of the system, be familiar with the code of practice, procedures and incident response protocol, and be thoroughly trained. The operation of the scheme should be monitored regularly and a longer-term independent audit put in place.

Remote monitoring

One CCTV security company specialising in the remote monitoring of commercial property claims savings of up to 75 per cent over traditional manned guarding security. From a central remote monitoring facility, the company controls barriers to allow a vehicle through a site to a chosen building, monitors (un)loading of the vehicle and allows the vehicle to exit the site.

Such an arrangement also enables remote control of lighting, air conditioning and pumps, especially in emergency situations. The software provides visual perimeter protection using complex programmable dome cameras combined with live audio facilities. This enables verbal communication between monitoring-centre operators and unauthorised people picked up on camera, or to verify visitors' identification.

Other companies offer remote desktop video surveillance over any distance to enable monitoring of remote or unmanned premises with a PC or notebook computer. Costs of such systems are usually affordable, even to small businesses.

Low-light CCTV cameras can be used to identify vehicle number plates near remote facilities where there can be problems from vehicle headlights dazzling conventional cameras, or there are poor light levels.

Security review

Any CCTV installation should be treated as part of an overall security review. Apart from any security systems, this should also include:

- integration of CCTV with any manned security
- establishment of correct security and safety procedures
- promotion of an organisation-wide security culture
- the training to achieve these objectives.

Recordings

Recordings can be stored on videotape, disk or other electronic media to be viewed offline or in case of an incident. Information recorded must be adequate, relevant and not exceed what is necessary to fulfil the agreed objectives. If recordings are to be used as evidence in the case of criminal action, they must have been handled in accordance with Home Office guidelines[1].

Guidelines for handling recorded media include the following:

- Recordings must be indelibly marked with date, time and camera, and be labelled.

- All record-keeping must be accurate and complete.

- Tapes should be kept for 31 days before being wiped clean and reused.

- Tapes should not be reused more than six times.

- Storage of tapes and disks must be secure, especially where they contain incident data, both for protection of potential evidence, and for the protection of individuals' privacy.

- Access to storage must be controlled.

- Ensure good practice in the use of tapes and disks, and release of tapes to third parties. Destruction of tapes should be secure and controlled.

Data protection

The *Data Protection Act 1998* covers CCTV recordings of individuals who can be identified and where the system can be programmed to search for a specific part of a recording if it is known that an image of a suspected individual is recorded. If your system is capable of this you are obliged by law to register with the Data Protection Registrar. Do this as soon as you decide on such a system – to stay within the law you will have to take into account the principles behind the Act when designing the scheme.

Violence and aggression in the workplace

The objective of an aggressive act is typically the attainment of some material benefit, such as cash or high value goods. Aggression, expressed as violence, is essentially an issue between the people involved, comprising the aggressor, the aggressed, colleagues of the aggressed and bystanders who happen to be in the area.

At-risk areas

Aggression often takes place in areas accessible to the public. Typically these include:

- shops, post offices and petrol stations
- retail finance services
- DSS and local government enquiry offices
- transport ticketing areas
- hospitals and schools.

The common thread is the interface between the public and members of staff. All these environments exist for the purpose of serving the public and accessibility is therefore a necessary part of that service. The thrust of management effort has been to provide a better service to customers. The dilemma is that unrestricted access is the antithesis of good security.

Studies by criminologists have shown that crimes, particularly those involving violence, take place in environments where the aggressors believe that:

- they are unlikely to be seen by the public, police or security officers

- if seen, there is little likelihood of being identified

- there are few people to report the crime in time for there to be an effective reaction

- there are many good escape routes by foot and vehicle.

The people involved

- **Staff** – staff at transaction counters are mainly under 30 years old and most are female. Their objectives and reactions are predictable in that their objective is minimum injury and their reaction can be trained and managed.

- **Raiders** – raiders are also mainly under 30 years old, most are male and are aware of the risks of being apprehended and the various penalties that will be suffered if caught following a raid, with or without injury. A raider, operating alone or as part of an organised group, relies on the ability to dominate the situation by surprise, threats and violence. To stay and take a hostage will incur delay – to delay is to invite capture and to injure will intensify the police hunt and increase the penalty.

- **Public** – customers or members of the public who are present when a raid occurs are wholly unpredictable. However, in most cases people are initially shocked and take no action.

Personal safety – training and counselling

Courses in personal safety in the workplace seek to train staff how to recognise and remedy confrontational behaviour in others, examine their own attitudes and eliminate areas that can spark aggression. Typical course content would include: planning safety in travel to, from and during work; controlling stress and tension; and non-verbal communication. Importance should be placed on taking control in the event of an attack, getting away and the consequences of fighting back. Assertiveness and the law on self-defence needs to be discussed and risks should be put into perspective, backed up by statistics.

A crisis management team needs to be put in place to provide a proactive response to any incident. In addition, management must identify external sources of assistance, and build a model of intervention. With adequate crisis intervention, there should be fewer individual long-term needs.

Principal strategies for defence

These are:

- **Hardening the target** – cash transaction counters can be equipped with armoured doors, walls and windows, akin to a bank vault. However, this can be unwelcoming to the customer and there are weak points of visibility/access at the windows and doors.

- **Removing the target** – removing cash into an armoured enclosure as above is one solution, but is not available to most transaction counters where there is a tradition of open access across the counter.

- **Removing the means** – raiders rely on the tactic of surprise to achieve immediate and total dominance of the area by fear and aggression. Conventional transaction counters have no active defence. This advantage should be removed. Some counters are equipped with bullet-resistant glazing and offer a degree of passive protection, but still no active defence.

- **Reducing the pay-off** – good cash management by the use of teller-assist units and time-locked mini-safes can reduce the amount of money lost to a raider.

- **Surveillance** – this serves no purpose unless there is a practical action that can be taken as a result of the surveillance revealing a threatening situation. CCTV is only a passive deterrence against violence which can also help identify offenders.

These strategies for effective defence against crime can be adopted on their own or in any combination. Adopting all strategies in different facets of the overall security is usually seen to offer the best strategy.

Access control, asset protection and guarding

Access to the workplace should achieve a balance between convenience for employees and bona fide visitors, and the denial of access to areas where people do not have a need or right to be. Access control must not interfere with escape in case of emergency or fire. Advice is available from security consultants, approved security retailers, the police and the local fire service.

Access risk analysis

Access must be a basic consideration at the risks analysis stage – every workplace is different, with variations in the business activity and risks. Risks will range from opportunistic or organised crime to the ignorance and carelessness of staff. When assessing access risk:

- Start at the perimeter of the property and work in to the main door(s) of the building, other external doors and windows, the reception area, and on to all internal doors.

- Decide who is to be allowed free or controlled access at these various points and at what times.

- Consider how to secure and allow entry and egress through access points.

- Consider how to identify people who are authorised to be on-site.

Security measures

Access restriction

Access restriction serves to deter attempted entry and prohibit actual entry. The restriction of access to an area that any member of the public needs to enter will inevitably be a compromise between security needs and the business needs of the organisation. With staff-controlled door systems, staff can be actively involved in deciding who they allow to enter their premises and exclude any suspicious characters.

Perimeter boundary

Consider the following:

- Invisible barriers can be created by infra-red beam systems.

- Fences or walls have to fit design criteria and be aesthetically appropriate – but check planning permission.

- Power fencing conforming to health and safety standards can be used to deliver a low voltage electric shock to intruders.

- Tunnels, culverts and manholes giving access to the premises should be secured.

- Perimeter entry points need to be kept to a minimum, but should allow for smooth flow of traffic at peak times.

- Gates should be high and strong enough to deter entry when locked.

Building exteriors

Consider the following:

- How vulnerable is the building exterior at quiet times or at night when the premises are empty?

- Keep entrance doors to a minimum, and locked when not in use.

- All windows should have locks.

- How easy is access from roads, footpaths, flat roofs, roof lights and fire escapes?

- Secure ground-floor windows with steel bars or wire mesh.

- Ensure goods in and out are always manned during opening hours.

- Good external lighting is a deterrent to intruders in areas with good natural surveillance.

For external doors and doors leading to vulnerable areas, fit as a minimum thief-resistant mortise deadlocks conforming to *British Standard 3621*. Specialised advice on locks should always be sought. Always buy from a member of the Master Locksmiths Association.

Rising screens

Rising screens are designed to protect personnel against actual and threatened violence (both physical and psychological). They have a track record of successfully defeating violent raids in a number of countries, environments and cultures. Rising screens are installed into the service counter where staff and public have direct contact, and provide a tangible barrier to projectiles, syringes and physical contact at the touch of a button. Aggression is restricted to the fraction of a second between realisation of a raid and the action of raising the screen. Staff are able to remove the threat the moment the presence or threat of a raider is perceived or suspected.

Screens are housed in a steel body shell which is built into and supports the counter. The screen is a telescopic arrangement of two sheets powered pneumatically to rise from the counter to the ceiling – body and lower screen panels can resist bullet penetration from powerful handguns (.44 Magnum and sawn-off shotgun with solid ball shot). Upper panels – not generally required to be bullet resistant – are made of sheet aluminium and impenetrable to sight, sound and thrown objects. Special situations can have panels resistant to 7.62mm armour-piercing ammunition.

Authorised entrants

ID badges can form part of an access control strategy; they need to be unique to a facility and not easily copied. Electronic access control systems can combine security with convenience. They allow doors to remain locked, giving continuous security, but automatically unlock them when authorised employees or visitors are identified by their unique codes. Individuals can be identified by voice entry, pin pads into which numbers are keyed, contact systems such as magnetic swipe systems, non-contact systems where cards or tags pass within range of readers, or new technologies such as biometric fingerprint or eye retinal reading systems.

Intruder alarms

Intruder alarms are a good visible and audible deterrent. They should conform to *British Standard 4737*. Do get advice from insurers first, and only use installation companies who are members of, or approved by, an appropriate body. There are two basic types of intruder alarm: audible-only or monitored, where the system is connected to a 24-hour alarm-receiving centre (ARC) by telephone or radio link.

Over 90 per cent of alarms are triggered by events other than genuine break-ins. The Association of Chief Police Officers has reached an agreement with NACOSS (National Approval Council for Security Systems), BSIA (British Security Industry Association), ABI (Association of British Insurers) and the British Retail Consortium to reduce the number of false alarms by 10 per cent each year.

The police have identified three levels of response:

- level 1 – immediate
- level 2 – response may be delayed due to higher priorities
- level 3 – no police response, key holders only.

Newly-installed and properly monitored systems, or where the presence of an intruder is suspected, receive response level 1. If four false alarm calls are reported within 12 months, response drops to level 2. If seven false calls are reported in the next 12 months, response drops to level 3. Restoration to a higher level will only be achieved when an organisation can prove that no false alarms have been made for three months.

Personal attack alarms

Personal attack alarms serve to summon assistance in the event of an incident. They can be interfaced to other systems to attract a security officer's attention at a CCTV console to start a recording sequence, sound a siren or start a strobe light. The alarms, of course, cannot stop the aggression, but may deter the raider.

Asset protection

Cash, stock and equipment are prime targets for thieves – both internal and external. Large items of electrical equipment and any easily portable equipment, such as tools, laptops and mobile phones, are vulnerable to theft and burglary, on and off the business premises. The following good practice tips should help minimise the risk.

Company cash and valuables

- Consult insurers and train staff in cash handling.
- Payment of wages by cheque, credit transfer or giro reduces the need to carry cash.
- Department petty cash should be monitored and managed by accounts staff.
- Cash should be banked frequently.

Stock

- Do not carry high levels of inventory.
- Employ trustworthy people.
- Access control should only admit authorised personnel.
- Check goods issued and receipts.
- Issue standard quantities for specific use.
- Perform regular spot stock checks.

Equipment

- Encourage employees to carry laptops inside a bag – business people carrying laptops are frequently mugged.
- Clear security marking of assets is a simple way to deter thieves and identify items if stolen.

- Security guards can check parcels or equipment being taken off the premises.

- Consider having spot checks of staff leaving the premises to deter internal thieves; a code of practice should be drawn up and clauses written into staff contracts which authorises the procedure (search is only possible with the agreement of the individual).

Manned guarding

If manned guarding of the premises is to be part of an overall security system, a decision must be made to employ staff directly or to outsource the service to an external supplier. This will be determined by the size and nature of the organisation and other measures, such as CCTV. Outsourced guarding can either be static – on the premises continuously as in-house staff would be – or mobile – a patrol which tours a number of premises out of hours, calling in to check each one at regular intervals.

Private Security Industry Act

The *Private Security Industry Act 2001* became law in May 2001. This means the security industry in the private sector in England and Wales is now subject to a regulatory system, as in other EU member states. A Security Industry Authority has been created to license and approve security firms and the individuals (employees, directors and partners) who work in them. Licences will last three years, providing conditions are not broken.

In-house security departments are exempt from the legislation.

Security personnel

Security personnel need detailed job descriptions, called 'assignment instructions'. These should cover all duties and responsibilities, which may include access control, issue and control of ID badges, record-keeping, CCTV monitoring, and incident and emergency response. Guards may also need to make regular premises patrols.

Existing staff taking on security responsibilites must receive appropriate training, which is available through the Security Industry Training Organisation. Security staff need an understanding of the limits of their powers of search and arrest, as specified in the *Police and Criminal Evidence Act 1984*. Security staff should also be trained and certified as first aid providers and in fire safety. All training should be regularly updated.

Information protection

The continuity and survival of a business depends increasingly on its information. Analysis of the potential risks to an organisation of the loss of information should take into account:

- production processes and design drawings

- proprietary software programs

- customer lists, marketing plans and tender information
- financial data
- legal records
- personnel records.

In addition, business documents need to be protected against disclosure, copying, theft, fire and vandalism.

Electronic information is vulnerable in very specific ways: networks can be hacked into, emails read, information copied or corrupted, and virus infections introduced. An information security policy should be formulated following an assessment of the risks and with reference to business objectives.

All companies should be aware of the provisions of the *Data Protection Act 1998* which sets out rules for handling personal data about any living, identifiable individual, held or processed by computer or other technology.

Fire risk

Fire poses a devastating risk to any business. Minimising the risk of fires is fundamental to any safety strategy.

Causes of fire

As the following list of the commonest causes of fires shows, most fires are caused by people doing something they should not or by not doing something that they should:

- fire raising and arson
- careless disposal of cigarettes or matches
- combustible material left near a source of heat
- accumulation of easily ignitable rubbish or paper
- carelessness on the part of contractors and maintenance workers
- electrical equipment left switched on when not in use
- misuse of portable heaters
- obstructing ventilation of heaters, machinery or office equipment.

Fire is a chemical reaction, requiring three fundamental elements to be in place: oxygen (always present), fuel (the combustible substance which can be a solid, liquid or gas) and ignition (source of heat energy). As all three points of the fire triangle must be in place to cause a fire, it follows that managers should attempt to prevent this from happening. Both managers and employees should strive to prevent sources of fuel and ignition from coming together.

Minimising fire risk

Poor housekeeping is the greatest single cause of fire. This checklist of best practice guidelines is recommended to minimise risk:

- Where smoking is permitted, suitable deep metal ashtrays should be provided. Ashtrays should not be emptied into combustible waste unless the waste is to be removed from the building immediately. It is recommended that smoking ceases one hour before close of work, so that if smouldering occurs it will be detected before staff leave the premises.

- Combustible waste and contaminated rags should be kept in separate metal bins with close-fitting metal lids.

- Cleaners should preferably be employed in the evenings when work ceases. This will ensure that combustible rubbish is removed from the building to a place of safety before the premises are left unoccupied.

- Rubbish should not be kept in the building overnight or stored nearby.

- No-smoking areas should be strictly enforced, especially in places which are infrequently used, such as stationery stores and oil stores. Suitable 'No smoking' notices should be displayed.

- Where no smoking is enforced due to legal requirements (areas where flammable liquids are used or stored, for example) or in areas of high risk or high loss effect, it is recommended that the notice reads 'Smoking prohibited – dismissal offence'.

- Materials should not be stored on cupboard tops, and all filing cabinets should be properly closed and locked at the end of each day.

Anything that burns can be regarded as fuel. A premises' structure may be made of materials which will readily burn when exposed to fire or flame. Some potential sources of fuel commonly found in premises are:

- upholstered furniture, carpets and curtains

- office storage, filing and other storage cabinets

- wood and paper

- packaging materials

- paints and adhesives

- petrol and paraffin

- liquefied petroleum gas.

A good housekeeping approach assists in reducing risk to an acceptable level.

Statutory requirements

Note that in the wealth of fire legislation, premises are not policed by enforcing authorities. Employers are required to find out for themselves how to comply with the legislation. Consequently many companies buy in fire safety advice as and when needed from an independent fire safety consultant. A list of consultants is available from the Institution of Fire Engineers. See **Complying with health and safety law: fire safety, p 45** for statutory requirements relating to fire risk assessment.

Information

Association of British Insurers, tel: 020 7600 3333

Association of Security Consultants, tel: 07071 224865

British Computer Society, tel: 01793 417417, *www.bcs.org.uk*

British Security Industry Association, tel: 01905 21464, *www.bsia.co.uk*

CCTV User Group, for model code of practice and model procedural manual, tel: 01252 627970

The Centre for Crisis Psychology, tel: 01756 796383

Data Protection Registrar, tel: 01625 545745, *www.dataprotection.gov.uk/summary.htm*

Institution of Fire Engineers, tel: 0116 2553654, *www.ife.org.uk*

International Institute of Security, tel: 01803 663275

International Professional Security Association, tel: 01495 757153, *www.ipsa.org.uk*

Master Locksmiths Association, tel: 01327 262255, *www.locksmiths.co.uk*

NACOSS (National Approval Council for Security Systems), tel: 01628 637512, *www.nacoss.org.uk*

National Security Inspectorate, tel: 0870 2050000

Security Systems and Alarms Inspection Board, tel: 0191 2963242

Security Industry Authority, *www.the-sia.org.uk*

1 See the Home Office booklet on using and storing tapes as evidence: *CCTV – Looking out for you*, available from the Stationery Office, tel: 020 7873 9090.

13 Maintenance and Repair

Frank Booty

All properties and facilities need maintaining and, for many, maintenance is at the core of the facilities management role. Organisations are beginning to realise that planned preventative maintenance is more economical than ad hoc replacement of parts when they fail. As well as ensuring a planned maintenance schedule is effective, facilities managers must be careful to comply with statutory requirements relating to both electrical systems' testing and workers' safety.

Facilities managers also need a strategy in place for maintaining critical IT equipment. Whereas vendor-specific service agreements offer excellent service and assurance, such provision is compromised when a number of products from different vendors exist within one workplace. What solutions are available to the facilities manager, concerned with keeping the administrative burden of dealing with contracts to a minimum and ensuring that downtime does not affect the bottom line?

Plant and property maintenance

Statutory requirements

Construction (Design and Management) Regulations

A growing number of larger companies, local authorities and other public bodies have been pursuing increasingly formalised procedures for checking the health and safety standards of contractors wishing to work for them. This process has been accelerated by the introduction of the *Construction (Design and Management) Regulations 1994* which require organisations to satisfy themselves that potential principal contractors are capable of dealing with the health and safety issues associated with projects relating to their premises (see **Complying with health and safety law: Construction work and building management, p 65**).

Statutory maintenance tests

Do note the important issue of statutory maintenance tasks. Failure to check your equipment, system or process and record the results at the prescribed frequencies is serious. There are also certain facilities, such as lifts or elevators, where insurance implications mean a relevant official has to inspect the system during the maintenance process.

Costs

Costs for maintaining different types of building range from £2,700 per 100m^2 per year for air conditioned offices down to £950 per 100m^2 per year for warehouses[1]. Annual maintenance expenditure typically covers areas such as decorations, fabric, services, cleaning, utilities, administrative costs, overheads and external works[2]. Total expenditure on building maintenance in the UK rose for the eighth successive year in 2001 – with an estimated total value of £50.5 million. The cost of maintenance rose by 7.6 per cent over the year to October 2002.

When maintaining properties, fabric costs relate to the floor to wall ratio, the density of partitioning, the standards of fittings and frequency of use. Any services maintenance programme will depend on the quality, age and condition of the heating, ventilation and air conditioning systems installed. The amount of churn within a company will also affect maintenance costs.

Types of maintenance

According to British Standards, maintenance is a combination of all technical and associated administrative actions needed to retain an item or system in (or restore it to) a state in which it can perform its required function efficiently and as expected. Essentially there are two types of maintenance:

- **planned** (programmed, preventative and cyclical)
- **unplanned** (reactive, normal response, and emergency response).

Planned maintenance is maintenance organised and executed with forethought, control and application of records. It encompasses condition-based maintenance, which is progressed following information received about a system or structure's condition from routine or continuous monitoring processes.

Unplanned maintenance includes breakdown, corrective and emergency maintenance. A repair is the restoration of an item or system to an acceptable state through renewing, replacing or mending worn out or damaged parts. It is typically considered that the ups and downs of unplanned maintenance work should be run alongside planned work schedules. The reaction to unknown and unplanned events can thus be offset against meeting statutory obligations and service needs.

Condition assessments

Sound property management involves regularly checking a building's health. Condition assessments are now recognised as key tools for both strategic capital planning and tactical project prioritisation. Such systems integrate life-cycle data and condition assessment information with other facilities management technology systems, such as computerised monitoring and management systems and project management software.

Facilities managers can identify problems at their earliest stages and evaluate a building's future maintenance and repair needs through a systematic approach to assessing the condition of a variety of building components and systems. These may include building structure, building envelope, mechanical systems, electrical systems, interior finishes and lift safety. Building assessment protocols are applied to each component or system defining the scope of the audit for that category, the procedure to be followed and items that should typically be measured. Checksheets highlighting potential problem areas should be provided to assist facilities managers in conducting the assessments. From there, facilities managers will be able to judge how much work would be involved in repairing areas that require attention. The protocols can also be used to refer to relevant coding standards to assist companies in evaluating how well a given area complies with appropriate standards.

Refurbishment costs

Building owners/developers considering the relative merits of refurbishment compared to new build may be surprised to discover renovation projects can exceed 80 per cent of the cost of building a similar facility from scratch and are often about 66 per cent, according to a report from Building Maintenance Information (BMI). The *BMI Special Report 319 – Review of Rehabilitation Costs*[3] provides data on the average refurbishment costs of over 150 types of building, with information based on analysis of over 2,250 building projects. While the exact content of each project is not defined, all examples used cover the complete refurbishment of a building and have been converted to 3rd quarter 2002 levels to make them properly comparable. Figures for some building types are given below:

Building type	Rehabilitation Mean cost (£/m^2)	New build Mean cost (£/m^2)	Ratio of rehabilitation to new build
Offices	620	1,024	61%
General hospitals	856	1,225	70%
Schools	543	923	59%
Banks/building societies	730	1,334	55%
Flats	569	685	83%

BMI, which collects and analyses data on property occupancy cost from subscribers, is a service of RICS Building Cost Information Service Ltd.

Serviceability

Serviceability is defined as the ease with which corrective maintenance or preventative maintenance can be performed on a system. Higher serviceability improves availability and reduces service cost. Independent cost analysis studies indicate a large proportion of overall life-cycle costs of most systems/products is given over to maintenance and support. Indeed for some systems, maintenance and support has been demonstrated to account for up to 75 per cent of overall life-cycle costs. As long-term cost-effectiveness is a key competitive advantage in the current global marketplace, more and more companies are making plans to reduce system maintenance and support costs.

Managing maintenance contracts

All critical systems and response times should be detailed in specific service level agreements (SLAs) (see **Outsourcing: service level agreements, p 242**). Facilities managers can measure the performance of a particular service against the target given in the SLA through a helpdesk or computer-aided facilities management (CAFM) system (see **Space design and management: CAFM, p 343**).

Voucher systems

Maintenance systems, run as a part of a helpdesk or CAFM system, typically utilise job tickets or vouchers. These are issued to relevant tradesmen or contractors, providing them with information such as the location of the fault, description, agreed response time and estimated time for the work to be completed. Planned maintenance vouchers often include service routine details to assist personnel to process the required work. Cost codes track labour costs and all spare parts and consumables utilised during the work, so that these can be recharged efficiently and appropriately.

Software features

Many modern maintenance software packages use barcodes to collect data and costings on particular jobs, which saves a lot of time and effort otherwise expended on manual data entry. Such software packages can also be used to chart the history of items of plant, systems and schedules, as well as to make records of maintenance frequencies and issuing of spares. They can also assist in the processes necessary to perform statutory maintenance tests required on certain systems (electrical installations, for example).

Number and frequency of maintenance visits

There will be occasions when a planned maintenance service will have to be rescheduled. Companies will always want to know that the precise number of planned maintenance calls agreed in the SLA or contract have been actioned or delivered, so recording an event that has been pushed forward or back must take place.

The frequency of maintenance visits should be agreed, usually according to manufacturers' service requirements or recommendations. Maintenance software packages often feature the ability to plan workloads over defined periods to enable the best possible fit with the resources available to perform tasks. Unplanned activities can also be allowed for.

Managing the maintenance schedule

- Check to see if any statutory obligations have to be complied with.

- Find out exactly what plant and equipment there is within the estate and produce a detailed asset register (most likely this will be computerised), which should be checked and updated regularly.

- Ensure all heath and safety regulations are being followed.

- Conduct a risk assessment on all systems and tasks.

- Make sure all systems and components essential to the company's business continuity plan are known and that they are properly included in maintenance priorities.

- Develop a planned preventative maintenance schedule for all essential items of equipment, systems and fittings.

- Make sure an accessible maintenance and test-result recording and documentation system is operational.

- Set up a helpdesk (or at least a work request system) which links to all other procedures and systems within a company.

- Anticipate unplanned maintenance work and agree relevant charging structures.

- Make friends with the finance director, as capital investment budgets will need to be drawn up and life cycle costing exercises undertaken.

- Keep your team informed.

- Talk to your customers. Ask them what they think of your services (by conducting regular surveys), and find out what they want.

Employee safety

Effective maintenance is key to ensuring a healthy and safe workplace. Managers who control premises have a legal duty to ensure the safety of employees (see **Complying with health and safety law: maintenance and repair, p 41**). Facilities managers also have to be satisfied any contractors working on site are complying with health and safety guidance and regulations, and that they have conducted risk assessments where necessary. Compliance with health and safety should typically be embedded in specifications or SLAs from the outset, and regular two-way communication on health and safety matters is recommended.

Risk assessments

(See **Complying with health and safety law, pp 1–86**.)

Workplace injuries (or worse) are substantially reduced through the adoption of rigorous risk assessment practices, which highlight areas where maintenance is necessary. Risk assessments can be conducted using software systems or on paper and should be undertaken for workplace tasks or issues such as:

- air quality, humidity and temperature

- manual handling

- DSE-related issues – checking closeness to screens, rest breaks, etc

- first aid facilities

- static on carpets

- cleaning

- adequate lighting

- cable runs and any 'rogue' trailing leads

- control of substances hazardous to health

- noise.

Facilities managers should compile a risk register, where known risks can be ranked from low to high. As insurance companies will give reduced premiums against companies which can demonstrate where risks are low rather than high, the facilities manager who acts proactively here will be fondly welcomed by the finance department.

Preventative maintenance programmes

Preventative maintenance is maintenance carried out at predetermined intervals or according to prescribed criteria, with the intention of reducing the probability of failure or performance degradation of a system or structure. A preventative maintenance programme allocates specific maintenance tasks to particular periods in a timetable.

Preventative maintenance programmes save money and eliminate downtime. Maintenance programmes range from basic essential checks to comprehensive tests run according to manufacturers' specifications. Generally, full maintenance programmes are carried out at the end of a season when systems are shut down after several months of operation. This ensures readiness for the next period of operation. Ideally, a system should also be checked out immediately before start-up to make sure it is ready when needed. This applies particularly to heating systems in hotels but is equally valid in industrial premises.

Providing site owners authorise a full inspection and maintenance programme, with replacement of parts where required, they should be able to rely on the findings of such a programme for the forthcoming season of operation.

Reading the signs

Maintenance engineers should be trained to spot the tell-tale signals from ionisation probes and ultraviolet cells which indicate the condition of parts of a system. They should also take full-load current and bearing temperature readings from system motors, which verify their state of health.

Companies new to this process are recommended to have a full inventory check or technical audit of the heating, plumbing and ventilating plant at a site. A planned preventative maintenance schedule can then be worked out to cover all the equipment.

This might, for example, require inspection of oil burners every three months. If the planned maintenance schedule complies with the manufacturer's specifications, the system is unlikely to malfunction.

However, any deviation from these specifications – any cutting corners or cost savings – will inevitably result in unplanned maintenance problems and increased costs. System operating costs will increase with the age of the system, as will maintenance costs and system downtime.

Faults with new installations

Of course, installing a brand new system is no guarantee of trouble-free operation and new systems also require planned maintenance. The frequency of major failures due to poor installation or inadequate design is surprisingly high. This is where a site survey procedure often highlights system faults and design defects, which can be rectified economically early in the life of the system. Before the end of the first year of operation, it makes sense to have all the building systems checked for defects, while the installers remain liable for rectifying any installation faults. It is common to find access control panels that are not wired correctly, and missing thermostats.

Spare parts holding

To support the maintenance programme, a minimum spares holding is recommended. This would include belts for motor drives – inexpensive items but nevertheless essential for the system to operate correctly.

Air conditioning

Preventative maintenance is equally valid for air conditioning systems. Filter elements need replacing regularly or the consequence can be costly.

One company had a unit with a badly blocked filter element, which had been pulled out of its track and was resting on the drive belt. Friction burn marks were evident on the element. This might have caused a serious fire but was, fortunately, spotted in time. The antidote is to maintain a spare parts holding of filter elements, costing £200. A spare parts holding of under £1,000 guarantees minimal maintenance costs, and assures minimal downtime and system reliability – insurance which is well worth considering.

Test instrumentation

Sophisticated monitoring equipment is essential. All engineers should carry flue gas analysers and be able to interpret the results to achieve safety and maximum efficiency. This can often save money over time. Engineers have been known to encounter boilers which are operating at efficiency levels as low as 40 per cent, when they should be operating at about 80 per cent. This increases the fuel consumption of the system and, more importantly, can lead to blocked and sooted-up flues, which, in turn, can lead to carbon monoxide emission hazards.

Staff training needs

Frequently there are basic maintenance procedures which can be carried out by staff without the need for a maintenance engineer. These range from the act of pressing a boiler reset button to restarting an entire system. For example, replacing filter elements at prescribed intervals is a relatively simple task which can realistically be carried out in-house, provided the necessary instruction has been provided.

When it comes to complex computer-based building management systems, property managers need to be able to interpret the mass of information they are provided with and training is, again, a key requirement.

Environmental issues

Some of the latest sites have been designed to reduce nitrous oxide emissions, which are known to affect the composition of the ozone layer. Awareness of nitrous oxide gas emissions is something with which everyone in the industry should be increasingly concerned. There may also be future standards for the operation of energy controls, including those applying to building management systems (BMS).

Turnkey service management

When buying a new electrical appliance, facilities managers must decide whether to take out a service management agreement. With technology advancing at exponential rates, and appliances now supporting more and more critical applications, any downtime due to appliance failure becomes less and less acceptable. Yet, despite manufacturers' claims, nothing is infallible. There will be occasions (albeit infrequent) when problems arise and repairs are necessary. This is when the service engineer becomes your best friend.

Manufacturers offer numerous after-sales packages to provide users with the assurance that, should a product suffer from a failure of some kind, a service engineer will be on standby to offer assistance. Domestically speaking, such service management agreements (usually defined as extended warranty packages) may initially appear costly, but when weighed against an independent engineer's call-out and hourly charges, they could bring benefits after only a single use.

Within the corporate arena, service management agreements play a more integral role in the initial purchase of a product. When committing to purchase a new piece of equipment, assurance is necessary that not only is the organisation purchasing at the best price available, but also that the equipment is accompanied by a comprehensive service package. In the event of failure, the cost to the organisation in loss of productivity alone could easily outstrip the initial capital outlay for the equipment.

Managing multiple vendors

With so many organisations looking for the best deals each time they buy new equipment, it is unlikely that every appliance will be supplied by the same vendor – which has ramifications for the service manager. Organisations looking to manage multiple electronic devices, for example, should consider a single maintenance contractor.

Each individual vendor may offer a uniquely tailored service solution for its own range of products, which means an organisation may end up holding multiple agreements with multiple vendors. For example, consider the possibility that 'brand-X' operates six different products within a particular company, as do four other vendors, each in turn offering a tailored service agreement for each product (email server, network printer, uninterruptible power supply (UPS), PCs, and so on). In the event of one of these products failing and an engineering call-out being required, the host organisation must sift through numerous contracts in order to find the correct one for the correct piece of equipment. The amount of time taken simply to identify the appropriate service department or contact may have potentially cost the organisation thousands of pounds in lost productivity.

The complete service solution

In essence, the complete service solution is a simple idea – one organisation provides the complete service management for all devices. In practice, it is not quite that simple – it is unlikely that a photocopier engineer could provide technical support for a server fault, for example.

Behind the complete service solution lies the fundamental premise of service management – expert technical assistance. As such, the complete service solution offers expert assistance for a specific set of products, be they photocopiers or UPSs. Consider the UPS as the example in this case. The UPS is a niche product (particularly in the high-end segment where a single unit may involve a five figure capital outlay), and each unit can be fundamentally different. It is hard to directly compare the UPSs of two manufacturers, as each unit integrates inherently individual technology and specifications around a common design – that of offering power protection and assurance 24/7.

Within the UPS marketplace, an immediate response to any service need is imperative. This is why certain manufacturers in the industry have paid close attention to the traditional service management problems, and have devoted time to evolve this practice into a complete one-stop service solution.

The UPS industry has devised two modes of service management:

Third-party service management

Within this model, a single manufacturer operates as the sole service provider to the customer, thus providing direct service and support to every brand within the host organisation. In the event of a failure, the user contacts the manufacturer, and it will send one of its service engineers to address the technical problem. Despite the apparent advantages of this method (one contract for all servicing needs), the manufacturer must be able to service all brands of UPS to a high level. As mentioned already, all UPSs encompass individual specifications and technologies, so it would be essential for the managing organisation to employ expert engineers in all of the UPSs currently in the marketplace.

Outsourced management ('total support')

Operating along similar lines to the model above, the outsourced management solution is executed through a single manufacturer acting as a service facilitator (or agreement host). In the event of a failure, the user contacts the chosen host manufacturer for technical support. Once the call has been received, it is analysed to discover which particular brand of UPS is at fault and whether the agreement host is equipped to support the device in question. Instead of sending the host manufacturer's own service engineer to service all manner of units, this service model means the host manufacturer will (where necessary) outsource the maintenance of a particular unit to the specific vendor. Through this practice, the user is benefiting from cost-effective, vendor-specific service management while enjoying a centralised support contact process.

Of the two models above, the outsourced management method offers the user the advantages of a focused service management agreement without the aggravation of having to deal with multiple contracts. Within the high-end UPS sector, total support has been recognised as the optimum service management method and has received recognition from many well-known organisations, such as Tesco and Bank of Scotland. But should this practice be restricted to just the high-end electronics industry?

Needs of smaller organisations

Traditionally, smaller units have not been covered by total support service management agreements, but with advancing technology allowing smaller and smaller units to support larger systems, smaller unit users are demanding the same level of service management as their larger counterparts.

As a result, manufacturers have adapted the total support model to cater for this sector. For example, in supermarkets the organisation-wide EPoS (electronic point-of-sale) cashier system may be supported by a large UPS, but individual tills will still have their own separate UPSs. Larger UPSs may require specialised support (from the host organisation or outsourced vendor), but in most cases involving smaller UPSs, immediate support can be offered by the host organisation as the majority of failures in these units are due to the natural lifespan of the internal batteries. In cases such as these, the host is able to 'hot-swap' the batteries on site no matter what brand of UPS is being operated. In this way, the supermarket can call on technical support for all sizes of UPSs, thus assuring power protection for all of its systems.

E-business solutions for support

The potential now exists for manufacturers to combine thousands of pages of maintenance manuals, parts illustrations, service bulletins and parts catalogues on a web-based system into intelligent, extensible software applications, providing their customers and channel partners with an e-business platform that improves equipment maintenance and drives additional spare parts sales. The combination of solutions gives manufacturers and operators of high-value equipment shared access to the product support information that enables them to service their revenue-producing assets more effectively and efficiently, resulting in less downtime and improved field staff productivity. Such a combined solution also provides collaboration and transaction capabilities that support post-sale business processes such as order management, warranty management, channel management, shop-floor task execution and inventory management.

Information

Building Maintenance Information (BMI) and Building Cost Information Service (BCIS), tel: 020 7695 1500, *www.bcis.co.uk*

CORGI (Council for Registered Gas Installers), tel: 01256 372200, *www.corgi-gas.com*

NICEIC (National Inspection Council for Electrical Installation Contracting), tel: 020 7564 2323, *www.niceic.org.uk*

1 Costs computed for different types of building by Building Maintenance Information (BMI) in its *BMI Building Maintenance Price Book 2003*.
2 The Building Cost Information Service (BCIS) provides a map of the UK detailing the costs of carrying out a maintenance contract, showing regional pricing levels, available in the appendices of the above publication.
3 *BMI Special Report 319 – Review of Rehabilitation Costs* is available as part of the BMI Bulletin Service. Copies cost £30 each, tel: 020 7695 1500.

Appendix

Category	Sub-categories (Contract bundle items)	Principal examples/cost elements	Items included in costs	Items excluded
Services maintenance and repair	Heat and ventilation	boilers radiators chillers ductwork filters fire extinguishers humidifiers	handy-men supervisors blue-collar staff specialist services cleaning tenants areas service charge element water treatment PPM, emergency, ad hoc, etc smoke tests statutory testing	catering equipment new installations alterations improvements grounds lighting general management time security systems cleaning equipment computer installations
	Plumbing	sprinklers sanitary fittings water supplies drainage	emergency inspection and testing PAT tests legionnaire testing	data cabling churn line management
	Electrical	switchgear wiring internal lighting small power floor outlets fire alarms generators building management systems energy management systems UPS	hardwire testing testing and inspection of earth bonding	
	Lifts	lifts escalators		
Building maintenance and repair	Fabric	structural roofing partitions doors	handy-men supervisors blue-collar staff maintenance equipment tools	new installations alterations improvements management time churn

	Decorations	finishes	materials	office equipment grounds maintenance furniture
	Fixtures and fittings	fixtures fittings	tenants areas service charge element signage essential spares plantroom cleaning gutter clearance	internal landscaping
Grounds maintenance and repair	Maintenance	services (including drain clearance) hard landscaping (fences, pavings) soft landscaping (planted areas, lawns)	gardening horticulture tree surgery fences	
	Cleaning	power washing	service charges snow clearance car park areas road maintenance (including gritting)	
	Utilities	lighting		
	Security	special grounds patrols/guarding specialist grounds security system maintenance		
Furniture maintenance and repair	Maintenance	chairs desks	service charge element	additional purchases moves special aids and adaptations
	Repairs			
	ISOLATED replacements	(only considered if uneconomic to repair)		
Equipment maintenance and repair	Maintenance	loose electrical appliances	service charge element	additional purchases blinds and curtains IT equipment photocopiers
	Fitting out	AV equipment		
	Repairs	rental costs		
	ISOLATED replacements	(only considered if uneconomic to repair)		
Alterations and fitting out	Churn	moves and changes costs	construction project management professional fees statutory fees furniture and fittings	major refurbishment statutory improvement
	Fitting out			
	Improvement			
	Adaptations			
Cleaning	Windows and cladding	windows external walls	deep clean toilets carpet shampoos stain removal cleaning materials	deep clean kitchens catering area cleaning contract management time cleans due to churn
	Internal areas	floors internal walls		

Appendix – continued

Category	Sub-categories (Contract bundle items)	Principal examples/cost elements	Items included in costs	Items excluded
Cleaning – *continued*		ceilings sanitary fittings toilet area surfaces	supervisors tenants' areas service charge element graffiti removal atria glazing roofs and integral gutters litter picking cleaning equipment maintnenance health and safety requirements (eg, slippery surface signs)	plantroom cleans grounds cleaning
	Supplies	janitorial supplies		
	Furniture and equipment	furniture, fittings and business equipment		
	Special cleans	exposed services catering special cleans computer special cleans lighting special cleans ductwork special cleans lift shaft special cleans		
	Pest control	pest control	wires, nets, poisons (eradication contract)	
	Waste disposal	general office waste disposal waste recycling service hazardous/environmentally sensitive waste disposal secure waste disposal	equipment maintenance (eg, shredders) hire of containers	
Laundry	Laundry services	uniforms pillows sheets towels	consumables dedicated staff costs contract costs linen hire	tablecloths chefs' whites new linen/towels, etc.
Security & reception	Reception	reception door guard/commissionaire	staff costs day guards (external and internal) night patrols (external and internal) uniforms radios security cards camera operators tenants' areas service charge element barriers swipe cards	fire alarms new installations alterations improvements management time changes due to churn
	Guarding	external guarding internal guarding		
	Surveillance	external surveillance internal surveillance		
	Duties	visitor escorting lost property		
	Security system maintenance	car parking control card readers		

Category	Subcategory	CCTV equipment	CCTV pass issue key management tenants' areas service charge element	telephones management time environmental testing
Utilities	Energy	electricity gas oil		
	Water and sewerage	water sewerage		
Internal door	Horticultural	trees cut flowers planters	contract charges cleaning costs	
	Objets d'art	objets d'art	insurance premiums	
Archiving		physical documents electronic media film-based media document/file disposal specialist filing systems	contract charges maintenance contracts	
Reprographics	Machines	convenience copiers central black and white photocopying central colour photocopying origination/DTP controller	paper management maintenance leases	utilities
	Consumables	off-site printing laminating equipment binding equipment and consumables		
	Dedicated staff			
Stationery	Departmental	standard paper products bespoke paper products (headed paper, etc.) non-paper consumables	envelopes	paper for photocopiers writing materials
	Personal		office equipment other: cards/diaries/files flip-charts/foils/pens line management	
	Storage materials			
	Management			
IT Communications	Switchboard	switchboard service operation switchboard service maintenance	staff costs equipment maintenance	

Appendix – continued

Category	Sub-categories (Contract bundle items)	Principal examples/cost elements	Items included in costs	Items excluded
IT Communications – *continued*	Equipment maintenance	telephone/fax equipment maintenance radio pagers/DECT mobiles maintenance audio-visual conferencing equipment main tenance telephone cable maintenance	line management	
	Call charges	mobile phone charges national line charges inter-site leased line charges international line charges bureau services charges		
IT Computers	PC equipment	PC equipment maintenance	equipment/hardware costs lease costs ISDN/other line costs ISP subscriptions domain subscriptions consultancy costs maintenance contracts	new purchases (hardware and software)
	Software	software maintenance line charges website management		
Distribution (Mail/Post room)	Mail processing/delivery	processing and delivery of incoming mail collection and preparation of mail for external distribution processing and delivery of internal mail/messages	dedicated staff uniforms equipment maintenance dedicated IT scanning/X-ray postal charges courier charges packaging (ie. jiffy bags, bubble wrap, etc.)	
	Charges	post office charges		
	Couriers	local couriers' charges national couriers' charges international couriers' charges		
	Equipment	post room equipment maintenance		
Text preparation	Typing services operation	Typing services operation	staff costs equipment costs	
	Bureau charges	Bureau charges		

Transport/fleet management	Pool cars	pool cars maintenance pool cars cleaning pool cars operation/chauffeurs	staff costs equipment costs uniforms overalls	fitting out general cleaners utilities purchase finance
	Delivery vans	pool delivery van maintenance pool delivery van cleaning pool delivery van operation/drivers		
	Service vehicles	service vehicle maintenance service vehicle cleaning service vehicle operation/drivers		
Catering	Staff dining	staff dining: breakfast menu staff dining: lunch menu staff dining: sandwich bar staff dining: snacks and beverages	subsidy costs chef, cooks, supervisors, waiters, servers, till staff specialist cleaners	
	Vending	vending: sandwiches vending: confectionery and snack products vending: canned/bottled drinks vending: beverages	preparation food cost drink cost alcohol sandwiches	
	Hospitality	hospitality: sandwich lunches hospitality: beverage service hospitality: cold buffet lunches hospitality: hot buffet lunches	leases, rental crockery disposables linen	
	Private dining	private dining rooms: breakfast menu (silver service) private dining rooms: lunch menu (silver service)	laundry	
	Special functions	special functions: seated dinners (silver service) special functions: buffets (silver service) special functions: cocktail parties	consumables deep cleaning/specialist cleaning income from till receipts catering contractor management fee consultants	
	Bar	bar: coffee lounge bar: alcoholic and soft drinks		
	Maintenance and repair	catering equipment maintenance		
Porterage		workplace removals general services	supervision staff uniforms trolleys	waste disposal moves

Appendix – continued

Category	Sub-categories (Contract bundle items)	Principal examples/cost elements	Items included in costs	Items excluded
Helpdesk/MIS		helpdesk operation booking services equipment/software maintenance	supervision staff uniforms specialist equipment/software maintenance	
Travel		booking service operation travel charges		
Fitness centre		fitness centre management fitness centre equipment maintenance		
Nursery/crèche		nursery/crèche management nursery/crèche equipment maintenance		
General management		intelligent client function (ICF) management agency	senior/strategic management salaries benefits overheads contract management (in-house and outsourced contracts) expenses equipment course fees professional subs	blue-collar workers task supervisors
Professional services		health and safety management project management estate management space management conference/meeting room management	facilities consultants	blue-collar workers task supervisors

Notes

All categories to include outsourced contracts and in-house staff

In-house staff costs to include benefits and overhead allowances

All costs to be exclusive of VAT

Costs of space occupied by category to be excluded but may be shown separately

Depreciation and amortisation costs are not included within the categories but may be shown separately

Index

[all references are to page number]

Access risk analysis
  access to workplace, and, 357
Access to workplace
  access risk analysis, 357
  authorised entrants, 359
  building exteriors, 358
  company cash, 360
  equipment, 360–361
  information protection, 361–362
  introduction, 357
  intruder alarms, 359–360
  manned guarding, 361
  perimeter boundary, 358
  personal attack alarms, 360
  private security, 361
  restriction of access, 358
  rising screens, 359
  security measures, 358–360
  stock, 360
  valuables, 360
Accounting valuations
  depreciated replacement cost, 159–160
  existing use, 159
  FRS 15, 160
  investment, development or disposal property, 160
Acquisition of property
  completion, 123–124
  costs, 124–125
  exchange of contracts, 123
  fees, 125
  introduction, 121
  land registry fees, 125
  local land charges searches, 125
  ownership, 121
  procedure
    completion, 123–124
    costs, 124–125
    exchange of contracts, 123
    fees, 125
    generally, 123
  registration system, 122
  role of professional advisers, 122–123
  stamp duty, 124
  valuation of property, and
    further investigations, 158–159
    'hope' value, 158
    market value, 157–158
    net realisation proceeds, 159
    special purchasers, 158
  value added tax, 124–125

Adjacencies
  space design and management, and, 336
Adoption leave
  generally, 95
  reform proposals, 120
Aesthetics
  space design and management, and, 337–338
Agency workers
  employment law, and, 98
Aggression in workplace
  at-risk areas, 355–356
  counselling, 356
  defensive strategies, 356–357
  introduction, 355
  persons involved, 356
  training, 356
Air conditioning
  close control systems, 299
  fixed systems, 298
  introduction, 298
  need, 298
  portable systems, 299
  preventative maintenance programmes, and, 371
  refrigerant policy, 300
  temperature control systems, 299–300
Air quality
  humidity, 33–34
  passive smoking
    case law, 34
    generally, 34–35
  temperature, 32–33
  ventilation, 33
Alterations
  business leases, and, 131
Annual leave
  part-time workers, and, 90
Appeals
  flexible working, and, 88–89
  planning, and
    challenges, 144
    enforcement, and, 147
    generally, 143–144
    human rights, and, 144
Asbestos, control of
  health and safety regulations, and, 9
Asbestos-related diseases
  employers' duty, 27
  introduction, 25
  leaving in place, 26
  repair and removal, 26–27
  surveys and logs, 25–26

Assignment
business leases, and, 130
Audio-conferencing
introduction, 272–273
technology, 273

Back pain, avoidance of
environment, 19
individual's circumstances, 19
introduction, 18
load, 19
risk assessment, 18
task changes, 18–19
Barcode readers
managing maintenance contracts, and, 368
Behavioural effects
budgetary control, and, 170
transport plans, and, 260
introduction, 255
Benchmarking facilities costs
external comparison, 181–182
facilities audit, 182
internal comparison, 181–182
misinterpretation of value, 180
process
cost data, 183–184
facilities protocol, 186
graphics, 186–187
introduction, 182
obtaining comparable data, 185
parameters, 184–185
performance data, 183
reporting, 188
resource drivers, 182–183
statistics production, 186–187
troubleshooting diagnosis, 187–188
purpose, 179–181
wider perspective, 180–181
Best practice
business continuity, and, 232–233
financial management, and
and see below
generally, 166–175
prevention of water pollution, and
examples, 295
introduction, 293
key facts, 295
options, 293–294
transport plans, and, 260–261
Best practice financial management
budgetary control
behavioural effects, 170
change management, 171–172
communication, 170
coordination, 169–170
evaluation, 171
introduction, 166
planning, 166–167
preparation, 167–169
reporting and reconciliation, 170–171

Best practice financial management—*contd*
e-procurement
disadvantages, 175
growth, 174–175
introduction, 174
procurement
contracted-out provision, 172–173
in-house provision, 172–173
market capability. 173–174
scope of services, 173
strategic considerations, 172
Bluetooth
communications, and, 266
Budgetary control
behavioural effects, 170
change management, 171–172
communication, 170
computer-aided facilities management, and, 345
coordination, 169–170
evaluation, 171
introduction, 166
planning, 166–167
preparation
cost centres, 167–168
data, 168–171
introduction, 167
zero-based budgeting, 168
reporting and reconciliation, 170–171
Building alterations
disability discrimination, and, 110–111
Building exteriors
access to workplace, and, 358
Building management
Building Regulations, 77–79
computer-aided facilities management, and, 343
introduction, 73
permit to work procedures
generally, 76–77
method statements, 77
safe means of access
cleaning and maintenance, 75
cleaning windows, 74
effects of failure, 75
introduction, 73–74
key points, 76
using ladders, 74–75
safe systems of work, 76–77
Building operations
planning, and, 137
Building Regulations
construction, work, and, 77–79
planning, and, 148
Buildings insurance
introduction, 196
flood, 196–197
terrorism, 197
Business continuity
best practice procedures, 232–233

Business continuity—*contd*
  business impact analysis
    introduction, 222
    potential business impact analysis, 223–224
    potential risk analysis, 223
  business vulnerability, 221–222
  care of staff
    communication, 229–230
    introduction, 228–229
    post-event welfare, 230
    training, 229
  dealings with media, 230–231
  development of strategy
    business impact analysis, 222–224
    business vulnerability, 221–222
    effectiveness, 222
    introduction, 221
  implementation of strategy
    drawing up plan, 224–225
    rehearsal of plan, 226
    roles and responsibilities, 225–226
  introduction, 220
  inventory control, 231
  outsourcing disaster recovery
    considerations, 227–228
    introduction, 226–227
    selection of supplier, 227
  restoration of business, 232
  Turnbull report, 220
Business impact analysis
  introduction, 222
  potential business impact analysis, 223–224
  potential risk analysis, 223
Business leases
  access rights, 132
  alterations, 131
  assignment, 130
  breach of repairing obligations, 132
  dealings
    assignment, 130
    introduction, 130
    sharing occupation, 131
    sub-letting, 130
  demised premises, 127
  exceptions and reservations, 128
  fixtures and fittings, 127
  insurance, 132–133
  interest, 130
  introduction, 127
  landlord's remedies for tenant breaches
    non-payment of rent, 135
    other, 136
  new buildings, 131–132
  non-payment of rent, 135
  old buildings, 132
  options to terminate, 134–135
  parties, 127
  rates and taxes, 130

Business leases—*contd*
  rent
    generally, 129
    payment, 129–130
  rent review, 130
  repairs, 131
  reserve funds, 134
  rights granted, 128
  security of tenure
    compensation
      generally, 128
      landlords, notice, 128–129
    new lease, 129
    tenant's request for new tenancy, 129
    termination, 128
  service charges
    apportionment, 133
    introduction, 133
    management arrangements, 133
    objections, 134
    payment, 134
    services, 133
    sinking funds, 134
  sharing occupation, 131
  sinking funds, 134
  sub-letting, 130
  term, 128
  termination, 128–129
  use, 131
Business risk
  risk management, and, 208–209
Business vulnerability
  continuity of business, and, 221–222

Cabling
  computer-aided facilities management, and, 344
  floor boxes, 332
  generally, 331–332
  grommets, 332
  management, 332
Cabling categories
  communications, and, 269–270
Call centres
  business continuity, and, 232
Capital allowances
  buildings, 205–206
  introduction, 204
  plant and machinery, 204
Capital and revenue expenditure
  financial management, and, 203
Capital gains tax (CGT)
  financial management, and, 199–200
Car park management
  design, 262
  floor graphic advertising, 262
  introduction, 261
  lighting, 263
  plans, 261–262
  security, 263

Catering facilities
drinking water, 312
fast food, 312
food safety
 court proceedings, 81
 improvement notices, 80
 introduction, 79
 licensing, 84
 premises registration, 81
 prohibition order, 80–81
 statutory provisions, 79–80
future prospects, 316
health and safety, 83–84
hygiene
 drainage facilities, 82
 equipment, 82
 grease traps, 82
 introduction, 81–82
 management systems, 83
 pest proofing, 82
 premises, 82
 refuse material, 82
 services, 82
 waste material, 82
improvement notices, 80
introduction, 312–313
licensing, 84
menu, 313
prohibition order
 emergency, 81
 generally, 80–81
restaurant facilities
 ambience, 314–315
 caterer selection, 315–316
 costs, 314
 design, 313
 introduction, 312–313
 layout, 313–314
 management, 315
 siting, 313–314
 space, 314
 subsidies, 315
temperature control, 83
vending machines, 313
CDM Regulations
client, 67–68
design risk assessment, 72
designer, 69–70
generally, 66–67
health and safety file, 71–72
health and safety plan
 construction phase, 71
 pre-tender, 70–71
introduction, 8–9
maintenance and repair, and, 365
planning supervisor, 69
principal contractor, 70
Certificate of lawful use or development
planning, and, 147–148

Certificates
fire safety, and, 45–46
Change management
financial management, and, 171–172
Churn of space
benefits and costs, 339
cutting cost, 340
hotdesking, 341–343
introduction, 339
relocation, 340–341
CIBSE guidelines
cleaner indoor air, and, 300–301
Circulation
space design and management, and, 335–336
Civil compensation
health and safety, and, 17
Cleaner indoor air
CIBSE guidelines, 300–301
humidity
 employers' duties, 302
 introduction, 301
 management, 303
 measurement, 303
 staff discomfort, 302–303
 stress, 302
 symptom recognition, 302
introduction, 300
pollutants, 301
Cleaning windows
safe means of access, and, 74
Cleaning workplace facilities
contractor selection, 316–317
costs, 317
introduction, 316
market dynamics, 316
working time, 318
Climate change levy
energy efficiency, and
 emission reduction, 286–288
 introduction, 285–286
 objectives, 286
exemptions, 60–61
generally, 60
rates, 60
Closed circuit television (CCTV)
choice, 352–353
data protection, 354
generally, 351
operation, 353
recordings, 354–355
remote monitoring, 354
security audits, 352
threats, 351
Combined heat and power
CHP Club, 281
efficiency, 281
introduction, 280
Communication
financial management, and, 170

Communications
  conferencing
    introduction, 272–273
    technology, 273
  convergence of data and telecom
    Bluetooth, 266
    fixed network, 265–266
    future prospects, 267
    introduction, 265
    mobile telephony, 265
    voice to data conversion, 266
    Wi-Fi zones, 267
    wireless LANs, 267
  digital document systems
    establishment, 277
    introduction, 277
    paper storage, 277
  e-business
    e-mail negotiations, 275
    e-procurement, 275
    intranet services, 276
    intranet site, 276
    introduction, 274
    top-down approach, 274–275
  helpdesks, 276–277
  infrastructure management
    cabling categories, 269–270
    future-proofing, 268–269
    introduction, 268
  introduction, 265
  presentation
    introduction, 272–273
    technology, 273–274
  voice over IP (VoIP)
    data network integration, 271–272
    developments, 272
    features, 270–271
    introduction, 270
Company cash
  access to workplace, and, 360
Comparable workers
  part-time workers, and, 92–93
Compensation
  disability discrimination, and, 111
Complete service solution
  turnkey service management, and, 373–375
Completion
  acquisition of property, and, 123–124
Computer-aided facilities management (CAFM)
  budgetary control, 345
  buildings, 343
  cabling, 344
  choice of supplier, 346–348
  data protection, 348–349
  environmental issues, 344
  financial management, 345
  future-proofing, 347
  health and safety, 344
  helpdesks, 345

Computer-aided facilities management (CAFM)—
  contd
  introduction, 343
  inventory management, 345
  maintenance and repairs, 344–345
  networks, 344
  security, 345
  space usage, 343
  system implementation, 349–350
  transitional planning, 349
Computer telephony integration
  business continuity, and, 232
  generally, 272
Computer workstations
  upper limb disorders, and, 22–23
Condition assessment
  maintenance and repair, and, 366–367
Conferencing
  introduction, 272–273
  technology, 273
Confined spaces, working in
  generally, 44–45
  health and safety regulations, and, 8
Conservation areas
  planning, and, 139
Construction, design and management (CDM) regulations
  client, 67–68
  design risk assessment, 72
  designer, 69–70
  generally, 66–67
  health and safety file, 71–72
  health and safety plan
    construction phase, 71
    pre-tender, 70–71
  introduction, 8–9
  maintenance and repair, and, 365
  planning supervisor, 69
  principal contractor, 70
Construction work
  building management, 73–79
    Building Regulations, 77–79
    introduction, 73
    permit to work procedures, 76–77
    safe means of access, 73–76
  CDM Regulations
    client, 67–68
    design risk assessment, 72
    designer, 69–70
    generally, 66–67
    health and safety file, 71–72
    health and safety plan, 70–71
    planning supervisor, 69
    principal contractor, 70
  improvement notices, 65
  introduction, 65
  key issues, 66
  prohibition notices, 66
  refurbishment works, 72–73

Consultation with employees
employment law, and
European works councils, 104
introduction, 103–104
national works councils, 106–107
redundancies, 104–106
transfers, 105
health and safety regulations, and, 10
transport plans, and, 257–258
Contaminated land
generally, 149
introduction, 149
'polluter pays' principle, 149
reducing clean-up liability, 150
statutory basis, 149
Continuity of business
best practice procedures, 232–233
business impact analysis
introduction, 222
potential business impact analysis, 223–224
potential risk analysis, 223
business vulnerability, 221–222
care of staff
communication, 229–230
introduction, 228–229
post-event welfare, 230
training, 229
dealings with media, 230–231
development of strategy
business impact analysis, 222–224
business vulnerability, 221–222
effectiveness, 222
introduction, 221
implementation of strategy
drawing up plan, 224–225
rehearsal of plan, 226
roles and responsibilities, 225–226
introduction, 220
inventory control, 231
outsourcing disaster recovery
considerations, 227–228
introduction, 226–227
selection of supplier, 227
restoration of business, 232
Turnbull report, 220
Contract workers
disability discrimination, and, 112
Coordination
financial management, and, 169–170
Corporate killing
health and safety, and, 17
Corporate manslaughter
generally, 17
reform proposals, 86
Corporate social responsibility
environmental protection, and, 64
Corporation tax
financial management, and, 199

Cost centres
budgetary control, and, 167–168
Cost data
benchmarking facilities costs, and, 183–184
Cost/benefit analysis
financial analysis, and, 193
Costs
acquisition of property, and, 124–125
maintenance and repair, and, 366
Counselling
aggression in the workplace, and, 356
Criminal sanctions
corporate killing, 17
directors' responsibilities, 16–17
future legislation, 17
generally, 14–15
reform proposals, 16

Dangerous substances
health and safety regulations, and, 11–12
Data
budgetary control, and, 168–171
Data-conferencing
introduction, 272–273
technology, 273
Data protection
closed circuit television, and, 354
computer-aided facilities management, and,
348–349
Dealings with the media
continuity of business, and, 230–231
Demised premises
business leases, and, 127
Dependants' leave
generally, 96
Depreciated replacement cost
valuation of property, and, 159–160
Depreciation
facilities finance, and, 203–204
Designer
construction, design and management, and, 69–70
Development
planning, and, 137
Digital document systems
establishment, 277
introduction, 277
paper storage, 277
Digital risk
generally, 214
minimisation, 215
types, 214
Directors' responsibilities
health and safety, and, 16–17
Disability discrimination
building alterations, 110–111
compensation, 111
complaints, 111
contract workers, 111–112
Disability Rights Commission, 112

Disability discrimination—*contd*
  generally, 107–108
  leased premises, 110–111
  public access, 109–110
  reasonable adjustments, 108–109
  reform proposals, 120
Disciplinary procedure
  employment law, and, 118–119
Discounted cash flow
  financial analysis, and, 190–191
Display screen equipment
  health and safety regulations, and, 6–7
Disposal of property
  completion, 123–124
  costs, 124–125
  exchange of contracts, 123
  fees, 125
  introduction, 121
  land registry fees, 125
  local land charges searches, 125
  ownership, 121
  procedure
    completion, 123–124
    costs, 124–125
    exchange of contracts, 123
    fees, 125
    generally, 123
  registration system, 122
  role of professional advisers, 122–123
  stamp duty, 124
  valuation of property, and
    further investigations, 158–159
    'hope' value, 158
    market value, 157–158
    net realisation proceeds, 159
    special purchasers, 158
  value added tax, 124–125
Dispute resolution
  outsourcing, and, 245
Distributed workplace strategies
  sustainable property, and, 198
Document systems
  establishment, 277
  introduction, 277
  paper storage, 277
Drainage
  catering facility hygiene, and, 82
Drinking water
  catering facilities, and, 312
Driving
  flexible working, and, 58–59

E-business
  e-mail negotiations, 275
  e-procurement, 275
  intranet services, 276
  intranet site, 276
  introduction, 274
  maintenance and repair, and, 375
  top-down approach, 274–275

Economic structure of organisations
  facilities management costs, 164–165
  introduction, 163
  systems technology, 165–166
  universal principles, 163
Electricity at work
  health and safety regulations, and, 9
Electricity, purchase of
  avoidance of power failures, 283
  checking invoices, 283–285
  combined heat and power, 280–281
  introduction, 279
  meter-reading errors, 284–285
  NETA, 280
  open systems in building control, 282
  reverse auction agencies, 279
  totally integrated power, 281–282
Email use policy
  workplace surveillance, and, 117–118
Emergency exits
  means of escape, and, 53
Emergency lighting
  categories, 324
  escape routes, 324–325
  introduction, 323
  luminaries, 323
  maintenance, 325–326
  means of escape, and, 52–53
  safety signs, 325
  standards, 324–325
  testing, 325–326
Employees, consultation with
  employment law, and
    European works councils, 104
    introduction, 103–104
    national works councils, 106–107
    redundancies, 104–106
    transfers, 105
  health and safety regulations, and, 9–10
  transport plans, and, 257–258
Employees' duties
  fire safety, and, 53–54
  health and safety, and, 3
Employers' duties
  asbestos-related diseases, and, 27
  health and safety, and, 2–3
Employment law
  adoption leave
    generally, 95
    reform proposals, 120
  agency workers, 98
  dependants' leave, 96
  disability discrimination
    building alterations, 110–111
    compensation, 111
    complaints, 111
    contract workers, 111–112
    Disability Rights Commission, 112
    generally, 107–108

Employment law—*contd*
  disability discrimination—*contd*
    leased premises, 110–111
    public access, 109–110
    reasonable adjustments, 108–109
    reform proposals, 120
  disciplinary hearings, 118–119
  employee consultation
    European works councils, 104
    introduction, 103–104
    national works councils, 106–107
    redundancies, 104–106
    transfers, 105
  fixed-term contracts, 97
  flexible working
    appeals, 88–89
    introduction, 87
    reasons for refusal, 88
    reform proposals, 120
    right of request, 87–89
  48-hour week
    annual leave, 90
    enforcement, 92
    exceptions, 91–92
    generally, 89
    nightworkers, 90
    reform proposals, 120
    rest periods, 90
  grievance hearings, 118–119
  maternity leave, 95
  minimum wage, 119
  parental leave, 96
  part-time workers
    comparable full-timers, 92–93
    introduction, 92
    justification, 93
    pro-rata principle, 93
    regulatory guidance, 94
    remedies, 93–94
  paternity leave
    generally, 95
    reform proposals, 120
  redundancy
    generally, 104–105
    selection, 106
  reform proposals, 120
  transfer of undertakings (TUPE)
    amendments to regulations, 101–102
    case law, 99–101
    disadvantages, 103
    employee consultation, and, 105
    introduction, 98–99
    notification requirements, 102–103
    practical implications, 101
    reform proposals, 103
    Süzen decision, 99
  unfair dismissal
    automatically unfair reasons,113–114
    introduction, 113

Employment law—*contd*
  working time
    annual leave, 90
    enforcement, 92
    exceptions, 91–92
    generally, 89
    nightworkers, 90
    reform proposals, 120
    rest periods, 90
  workplace surveillance
    effect, 115–116
    email use policy, 117–118
    generally, 114
    Internet use policy, 117–118
    personal data Code, 117
    practical considerations, 117
    privacy laws, 116
    purpose, 114–115
  works councils
    European, 104
    national, 106–107
    reform proposals, 120
Energy efficiency measures and reports
  improvement programmes, 288–289
  introduction, 288
  measurement, 288
  metering data, 289–290
Enforcement notices
  planning, and, 147
Enforcement of health and safety law
  Health and Safety Commission, 2
  introduction, 2
Engineering operations
  planning, and, 137
Environment at work
  back pain avoidance, and, 19
Environmental issues
  preventative maintenance programmes, and, 372
Environmental liability (health and safety)
  climate change levy
    exemptions, 60–61
    generally, 60
    rates, 60
  corporate social responsibility, 64
  EU legislation, 64
  introduction, 60
  pollution, 63–64
  supply chain management, 65
  waste management
    duty of care, 62–63
    introduction, 61
    minimisation, 62
    Regulations, 61–62
Environmental liability (property)
  computer-aided facilities management, and, 344
  contaminated land, 149
  introduction, 149
  'polluter pays' principle, 149
  reducing clean-up liability, 150
  statutory basis, 149

E-procurement
　disadvantages, 175
　growth, 174–175
　introduction, 174
Ergonomic hazards
　risk assessment, and, 12
Escape, means of
　emergency exits, 53
　emergency lighting, 52–53
　generally, 51
　Home Office guidance, 51–52
Estate agents
　acquisition of property, and, 122
European Works Councils
　employment law, and, 104
Evaluation
　financial management, and, 171
Exchange of contracts
　acquisition of property, and, 123
Existing use value
　valuation of property, and, 159
Exit strategy
　outsourcing, and, 246
Explosive atmospheres
　health and safety regulations, and, 11–12

Facilities audit
　benchmarking facilities costs, and, 182
Facilities management costs
　financial management, and, 164–165
Fast food
　catering facilities, and, 312
Fees
　acquisition of property, and, 125
Financial analysis, techniques for
　application of, 193
　cost/benefit analysis, 193
　discounted cash flow, 190–191
　internal rate of return, 192–193
　introduction, 189
　net present value, 191–192
　pay-back period, 190
Financial management
　behavioural effects, 170
　benchmarking facilities costs
　　cost data, 183–184
　　external comparison, 181–182
　　facilities audit, 182
　　facilities protocol, 186
　　graphics, 186–187
　　internal comparison, 181–182
　　obtaining comparable data, 185
　　parameters, 184–185
　　performance data, 183
　　process, 182–188
　　purpose, 179–181
　　reporting, 188
　　resource drivers, 182–183
　　statistics production, 186–187
　　troubleshooting diagnosis, 187–188

Financial management—*contd*
　best practice
　　budgetary control, 166–172
　　procurement, 172–174
　budgetary control
　　behavioural effects, 170
　　change management, 171–172
　　communication, 170
　　coordination, 169–170
　　evaluation, 171
　　introduction, 166
　　planning, 166–167
　　preparation, 167–169
　　reporting and reconciliation, 170–171
　capital allowances
　　buildings, 205–206
　　introduction, 204
　　plant and machinery, 204
　capital and revenue expenditure, 203
　capital gains tax, 199–200
　change management, 171–172
　communication, 170
　computer-aided facilities management, and, 345
　coordination, 169–170
　corporation tax, 199
　cost centres, 167–168
　data, 168–171
　depreciation, 203–204
　economic structure of organisations
　　facilities management costs, 164–165
　　introduction, 163
　　systems technology, 165–166
　　universal principles, 163
　e-procurement
　　disadvantages, 175
　　growth, 174–175
　　introduction, 174
　evaluation, 171
　facilities management costs, 164–165
　financial analysis, techniques for
　　application of, 193
　　cost/benefit analysis, 193
　　discounted cash flow, 190–191
　　internal rate of return, 192–193
　　introduction, 189
　　net present value, 191–192
　　pay-back period, 190
　income tax, 199
　introduction, 163
　landfill tax, 203
　life cycle costing
　　financial analysis techniques, 189–193
　　introduction, 188
　　whole life costs, 189
　planning, 166–167
　preparation
　　cost centres, 167–168
　　data, 168–171
　　introduction, 167
　　zero-based budgeting, 168

Financial management—*contd*
  principles of facilities finance
    capital allowances, 204–206
    capital and revenue expenditure, 203
    depreciation, 203–204
    introduction, 198
    taxation, 198–203
  private finance initiative (PFI), 176
  procurement
    contracted-out provision, 172–173
    in-house provision, 172–173
    market capability. 173–174
    scope of services, 173
    strategic considerations, 172
  property costs
    buildings insurance, 196–197
    distributed workplace strategies, 198
    flood insurance, 196–197
    introduction, 194
    rates, 194–195
    rent, 194
    service charges, 195–196
    sustainable property, 197–198
    terrorism insurance, 197
  public private partnership (PPP)
    introduction, 175–176
    life cycle cost models, 177–178
    payment mechanisms, 178
    process, 176–177
  reporting and reconciliation, 170–171
  stamp duty, 202
  systems technology, 165–166
  taxation
    capital gains tax, 199–200
    corporation tax, 199
    income tax, 199
    introduction, 198–199
    landfill tax, 203
    stamp duty, 202
    value added tax, 200–202
  universal principles, 163
  value added tax
    exempt supplies, 201–202
    introduction, 200
    standard-rated supplies, 200–201
    zero-rated supplies, 201
  whole life economics
    financial analysis techniques, 189–193
    introduction, 188
    whole life costs, 189
    zero-based budgeting, 168
Fire risk
  causes of fire, 362–363
  introduction, 362
  minimisation, 363
  statutory requirements, 364
Fire safety
  assessment of risk
    checklist, 48–50

Fire safety—*contd*
  assessment of risk—*contd*
    'five steps' approach, 47–48
    generally, 47–48
    certificates, 45–46
    employees' responsibilities, 53–54
    equipment, 53
    evaluation of risk, 47
    hazard identification, 47
    introduction, 45
    means of escape
      emergency exits, 53
      emergency lighting, 52–53
      generally, 51
      Home Office guidance, 51–52
    notices, 53
    records, 47–48
    reform proposals, 54–55, 85
First aid
  health and safety regulations, and, 10
Fixed network
  communications, and, 265–266
Fixed-term contracts
  employment law, and, 97
Fixtures and fittings
  business leases, and, 127
Fleet management
  transport policies, and, 263–264
Flexible working
  appeals, 88–89
  health and safety law, and
    driving, 58–59
    homeworking, 56–58
    hotdesking, 56–57
    introduction, 56
    laptops, 57
    lone working, 59
  introduction, 87
  reasons for refusal, 88
  reform proposals, 120
  right of request, 87–89
Flood insurance
  property costs, and, 196–197
Floor graphic advertising
  car park management, and, 262
Flooring
  slips and trips, and, 37–38
Food-related facilities
  court proceedings, 81
  health and safety, 83–84
  hygiene
    drainage facilities, 82
    equipment, 82
    grease traps, 82
    introduction, 81–82
    management systems, 83
    pest proofing, 82
    premises, 82
    refuse material, 82

Food-related facilities—*contd*
  hygiene—*contd*
    services, 82
    waste material, 82
  improvement notices, 80
  introduction, 79
  licensing, 84
  premises registration, 81
  prohibition order
    emergency, 81
    generally, 80–81
  reform proposals, 86
  statutory provisions, 79–80
  temperature control, 83
Force majeure clause
  outsourcing, and, 243–244
48-hour week
  annual leave, 90
  enforcement, 92
  exceptions, 91–92
  generally, 89
  nightworkers, 90
  reform proposals, 120
  rest periods, 90
Foul drainage
  sewerage charges, and, 290–291
Freehold interests
  generally, 121
  valuation of property, and 160–161
Furniture
  height-adjustable desking, 310
  introduction, 308
  posture, 311
  purchase criteria, 311
  seating, 310–311
  selection, 309
  workspace design, 309–310
  workstations, 310

Gas and electricity supply
  avoidance of power failures, 283
  checking invoices, 283–285
  combined heat and power, 280–281
  introduction, 279
  meter-reading errors, 284–285
  NETA, 280
  open systems in building control, 282
  reverse auction agencies, 279
  totally integrated power, 281–282
General packet radio service (GPRS)
  communications, and, 265
Grease traps
  catering facility hygiene, and, 82
Grievance procedure
  employment law, and, 118–119
Group planning
  space design and management, and, 337

Hazard identification
  fire safety, and, 47
  risk assessment, and, 12
Hazardous substances
  health and safety regulations, and, 9
  risk assessment, and, 12
Health and Safety at Work Act 1974 (HASAWA)
  employees' duties, 3
  employers' duties, 2–3
  personal liability, 3
  safety policy, 3
  suppliers' duties, 3
Health and Safety Commission (HSC)
  generally, 2
Health and Safety Executive (HSE)
  generally, 2
Health and safety file
  construction, design and management, and, 71–72
Health and safety law
  asbestos-related diseases
    employers' duty, 27
    introduction, 25
    leaving in place, 26
    repair and removal, 26–27
    surveys and logs, 25–26
  back pain, avoidance of
    environment, 19
    individual's circumstances, 19
    introduction, 18
    load, 19
    risk assessment, 18
    task changes, 18–19
  building management
    Building Regulations, 77–79
    introduction, 73
    permit to work procedures, 76–77
    safe means of access, 73–76
  catering facilities
    court proceedings, 81
    health and safety, 83–84
    hygiene, 81–83
    improvement notices, 80
    introduction, 79
    licensing, 84
    premises registration, 81
    prohibition order, 80–81
    statutory provisions, 79–80
    temperature control, 83
  civil compensation, 17
  computer-aided facilities management, and, 344
  construction work
    building management, 73–79
    CDM Regulations, 66–72
    introduction, 65
    key issues, 66
    refurbishment works, 72–73
  criminal sanctions
    corporate killing, 17
    directors' responsibilities, 16–17

Health and safety law—*contd*
  criminal sanctions—*contd*
    future legislation, 17
    generally, 14–15
    reform proposals, 16
  enforcement, 2
  environmental protection and liability
    climate change levy, 60–61
    corporate social responsibility, 64
    EU legislation, 64
    introduction, 60
    pollution, 63–64
    supply chain management, 65
    waste management, 61–63
  fire safety
    certificates, 45–46
    employees' responsibilities, 53–54
    equipment, 53
    introduction, 45
    means of escape, 51–53
    notices, 53
    reform proposals, 54–55
    risk assessment, 46–50
  flexible working
    driving, 58–59
    homeworking, 56–58
    hotdesking, 56–57
    introduction, 56
    laptops, 57
    lone working, 59
  introduction, 1
  legionellosis
    control measures, 29
    designing out, 28–29
    introduction, 27
    legal duties, 28
    nature of disease, 27–28
    risk assessment, 29
  maintenance and repair
    confined spaces, 44–45
    introduction, 41
    managing of contractors, 41–43
    working at height, 43–44
  noise, reduction of
    control measures, 24–25
    introduction, 24
  occupational health promotion
    asbestos-related diseases, 25–27
    back pain, 18–19
    introduction, 18
    legionellosis, 27–29
    noise, 24–25
    upper limb disorders, 19–24
    well-being, 30–36
  policy
    arrangements, 4–5
    organisational responsibilities, 4
    statement of intent, 4
  reform proposals, 85–86

Health and safety law—*contd*
  regulations
    asbestos, 9
    confined spaces, 8
    construction design and management, 8–9
    consultation with employee, 9–10
    dangerous substances, 11–12
    display screen equipment, 6–7
    electricity, 9
    explosive atmospheres, 11–12
    first aid, 10
    hazardous substances, 9
    information for employees, 10
    lifting operations and equipment, 10
    management, 5
    manual handling operations, 7
    noise, 11
    protective equipment, 8
    reporting injuries, etc., 11
    safety representatives, 11
    safety signs and signals, 10
    work equipment, 7–8
    workplace, 6
  risk assessment
    control of risks, 13
    hazard identification, 12
    introduction, 12
    persons at risk, 12–13
    records, 13
    review and revision, 14
    suitability and sufficiency, 14
  safety in the workplace
    building management, 73–79
    catering facilities, 79–84
    construction work, 65–73
    environmental protection, 60–65
    equipment, 38–39
    fire safety, 45–56
    flexible working, 56–59
    maintenance and repair, 41–45
    means of escape, 51–53
    slips and trips, 37–38
    vehicles, 39–40
  slips and trips, prevention of
    case example, 38
    flooring, 37–38
    introduction, 37
  statutory basis
    employees' duties, 3
    employers' duties, 2–3
    personal liability, 3
    safety policy, 3
    suppliers' duties, 3
  vehicles at the workplace
    introduction, 39–40
    safe traffic routes, 40
  well-being, improvement of
    air quality, 32–35
    humidity, 33–34

Health and safety law—*contd*
well-being, improvement of—*contd*
introduction, 30
lighting, 31–32
natural light, 32
passive smoking, 34–35
photocopiers, 31
sick-building syndrome, 30–31
stress, 35–36
temperature, 32–33
violence, 36–37
ventilation, 33
work equipment, use of
introduction, 38–39
practical examples, 39
work-related upper limb disorders
computer workstations, 22–23
introduction, 19–20
manual handling checklist, 20–21
risk assessment, 21–22
seating, 23
solutions, 22
Health and safety policy
arrangements, 4–5
organisational responsibilities, 4
statement of intent, 4
Health and safety plan
construction, design and management, and,
70–71
Heating and ventilation
air conditioning
close control systems, 299
fixed systems, 298
introduction, 298
need, 298
portable systems, 299
refrigerant policy, 300
temperature control systems, 299–300
cleaner indoor air
CIBSE guidelines, 300–301
humidity, 301–303
introduction, 300
pollutants, 301
equipment choice, 297
indoor air quality
effect of equipment, 296
generally, 295–296
saving energy, 296
Height-adjustable desking
furniture, and, 310
Helpdesks
communications, and, 276–277
computer-aided facilities management, and, 345
Highway drainage
sewerage charges, and, 291
Home Office guidance
means of escape, and, 51–52
Homeworking
flexible working, and, 56–58

'Hope' value
valuation of property, and, 158
Hotdesking
communications, 342
efficient use, 342
employee/desk ratio, 341–342
flexible working, and, 56–57
furniture 342–343
introduction, 341
layout, 342
stationery, 343
storage, 342–343
Humidity
employers' duties, 302
improvement of well-being, and, 33–34
introduction, 301
management, 303
measurement, 303
staff discomfort, 302–303
stress, 302
symptom recognition, 302
Hygiene in catering facilities
drainage facilities, 82
equipment, 82
grease traps, 82
introduction, 81–82
management systems, 83
pest proofing, 82
premises, 82
refuse material, 82
services, 82
waste material, 82

Improvement notices
catering facilities, and, 80
construction work, and, 65
Income tax
financial management, and, 199
Indoor air quality
effect of equipment, 296
generally, 295–296
Information for employees
health and safety regulations, and, 10
Information protection
access to workplace, and, 361–362
Information technology (IT)
conferencing
introduction, 272–273
technology, 273
convergence of data and telecom
Bluetooth, 266
fixed network, 265–266
future prospects, 267
introduction, 265
mobile telephony, 265
voice to data conversion, 266
Wi-Fi zones, 267
wireless LANs, 267

Information technology (IT)—*contd*
  digital document systems
    establishment, 277
    introduction, 277
    paper storage, 277
  e-business
    e-mail negotiations, 275
    e-procurement, 275
    intranet services, 276
    intranet site, 276
    introduction, 274
    top-down approach, 274–275
  helpdesks, 276–277
  infrastructure management
    cabling categories, 269–270
    future-proofing, 268–269
    introduction, 268
  introduction, 265
  presentation
    introduction, 272–273
    technology, 273–274
  voice over IP (VoIP)
    data network integration, 271–272
    developments, 272
    features, 270–271
    introduction, 270
Injunctions
  planning, and, 147
Insurance
  business leases, and, 132–133
Interest
  business leases, and, 130
Internal rate of return
  financial analysis, and, 192–193
Internet protocol (IP)
  communications, and, 265
Internet use policy
  workplace surveillance, and, 117–118
Intruder alarms
  access to workplace, and, 359–360
Inventory control
  business continuity, and, 231
  computer-aided facilities management, and, 345
Invitation to tender
  outsourcing, and, 239–240

Justification
  part-time workers, and, 93

Ladders, use of
  safe means of access, and, 74–75
Land registry fees
  acquisition of property, and, 125
Landfill tax
  financial management, and, 203
Laptop computers
  flexible working, and, 57
Leasehold interests
  generally, 125–126

Leasehold interests—*contd*
  introduction, 121
  ongoing liability, 126–127
  valuation of property, and, 161
Lease of business premises
  access rights, 132
  alterations, 131
  assignment, 130
  breach of repairing obligations, 132
  dealings
    assignment, 130
    introduction, 130
    sharing occupation, 131
    sub-letting, 130
  demised premises, 127
  exceptions and reservations, 128
  fixtures and fittings, 127
  insurance, 132–133
  interest, 130
  introduction, 127
  landlord's remedies for tenant breaches
    non-payment of rent, 135
    other, 136
  new buildings, 131–132
  non-payment of rent, 135
  old buildings, 132
  options to terminate, 134–135
  parties, 127
  rates and taxes, 130
  rent
    generally, 129
    payment, 129–130
  rent review, 130
  repairs, 131
  reserve funds, 134
  rights granted, 128
  security of tenure
    compensation
      generally, 128
      landlords, notice, 128–129
      new lease, 129
      tenant's request for new tenancy, 129
    termination, 128
  service charges
    apportionment, 133
    introduction, 133
    management arrangements, 133
    objections, 134
    payment, 134
    services, 133
    sinking funds, 134
  sharing occupation, 131
  sinking funds, 134
  sub-letting, 130
  term, 128
  termination, 128–129
  use, 131
Leased premises
  disability discrimination, and, 110–111

Legionellosis
control measures, 29
designing out, 28–29
introduction, 27
legal duties, 28
nature of disease, 27–28
risk assessment, 29

Licensing
catering facilities, and, 84

Lifecycle costing
financial analysis, techniques for
application of, 193
cost/benefit analysis, 193
discounted cash flow, 190–191
internal rate of return, 192–193
introduction, 189
net present value, 191–192
pay-back period, 190
introduction, 188
whole life costs, 189

Lifting operations and equipment
generally, 10
safe means of access, and, 74

Lighting
car park management, and, 263
computer-controlled systems, 322–323
electric lighting, 319–320
emergency lighting
categories, 324
escape routes, 324–325
introduction, 323
luminaries, 323
maintenance, 325–326
safety signs, 325
standards, 324–325
testing, 325–326
energy efficiency, 318
health and safety, and
generally, 31
risk assessment, 31–32
management systems, 322–323
means of escape, and, 52–53
natural lighting, 319
objectives, 318–319
output, 320
quality, 321–322
sources
electric, 319–320
natural, 319
standards, 320

Listed buildings
planning, and, 139

Load
back pain avoidance, and, 19

Local land charges searches
acquisition of property, and, 125

LOLER 1998
generally, 10
safe means of access, and, 74

Lone working
flexible working, and, 59

Maintenance and repair
CDM Regulations, 365
computer-aided facilities management, and
generally, 344–345
introduction, 368
condition assessment, 366–367
confined spaces, and, 44–45
costs, 366
e-business solutions, 375
employee safety
introduction, 369
risk assessments, 369–370
health and safety, and
confined spaces, 44–45
introduction, 41
managing of contractors, 41–43
working at height, 43–44
introduction, 365
maintenance checks, 365
managing contracts
barcode readers, 368
checklist, 369
frequency of visits, 368
introduction, 368
number of visits, 368
software features, 368
voucher systems, 368
managing of contractors, and
introduction, 41
key steps, 42
legal duty, 41–42
purpose of employers' liability, 43
outsourcing, 374
preventative programmes
air conditioning, 371
environmental issues, 372
introduction, 370
new installations faults, 371
spare parts holding, 371
staff training, 372
tell-tale signals, 371
test instrumentation, 372
refurbishment costs, 367
risk assessments, 369–370
service level agreements, 368
serviceability, 367–368
statutory requirements, 365
turnkey service management
complete service solution, 373–375
generally, 372–373
multiple vendor management, 373
outsourced support, 374
smaller organisations' needs, 374–375
third-party service management, 374
total support, 374
types, 366
working at height, and, 43–44

Maintenance checks
maintenance and repair, and, 365
Management of health and safety
generally, 5
safe means of access, and, 74
Managing maintenance contracts
barcode readers, 368
checklist, 369
frequency of visits, 368
introduction, 368
number of visits, 368
software features, 368
voucher systems, 368
Managing of contractors
introduction, 41
key steps, 42
legal duty, 41–42
purpose of employers' liability, 43
Manned guarding
access to workplace, and, 361
Manual handling operations
health and safety regulations, and, 7
upper limb disorders, and, 20–21
Market value
valuation of property, and, 157–158
Material change of use
planning, and, 138–139
Maternity leave
employment law, and, 95
Means of escape
emergency exits, 53
emergency lighting, 52–53
generally, 51
Home Office guidance, 51–52
Meeting room
space design and management, and, 335
Metering
sewerage charges, and, 292
Meter-reading errors
gas and electricity, and, 284–285
Method statements
safe systems of work, and, 77
Minimum wage
employment law, and, 119
Mining operations
planning, and, 137
Mitigation
risk management, and, 207
Mobile phones
flexible working, and, 59
Mobile telephony
communications, and, 265

National works councils
employment law, and, 106–107
Natural light
improvement of well-being, and, 32
Net present value
financial analysis, and, 191–192

Net realisation proceeds
valuation of property, and, 159
NETA
gas and electricity, and, 280
New installations, faults in
preventative maintenance programmes, and, 371
Nightworkers
part-time workers, and, 90
Noise and vibration at work
advice, 308
health and safety, and
control measures, 24–25
generally, 24
introduction, 11
reform proposals, 85
hearing damage, 306
introduction, 305
minimisation through design, 307
sound perception, 306
sound power level, 306–307
source control, 308
Non-employees, duties to
health and safety, and, 3
Non-payment of rent
generally, 135
landlord's remedies, 135
Notices
fire safety, and, 53

Obligations
planning, and, 143
Occupational health promotion
asbestos-related diseases
employers' duty, 27
introduction, 25
leaving in place, 26
repair and removal, 26–27
surveys and logs, 25–26
back pain, avoidance of
environment, 19
individual's circumstances, 19
introduction, 18
load, 19
risk assessment, 18
task changes, 18–19
introduction, 18
legionellosis
control measures, 29
designing out, 28–29
introduction, 27
legal duties, 28
nature of disease, 27–28
risk assessment, 29
noise, reduction of
control measures, 24–25
introduction, 24
well-being, improvement of
air quality, 32–35
humidity, 33–34

Occupational health promotion—*contd*
  well-being, improvement of—*contd*
    introduction, 30
    lighting, 31–32
    natural light, 32
    passive smoking, 34–35
    photocopiers, 31
    sick-building syndrome, 30–31
    stress, 35–36
    temperature, 32–33
    violence, 36–37
    ventilation, 33
  work-related upper limb disorders
    computer workstations, 22–23
    introduction, 19–20
    manual handling checklist, 20–21
    risk assessment, 21–22
    seating, 23
    solutions, 22
Occupiers' liability
  case study, 150–154
  generally, 150
Open-plan
  space design and management, and, 334–335
Operational development
  planning, and, 137
Options to terminate
  business leases, and, 134–135
Outsourcing
  anticipating pitfalls
    business change, 238
    introduction, 237
    people issues, 237–238
    process change, 238–239
  case study, 253–254
  contract management, 246
  contractor selection
    final negotiations, 240–241
    final selection, 240
    invitation to tender, 239–240
    supplier market, 242
    tender document, 239
  contractual arrangements
    contract management, 246
    decision-making, 246
    dispute resolution, 245
    exit strategy, 246
    flexibility, 245
    function, 244–245
    introduction, 244
  decision-making, 246
  dispute resolution, 245
  disaster recovery, and
    considerations, 227–228
    introduction, 226–227
    selection of supplier, 227
  exit strategy, 246
  extent
    core activities, 236–237

Outsourcing—*contd*
  extent—*contd*
    introduction, 235–236
    non-core activities, 236–237
  final negotiations
    creating synergy, 241
    flexibility, 241
    introduction, 240
  final selection, 240
  introduction, 235
  invitation to tender, 239–240
  maintenance and repair, and, 374
  performance indicators
    balanced scorecard, 246–247
    client satisfaction, 247–248
  relationship building
    anticipating problems, 250–251
    continuous improvement model, 248–249
    coordinating standards, 250
    defining added value, 249
    good communication, 249–250
    introduction, 248
    reviews, 251
    team dynamics, 251
  scope, 235–236
  service level agreements
    force majeure clauses, 243–244
    generally, 242–243
    incentives, 243
    penalties, 243
  space design and management, and, 339
  tender document, 239
  termination management
    introduction, 252
    key lessons, 252–253
Ownership
  property law, and, 121

Parameters
  benchmarking facilities costs, and, 184–185
Parental leave
  employment law, and, 96
Partitioning
  space design and management, and, 330–331
Part-time workers
  comparable full-timers, 92–93
  introduction, 92
  justification, 93
  pro-rata principle, 93
  regulatory guidance, 94
  remedies, 93–94
Passive smoking
  case law, 34
  generally, 34–35
Paternity leave
  generally, 95
  reform proposals, 120
Pay-back period
  financial analysis, and, 190

Performance data
  benchmarking facilities costs, and, 183
Performance indicators
  outsourcing, and
    balanced scorecard, 246–247
    client satisfaction, 247–248
Perimeter boundary
  access to workplace, and, 358
Permit to work procedures
  generally, 76–77
  method statements, 77
Permitted development
  demolition works, 145
  external works, 145–146
  internal work, 145
  introduction, 144–145
  Regulations, 145–146
Personal attack alarms
  access to workplace, and, 360
Personal data
  workplace surveillance, and, 117
Personal liability
  health and safety, and, 3
Personal protective equipment regulations
  generally, 8
  reform proposals, 85
Pest proofing
  catering facility hygiene, and, 82
Photocopiers
  improvement of well-being, and, 31
Physical hazards
  risk assessment, and, 12
Planning
  appeals
    challenges, 144
    enforcement, and, 147
    generally, 143–144
    human rights, and, 144
  application for permission
    architects' role, 139–140
    form, 140–141
    planning consultants' role, 139–140
    process, 141
    solicitors' role, 140
  building operations, 137
  building regulations, 148
  certificate of lawful use or development, 147–148
  conservation areas, 139
  decision on application
    deemed refusal, 142
    grant in full, 143
    grant in outline, 142–143
    refusal, 142
  development, 137
  enforcement
    appeals, 147
    building regulations, 148
    enforcement notices, 147
    entry powers, 146

Planning—*contd*
  enforcement—*contd*
    injunctions, 147
    inspection powers, 146
    introduction, 146
    stop notices, 147
  enforcement notices, 147
  engineering operations, 137
  injunctions, 147
  introduction, 136
  listed buildings, 139
  material change of use, 138–139
  mining operations, 137
  obligations, 143
  operational development, 137
  permitted development
    demolition works, 145
    external works, 145–146
    internal work, 145
    introduction, 144–145
    Regulations, 145–146
  requirement for planning permission
    conservation areas, 139
    development, 137
    introduction, 136–137
    listed buildings, 139
    operational development, 137
    use of land, 137–139
  statutory basis, 146
  stop notices, 147
  use of land
    contractually permitted, 137–138
    introduction, 137
    lawful, 138
    material change, 138–139
Planning supervisor
  construction, design and management, and, 69
Policy for health and safety
  arrangements, 4–5
  organisational responsibilities, 4
  statement of intent, 4
'Polluter pays' principle
  contaminated land, and, 149
Pollution
  environmental protection, and, 63–64
Post traumatic stress disorder (PTSD)
  business continuity, and, 230
Posture
  seating, and, 311
Premises registration
  catering facilities, and, 81
Presentation
  introduction, 272–273
  technology, 273–274
Preventative maintenance programmes
  air conditioning, 371
  environmental issues, 372
  introduction, 370
  new installations faults, 371

Preventative maintenance programmes—*contd*
spare parts holding, 371
staff training, 372
tell-tale signals, 371
test instrumentation, 372
Principal contractor
construction, design and management, and, 70
Privacy
workplace surveillance, and, 116
Private finance initiative (PFI)
financial management, and, 176
Private security
access to workplace, and, 361
Procurement
contracted-out provision, 172–173
in-house provision, 172–173
market capability. 173–174
scope of services, 173
strategic considerations, 172
Prohibition notices
construction work, and, 66
Prohibition orders
emergency, 81
generally, 80–81
Property costs
buildings insurance
flood, 196–197
introduction, 196–197
terrorism, 197
distributed workplace strategies, 198
introduction, 194
rates, 194–195
rent, 194
service charges, 195–196
sustainable property, 197–198
Property law
acquisition and disposal
completion, 123–124
costs, 124–125
exchange of contracts, 123
fees, 125
introduction, 121
land registry fees, 125
local land charges searches, 125
ownership, 121
purchase procedure, 123–127
registration system, 122
role of professional advisers, 122–123
stamp duty, 124
value added tax, 124–125
business leases
access rights, 132
alterations, 131
assignment, 130
breach of repairing obligations, 132
dealings, 130–131
demised premises, 127
exceptions and reservations, 128
fixtures and fittings, 127

Property law—*contd*
business leases—*contd*
insurance, 132–133
interest, 130
introduction, 127
landlord's remedies for tenant breaches, 135–136
new buildings, 131–132
non-payment of rent, 135
old buildings, 132
options to terminate, 134–135
parties, 127
rates and taxes, 130
rent, 129–130
rent review, 130
repairs, 131
reserve funds, 134
rights granted, 128
security of tenure, 128–129
service charges, 133–134
sharing occupation, 131
sinking funds, 134
sub-letting, 130
term, 128
termination, 128–129
use, 131
environmental matters
contaminated land, 149
introduction, 149
'polluter pays' principle, 149
reducing clean-up liability, 150
statutory basis, 149
freehold, 121
introduction, 121
leasehold
generally, 125–126
introduction, 121
ongoing liability, 126–127
occupiers' liability
case study, 150–154
generally, 150
ownership, 121
planning
appeals, 143–144
application for permission, 139–141
decision on application, 142–143
enforcement, 146–148
introduction, 136
obligations, 143
permitted development, 144–146
requirement for planning permission, 136–139
statutory basis, 146
portfolio knowledge
generally, 154–155
key requirements, 155
registration system, 122
role of professional advisers
estate agents, 122
solicitors, 122–123
surveyors, 122

Property law—*contd*
  valuation
    accounting, for, 159–160
    acquisition/disposal, for, 157–159
    approaches, 160–161
    commissioning procedure, 156–157
    introduction, 155–156
    negotiation of lease terms, for, 161–162
    purpose, 157
    regulatory framework, 156
Pro-rata principle
  part-time workers, and, 93
Provision and use of work equipment
  generally, 7
  safe means of access, and, 74
Psychological hazards
  risk assessment, and, 12
Public access
  disability discrimination, and, 109–110
Public private partnership (PPP)
  introduction, 175–176
  life cycle cost models, 177–178
  payment mechanisms, 178
  process, 176–177
Pure risk
  risk management, and, 208
PUWER 1998
  generally, 7
  safe means of access, and, 74

Quality process
  risk management, and, 215

Rates
  business leases, and, 130
  property costs, and, 194–195
Reasonable adjustments
  disability discrimination, and, 108–109
Records
  asbestos-related diseases, and, 25–26
  fire safety, and, 47–48
  risk assessment, and, 13
'Red book'
  valuation of property, and, 156
Redundancy
  generally, 104–105
  selection, 106
Reform proposals
  employment law, and, 120
  health and safety, and
    criminal sanctions, 16
    fire safety, 54–55
    generally, 85–86
Refrigerant policy
  air conditioning, and, 300
Refurbishment costs
  maintenance and repair, and, 367
Refuse material
  catering facility hygiene, and, 82

Registration of land
  property law, and, 122
Regulations (health and safety)
  asbestos, 9
  confined spaces, 8
  construction design and management, 8–9
  consultation with employee, 9–10
  dangerous substances, 11–12
  display screen equipment, 6–7
  electricity, 9
  explosive atmospheres, 11–12
  first aid, 10
  hazardous substances, 9
  information for employees, 10
  lifting operations and equipment, 10
  management, 5
  manual handling operations, 7
  noise, 11
  protective equipment, 8
  reporting injuries, etc., 11
  safety representatives, 11
  safety signs and signals, 10
  work equipment, 7–8
Relocation
  space design and management, and, 340–341
Remote metering
  sewerage charges, and, 292
Remote monitoring
  closed circuit television, and, 354
Rent on business leases
  financial management, and, 194
  generally, 129
  non-payment
    generally, 135
    landlord's remedies, 135
  payment, 129–130
  review, 130
Repairs
  asbestos-related diseases, and, 26–27
  business leases, and, 131
Repetitive strain disorder (RSI)
  computer workstations, 22–23
  introduction, 19–20
  manual handling checklist, 20–21
  risk assessment, 21–22
  seating, 23
  solutions, 22
Reporting injuries, diseases and dangerous occurrences
  health and safety regulations, and, 11
Reserve funds
  business leases, and, 134
Rest periods
  part-time workers, and, 90
Restaurant facilities
  ambience, 314–315
  caterer selection, 315–316
  costs, 314
  design, 313

Restaurant facilities—*contd*
introduction, 312–313
layout, 313–314
management, 315
siting, 313–314
space, 314
subsidies, 315
Restoration of business
business continuity, and, 232
Reverse auction agencies
gas and electricity, and, 279
Revitalising Health and Safety (**Home Office**)
criminal sanctions, and, 16
RIDDOR 1995
health and safety regulations, and, 11
Rising screens
access to workplace, and, 359
Risk analysis
generally, 207
Risk assessment
back pain avoidance, and, 18
construction, design and management, and, 72
control of risks, 13
fire safety, and
checklist, 48–50
'five steps' approach, 47–48
generally, 47–48
hazard identification, 12
introduction, 12
legionellosis, and, 29
lighting, and, 31–32
maintenance and repair, and, 369–370
persons at risk, 12–13
records, 13
review and revision, 14
suitability and sufficiency, 14
upper limb disorders, and, 21–22
Risk management
analysis, 207
assessment, 207
business risk, 208–209
development of strategy
information security standard, 210
introduction, 210
outsourcing risk, 211–212
prioritising risk, 210–211
digital risk
generally, 214
minimisation, 215
types, 214
generally, 208
introduction, 207
linking to quality process, 215
mitigation, 207
phases, 207
planning, 213
practice, in
addressing internal issues, 217–218
case study, 218–219

Risk management—*contd*
practice, in—*contd*
conclusion, 218
defining the problem, 216
immediate changes, 216–217
introduction, 215–216
tackling harder issues, 217
pure risk, 208
responsibilities
generally, 213
Turnbull recommendations, 212
types, 208–209

Safe means of access
cleaning and maintenance, 75
cleaning windows, 74
effects of failure, 75
introduction, 73–74
key points, 76
using ladders, 74–75
Safe systems of work
generally, 76–77
method statements, 77
Safe traffic routes
vehicles in the workplace, and, 40
Safety in the workplace
building management, 73–79
catering facilities, 79–84
construction work, 65–73
environmental protection, 60–65
equipment, 38–39
fire safety, 45–56
flexible working, 56–59
maintenance and repair, 41–45
means of escape, 51–53
slips and trips, 37–38
vehicles, 39–40
Safety policy
health and safety, and, 3
Safety representatives
health and safety regulations, and, 11
Safety signs and signals
health and safety regulations, and, 10
lighting, and, 325
Seating
furniture, and, 310–311
upper limb disorders, and, 23
Security
access to workplace
access risk analysis, 357
authorised entrants, 359
building exteriors, 358
company cash, 360
equipment, 360–361
information protection, 361–362
introduction, 357
intruder alarms, 359–360
manned guarding, 361

Security—*contd*
  access to workplace—*contd*
    perimeter boundary, 358
    personal attack alarms, 360
    private security, 361
    restriction of access, 358
    rising screens, 359
    security measures, 358–360
    stock, 360
    valuables, 360
  aggression in workplace
    at-risk areas, 355–356
    counselling, 356
    defensive strategies, 356–357
    introduction, 355
    persons involved, 356
    training, 356
  closed circuit television (CCTV)
    choice, 352–353
    data protection, 354
    generally, 351
    operation, 353
    recordings, 354–355
    remote monitoring, 354
    security audits, 352
    threats, 351
  fire risk
    causes of fire, 362–363
    introduction, 362
    minimisation, 363
    statutory requirements, 364
  introduction, 351
Security audits
  closed circuit television, and, 352
Security of tenure
  compensation
  generally, 128
  landlords, notice, 128–129
  new lease, 129
  tenant's request for new tenancy, 129
  termination, 128
Service charges
  apportionment, 133
  financial management, and, 195–196
  introduction, 133
  management arrangements, 133
  objections, 134
  payment, 134
  services, 133
  sinking funds, 134
Service level agreement (SLA)
  force majeure clauses, 243–244
  generally, 242–243
  incentives, 243
  maintenance and repair, and, 368
  penalties, 243
Serviceability
  maintenance and repair, and, 367–368

Sewerage, charges for
  allowances, 292
  EC Directives, 292
  foul drainage, 290–291
  highway drainage, 291
  introduction, 290
  metering, 292
  remote metering, 292
  surface drainage, 291
  trade effluent, 291
Sharing occupation
  business leases, and, 131
Sick building syndrome
  at-risk buildings, 30
  introduction, 30
  solutions, 31
  symptoms, 30
Sinking funds
  business leases, and, 134
'Six-pack' regulations
  asbestos, 9
  confined spaces, 8
  construction design and management, 8–9
  consultation with employee, 9–10
  dangerous substances, 11–12
  display screen equipment, 6–7
  electricity, 9
  explosive atmospheres, 11–12
  first aid, 10
  hazardous substances, 9
  information for employees, 10
  lifting operations and equipment, 10
  management, 5
  manual handling operations, 7
  noise, 11
  protective equipment, 8
  reporting injuries, etc., 11
  safety representatives, 11
  safety signs and signals, 10
  work equipment, 7–8
  workplace, 6
Slips and trips, prevention of
  case example, 38
  flooring, 37–38
  introduction, 37
Solicitors
  acquisition of property, and, 122–123
Space design and management
  adjacencies, 336
  aesthetics, 337–338
  cabling
    floor boxes, 332
    generally, 331–332
    grommets, 332
    management, 332
  churn
    benefits and costs, 339
    cutting cost, 340
    hotdesking, 341–343

Space design and management—*contd*
  churn—*contd*
    introduction, 339
    relocation, 340–341
  circulation, 335–336
  computer-aided systems, 343–344
  group planning, 337
  hotdesking
    communications, 342
    efficient use, 342
    employee/desk ratio, 341–342
    furniture 342–343
    introduction, 341
    layout, 342
    stationery, 343
    storage, 342–343
  introduction, 329
  measuring space, 329–330
  options
    introduction, 333–334
    meeting rooms, 335
    open-plan, 334–335
  outsourcing, and, 339
  partitioning, 330–331
  per person requirements, 332–333
  planning
    grids, 330
    measuring space, 329–330
  properties of building materials, 330
  relocation, 340–341
  space records, 337
  space-saving tips, 338–339
  universal footprint, 333
Spare parts holdings
  preventative maintenance programmes, and, 371
Stamp duty
  acquisition of property, and, 124
  financial management, and, 202
Stock
  access to workplace, and, 360
Stop notices
  planning, and, 147
Stress
  causes and prevention, 35–36
  generally, 35
  humidity, and, 302
  stressful buildings, 36
Sub-letting
  business leases, and, 130
Suppliers' duties
  health and safety, and, 3
Supply chain management
  environmental protection, and, 65
Surface drainage
  sewerage charges, and, 291
Surveyors
  acquisition of property, and, 122
Surveys
  asbestos-related diseases, and, 25–26

Sustainable property
  property costs, and, 197–198

Taxation
  capital gains tax, 199–200
  corporation tax, 199
  income tax, 199
  introduction, 198–199
  landfill tax, 203
  stamp duty, 202
  value added tax
    exempt supplies, 201–202
    introduction, 200
    standard-rated supplies, 200–201
    zero-rated supplies, 201
Tele-conferencing
  introduction, 272–273
  technology, 273
Temperature
  and see HEATING AND VENTILATION
  catering facilities, and, 83
  improvement of well-being, and, 32–33
Temperature control
  air conditioning, and, 299–300
Tender document
  outsourcing, and, 239
Termination
  business leases, and, 128–129
Terrorism insurance
  property costs, and, 197
Test instrumentation
  preventative maintenance programmes, and, 372
Third-party service management
  turnkey service management, and, 374
Threats
  closed circuit television, and, 351
Total support
  turnkey service management, and, 374
Totally integrated power
  gas and electricity, and, 281–282
Trade effluent
  sewerage charges, and, 291
Training
  aggression in the workplace, and, 356
  preventative maintenance programmes, and, 372
Transfer of undertakings (TUPE)
  amendments to regulations, 101–102
  case law, 99–101
  disadvantages, 103
  employee consultation, and, 105
  introduction, 98–99
  notification requirements, 102–103
  practical implications, 101
  reform proposals, 103
  Süzen decision, 99
Transport plans
  adoption, 258
  baseline, 257
  behavioural change, 260

Transport plans—*contd*
  Best Practice programme, 260–261
  complementary measures package, 257
  consultation with employees, 257–258
  director-level support, 256
  evaluation, 260
  implementation resources, 258
  introduction, 255–256
  marketing, 259
  monitoring, 260
  objectives, 256
  project management, 258–259
  target setting, 259–260
Transport policies
  car park management
    design, 262
    floor graphic advertising, 262
    introduction, 261
    lighting, 263
    plans, 261–262
    security, 263
  fleet management, 263–264
  introduction, 255
  travel plans
    and see TRAVEL PLANS
    generally, 255–260
Turnbull report
  business continuity, and, 220
  risk management, and, 212
Turnkey service management
  complete service solution, 373–375
  generally, 372–373
  multiple vendor management, 373
  outsourced support, 374
  smaller organisations' needs, 374–375
  third-party service management, 374
  total support, 374

Unfair dismissal
  automatically unfair reasons, 113–114
  introduction, 113
Universal footprint
  space design and management, and, 333
Universal mobile telecom system (UMTS)
  communications, and, 265
Upper limb disorders
  computer workstations, 22–23
  introduction, 19–20
  manual handling checklist, 20–21
  risk assessment, 21–22
  seating, 23
  solutions, 22
Use of land
  contractually permitted, 137–138
  introduction, 137
  lawful, 138
  material change, 138–139
User
  business leases, and, 131

Using ladders
  safe means of access, and, 74–75

Valuables
  access to workplace, and, 360
Valuation of property
  accounting, for
    depreciated replacement cost, 159–160
    existing use, 159
    FRS 15, 160
    investment, development or disposal property, 160
  acquisition/disposal, for
    further investigations, 158–159
    'hope' value, 158
    market value, 157–158
    net realisation proceeds, 159
    special purchasers, 158
  approaches
    freehold interests, 160–161
    long leasehold interests, 161
    short leasehold interests, 161
  commissioning procedure, 156–157
  introduction, 155–156
  negotiation of lease terms, for, 161–162
  purpose, 157
  'red book', 156
  regulatory framework, 156
Value added tax
  acquisition of property, and, 124–125
  exempt supplies, 201–202
  introduction, 200
  standard-rated supplies, 200–201
  zero-rated supplies, 201
Vehicles at the workplace
  introduction, 39–40
  safe traffic routes, 40
Vending machines
  catering facilities, and, 313
Violence
  improvement of well-being, and, 36–37
Ventilation
  improvement of well-being, and, 33
Video-conferencing
  introduction, 272–273
  technology, 273
Violence in workplace
  at-risk areas, 355–356
  counselling, 356
  defensive strategies, 356–357
  introduction, 355
  persons involved, 356
  training, 356
Voice over IP (VoIP)
  business continuity, and, 232
  data network integration
    introduction, 271
    quality, 271–272
    security, 272
    standards, 272

Voice over IP (VoIP)—*contd*
developments, 272
features, 270–271
introduction, 270
Voice to data conversion
communications, and, 266
Voucher systems
managing maintenance contracts, and, 368

Waste management
disposal, 304
health and safety, and
duty of care, 62–63
introduction, 61
minimisation, 62
Regulations, 61–62
introduction, 303–304
responsibility, 304
savings, 305
sustainability, 304–305
Waste material
catering facility hygiene, and, 82
Waste water management
introduction, 290
sewerage charges
allowances, 292
EC Directives, 292
foul drainage, 290–291
highway drainage, 291
introduction, 290
metering, 292
remote metering, 292
surface drainage, 291
trade effluent, 291
water pollution prevention
best management practices, 293–295
causes of contamination, 293
introduction, 293
Water pollution, prevention of
best management practices
examples, 295
introduction, 293
key facts, 295
options, 293–294
causes of contamination, 293
introduction, 293
Water supply
generally, 283
Well-being, improvement of
air quality
humidity, 33–34
passive smoking, 34–35
temperature, 32–33
ventilation, 33
humidity, 33–34
introduction, 30
lighting
generally, 31
risk assessment, 31–32

Well-being, improvement of—*contd*
natural light, 32
passive smoking
case law, 34
generally, 34–35
photocopiers, 31
sick-building syndrome
at-risk buildings, 30
introduction, 30
solutions, 31
symptoms, 30
stress
causes and prevention, 35–36
generally, 35
stressful buildings, 36
violence, 36–37
temperature, 32–33
violence, 36–37
ventilation, 33
Wi-Fi zones
communications, and, 267
Window cleaning
safe means of access, and, 74
Wireless LANs
communications, and, 267
Work environment
back pain avoidance, and, 19
risk assessment, and, 12
Work equipment, use of
health and safety regulations, and, 7–8
introduction, 38–39
practical examples, 39
safe means of access, and, 74
Whole life costs
financial analysis techniques, 189–193
introduction, 188
whole life costs, 189
Work place regulations
generally, 6
reform proposals, 85
Working at height
generally, 43–44
reform proposals, 85
Working time
annual leave, 90
enforcement, 92
exceptions, 91–92
generally, 89
nightworkers, 90
reform proposals, 120
rest periods, 90
Workplace facilities
air conditioning
close control systems, 299
fixed systems, 298
introduction, 298
need, 298
portable systems, 299
refrigerant policy, 300
temperature control systems, 299–300

Workplace facilities—*contd*
  catering facilities
    drinking water, 312
    fast food, 312
    future prospects, 316
    introduction, 312–313
    menu, 313
    restaurant facility, 312–316
    vending machines, 313
  cleaner indoor air
    CIBSE guidelines, 300–301
    humidity, 301–303
    introduction, 300
    pollutants, 301
  cleaning
    contractor selection, 316–317
    costs, 317
    introduction, 316
    market dynamics, 316
    working time, 318
  climate change levy
    emission reduction, 286–288
    introduction, 285–286
    objectives, 286
  combined heat and power
    CHP Club, 281
    efficiency, 281
    introduction, 280
  emergency lighting
    categories, 324
    escape routes, 324–325
    introduction, 323
    luminaries, 323
    maintenance, 325–326
    safety signs, 325
    standards, 324–325
    testing, 325–326
  energy efficiency measures and reports
    improvement programmes, 288–289
    introduction, 288
    measurement, 288
    metering data, 289–290
  furniture
    height-adjustable desking, 310
    introduction, 308
    posture, 311
    purchase criteria, 311
    seating, 310–311
    selection, 309
    workspace design, 309–310
    workstations, 310
  gas and electricity supply
    avoidance of power failures, 283
    checking invoices, 283–285
    combined heat and power, 280–281
    introduction, 279
    meter-reading errors, 284–285
    NETA, 280
    open systems in building control, 282

Workplace facilities—*contd*
  gas and electricity supply—*contd*
    reverse auction agencies, 279
    totally integrated power, 281–282
  heating, ventilation and air conditioning
    air conditioning, 298–300
    cleaner air promotion, 300–303
    equipment choice, 297
    indoor air quality, 295–296
    saving energy, 296
  humidity
    employers' duties, 302
    introduction, 301
    management, 303
    measurement, 303
    staff discomfort, 302–303
    stress, 302
    symptom recognition, 302
  introduction, 279
  lighting
    computer-controlled systems, 322–323
    electric lighting, 319–320
    emergency lighting, 323–326
    energy efficiency, 318
    management systems, 322–323
    natural lighting, 319
    objectives, 318–319
    output, 320
    quality, 321–322
    sources, 319–320
    standards, 320
  noise and vibration
    advice, 308
    hearing damage, 306
    introduction, 305
    minimisation through design, 307
    sound perception, 306
    sound power level, 306–307
    source control, 308
  restaurant facilities
    ambience, 314–315
    caterer selection, 315–316
    costs, 314
    design, 313
    introduction, 312–313
    layout, 313–314
    management, 315
    siting, 313–314
    space, 314
    subsidies, 315
  sewerage
    allowances, 292
    EC Directives, 292
    foul drainage, 290–291
    highway drainage, 291
    introduction, 290
    metering, 292
    remote metering, 292
    surface drainage, 291
    trade effluent, 291

Workplace facilities—*contd*
  waste management
    disposal, 304
    introduction, 303–304
    responsibility, 304
    savings, 305
    sustainability, 304–305
  waste water management
    introduction, 290
    sewerage charges, 290–292
    water pollution prevention, 293–295
  water pollution, prevention of
    best management practices, 293–295
    causes of contamination, 293
    introduction, 293
  water supply, 283
Workplace surveillance
  effect, 115–116
  email use policy, 117–118
  generally, 114
  Internet use policy, 117–118
  Personal data code, 117

Workplace surveillance—*contd*
  practical considerations, 117
  privacy laws, 116
  purpose, 114–115
Work-related upper limb disorders
  computer workstations, 22–23
  introduction, 19–20
  manual handling checklist, 20–21
  risk assessment, 21–22
  seating, 23
  solutions, 22
Workspace design
  furniture, and, 309–310
Works councils
  European, 104
  national, 106–107
  reform proposals, 120
Workstations
  furniture, and, 310
  upper limb disorders, and, 22–23
Zero-based budgeting
  budgetary control, and, 168